FUNDAMENTALS OF STRATEGY

Gerry Johnson
Lancaster University Management School

Kevan Scholes
Sheffield Hallam University

Richard Whittington
Saïd Business School, University of Oxford

FT Prentice Hall
FINANCIAL TIMES

An imprint of Pearson Education
Harlow, England • London • New York • Boston • San Francisco • Toronto
Sydney • Tokyo • Singapore • Hong Kong • Seoul • Taipei • New Delhi
Cape Town • Madrid • Mexico City • Amsterdam • Munich • Paris • Milan

Pearson Education Limited

Edinburgh Gate
Harlow
Essex CM20 2JE
England

and Associated Companies throughout the world

Visit us on the World Wide Web at:
www.pearsoned.co.uk

First published 2009

ISBN: 978-0-273-71310-4

British Library Cataloguing-in-Publication Data
A catalogue record for this book is available from the British Library

Library of Congress Cataloging-in-Publication Data
Johnson, Gerry.
Fundamentals of strategy / Gerry Johnson, Kevan Scholes, Richard Whittington.
p. cm.
Includes bibliographical references and index.
ISBN 978-0-273-71310-4 (pbk. : alk. paper) 1. Business planning. 2. Strategic planning. 3. Business planning – Case studies. 4. Strategic planning – Case studies. I. Scholes, Kevan. II. Whittington, Richard, 1958– III. Title.
HD30.28.J6495 2008
658.4′012—dc22

2008034650

10 9 8 7 6 5 4 3
12 11 10

Typeset in 9.5/13 Linoletter by 35
Printed and bound by Graficas Estella, Spain

Welcome to
FUNDAMENTALS OF STRATEGY

Strategy is a fascinating subject. It's about the overall direction of all kinds of organisations, from multinationals to entrepreneurial start-ups, from charities to ... ore. **Strategy raises the big questions** about ... w, how they innovate and how they change. As a ... **you will be involved** in influencing, implementing ...

... *Strategy* is to give you a **clear understanding** of ... ques of strategy, and to **help you get a great** ... ow you might make the most of the text:

... n the fundamental areas of strategy in just ...

... **case examples** to **clarify your understanding** of ... anslate into an easily recognisable, real-world ...

... **d readings** at the end of each chapter. They're ... and valuable sources that will enhance your ... edge in your course work.

... ts and Audio Summary ... to the website at ... here you can ...

KEY CONCEPT

AUDIO SUMMARY

... rstanding of key concepts using **self-assessment** ... and interactive exercises, and ... nic flashcards and a glossary in 6 languages.

... *gy* to give you what you need: a clear and concise ... o put that into practice, and – of course – success ... u'll be just as intrigued by the key issues of ...

... d luck!

Gerry Johnson
Kevan Scholes
Richard Whittington

* P.S. In order **to log in to the website**, you'll need to register with the **access code** included with all new copies of the book.

Gerry Johnson BA, PhD (left) is Professor of Strategic Management at Lancaster University Management School and a Senior Fellow of the UK Advanced Institute of Management (AIM) Research. He is the author of numerous books, has published papers in many of the foremost management research journals in the world and is a regular speaker at the major academic conferences throughout the world. He also serves on the editorial boards of the *Academy of Management Journal*, the *Strategic Management Journal* and the *Journal of Management Studies*. His research is into strategic management practice, processes of strategy development and strategic change in organisations. As a consultant he works with senior management teams on issues of strategy development and strategic change where he applies many of the concepts from *Exploring Corporate Strategy* to help them challenge, question and develop the strategies of their organisations.

Kevan Scholes MA, PhD, DMS, CIMgt, FRSA (centre) is Principal Partner of Scholes Associates – specialising in strategic management. He is also Visiting Professor of Strategic Management and formerly Director of the Sheffield Business School, UK. He has extensive experience of teaching strategy to both undergraduate and postgraduate students at several universities. In addition his corporate management development work includes organisations in manufacturing, many service sectors and a wide range of public service organisations. He has regular commitments outside the UK – including Ireland, Australia and New Zealand. He has also been an advisor on management development to a number of national bodies and is a Companion of The Chartered Management Institute.

Richard Whittington MA, MBA, PhD (right) is Professor of Strategic Management at the Saïd Business School and Millman Fellow at New College, University of Oxford. He is author or co-author of eight books and has published many journal articles. He is a senior editor of *Organization Studies* and serves on the editorial boards of *Organization Science*, the *Strategic Management Journal* and *Long Range Planning*, amongst others. He has had full or visiting positions at the Harvard Business School, HEC Paris, Imperial College London, the University of Toulouse and the University of Warwick. He is active in executive education and consulting, working with organisations from across Europe, the USA and Asia. His current research is focused on strategy practice and international management.

Contents

Supporting resources

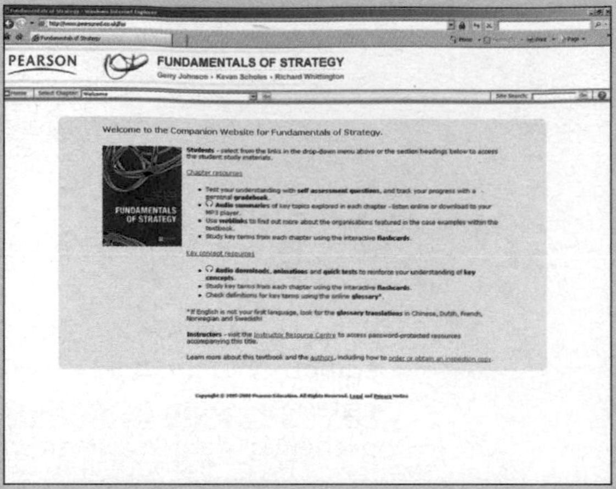

Visit the *Fundamentals of Strategy* Companion Website at **www.pearsoned.co.uk/fos**

Register to create your own personal account using the access code supplied with the copy of the book. Access the following teaching and learning resources:

Resources for students

- **Key concepts: audio downloads, animations** and **quick tests** to reinforce your understanding
- **Chapter audio summaries** that you can download or listen to online
- **Self assessment questions** and a **personal gradebook** so you can test your learning and track your progress
- **Revision flashcards** to help you prepare for your exams
- A **multi-lingual online glossary** to explain key concepts
- Guidance on **how to analyse a case study**
- **Links** to relevant sites on the web so you can explore more about the organisations featured in the case examples and case studies

Also: The student Companion Website with Grade Tracker provides the following features:

- Enables students to save their scores from self assessment questions, and lecturers to monitor the scores of their class
- Search tool to help locate specific items of content
- Online help and support to assist with website usage and troubleshooting

Resources for instructors

- **Instructor's manual**, including extensive teaching notes for cases and suggested teaching plans
- Media-rich downloadable **PowerPoint slides**, including animations, video clips and key exhibits from the book
- **Classic cases** – over 30 case studies from previous editions of the book
- **Secure testbank** containing over 600 questions

Also: the following instructor resources are available off-line:

- Instructor's manual in hard copy, with CD containing PowerPoint slides and classic cases
- Video resources on DVD

For more information please contact your local Pearson Education sales representative or visit **www.pearsoned.co.uk/fos**

Preface

About *Fundamentals of Strategy*

We are delighted to introduce *Fundamentals of Strategy*. Based on the eighth edition of the market-leading *Exploring Corporate Strategy*, this book concentrates on the fundamental issues and techniques of strategy. *Fundamentals* will particularly suit those on short courses in strategy – for example, doing an initial course at undergraduate, postgraduate or post-experience level, or studying strategy as part of a wider degree in the sciences or engineering perhaps.

Students can be sure that they have the essential materials in this book, while knowing that they can easily go deeper into particular topics by referring to the complete *Exploring Corporate Strategy*. Teachers familiar with *Exploring Corporate Strategy* will find that the definitions and the content of *Fundamentals of Strategy* are entirely consistent, making it easy to teach courses using the different books in parallel.

Fundamentals of Strategy has ten chapters, with the emphasis on what *Exploring Corporate Strategy* terms the 'strategic position' and 'strategic choices'. Under 'strategic position', *Fundamentals* introduces environmental analysis, strategic capability, strategic purpose and culture and strategy. Under 'strategic choices', the book addresses business-level strategy, corporate-level strategy, international strategy and strategy methods and evaluation. The final tenth chapter, Strategy in Action, raises implementation issues such as organisational structure, management processes and strategic change.

Wider and more extensive treatments of other issues, such as the practice and resourcing of strategy, deeper analysis through 'key debates', 'strategy lenses' and 'commentaries', and many more cases can all be found in *Exploring Corporate Strategy*. A brief contents of *Exploring Corporate Strategy* can be found on page xv.

We are excited to be launching this new *Fundamentals of Strategy*, believing that it will bring the proven benefits of *Exploring Corporate Strategy* to the growing number of students on shorter courses. A guide to getting the most from the features and learning materials of the book follows this preface.

We hope that you will benefit from and enjoy using the *Fundamentals of Strategy*. We are always happy to receive your feedback; you can contact us at the email addresses given below.

Gerry Johnson (gerry.johnson@lancaster.ac.uk)
Kevan Scholes (KScholes@scholes.u-net.com)
Richard Whittington (richard.whittington@sbs.ox.ac.uk)
November 2008

Authors' Acknowledgements

Many people helped us with the development of the eighth edition of *Exploring Corporate Strategy*, from which this new textbook derives.

Special thanks are due to the following members of the Advisory Board for their valued, insightful and constructive comments.

Anders Soderholm, Umea Universiteit
Antony Beckett, University Of West England
Bruce Millett, University of Southern Queensland
Erik Dirksen, Universiteit Van Amsterdam
Frederic Frery, ESCP-EAP, Paris
Ian McKeown, University of Wolverhampton
James Cunningham, National University of Ireland, Galway
Jamie Weatherston, University Of Northumbria
Jesper Norus, Copenhagen Business School (F)
Jill Shepherd, Simon Fraser University
John Toth, Leeds Metropolitan University
Keld Harbo, Aarhus School of Business
Mary Klemm, Bradford University
Mike Danilovic, Jonkoping Business School
Hans Roosendaal, University of Twente
Rehan Ul Haq, University Of Birmingham
Robert Morgan, Cardiff University
Ron Livingstone, Glasgow Caledonian University
Sarah Dixon, Kingston University
Tina McGuiness, Sheffield University

We are also grateful to the following reviewers, who provided comment on draft chapters of *Fundamentals of Strategy*. Their feedback helped to confirm the selection of content from the eighth edition to ensure that *Fundamentals of Strategy* fits the needs of the short courses for which it is designed.

Declan Bannon, University of the West of Scotland
Laure Cabantous, Nottingham University
Marko Kohtamäki, University of Vaasa
Olivier Furrer, Radboud University, Nijmegen
Sue Hornibrook, University of Kent
Volker Mahnke, Copenhagen Business School

In addition to those acknowledged above, many other users of the book provide more informal advice and suggestions. We are grateful to both teachers – many of whom we have had the pleasure of meeting at our annual workshops – and our students and clients at Sheffield, Strathclyde, Lancaster and Oxford and in many other places around the world for this invaluable feedback.

We would like to thank those who have contributed directly to the book by providing case studies and illustrations, and those organisations that have been brave enough to be featured in these. These organisations sometimes face difficulties in responding to enquiries from tutors and students relating to the cases, and so we hope that you will respect their request not to contact them directly for further information.

There are many colleagues that we would like to thank for helping to keep us up to date in particular aspects of the subject and related areas. So thank you to, Julia Balogun, John Barbour, George Burt, Stéphane Girod, Mark Gilmartin, Royston Greenwood, Paula Jarzabkowski, Phyl Johnson, Aidan McQuade, Michael Mayer, Jill Shepherd, Angela Sutherland, Thomas Powell and Basak Yakis.

Thanks are also due to Christine Reid and Scott McGowan at Strathclyde for their valuable assistance with references, as well as to Lorna Carlaw at Strathclyde and Kate Goodman at Oxford for their part in preparing the manuscript for the book.

Getting the Most from *Fundamentals of Strategy*

Fundamentals of Strategy builds on the established strengths of *Exploring Corporate Strategy,* proven over eight best-selling editions. A range of in-text features and supplementary resources have been developed to enable you and your students to gain maximum added value to the teaching and learning of strategy.

- **Outstanding pedagogical features**. Each chapter has clear learning outcomes, definitions of key concepts in the margins, practical questions associated with real-life Illustrations, and concise end-of-chapter case examples through which students can easily apply what they have learnt.
- **Up-to-date materials**. The *Fundamentals of Strategy* is based on the latest 8th edition of *Exploring Corporate Strategy*. Our references are up to date, so that you can easily access the latest research. Cases and examples are fresh and engage with student interests and day-to-day experience.
- **Range of examples**. This edition maintains the wide range of examples used in the text, Illustrations and cases. We draw from all over the world, with no bias to North America, and use examples from the public and voluntary sectors as well as the private.

  Fundamentals of Strategy does not include any longer cases. If you wish to supplement the book with any of the case studies included in *Exploring Corporate Strategy,* please consult your local Pearson Education representative to find out what their Custom Publishing programme can do for you.
- **Attractive text layout and design**. We make careful use of colour and photography to improve clarity and ease of 'navigation' through the text. Reading the text should be an enjoyable and straight forward process.
- **Teaching and learning support**. You and your students can access a wealth of resources at **www.pearsoned.co.uk/fos**, including the following:

  For students
  - audio material to explain key concepts
  - self-assessment questions to measure progress and understanding
  - flashcards, a multilingual glossary, and weblinks for revision and research

  For instructors
  - an Instructor's Manual which provides a comprehensive set of teaching support, including guidance on the use of case studies and assignments, and advice on how to plan a programme using the text
  - PowerPoint slides

- a test-bank of assessment questions
- Classic cases from previous editions of the book

In addition to the website, a printed copy of the Instructor's Manual is also available.

- **Video resources on DVD**. A DVD has been specially created for in-class use and contains briefings on selected topics from the authors, and material to support some of the case studies in *Exploring Corporate Strategy*: Some of this material may also be relevant for users of *Fundamentals of Strategy*.

  1. 'With the Experts' (the authors explain key concepts)
     Strategy in Different Contexts
     Porter's Five Forces
     Core Competences
     Strategic Drift and the Cultural Web
  2. Case Study organisations
     SAB Miller – international development
     eBay – success and sustainability
     Amazon.com – business level strategy
     Eurotunnel – a clash of national cultures
     Manchester United – football club or business?
     easyJet – competitive strategy
     Marks & Spencer – two CEOs on managing turnaround

  You can order and find out more about these resources from your local Pearson Education representative (**www.pearsoned.co.uk/replocator**).

- **Teachers' Workshop**. We run an annual workshop to facilitate discussion of key challenges and solutions in the teaching of strategic management. Details of forthcoming workshops can be found at **www.pearsoned.co.uk/ecsworkshop**.

- **Complementary textbooks**. In addition to *Exploring Corporate Strategy*, four further textbooks, written in collaboration with Gerry Johnson and Kevan Scholes, build on key themes of *Exploring Corporate Strategy* and examine these in more depth. These are all available from Pearson Education:

  Exploring Strategic Change (3rd edition, 2008); J. Balogun and V. Hope Hailey
  *Exploring Public Sector Strategy (*2001); G. Johnson and K. Scholes (editors)
  Exploring Techniques of Analysis and Evaluation in Strategic Management (1998); V. Ambrosini
  *Exploring Strategic Financial Management (*1998); T. Grundy

As indicated above, *Exploring Corporate Strategy* provides deeper and more extensive coverage of the theory and practice of strategy. A brief table of contents from the eighth edition is listed below:

Guided Tour

→ Strategy in context

Illustrations showcase the application of specific strategic issues in the real world so you can identify and relate theory and practice.

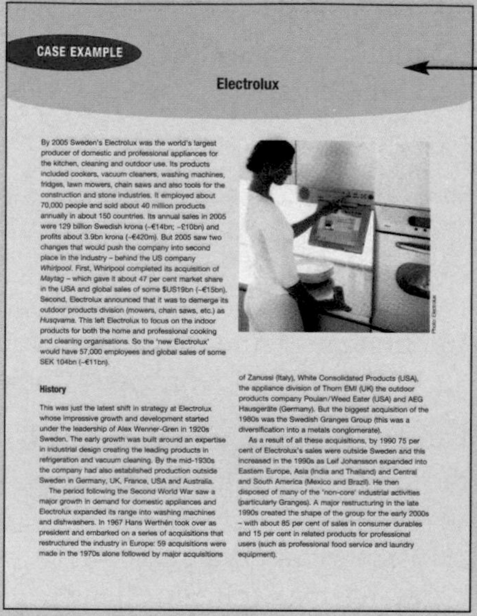

The **Case example** at the end of each chapter provides a broad view of the topic of the chapter in the context of a wide range of global organisations and in a variety of sectors.

→ Checking your understanding

Chapter summaries recap and reinforce the key points to take away from the chapter. Download or listen online to the **audio summaries** on the companion website.

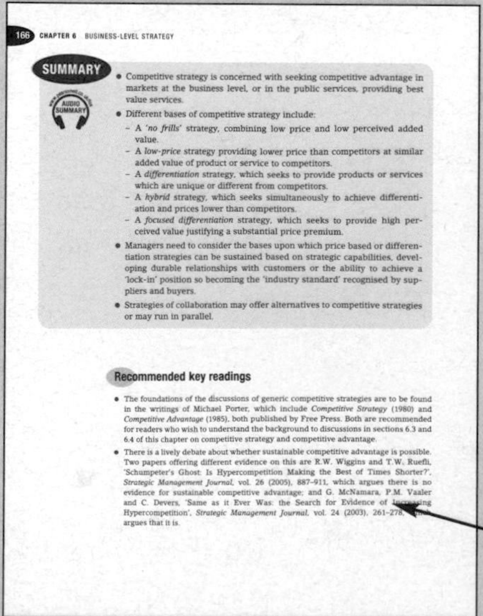

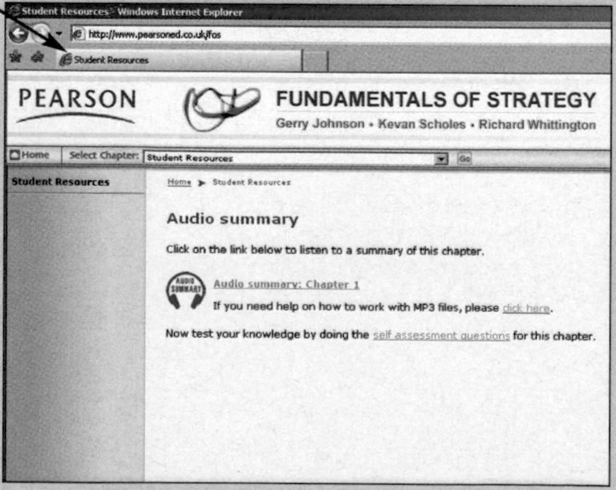

Recommended key readings direct you to other relevant sources so that you can read and research further into the key topics discussed in the chapter.

→ Checking your understanding (continued)

Key terms are highlighted in the text with a brief explanation in the margin when they first appear. These terms are also included in the **Glossary** at the end of the book and on the companion website where you can find them in six languages. You can test your understanding of these key terms using **flashcards** on the website.

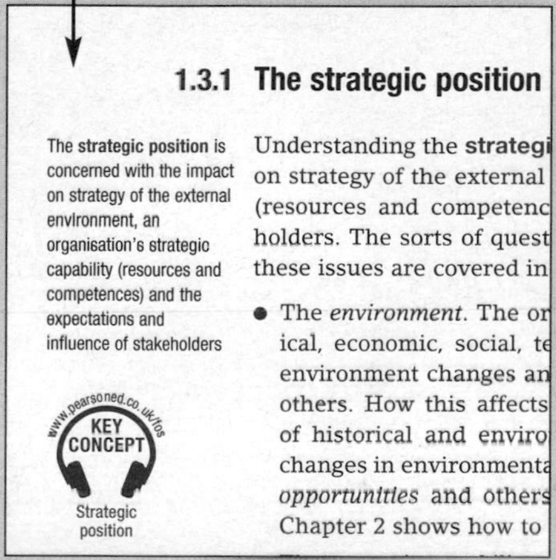

1.3.1 The strategic position

The **strategic position** is concerned with the impact on strategy of the external environment, an organisation's strategic capability (resources and competences) and the expectations and influence of stakeholders

Understanding the **strategi**
on strategy of the external
(resources and competenc
holders. The sorts of quest
these issues are covered in

- The *environment*. The or
ical, economic, social, te
environment changes an
others. How this affects
of historical and enviro
changes in environmenta
opportunities and others
Chapter 2 shows how to

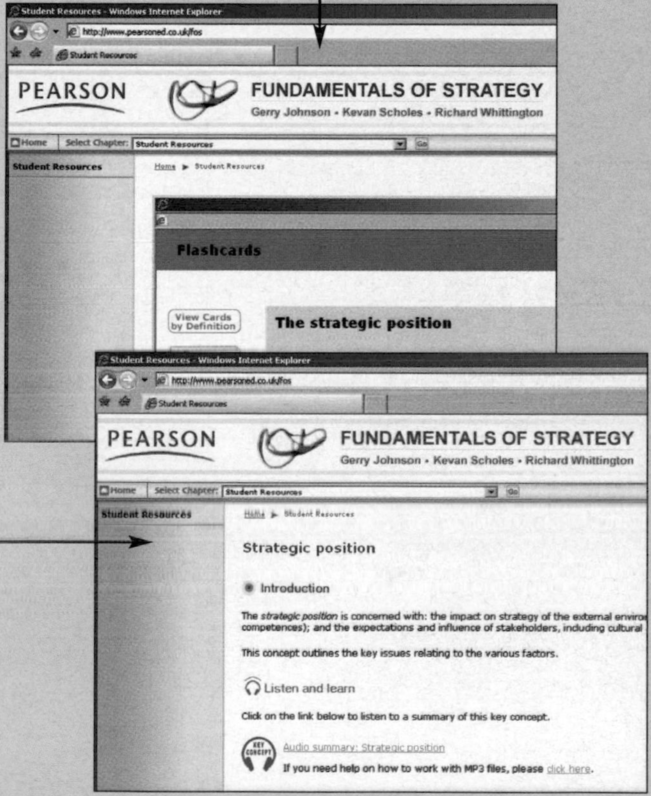

Key concept icons in the text direct you to audio and other resources on the companion website where you can check and reinforce your understanding of key concepts.

→ Assessing your progress

Use the **Self-assessment questions** on the companion website to test your knowledge. Save your score in a personal gradebook and track your progress.

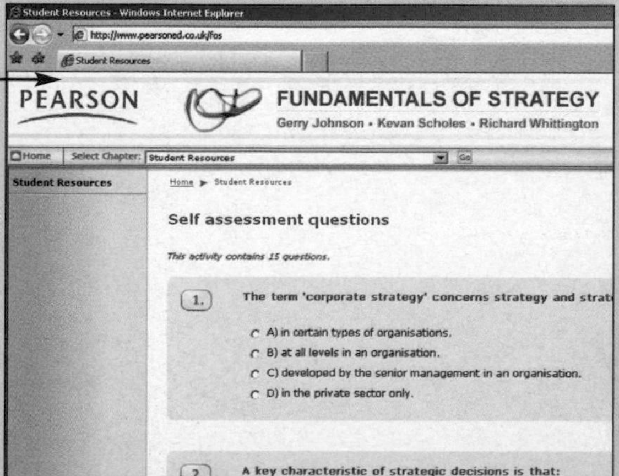

1

Introducing Strategy

LEARNING OUTCOMES

After reading this chapter you should be able to:

- → Understand the characteristics of strategic decisions and what is meant by strategy and strategic management, distinguishing them from operational management;
- → Understand how strategic priorities vary by level: corporate, business and operational;
- → Understand the basic vocabulary of strategy, as used in different contexts;
- → Understand the fundamental elements of the *Exploring Corporate Strategy* strategic management model: strategic position, strategic choices and strategy in action.

Photo: Dennis Gilbert/View Pictures Ltd

1.1 INTRODUCTION

In November 2006 Yahoo! manager Brad Garlinghouse issued a memo that directly challenged the senior management of the internet giant. Leaked to the media as 'The Peanut Butter Manifesto', his memo accused Yahoo!'s leadership of lacking strategic direction. Growth had slowed, Google had overtaken Yahoo! in terms of on-line advertising revenues, and the share price had fallen by nearly a third since the start of the year. According to Brad Garlinghouse, Yahoo! was spread too thin, like peanut butter. It was time for strategic change.

All organisations are faced with the challenges of strategic direction: some from a desire to grasp new opportunities, others to overcome significant problems, as at Yahoo!. This book deals with why changes in strategic direction take place in organisations, why they are important, how such decisions are taken, and the concepts that can be useful in understanding these issues. This introductory chapter addresses particularly the meaning of 'strategy' and 'strategic management', why they are so important and what distinguishes them from other organisational challenges, tasks and decisions. The chapter will draw on the Yahoo! example in Illustration 1.1 to illustrate its points.

1.2 WHAT IS STRATEGY?

Why were the issues facing Yahoo! described as 'strategic'?[1] What types of issues are strategic and what distinguishes them from operational issues in organisations?

1.2.1 The characteristics of strategic decisions

www.pearsoned.co.uk/fos
KEY CONCEPT
Strategy

The words 'strategy' and 'strategic decisions' are typically associated with issues like these:

- *The long-term direction* of an organisation. Brad Garlinghouse explicitly recognised that strategic change in Yahoo! would require a 'marathon and not a sprint'. Strategy at Yahoo! involved long-term decisions about what sort of company it should be, and realising these decisions would take plenty of time.
- *The scope of an organisation's activities*. For example, should the organisation concentrate on one area of activity, or should it have many? Brad Garlinghouse believed that Yahoo! was spread too thinly over too many different activities.

- *Advantage* for the organisation over competition. The problem at Yahoo! was that it was losing its advantage to faster-growing companies such as Google. Advantage may be achieved in different ways and may also mean different things. For example, in the public sector, strategic advantage could be thought of as providing better value services than other providers, thus attracting support and funding from government.
- *Strategic fit with the business environment.* Organisations need appropriate *positioning* in their environment, for example in terms of the extent to which products or services meet clearly identified market needs. This might take the form of a small business trying to find a particular niche in a market, or a multinational corporation seeking to buy up businesses that have already found successful market positions. According to Brad Garlinghouse, Yahoo! was trying to succeed in too many environments.
- *The organisation's resources and competences.*[2] Following 'the resource-based view' of strategy, strategy is about exploiting the strategic capability of an organisation, in terms of its resources and competences, to provide competitive advantage and/or yield new opportunities. For example, an organisation might try to leverage resources such as technology skills or strong brands. Yahoo! claims a brand 'synonymous with the Internet', theoretically giving it clear advantage in that environment.
- *The values and expectations* of powerful actors in and around the organisation. These actors – individuals, groups or even other organisations – can drive fundamental issues such as whether an organisation is expansionist or more concerned with consolidation, or where the boundaries are drawn for the organisation's activities. At Yahoo!, the senior managers may have pursued growth in too many directions, and been too reluctant to hold themselves accountable. But lower-level managers, ordinary employees, suppliers, customers and Internet users all have a stake in the future of Yahoo! too. The beliefs and values of these *stakeholders* will have a greater or lesser influence on the strategy development of an organisation, depending on the power of each. Certainly, Brad Garlinghouse was making a bold bid for influence over what seemed to be a failing strategy.

Overall, the most basic definition of strategy might be 'the long-term direction of an organisation'. However, the characteristics described above can provide the basis for a fuller definition:

Strategy is the *direction* and *scope* of an organisation over the *long term*, which achieves *advantage* in a changing *environment* through its configuration of *resources and competences* with the aim of fulfilling *stakeholder* expectations.

Strategy is the *direction* and *scope* of an organisation over the *long term*, which achieves *advantage* in a changing *environment* through its configuration of *resources and competences* with the aim of fulfilling *stakeholder expectations*

Illustration 1.1

Yahoo!'s peanut butter manifesto

Strategy can involve hard decisions about the scope of the business, its management and its organisation structure.

In November 2006, Brad Garlinghouse, MBA graduate and a Yahoo! senior vice president, wrote a memo to his top managers arguing that Yahoo!, the diversified Internet company, was spreading its resources too thinly, like peanut butter on a slice of bread. Edited extracts from the memo follow:

Three and half years ago, I enthusiastically joined Yahoo!. The magnitude of the opportunity was only matched by the magnitude of the assets. And an amazing team has been responsible for rebuilding Yahoo!. . . .

But all is not well. . . .

I imagine there's much discussion amongst the Company's senior-most leadership around the challenges we face. At the risk of being redundant, I wanted to share my take on our current situation and offer a recommended path forward, an attempt to be part of the solution rather than part of the problem.

RECOGNIZING OUR PROBLEMS

We lack a focused, cohesive vision for our company. We want to do everything and be everything – to everyone. We've known this for years, talk about it incessantly, but do nothing to fundamentally address it. We are scared to be left out. We are reactive instead of charting an unwavering course. We are separated into silos that far too frequently don't talk to each other. And when we do talk, it isn't to collaborate on a clearly focused strategy, but rather to argue and fight about ownership, strategies and tactics. . . .

I've heard our strategy described as spreading peanut butter across the myriad opportunities that continue to evolve in the online world. The result: a thin layer of investment spread across everything we do and thus we focus on nothing in particular.

I hate peanut butter. We all should.

We lack clarity of ownership and accountability. The most painful manifestation of this is the massive redundancy that exists throughout the organization. We now operate in an organizational structure – admittedly created with the best of intentions – that has become overly bureaucratic. For far too many employees, there is another person with dramatically similar and overlapping responsibilities. This slows us down and burdens the company with unnecessary costs.

There's a reason why a centerfielder and a left fielder have clear areas of ownership. Pursuing the same ball repeatedly results in either collisions or dropped balls. Knowing that someone else is pursuing the ball and hoping to avoid that collision – we have become timid in our pursuit. Again, the ball drops.

We lack decisiveness. Combine a lack of focus with unclear ownership, and the result is that decisions are either not made or are made when it is already too late. Without a clear and focused vision, and without complete clarity of ownership, we lack a macro perspective to guide our decisions and visibility into who should make those decisions. We are repeatedly stymied by challenging and hairy decisions. We are held hostage by our analysis paralysis.

We end up with competing (or redundant) initiatives and synergistic opportunities living in the different silos of our company. . . .

SOLVING OUR PROBLEMS

We have awesome assets. Nearly every media and communications company is painfully jealous of our position. We have the largest audience, they are highly engaged and our brand is synonymous with the Internet.

If we get back up, embrace dramatic change, we will win.

I don't pretend there is only one path forward available to us. However, at a minimum, I want to be part of the solution and thus have outlined a plan here that I believe can work. It is my strong belief that we need to act very quickly or risk going further down a slippery slope. The plan here is not perfect; it is, however, FAR better than no action at all.

There are three pillars to my plan:

1 Focus the vision.
2 Restore accountability and clarity of ownership.
3 Execute a radical reorganization.

1 Focus the vision

a) We need to boldly and definitively declare what we are and what we are not.
b) We need to exit (sell?) non core businesses and eliminate duplicative projects and businesses.

My belief is that the smoothly spread peanut butter needs to turn into a deliberately sculpted strategy – that is narrowly focused. . . .

2 Restore accountability and clarity of ownership

a) Existing business owners must be held accountable for where we find ourselves today – heads must roll,
b) We must thoughtfully create senior roles that have holistic accountability for a particular line of business. . . .
c) We must redesign our performance and incentive systems.

I believe there are too many BU [Business Unit] leaders who have gotten away with unacceptable results and worse – unacceptable leadership. Too often they (we!) are the worst offenders of the problems outlined here. We must signal to both the employees and to our shareholders that we will hold these leaders (ourselves) accountable and implement change. . . .

3 Execute a radical reorganization

a) The current business unit structure must go away.
b) We must dramatically decentralize and eliminate as much of the matrix as possible.
c) We must reduce our headcount by 15–20%.

I emphatically believe we simply must eliminate the redundancies we have created and the first step in doing this is by restructuring our organization. We can be more efficient with fewer people and we can get more done, more quickly. We need to return more decision making to a new set of business units and their leadership. But we can't achieve this with baby step changes. We need to fundamentally rethink how we organize to win. . . .

I love Yahoo!. I'm proud to admit that I bleed purple and yellow. I'm proud to admit that I shaved a Y in the back of my head.

My motivation for this memo is the adamant belief that, as before, we have a tremendous opportunity ahead. I don't pretend that I have the only available answers, but we need to get the discussion going; change is needed and it is needed soon. We can be a stronger and faster company – a company with a clearer vision and clearer ownership and clearer accountability.

We may have fallen down, but the race is a marathon and not a sprint. I don't pretend that this will be easy. It will take courage, conviction, insight and tremendous commitment. I very much look forward to the challenge.

So let's get back up.
Catch the balls.
And stop eating peanut butter.

Source: Extracts from Brad Garlinghouse's memo to Yahoo! managers, November 2006. Reprinted in *Wall Street Journal*, 16 November 2006.

Questions

1 Why were the issues facing Yahoo! described as strategic? Refer to Exhibit 1.1.

2 Identify examples of issues that fit each of the circles of the model in Exhibit 1.3.

Exhibit 1.1 summarises these characteristics of strategic decisions and also highlights some of the implications:

- *Complexity* is a defining feature of strategy and strategic decisions and is especially so in organisations with wide geographical scope, such as multinational firms, or wide ranges of products or services. For example, Yahoo! faces the complexity both of a fast-moving market environment and poorly-organised internal businesses.
- *Uncertainty* is inherent in strategy, because nobody can be sure about the future. For Yahoo!, the Internet environment is one of constant and unforeseeable innovation.
- *Operational decisions* are linked to strategy. For example, any attempt to coordinate Yahoo!'s business units more closely will have knock-on effects on web-page designs and links, career development and advertiser relationships. This link between overall strategy and operational aspects of the

Exhibit 1.1 Strategic decisions

Strategic decisions are about:

- The **long-term** direction of an organisation
- The **scope** of an organisation's activities
- Gaining **advantage** over competitors
- Addressing changes in the **business environment**
- Building on resources and competences (**capability**)
- **Values and expectations** of stakeholders

Therefore they are likely to:

- Be **complex** in nature
- Be made in situations of **uncertainty**
- Affect **operational** decisions
- Require an **integrated** approach (both inside and outside an organisation)
- Involve considerable **change**

organisation is important for two other reasons. First, if the operational aspects of the organisation are not in line with the strategy, then, no matter how well considered the strategy is, it will not succeed. Second, it is at the operational level that real strategic advantage can be achieved. Indeed, competence in particular operational activities might determine which strategic developments might make most sense.

- *Integration* is required for effective strategy. Managers have to cross functional and operational boundaries to deal with strategic problems and come to agreements with other managers who, inevitably, have different interests and perhaps different priorities. Yahoo! for example needs an integrated approach to powerful advertisers such as Sony and Vodafone from across all its businesses.
- *Relationships and networks* outside the organisation are important in strategy, for example with suppliers, distributors and customers. For Yahoo!, advertisers and users are crucial sets of relationships.
- *Change* is typically a crucial component of strategy. Change is often difficult because of the heritage of resources and because of organisational culture. According to Brad Garlinghouse at least, Yahoo!'s barriers to change seem to include a top management that is afraid of taking hard decisions and a lack of clear accountability amongst lower-level management.

1.2.2 Levels of strategy

Corporate-level strategy is concerned with the overall purpose and scope of an organisation and how value will be added to the different parts (business units) of the organisation

Strategies exist at a number of levels in an organisation. Taking Yahoo! again as an example, it is possible to distinguish at least three different levels of strategy. The top level is **corporate-level strategy**, concerned with the overall scope of an organisation and how value will be added to the different parts (business units) of the organisation. This could include issues of geographical coverage, diversity of products/services or business units, and how resources are to be allocated between the different parts of the organisation. For Yahoo!, whether to sell some of its existing businesses is clearly a crucial corporate-level decision. In general, corporate-level strategy is also likely to be concerned with the expectations of owners – the shareholders and the stock market. It may well take form in an explicit or implicit statement of 'mission' that reflects such expectations. Being clear about corporate-level strategy is important: determining the range of business to include is the *basis* of other strategic decisions.

Business-level strategy is about how to compete successfully in particular markets

The second level is **business-level strategy**, which is about how the various businesses included in the corporate strategy should compete in their particular markets (for this reason, business-level strategy is sometimes called 'competitive strategy'). In the public sector, the equivalent of business-level strategy is decisions about how units should provide best value services. This typically concerns issues such as pricing strategy, innovation or differentiation, for instance by better quality or a distinctive distribution channel. So, whereas corporate-level strategy involves decisions about the organisation as a whole, strategic decisions relate to particular strategic business units (SBU) within the overall organisation. A **strategic business unit** is a part of an organisation for which there is a distinct external market for goods or services that is different from another SBU. Yahoo!'s strategic business units include businesses such as Yahoo! Photos and Yahoo! Music.

A strategic business unit is a part of an organisation for which there is a distinct external market for goods or services that is different from another SBU

Of course, in very simple organisations with only one business, the corporate strategy and the business-level strategy are nearly identical. None the less, even here, it is useful to distinguish a corporate-level strategy, because this provides the framework for whether and under what conditions other business opportunities might be added or rejected. Where the corporate strategy does include several businesses, there should be a clear link between strategies at an SBU level and the corporate level. In the case of Yahoo!, relationships with online advertisers stretch across different business units, and using, protecting and enhancing the Yahoo! brand is vital for all. The corporate strategy with regard to the brand should support the SBUs, but at the same time the SBUs have to make sure their business-level strategies do not damage the corporate whole or other SBUs in the group.

The third level of strategy is at the operating end of an organisation. Here there are **operational strategies**, which are concerned with how the component parts of an organisation deliver effectively the corporate- and business-level strategies in terms of resources, processes and people. For example, Yahoo! has web-page designers in each of its businesses, for whom there are appropriate operational strategies in terms of design, layout and renewal. Indeed, in most businesses, successful business strategies depend to a large extent on decisions that are taken, or activities that occur, at the operational level. The integration of operational decisions and strategy is therefore of great importance, as mentioned earlier.

Operational strategies are concerned with how the component parts of an organisation deliver effectively the corporate- and business-level strategies in terms of resources, processes and people

1.2.3 The vocabulary of strategy

You will find a variety of terms used in relation to strategy, so it is worth devoting a little space to clarifying some of these. Exhibit 1.2 and Illustration 1.2 employ some of the terms that readers will come across in this and other books on strategy and in everyday business usage. Exhibit 1.2 explains these in relation to a personal strategy readers may have followed themselves – improving physical fitness.

Not all these terms are always used in organisations or in strategy books: indeed, in this book the word 'goal' is rarely used. It will also be seen, through the many examples in this book, that terminology is not used consistently across organisations (see also Illustration 1.2). Managers and students of strategy need to be aware of this. Moreover, it may or may not be that mission, goals, objectives, strategies and so on are written down precisely. In some organisations this is done very formally; in others a mission or strategy might

Exhibit 1.2 The vocabulary of strategy

Term	Definition	A personal example
Mission	Overriding purpose in line with the values or expectations of stakeholders	Be healthy and fit
Vision or strategic intent	Desired future state: the aspiration of the organisation	To run the London Marathon
Goal	General statement of aim or purpose	Lose weight and strengthen muscles
Objective	Quantification (if possible) or more precise statement of the goal	Lose 5 kilos by 1 September and run the marathon next year
Strategic capability	Resources, activities and processes. Some will be unique and provide 'competitive advantage'	Proximity to a fitness centre, a successful diet
Strategies	Long-term direction	Exercise regularly, compete in marathons locally, stick to appropriate diet
Business model	How product, service and information 'flow' between participating parties	Associate with a collaborative network (e.g. join running club)
Control	The monitoring of action steps to: • assess effectiveness of strategies and actions • modify as necessary strategies and/or actions	Monitor weight, kilometres run and measure times: if progress satisfactory, do nothing; if not, consider other strategies and actions

be implicit and, therefore, must be deduced from what an organisation is doing. However, as a general guideline the following terms are often used.

- A *mission* is a general expression of the overall purpose of the organisation, which, ideally, is in line with the values and expectations of major stakeholders and concerned with the scope and boundaries of the organisation. It is sometimes referred to in terms of the apparently simple but challenging question: *'What business are we in?'*
- A *vision* or *strategic intent* is the desired future state of the organisation. It is an aspiration around which a strategist, perhaps a chief executive, might seek to focus the attention and energies of members of the organisation.
- If the word *goal* is used, it usually means a general aim in line with the mission. It may well be qualitative in nature.
- On the other hand, an *objective* is more likely to be quantified, or at least to be a more precise aim in line with the goal. In this book the word 'objective' is used whether or not there is quantification.

Illustration 1.2

The vocabulary of strategy in different contexts

All sorts of organisations use the vocabulary of strategy. Compare these extracts from the statements of communications giant Nokia and Kingston University, a public institution based in London with 20,000 students.

Nokia

Vision and Mission: Connecting is about helping people to feel close to what matters. Wherever, whenever, Nokia believes in communicating, sharing, and in the awesome potential in connecting the 2 billion who do with the 4 billion who don't.

If we focus on people, and use technology to help people feel close to what matters, then growth will follow. In a world where everyone can be connected, Nokia takes a very human approach to technology.

Strategy: At Nokia, customers remain our top priority. Customer focus and consumer understanding must always drive our day-to-day business behavior. Nokia's priority is to be the most preferred partner to operators, retailers and enterprises.

Nokia will continue to be a growth company, and we will expand to new markets and businesses. World leading productivity is critical for our future success. Our brand goal is for Nokia to become the brand most loved by our customers.

In line with these priorities, Nokia's business portfolio strategy focuses on five areas, with each having long-term objectives: create winning devices; embrace consumer Internet services; deliver enterprise solutions; build scale in networks; expand professional services.

There are three strategic assets that Nokia will invest in and prioritize: brand and design; customer engagement and fulfilment; technology and architecture.

Kingston University, London

Mission: The mission of Kingston University is to promote participation in higher education, which it regards as a democratic entitlement; to strive for excellence in learning, teaching and research; to realise the creative potential and fire the imagination of all its members; and to equip its students to make effective contributions to society and the economy.

Vision: Kingston University aims to be a comprehensive and community University. Our ambition is to create a University that is not constrained by present possibilities, but has a grander and more aspirational vision of its future.

Goals:

- To provide all our current and future students with equal opportunities to realise their learning ambition.
- To provide a comprehensive range of high-quality courses and a supportive environment that encourages critical learning and develops personal, social and employable skills.
- To create authority in research and professional practice for the benefit of individuals, society and the economy.
- To develop collaborative links with providers and stakeholders within the region, nationally and internationally.
- To make the University's organisation, structure, culture and systems appropriate for the delivery of its Mission and Goals.
- To manage and develop its human, physical and financial resources to achieve the best possible academic value and value-for-money.

Sources: www.nokia.com; Kingston University Plan, 2006–2010 (www.kingston.ac.uk).

Questions

1. How do the vocabularies of Nokia and Kingston University fit with each other and with the definitions given in Exhibit 1.2?
2. To what extent is strategy different for a commercial organisation such as Nokia and a public organisation like Kingston University?
3. Compare your university's (or employer's) strategic statements with Kingston's or Nokia's (use a web search with your organisation's name and terms such as 'strategy', 'vision' and 'mission'). What implications might there be for you from any similarities and differences?

- *Strategic capability* is concerned with the *resources and competences* that an organisation can use to provide value to customers or clients. *Unique resources* and *core competences* are the bases upon which an organisation achieves strategic advantage and is distinguished from competitors.
- The concept of *strategy* has already been defined. It is the long-term direction of the organisation. It is likely to be expressed in broad statements both about the direction that the organisation should be taking and the types of action required to achieve objectives. For example, it may be stated in terms of market entry, new products or services, or ways of operating.
- A *business model* describes the structure of product, service and information flows and the roles of the participating parties. For example, a traditional model for manufactured products is a linear flow of product from component manufacturers to product manufacturers to distributor to retailers to consumers. But information may flow directly between the product manufacturer and the final consumer (advertising and market research).
- *Strategic control* involves monitoring the extent to which the strategy is achieving the objectives and suggesting corrective action (or a reconsideration of the objectives).

As the book develops, many other terms will be introduced and explained. These are the basics with which to begin.

Illustration 1.2 compares strategy vocabulary from two organisations operating in very different *contexts*. Nokia is a private sector communications giant, competing against global corporations such as Motorola and Samsung. Profit is vital to Nokia, but still it sees its vision and mission in terms of connecting more people around the world. Kingston University, on the other hand, is a public university, with a commitment to increasing participation in higher education. But it too must earn revenues, and needs to make a surplus in order to be able to invest in the future. Kingston University is also competing for students and research funds, going head-to-head with similar universities in the UK and around the world. Corporate-level and business-level strategies are no less important for a public body such as Kingston University as a commercial one like Nokia.

Strategy vocabulary, therefore, is relevant to a wide range of contexts. A small entrepreneurial start-up will need a strategy statement to persuade investors and lenders of its viability. Public sector organisations need strategy statements not only to know what to do, but also to reassure their funders and regulators that what they do is what they should be doing. Voluntary organisations need to communicate exciting strategies in order to inspire volunteers and donors. If they are to prosper within the larger organisation, SBU managers need to propose clear strategies that are consistent with the objectives of their corporate owners and with the needs of other SBUs within the corporate whole. Even privately-held organisations need persuasive strategy statements to motivate their employees and to build long-term relationships with their key customers or suppliers. Strategy vocabulary, therefore, is used in many different contexts, for many different purposes. Strategy is part of the everyday language of work.

1.3 STRATEGIC MANAGEMENT

Strategic management includes *understanding the strategic position* of an organisation, *strategic choices* for the future and managing *strategy in action*

The term ***strategic management*** underlines the importance of managers with regard to strategy. Strategies do not happen just by themselves. Strategy involves people, especially the managers who decide and implement strategy. Thus this book uses strategic management to emphasise the human element of strategy.

The strategic management role is different in nature from other aspects of management. An operational manager is most often required to deal with problems of operational control, such as the efficient production of goods, the management of a salesforce, the monitoring of financial performance or the design of some new system that will improve the level of customer service. These are all very important tasks, but they are essentially concerned with effectively managing resources already deployed, often in a limited part of the organisation within the context of an existing strategy. Operational control is what managers are involved in for most of their time. It is vital to the success of strategy, but it is not the same as strategic management.

For managers, strategic management involves a greater scope than that of any one area of operational management. Strategic management is concerned with complexity arising out of ambiguous and non-routine situations with organisation-wide rather than operation-specific implications. This is a major challenge for managers who are used to managing on a day-to-day basis the resources they control. It can be a particular problem because of the background of managers who may typically have been trained, perhaps over many years, to undertake operational tasks and to take operational responsibility. Accountants find that they still tend to see problems in financial terms, IT managers in IT terms, marketing managers in marketing terms, and so on. Of course, each of these aspects is important, but none is adequate alone. The manager who aspires to manage or influence strategy needs to develop a capability to take an overview, to conceive of the whole rather than just the parts of the situation facing an organisation. This is often referred to as the 'helicopter view'.

Because strategic management is characterised by its complexity, it is also necessary to make decisions and judgements based on the *conceptualisation* of difficult issues. Yet the early training and experience of managers is often about taking action, or about detailed *planning* or *analysis*. This book explains many analytical approaches to strategy, and it is concerned too with action related to the management of strategy. However, the major emphasis is on the importance of understanding the *strategic concepts* which inform this analysis and action.

Strategic management can be thought of as having three main elements: understanding *the strategic position* of an organisation, making *strategic choices* for the future and managing *strategy in action* (see Exhibit 1.3). As this book is about the fundamentals of strategy, it concentrates on the first two elements, position and choice. There is less emphasis on the management issues of strategy in action: this book focuses simply on key issues such as managing strategic change and putting in structures and processes to deliver the chosen strategy. Other issues to do with strategy in action – such as resourcing and the practice of strategy – are dealt with more fully in *Exploring Corporate Strategy*.[3] Nonetheless, it is important to understand why the three circles in Exhibit 1.3 have been drawn in this particular way.

Exhibit 1.3 could have shown the three elements of strategic management in a linear sequence – first understanding the strategic position, then strategic choices and finally putting strategy in action. Indeed, many texts on the subject do just this. However, in practice, the elements of strategic management do not follow this linear sequence – they are interlinked and feedback on each other. For example, in some circumstances an understanding of the

Exhibit 1.3 **The fundamentals of the *Exploring Corporate Strategy* strategic management model**

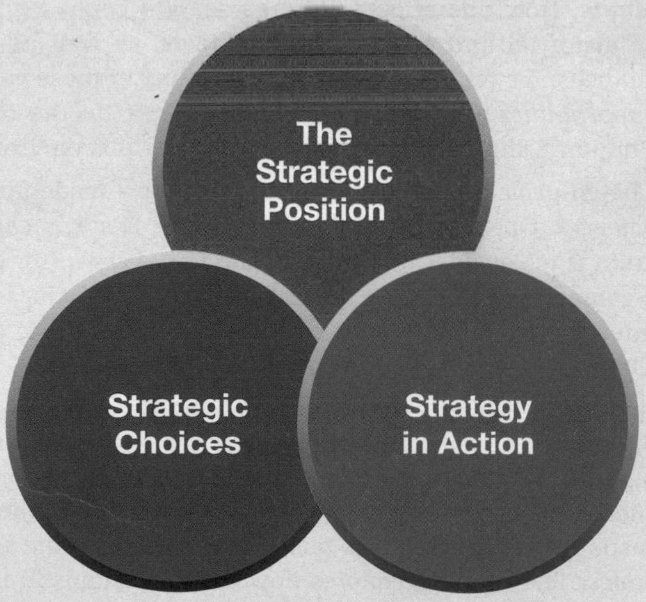

Source: Based on G. Johnson, K. Scholes and R. Whittington, *Exploring Corporate Strategy*, 8th edition, Pearson Education.

strategic position may best be built up from the experience of trying a strategy out in practice. Test marketing a prototype would be a good example. Here strategy in action informs understanding of the strategic position.

The inter-connected circles of Exhibit 1.3 are designed to emphasise this non-linear nature of strategy. Position, choices and action should be seen as closely related, and in practice none has priority over another. It is only for structural convenience that this book starts with strategic position, continues with important choices such as diversification and internationalisation, and then concludes with strategy in action. This sequence is not meant to suggest that the process of strategic management must follow a neat and tidy path. Indeed, the evidence on how strategic management happens in practice suggests that it usually does not occur in tidy ways.

1.3.1 The strategic position

The **strategic position** is concerned with the impact on strategy of the external environment, an organisation's strategic capability (resources and competences) and the expectations and influence of stakeholders

www.pearsoned.co.uk/fos KEY CONCEPT Strategic position

Understanding the **strategic position** is concerned with identifying the impact on strategy of the external environment, an organisation's strategic capability (resources and competences) and the expectations and influence of stakeholders. The sorts of questions this raises are central to future strategies and these issues are covered in Chapters 2 to 5 of this book:

- The *environment*. The organisation exists in the context of a complex political, economic, social, technological, environmental and legal world. This environment changes and is more complex for some organisations than for others. How this affects the organisation could include an understanding of historical and environmental effects, as well as expected or potential changes in environmental variables. Many of those variables will give rise to *opportunities* and others will exert *threats* on the organisation – or both. Chapter 2 shows how to analyse these various environmental factors.
- The *strategic capability* of the organisation – made up of *resources and competences*. One way of thinking about the strategic capability of an organisation is to consider its *strengths* and *weaknesses* (for example, where it is at a competitive advantage or disadvantage). The aim is to form a view of the internal influences – and constraints – on strategic choices for the future. Chapter 3 examines strategic capability in detail.
- Chapter 4 explores the major influences of *stakeholder expectations* on an organisation's *purposes*. Purpose is encapsulated in an organisation's *vision, mission* and *values*. Here the issue of *corporate governance* is important: who *should* the organisation primarily serve and how should managers be held responsible for this? This raises issues of *corporate social responsibility* and *ethics*. The chapter explores how both variations in international corporate governance systems and the *power* configurations within particular organisations can influence purpose.

- Chapter 5 examines *cultural and historical influences* can also influence strategy. Cultural influences can be *organisational*, *sectoral* or *national*. Historical influences can create *lock-in* on particular strategic trajectories. The impact of these influences can be *strategic drift*, a failure to create necessary change. The chapter demonstrates how managers can analyse and challenge these historical and cultural influences on strategy.

These positioning issues were all important for Yahoo! as it faced its crisis in 2006. The external environment offered the threat of growing competition from Google. Its strong Internet brand and existing audience were key resources for defending its position. The company was struggling with its purposes, with top management apparently indecisive. The company none the less had inherited a strong culture, powerful enough to make Brad Garlinghouse shave a Y on his head and believe that his blood bled in the corporate colours of his employer.

1.3.2 Strategic choices

Strategic choices involve understanding the underlying bases for future strategy at both the business unit and corporate levels and the options for developing strategy in terms of both the directions and methods of development

Strategic choices involve the options for strategy in terms of both the directions in which strategy might move and the methods by which strategy might be pursued. For example, an organisation might have to choose between alternative diversification moves, for example entering into new products and markets. As it diversifies, it has different methods available to it, for example developing a new product itself or acquiring an organisation already active in the area. Typical options and methods are covered in Chapters 6 to 9, as follows:

- There are strategic choices in terms of how the organisation seeks to compete at the *business level*. Typically these involve pricing and differentiation strategies, and decisions about how to compete or collaborate with competitors. These issues of business-level strategies will be discussed in Chapter 6.
- At the highest level in an organisation there are issues of *corporate-level strategy*, which are concerned with the scope, or breadth, of an organisation. These include *diversification* decisions about the portfolio of products and the spread of markets. For Yahoo!, being spread over too many businesses seems to be the major strategic problem. Corporate-level strategy is also concerned with the relationship between the separate parts of the business and how the corporate 'parent' adds value to these various parts. At Yahoo!, it is not clear how much the corporate parent is adding value to its constituent parts. These issues about the role of the centre and how it adds value are *parenting* issues and will be discussed in Chapter 7.
- *International strategy* is a form of diversification, into new geographical markets. It is often at least as challenging as diversification. Chapter 8 examines choices organisations have to make about which geographical markets

to prioritise and how to enter them, by export, licensing, direct investment or acquisition.

- Organisations have to make choices about the *methods* by which they pursue their strategies. Many organisations prefer to grow 'organically', in other words by building new businesses with their own resources. Other organisations might develop by mergers/acquisitions and/or strategic alliances with other organisations. These alternative methods are discussed in Chapter 9.

1.3.3 Strategy in action

Strategy in action is concerned with ensuring that strategies are working in practice

Strategy in action is concerned with ensuring that chosen strategies are actually put into practice. Chapter 10 covers three key issues for strategy in action:

- *Structuring* an organisation to support successful performance. According to Brad Garlinghouse, structural silos, matrix organisation and bureaucracy were all big problems for Yahoo!.
- *Processes* are required to control the way in which strategy is implemented. Managers need to ensure that strategies are implemented according to plan, check on progress and make necessary adjustments on the way.
- Managing s*trategic change* is typically an important part of putting strategy into action. This includes the need to understand how the context of an organisation should influence the approach to change and the different types of *roles* for people in managing change. It also looks at the *styles* that can be adopted for managing change and the *levers* by which change can be effected.

Chapter 10 is an introduction to strategy in action: these issues, and related ones, are dealt with more extensively in the same authors' *Exploring Corporate Strategy*.

1.4 STRATEGY DEVELOPMENT PROCESSES

The previous section introduced strategic position, strategic choices and strategy in action. Implicit so far is that strategies are the product of careful analysis and choices. However, this is not the only way that strategies develop in organisations. There are two broad explanations of strategy development:

- The *rational-analytic view* of strategy development is the conventional explanation. Here strategies are developed through rational and analytical processes, led typically by top managers. There is a linear sequence. First the strategic position is analysed; then, after weighing up the options, strategic choices are made; finally, structures, processes and change procedures are put in place to allow effective implementation. Often formal strategic planning systems are important to the analysis and formulation of the strategy. In this view, strategies are *intended*, in other words the product of deliberate choices.

- The *emergent strategy* view is the alternative broad explanation of how strategies develop. In this view, strategies often do not develop as intended or planned, but tend to emerge in organisations over time as a result of ad hoc, incremental or even accidental actions. Good ideas and opportunities often come from practical experience at the bottom of the organisation, rather than from top management and formal strategic plans. Even the best laid plans may need to be abandoned as new opportunities arise or the organisation learns from the marketplace.

The two views are not mutually exclusive. Intended strategies can often succeed, especially in stable markets where there are few surprises. Moreover, an organisation's key stakeholders – employees, owners, customers, regulators and so on – will typically want to see evidence of deliberate strategy-making: it is rarely acceptable to say that everything is simply emergent. The tools and concepts throughout the book, but particularly in Chapters 2, 3 and 6–9, are particularly helpful in this deliberate strategy-making. But it is wise to be open as well to the possibilities of emergence. Inflexible plans can hinder learning and prevent the seizing of opportunities. Moreover, strategic choices do not always come about as a result of simple rational analysis: *cultural and political processes* in organisations can also drive changes in strategy, as will become apparent in the discussions in Chapters 4 and 5.

This book allows for *both* the rational-analytical view and the emergent view. Indeed, the interconnected circles of the *Exploring Corporate Strategy* model in Exhibit 1.3 deliberately underline the possibly non-linear aspects of strategy. It is not just a matter of putting strategic choices into action in a logical sequence leading from strategy formulation to strategy implementation. Strategy in action often creates the strategic choices in the first place, as new opportunities and constraints are discovered in practice. Implementation can lead to formulation as well.[4]

SUMMARY

www.pearsoned.co.uk/fos
AUDIO SUMMARY

- Strategy is the *direction* and *scope* of an organisation over the *long term*, which achieves *advantage* in a changing *environment* through its configuration of *resources and competences* with the aim of fulfilling *stakeholder* expectations.
- Strategic decisions are made at a number of levels in organisations. *Corporate-level strategy* is concerned with an organisation's overall purpose and scope; *business-level (or competitive) strategy* with how to compete successfully in a market; and *operational strategies* with how resources, processes and people can effectively deliver corporate- and business-level strategies. Strategic management is distinguished from day-to-day operational management by the complexity of influences on decisions, the organisation-wide implications and their long-term implications.
- Strategic management has three major elements: understanding the *strategic position*, *strategic choices* for the future and *strategy in action*. The strategic position of an organisation is influenced by the external environment, internal strategic capability and the expectations and influence of stakeholders. Strategic choices include the underlying bases of strategy at both the corporate and business levels and the directions and methods of development. Strategy in action is concerned with issues of structure and processes for implementing strategy and the managing of change.

Recommended key readings

It is always useful to read around a topic. As well as the specific references below, we particularly highlight:

- For general overviews of the evolving nature of the strategy discipline, R. Whittington, *What is strategy – and does it matter?* 2nd edition, International Thompson, 2000; and H. Mintzberg, B. Ahlstrand and J. Lampel, *Strategy Safari: a Guided tour through the wilds of Strategic Management*, Simon and Schuster, 2000.
- For contemporary developments in strategy practice, business newspapers such as the *Financial Times*, *Les Echos* and the *Wall Street Journal*, and business magazines such as *Business Week*, the *Economist*, *L'Expansion* and *Manager-Magazin*. See also the websites of the leading strategy consulting firms: www.mckinsey.com; www.bcg.com; www.bain.com.

References

1. The question 'What is strategy?' has been discussed in R. Whittington, *What is strategy – and does it matter?* (1993/2000), International Thompson; M. Porter, 'What is strategy?', *Harvard Business Review*, November–December (1996), pp. 61–78; and F. Fréry, 'The fundamental dimensions of strategy', *MIT Sloan Management Review*, vol. 48, no. 1 (2006), pp. 71–75.
2. The Harvard 'business policy' tradition is discussed in L. Greiner, A. Bhambri and T. Cummins, 'Searching for a strategy to teach strategy', *Academy of Management Learning and Education*, vol. 2, no. 4 (2003), pp. 401–420.
3. G. Johnson, K. Scholes and R. Whittington, *Exploring Corporate Strategy*, 8th edition (2008), Pearson.
4. The classic discussion of the roles of rational strategy formulation and strategy implementation is in H. Mintzberg, 'The design school: reconsidering the basic premises of strategic management', *Strategic Management Journal*, vol. 11 (1991), pp. 171–195 and H.I. Ansoff, 'Critique of Henry Mintzberg's The Design School', *Strategic Management Journal*, vol. 11 (1991), 449–461.

CASE EXAMPLE

Electrolux

By 2005 Sweden's Electrolux was the world's largest producer of domestic and professional appliances for the kitchen, cleaning and outdoor use. Its products included cookers, vacuum cleaners, washing machines, fridges, lawn mowers, chain saws and also tools for the construction and stone industries. It employed about 70,000 people and sold about 40 million products annually in about 150 countries. Its annual sales in 2005 were 129 billion Swedish krona (~€14bn; ~£10bn) and profits about 3.9bn krona (~€420m). But 2005 saw two changes that would push the company into second place in the industry – behind the US company *Whirlpool*. First, Whirlpool completed its acquisition of *Maytag* – which gave it about 47 per cent market share in the USA and global sales of some $US19bn (~€15bn). Second, Electrolux announced that it was to demerge its outdoor products division (mowers, chain saws, etc.) as *Husqvarna*. This left Electrolux to focus on the indoor products for both the home and professional cooking and cleaning organisations. So the 'new Electrolux' would have 57,000 employees and global sales of some SEK 104bn (~€11bn).

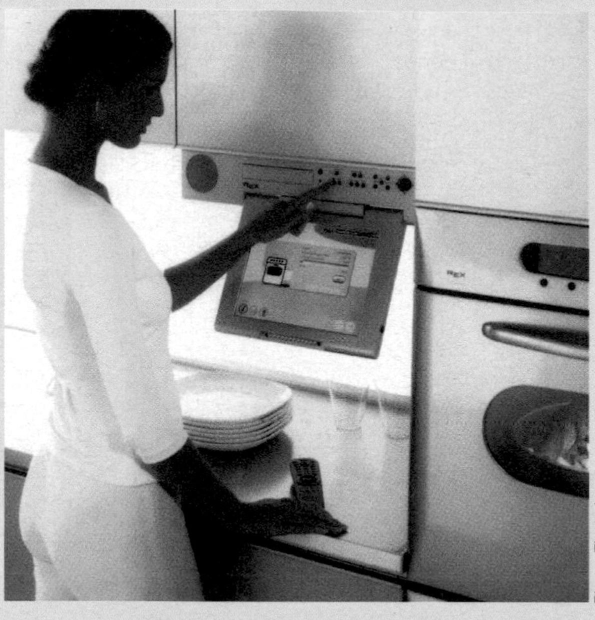

Photo: Electrolux

History

This was just the latest shift in strategy at Electrolux whose impressive growth and development started under the leadership of Alex Wenner-Gren in 1920s Sweden. The early growth was built around an expertise in industrial design creating the leading products in refrigeration and vacuum cleaning. By the mid-1930s the company had also established production outside Sweden in Germany, UK, France, USA and Australia.

The period following the Second World War saw a major growth in demand for domestic appliances and Electrolux expanded its range into washing machines and dishwashers. In 1967 Hans Werthén took over as president and embarked on a series of acquisitions that restructured the industry in Europe: 59 acquisitions were made in the 1970s alone followed by major acquisitions of Zanussi (Italy), White Consolidated Products (USA), the appliance division of Thorn EMI (UK) the outdoor products company Poulan/Weed Eater (USA) and AEG Hausgeräte (Germany). But the biggest acquisition of the 1980s was the Swedish Granges Group (this was a diversification into a metals conglomerate).

As a result of all these acquisitions, by 1990 75 per cent of Electrolux's sales were outside Sweden and this increased in the 1990s as Leif Johansson expanded into Eastern Europe, Asia (India and Thailand) and Central and South America (Mexico and Brazil). He then disposed of many of the 'non-core' industrial activities (particularly Granges). A major restructuring in the late 1990s created the shape of the group for the early 2000s – with about 85 per cent of sales in consumer durables and 15 per cent in related products for professional users (such as professional food service and laundry equipment).

The market

The 2005 annual report highlighted three critically important aspects of the company's markets that their strategies had to address:

Globalisation

'Electrolux operates in an industry with strong global competition. . . . Productivity within the industry has risen over the years, and consumers are offered increasingly better products at lower prices. More and more manufacturers are establishing plants in countries where production costs are considerably lower . . . and also purchasing more components there. In time, production costs for the major producers will essentially be at the same level. This will stimulate a shift of competitive focus to product development, marketing and brand-building.'

Market polarisation

'The combination of changing consumer preferences, the growth of global retail chains and greater global competition is leading to polarisation of the market. More consumers are demanding basic products. Companies that can improve efficiency in production and distribution will be able to achieve profitable growth in this segment. At the same time, demand for higher-price products is increasing.'

Consolidation of retailers

'The dealer structure in the household-appliances market [particularly in the USA] is being consolidated. Traditional dealers are losing market shares to large retail chains. The big chains benefit from high purchasing volumes and wide geographical coverage. This gives them greater opportunities to keep prices low. [But in turn, producers'] costs of serving large retailers is often lower than for traditional outlets, thanks to large volumes and efficient logistics.'

These three factors were also connected. For example, the rapid penetration of Asian producers (for example, LG and Samsung) into the US market was through securing big contracts with major US retailers (The Home Depot and Lowe's respectively).

Electrolux strategies

In the 2005 annual report the Chief Executive (Hans Stråberg) reflected on his first four years with the company and the challenges for the future:

Four years ago I took over as President and CEO of Electrolux. My goal was to accelerate the development of Electrolux as a market-driven company, based on greater understanding of customer needs. . . . We [said that we] would achieve [our goals] by:

- Continuing to cut costs and drive out complexity in all aspects of operations
- Increasing the rate of product renewal based on consumer insight
- Increasing our investment in marketing, and building the Electrolux brand as the global leader in our industry.

He continued by describing the major changes in strategy that had occurred over those four years whilst looking forward to the continuing and new challenges after the demerger in 2006:

Managing under-performers
We have divested or changed the business model for units that could be considered as non-core operations or in which profitability was too low. [For example], instead of continuing production of air-conditioners in the US, which was not profitable, we out-sourced these products to a manufacturer in China. Our operations in motors and compressors have been divested.

Moving production to low-cost countries
Maintaining competitive production costs is a prerequisite for survival in our markets. We will work on improving profitability either by divesting specific units or by changing the business model. It is also important to continue relocating production from high-cost to low-cost countries. . . . We have shut down plants where costs were much too high, and built new ones in countries with competitive cost levels. For example, we moved production of refrigerators from Greenville in the US to Juarez in Mexico. This has enabled us to cut costs and at the same time open a state-of-the-art production unit for serving the entire North American market. The goal is for these activities to be largely completed by late 2008.

More efficient production and logistics
We have put a good deal of time and effort into making production and logistics more efficient. This has involved reducing the number of product platforms, increasing productivity, reducing inventory levels and increasing delivery accuracy.

More efficient purchasing
Purchasing is another area where we have implemented changes in order to improve our cost position, mainly through better coordination at the global level. We have launched a project designed to drastically reduce the

number of suppliers. We have also intensified our cooperation with suppliers in order to cut the costs of components. [But] there is a good deal still to be done. Among other things, we are increasing the share of purchases from low-cost countries.

Intensified product renewal

Our future depends on how well we can combine a continued focus on costs with intensified product renewal and systematic development of both our brands and our personnel. . . . Our process for product development based on consumer insight reduces the risk of incorrect investment decisions. Achieving better impact in development of new products has involved making global coordination more efficient, which has given us a number of new global products. The result of our investments in product development over the past years is clearly reflected in the number of product launches for core appliances, which rose from about 200 in 2002 to about 370 in 2005. . . . Investment in product development has risen by SEK 500 million (~€77m) over the past three years. Our goal is to invest at least 2% of sales in product development. We will continue to launch new products at a high rate.

Access to competence

Over the past years we have established [talent management] processes and tools that ensure the Group of access to competence in the future. Active leadership development, international career opportunities and a result-oriented corporate culture enable us to successfully develop our human resources. In order to lead development in our industry, we will have to act fast and dare to do things differently. [We will also need] a strong environmental commitment and good relations with our suppliers.

Starting to build a strong global brand

When I took over as President and CEO in 2002 I stressed that we had to prioritise building of the Electrolux brand, both globally and across all product categories. A strong brand enables a significant price premium in the market, which leads to a sustainable long-term increase in margin. Work on building a strong brand has been very comprehensive. The share of products sold under the Electrolux brand has risen from 16% of sales in 2002 to almost 50% in 2005. We will continue to work on building the Electrolux brand as the global leader in our industry. Our goal is for our investment in brand-building to correspond to at least 2% of sales.

Looking ahead to the near future

Hans Stråberg concluded his review of the business by a look forward to the following year:

We expect the Group to report higher profitability again in 2006. . . . In both North America and Europe we are going to launch a number of important new products. Professional Indoor Products will improve its position in the North American market in 2006 by developing new distribution channels for food-service equipment. The success of our floor-care operation in the higher price segments will continue, among other things on the basis of higher volumes for cyclone vacuum cleaners.

There will be no change in the rate of relocation of production to low-cost countries. During the second half of 2006 we will see the full effect of the cost-savings generated by moving production from Greenville in the US to Juarez in Mexico. We expect that sales will be adversely affected by the strike at our appliance plant in Nuremberg, Germany [planned to close in 2007]. Continued reduction of purchasing costs is a very important factor for increasing our profitability in 2006.

The strategy that has been effectively implemented in recent years by everyone in our organisation is paying off. In 2006 we will continue this important work on strengthening the Electrolux brand, launching new products and reducing costs.

Sources: Company website (www.electrolux.com); annual report 2005.

Questions

1 Refer to section 1.2.1 and explain why the issues facing Electrolux were strategic. Try to find examples of all of the items cited in that section.

2 What levels of strategy can you identify at Electrolux? (Refer to section 1.2.2.)

3 Identify the main factors about the strategic position of Electrolux. List these separately under environment, capability and expectations (see section 1.3.1). In your opinion which are the most important factors?

4 Think about strategic choices for the company in relation to the issues raised in section 1.3.2.

5 What are the main issues about strategy into action that might determine the success or failure of Electrolux's strategies? (Refer to section 1.3.3.)

2

The Environment

LEARNING OUTCOMES

After reading this chapter, you should be able to:

- → Analyse the broad macro-environment of organisations in terms of political, economic, social, technological, environmental (green) and legal factors (PESTEL).
- → Identify key drivers in this macro-environment and use these key drivers to construct alternative scenarios with regard to environmental change.
- → Use five forces analysis in order to define the attractiveness of industries and sectors for investment and to identify their potential for change.
- → Identify strategic groups, market segments and critical success factors, and use them in order to recognise strategic gaps and opportunities in the market.

Photo: DBURKE/Alamy Images

2.1 INTRODUCTION

The environment is what gives organisations their means of survival. In the private sector, satisfied customers are what keep an organisation in business; in the public sector, it is government, clients, patients or students that typically play the same role. However, the environment is also the source of threats: for example, hostile shifts in market demand, new regulatory requirements, revolutionary technologies or the entry of new competitors. Environmental change can be fatal for organisations. To take one example, after 200 years of prosperity, print publisher Encyclopedia Britannica was nearly swept out of existence by the rise of electronic information sources, such as Microsoft's Encarta and the online Wikipedia. It is vital that managers analyse their environments carefully in order to anticipate and – if possible – influence environmental change.

This chapter therefore provides frameworks for analysing changing and complex environments. These frameworks are organised in a series of 'layers' briefly introduced here and summarised in Exhibit 2.1.

Exhibit 2.1 Layers of the business environment

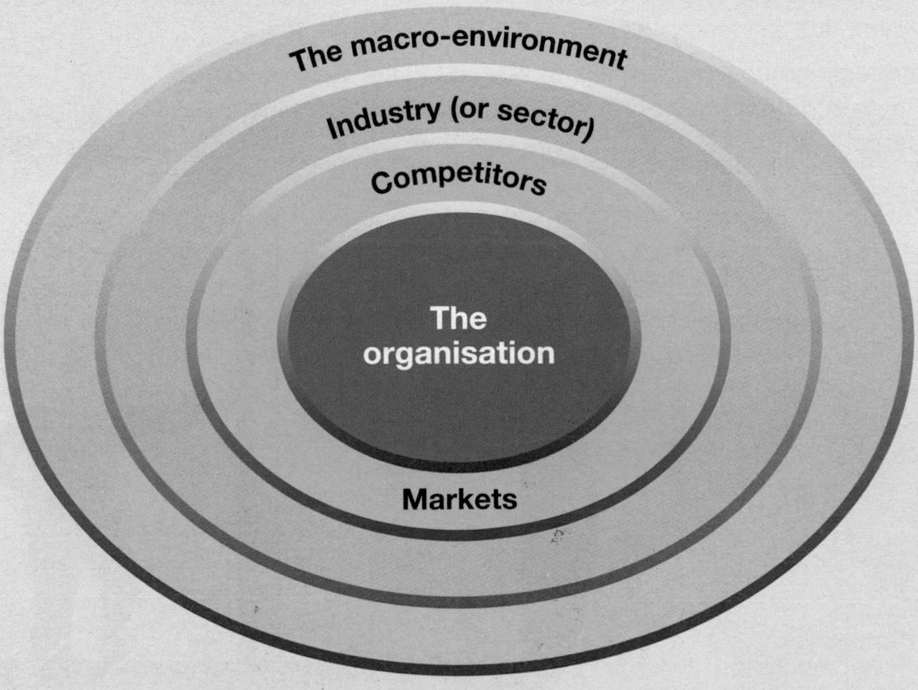

- *The macro-environment* is the highest-level layer. This consists of broad environmental factors that impact to a greater or lesser extent on almost all organisations. Here, the PESTEL framework can be used to identify how future trends in the *political, economic, social, technological, environmental ('green') and legal* environments might impinge on organisations. This PESTEL analysis provides the broad 'data' from which to identify *key drivers of change*. These key drivers can be used to construct *scenarios* of possible futures. Scenarios consider how strategies might need to change depending on the different ways in which the business environment *might* change.
- *Industry, or sector*, forms the next layer with this broad general environment. This is made up of organisations producing the same products or services. Here the *five forces* framework is particularly useful in understanding the attractiveness of particular industries or sectors and potential threats from outside the present set of competitors.
- *Competitors and markets* are the most immediate layer surrounding organisations. Within most industries or sectors there will be many different organisations with different characteristics and competing on different bases, some closer to a particular organisation, some more remote. The concept of *strategic groups* can help identify close and more remote competitors. Similarly, in the marketplace, customers' expectations are not all the same. They have a range of different requirements the importance of which can be understood through the concepts of *market segments* and *critical success factors*.

This chapter works through these three layers in turn, starting with the macro-environment.

2.2 THE MACRO-ENVIRONMENT

The three concepts in this section – PESTEL, key drivers and scenarios – are interrelated tools for analysing the broad macro-environment of an organisation. PESTEL provides a wide overview; key drivers helps focus on what is most important; and scenarios build on key drivers to explore different ways in which the macro-environment might change.

2.2.1 The PESTEL framework

The **PESTEL framework** categorises environmental influences into six main types: political, economic, social, technological, environmental and legal

The **PESTEL framework** (see Illustration 2.1) provides a comprehensive list of influences on the possible success or failure of particular strategies. PESTEL stands for Political, Economic, Social, Technological, Environmental and Legal.[1] Politics highlights the role of governments; Economics refers to macro-economic factors such as exchange rates, business cycles and differential economic growth rates around the world; Social influences include changing

Illustration 2.1

PESTEL analysis of the airline industry

Environmental influences on organisations can be summarised within six categories. For the airline industry, an initial list of influences under the six PESTEL analysis categories might include the following:

Political

- Government support for national carriers
- Security controls
- Restrictions on migration

Economic

- National growth rates
- Fuel prices

Social

- Rise in travel by elderly
- Student international study exchanges

Technological

- Fuel-efficient engines and airframes
- Security check technologies
- Teleconferencing for business

Environmental

- Noise pollution controls
- Energy consumption controls
- Land for growing airports

Legal

- Restrictions on mergers
- Preferential airport rights for some carriers

Questions

1 What additional environmental influences would you add to this initial list for the airline industry?

2 From your more comprehensive list, which of these influences would you highlight as likely to be the 'key drivers for change' for airlines in the coming five years?

www.pearsoned.co.uk/fos KEY CONCEPT PESTEL

cultures and demographics, for example, ageing populations in many Western societies; Technological influences refer to innovations such as the internet, nano-technology or the rise of new composite materials; Environmental stands specifically for 'green' issues, such as pollution and waste; and finally Legal embraces legislative constraints or changes, such as health and safety legislation or restrictions on company mergers and acquisitions.

For managers, it is important to analyse how these factors are changing now and how they are likely to change in the future, drawing out implications for the organisation. Many of these factors are linked together. For example, technology developments may simultaneously change economic factors (for example, creating new jobs), social factors (facilitating more leisure) and environmental factors (reducing pollution). As can be imagined, analysing these factors and their interrelationships can produce long and complex lists.

The **key drivers for change** are environmental factors that are likely to have a high impact on the success or failure of strategy

Rather than getting overwhelmed by a multitude of details, therefore, it is necessary to step back eventually to identify the **key drivers for change**. Key drivers for change are the high impact factors likely to affect significantly the success or failure of strategy. Typical key drivers will vary by industry or sector. For example, a clothing retailer may be primarily concerned with social changes driving customer tastes and behaviour, for example, forces encouraging out-of-town shopping. A computer manufacturer is likely to be concerned with technological change, for example increases in micro-processor speeds. Public sector managers are likely to be especially concerned with social change (for example, an ageing population), political change (changing government funding and policies) and legislative change (introducing new requirements). Identifying key drivers for change helps managers to focus on the PESTEL factors that are most important and which must be addressed as the highest priority. Many other changes will depend on these key drivers anyway (for example, an ageing population will drive changes in public policy and funding). Without a clear sense of the key drivers for change, managers will not be able to take the decisions that allow for effective action.

2.2.2 Building scenarios

When the business environment has high levels of uncertainty arising from either complexity or rapid change (or both), it is impossible to develop a single view of how environment influences might affect an organisation's strategies and indeed it would be dangerous to do so. Scenario analyses are carried out to allow for different possibilities and help prevent managers from closing their minds about alternatives. Thus **scenarios** offer plausible alternative views of how the business environment of an organisation might develop in the future.[2] They typically build on PESTEL analyses and the key drivers for change, but do not offer a single forecast of how the environment will change.

Scenarios are detailed and plausible views of how the business environment of an organisation might develop in the future based on key drivers for change about which there is a high level of uncertainty

Scenarios typically start from the key drivers with the greatest uncertainty. Such key drivers could create radically different views of the future according to how they turn out. For example, in the oil business, key drivers might be technological change, oil reserves, economic growth and international political stability. It might be assumed that technological change and oil reserves are relatively certain, while economic growth and political stability are not. Scenarios could be constructed around different views about future political stability and economic growth. These key drivers are of course interrelated: high political instability and low economic growth are likely to go together. Constructing plausible alternative views of how the business environment might develop in the future therefore depends on knitting together interrelated drivers into internally consistent scenarios. In this analysis so far, therefore,

Illustration 2.2

Scenarios for the biosciences in 2020

Nobody knows the future, but they can prepare for possible alternatives.

In 2006, researchers at the Wharton Business School collaborated with leading companies such as Hewlett Packard, Johnson & Johnson and Procter & Gamble to produce four scenarios for the future of biosciences in 2020. Biosciences include exciting high-tech industries such as genomics, stem cell therapy, cloning and regenerative medicine. The aim was to provide a broad framework for governments, business, researchers and doctors to work within as they considered the future for their particular specialities. The Wharton team were mindful that previous high-tech domains had failed to deliver on their initial promise: nuclear power for example fell radically out of favour from the late 1970s. The future for the biosciences is far from certain.

The Wharton team identified two fundamental but uncertain drivers for change: technological advance and public acceptance. On the first, the uncertainty was about the success of the technologies: after all, nuclear power had not deliverd the cheap energy originally hoped for. With regard to the second, public opinion regarding the biosciences is in the balance, with many calling for an end to stem cell research and cloning. The possibilities of technological success or failure, and public acceptance or rejection, define a matrix with four basic scenarios.

	Technology fails	Technology succeeds
Public acceptance	**Where's the beef?**	**New age of medicine**
Public rejection	**Much ado about nothing**	**Biosciences held hostage**

Source: Adapted from P.J.H. Schoemaker and M.S. Tomczyk (eds) *The Future of BioSciences*, The Mack Center for Technological Innovation and DSI, 2006.

Where's the beef proposes a world in which large corporate and government research initiatives has failed to deliver hoped-for cures for diseases such as Alzheimer's and AIDS, but the public still has high expectations. Companies would be under fire and at risk of political intervention. The *Much ado about nothing* scenario is a world in which the public becomes sceptical after many technological disappointments. The result is that government funding for company and university research dries up. *The Biosciences held hostage* scenario is a very different one, in which technological successes actually frighten the public into a reaction against technology, ethical and safety concerns driving tight restrictions on research, testing and marketing. Finally, the *New age of medicine* offers the prospect of both success and acceptance, a world in which private corporations and university research labs would prosper together as they delivered breakthrough innovations to a grateful public.

The point of the four scenarios is not to say that one is more likely than the others. The Wharton team show that all four scenarios are perfectly possible. Whereas bioscience companies might easily become too focused on the positive *New age* scenario, they need to bear in mind the other possibilities. The implication is that they should be cautious in their expectations of technological breakthroughs and manage public opinion skillfully, otherwise biosciences could become the nuclear industry of the twenty-first century.

Source: http://mackcenter.wharton.upenn.edu/biosciences.

Question

Over which of the two drivers – technological advance and public acceptance – do companies have the most influence? How should they exercise this influence?

two internally consistent and plausible scenarios could be proposed: one based on low growth and high instability, the other based on high growth and low instability.

Note that scenario planning does not attempt to predict the unpredictable: the point is to consider plausible alternative futures. Sharing and debating alternative scenarios improves organisational learning by making managers more perceptive about the forces in the business environment and what is really important. Managers should also evaluate and develop strategies (or contingency plans) for each scenario. They should then monitor the environment to see how it is actually unfolding and adjust strategies accordingly.

Because debating and learning are so valuable in the scenario building process, and scenarios deal with such high uncertainty, some scenario experts advise managers to avoid producing just three scenarios. Three scenarios tend to fall into a range of 'optimistic', 'middling' and 'pessimistic'. Managers naturally focus on the middling scenario and neglect the other two, reducing the amount of organisational learning and contingency planning. It is therefore typically better to have two or four scenarios, avoiding an easy mid-point. It does not matter if the scenarios do not come to pass: the value lies in the process of exploration and contingency planning that the scenarios set off.

Illustration 2.2 shows an example of scenario planning for the biosciences to 2020. Rather than incorporating a multitude of factors, the authors focus on two key drivers which (i) have high potential impact and (ii) are uncertain: technological advance and public acceptance. Both of these drivers may have different futures, which can be combined to create four internally-consistent scenarios of the future. These four scenarios are each given memorable titles, to facilitate communication and debate. The authors do not predict that one will prevail over the others, nor do they allocate relative probabilities. Prediction would close down debate and learning, while probabilities would imply a spurious kind of accuracy.

Scenarios are especially useful where there are a limited number of key drivers influencing the success of strategy; where there is a high level of uncertainty about such influences; where outcomes could be radically different; and where organisations have to make substantial commitments into the future that may be highly inflexible and hard to reverse in adverse circumstances. The oil industry, where companies must invest in exploring oilfields which may have lives of twenty years or more, has traditionally been a leader in the use of scenarios because it faces a combination of all four of these conditions.

2.3 INDUSTRIES AND SECTORS

The previous section looked at how forces in the macro-environment might influence the success or failure of an organisation's strategies. But the impact of these general factors tends to surface in the more immediate environment through changes in the competitive forces surrounding organisations. An important aspect of this for most organisations will be competition within their industry or sector. Economic theory defines an **industry** as 'a group of firms producing the same principal product'[3] or, more broadly, 'a group of firms producing products that are close substitutes for each other'.[4] This concept of an industry can be extended into the public services through the idea of a *sector*. Social services, health care or education also have many producers of the same kinds of services, which are effectively competing for resources. From a strategic management perspective it is useful for managers in any organisation to understand the competitive forces in their industry or sector since these will determine the attractiveness of that industry and the likely success or failure of particular organisations within it.

An **industry** is a group of firms producing the same principal product or service

This section looks at Michael Porter's *five forces framework* for industry analysis.

2.3.1 Competitive forces – the five forces framework

The **five forces framework** helps identify the attractiveness of an industry or sector in terms of competitive forces

www.pearsoned.co.uk/fos KEY CONCEPT

Porter's five forces

Porter's **five forces framework**[5] was originally developed as a way of assessing the attractiveness (profit potential) of different industries. The five forces constitute an industry's 'structure' (see Exhibit 2.2). Although initially developed with businesses in mind, industry structure analysis with the five forces framework is of value to most organisations. It can provide a useful starting point for strategic analysis even where profit criteria may not apply: in most parts of the public sector, each of the five forces has its equivalents. As well as assessing the attractiveness of an industry or sector, the five forces can help set an agenda for action on the various 'pinch-points' that they identify.

The five forces are: the *threat of entry* into an industry; the *threat of substitutes* to the industry's products or services; the *power of buyers* of the industry's products or services; the *power of suppliers* into the industry; and *the extent of rivalry* between competitors in the industry. Porter's essential message is that where these five forces are high, then industries are not attractive to compete in. There will be too much competition, and too much pressure, to allow reasonable profits. The rest of this section will introduce each of the five forces in more detail.

The threat of entry

How easy it is to enter the industry obviously influences the degree of competition. Threat of entry depends on the extent and height of **barriers to entry**. Barriers are the factors that need to be overcome by new entrants if they are to compete successfully. High barriers to entry are good for incumbents (existing competitors), because protecting them from new competitors coming in. Typical barriers are as follows:

Barriers to entry are factors that need to be overcome by new entrants if they are to compete successfully

Exhibit 2.2 The five forces framework

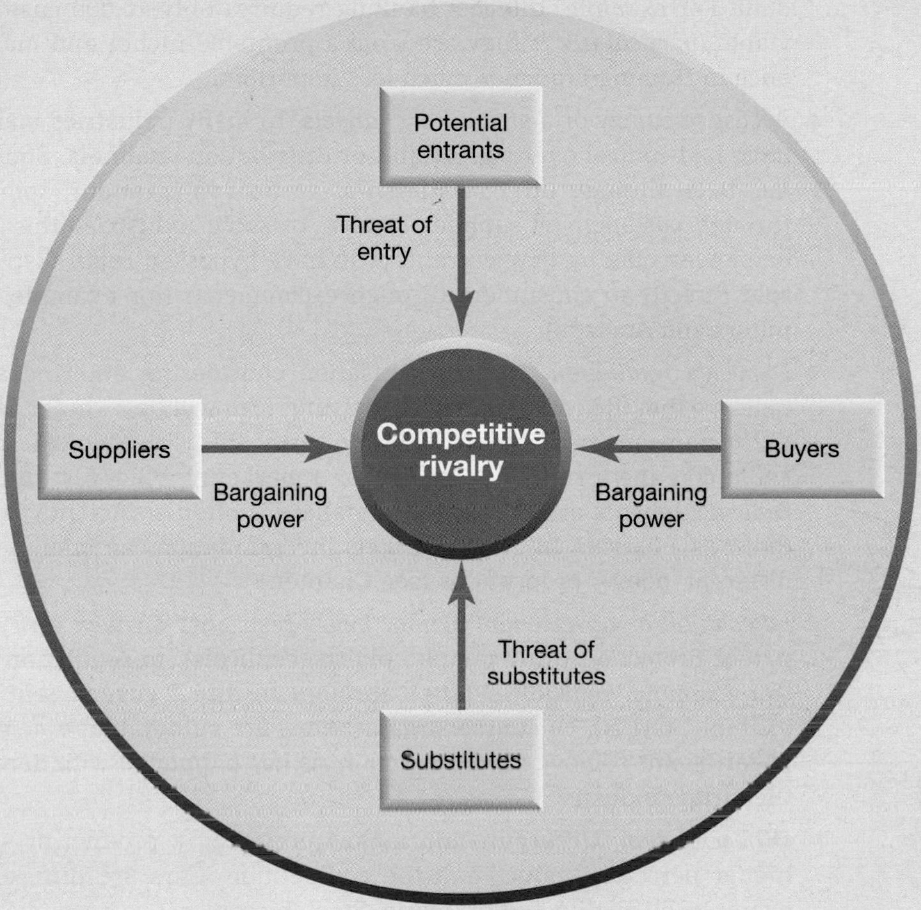

Source: Adapted with the permission of The Free Press, a Division of Simon & Schuster Adult Publishing Group, from *Competitive Strategy: Techniques for Analyzing Industries and Competitors* by Michael E. Porter. Copyright © 1980, 1998 by The Free Press. All rights reserved.

- *Scale and experience*. In some industries, *economies of scale* are extremely important: for example, in the production of automobiles or the advertising of fast-moving consumer goods. Once incumbents have reached large-scale production, it will be very expensive for new entrants to match them and until they reach a similar volume they will have higher unit costs. This scale effect is accentuated where there are high *investment requirements* for entry, for example, research costs in pharmaceuticals or capital equipment costs in automobiles. Barriers to entry also come from *experience curve* effects that give incumbents a cost advantage because they have learnt how to do things more efficiently than an inexperienced new entrant could possibly do (see

Chapter 3). Until the new entrant has built up equivalent experience over time, it will tend to produce at higher cost. Of course, changing 'business models' can alter scale effects or make certain kinds of experience redundant. For example, Internet banking requires only 10,000 customers to be viable (particularly if they are from a profitable niche) and makes experience in running branches much less important.

- *Access to supply or distribution channels*. In many industries manufacturers have had control over supply and/or distribution channels. Sometimes this has been through direct ownership (vertical integration); sometimes just through customer or supplier loyalty. In some industries this barrier has been overcome by new entrants who have bypassed retail distributors and sold directly to consumers through e-commerce (for example, Dell Computers and Amazon).
- *Expected retaliation*. If an organisation considering entering an industry believes that the retaliation of an existing firm will be so great as to prevent entry, or mean that entry would be too costly, this is also a barrier. Retaliation could take the form of a price war or a marketing blitz. Just the knowledge that incumbents are prepared to retaliate is often sufficiently discouraging to act as a barrier. In global markets this retaliation can take place at many different 'points' or locations (see Chapter 8).
- *Legislation or government action*. Legal restraints on new entry vary from patent protection (for example, pharmaceuticals), to regulation of markets (for example, pension selling), through to direct government action (for example, tariffs). Of course, organisations are vulnerable to new entrants if governments remove such protection, as has happened with deregulation of the airline industry.
- *Differentiation*. Differentiation means providing a product or service with higher perceived value than the competition. Cars are differentiated, for example, by quality and branding. Steel, by contrast, is by-and-large a commodity, undifferentiated and therefore sold by the tonne. Steel buyers will simply buy the cheapest. Differentiation reduces the threat of entry because increasing customer loyalty.

The threat of substitutes

Substitution reduces demand for a particular 'class' of products as customers switch to the alternatives

Substitutes are products or services that offer a similar benefit to an industry's products or services, but by a different process. For example, aluminium is a substitute for steel in automobiles; trains are a substitute for cars; films and theatre are substitutes for each other. Managers often focus on their competitors in their own industry, and neglect the threat posed by substitutes. Substitutes can reduce demand for a particular 'class' of products as customers switch to alternatives – even to the extent that this class of products or services becomes obsolete. However, there does not have to be much actual switching for the substitute threat to have an effect. The simple risk of substitution puts a cap on the prices that can be charged in an industry. Thus, although Eurostar has no direct competitors in terms of train services from Paris to London, the prices it can charge are ultimately limited by the cost of flights between the two cities.

There are two important points to bear in mind about substitutes:

- *The price/performance ratio* is critical to substitution threats. A substitute is still an effective threat even if more expensive, so long as it offers performance advantages that customers value. Thus aluminium is more expensive than steel, but its relative lightness and its resistance to corrosion give it an advantage in some automobile manufacturing applications. It is the ratio of price to performance that matters, rather than simple price.
- *Extra-industry effects* are the core of the substitution concept. Substitutes come from outside the incumbents' industry and should not be confused with competitors' threats from within the industry. The value of the substitution concept is to force managers to look outside their own industry to consider more distant threats and constraints. The more threats of substitution there are, the less attractive the industry is likely to be.

The power of buyers

Buyers are the organisation's immediate customers, not necessarily the ultimate consumers

Customers, of course, are essential for the survival of any business. But sometimes customers – here **buyers** – can have such high bargaining power that their suppliers are hard pressed to make any profits at all.

Buyer power is likely to be high when some of the following conditions prevail:

- *Concentrated buyers*. Where a few large customers account for the majority of sales, buyer power is increased. This is the case on items such as milk in the grocery sector in many European countries, where just a few retailers dominate the market. If a product or service accounts for a high percentage of the buyers' total purchases their power is also likely to increase as they are more likely to 'shop around' to get the best price and therefore 'squeeze' suppliers than they would for more trivial purchases.
- *Low switching costs*. Where buyers can easily switch between one supplier or another, they have a strong negotiating position and can squeeze suppliers who are desperate for their business. Switching costs are typically low for weakly differentiated commodities such as steel.
- *Buyer competition threat*. If the buyer has some facilities to supply itself, or if it has the possibility of acquiring such facilities, it tends to be powerful. In negotiation with its suppliers, it can raise the threat of doing the suppliers' job themselves. This is called *backward vertical integration*, moving back to sources of supply, and might occur if satisfactory prices or quality from suppliers cannot be obtained. For example, glass manufacturers have lost power against their buyers as some large window manufacturers have decided to produce some of their own glass.

It is very important that *buyers* are distinguished from *ultimate consumers*. Thus for companies like Nestlé or Unilever, their buyers are retailers such as Carrefour or Tesco, not ordinary consumers (see discussion of the 'strategic customer' in 2.4.3). Carrefour and Tesco have much more negotiating power than an ordinary consumer would have. The high buying power of such supermarkets has become a major source of pressure for the companies supplying them.

The power of suppliers

Suppliers supply the organisation with what is required to produce the product or service, and include labour and sources of finance

Suppliers are those who supply the organisation with what it needs to produce the product or service. As well as fuel, raw materials and equipment, this can include labour and sources of finance. The factors increasing supplier power are the converse to those for buyer power. Thus *supplier power* is likely to be high where there are:

- *Concentrated suppliers*. Where just a few producers dominate supply, suppliers have more power over buyers. The iron ore industry is now concentrated in the hands of three main producers, leaving the steel companies, relatively fragmented, in a very weak negotiating position for this essential raw material.
- *High switching cost*. If it is expensive or disruptive to move from one supplier to another, then the buyer becomes relatively dependent and correspondingly weak. Microsoft is a powerful supplier because of the high switching costs of moving from one operating system to another. Buyers are prepared to pay a premium to avoid the trouble, and Microsoft knows it.
- *Supplier competition threat*. Suppliers have increased power where they are able to cut out buyers who are acting as middlemen. Thus airlines have been able to negotiate tough contracts with travel agencies as the rise of online booking has allowed them to create a direct route to customers. This is called *forwards vertical integration*, moving up closer to the ultimate customer.

Most organisations have many suppliers, so it is necessary to concentrate the analysis on the most important ones or types. If their power is high, suppliers can capture all their buyers' own potential profits simply by raising their prices. Star football players have succeeded in raising their rewards to astronomical levels, while even the leading football clubs – their 'buyers' – struggle to make money.

Competitive rivalry

These wider competitive forces (the four arrows in the model) all impinge on the direct competitive rivalry between an organisation and its most immediate rivals. Thus low barriers to entry increase the number of rivals; powerful buyers with low switching costs force their suppliers to high rivalry in order to offer the best deals. The more competitive rivalry there is, the worse it is for incumbents within the industry.

Competitive rivals are organisations with similar products and services aimed at the same customer group

Competitive rivals are organisations with similar products and services aimed at the same customer group (i.e. not substitutes). In the European airline industry, Air France and British Airways are rivals; trains are a substitute. As well as the influence of the four previous forces, there are a number of additional factors directly affecting the degree of competitive rivalry in an industry or sector:

- *Competitor balance*. Where competitors are of roughly equal size there is the danger of intense competition as one competitor attempts to gain dominance over others. Conversely, less rivalrous industries tend to have one or two dominant organisations, with the smaller players reluctant to challenge the larger ones directly (for example, by focusing on niches to avoid the 'attention' of the dominant companies).
- *Industry growth rate*. In situations of strong growth, an organisation can grow with the market, but in situations of low growth or decline, any growth is likely to be at the expense of a rival, and meet with fierce resistance. Low growth markets are therefore often associated with price competition and low profitability. The *industry life cycle* influences growth rates, and hence competitive conditions.
- *High fixed costs*. Industries with high fixed costs, perhaps because requiring high investments in capital equipment or initial research, tend to be highly rivalrous. Companies will seek to reduce unit costs by increasing their volumes: to do so, they typically cut their prices, prompting competitors to do the same and thereby triggering price wars in which everyone in the industry suffers. Similarly, if extra capacity can only be added in large increments (as in many manufacturing sectors, for example, a chemical or glass factory), the competitor making such an addition is likely to create short-term overcapacity in the industry, leading to increased competition to use capacity.
- *High exit barriers*. The existence of high barriers to exit – in other words, closure or disinvestment – tends to increase rivalry, especially in declining industries. Excess capacity persists and consequently incumbents fight to maintain market share. Exit barriers might be high for a variety of reasons: for example, high redundancy costs or high investment in specific assets such as plant and equipment that others would not buy.
- *Low differentiation*. In a commodity market, where products or services are poorly differentiated, rivalry is increased because there is little to stop customers switching between competitors and the only way to compete is on price.

2.3.2 Implications of five forces analysis

The five forces framework provides useful insights into the forces at work in the industry or sector environment of an organisation. Illustration 2.3 describes the five forces in the changing steel industry. It is important, however,

Illustration 2.3

The consolidating steel industry

Five forces analysis helps understand the changing attractiveness of an industry.

For a long time, the steel industry was seen as a static and unprofitable one. Producers were nationally based, often state owned and frequently unprofitable – between the late 1990s and 2003, more than 50 independent steel producers went into bankruptcy in the USA. The twenty-first century has seen a revolution. For example, during 2006, Mittal Steel paid \$35bn (£19.6bn; €28bn) to buy European steel giant Arcelor, creating the world's largest steel company. The following year, Indian conglomerate Tata bought Anglo-Dutch steel company Corus for \$13bn. These high prices indicated considerable confidence in being able to turn the industry round.

New entrants

In the last 10 years, two powerful groups have entered world steel markets. First, after a period of privatisation and reorganisation, large Russian producers such as Severstal and Evraz entered export markets, exporting 30 million tonnes of steel by 2005. At the same time, Chinese producers have been investing in new production facilities, in the period 2003–2005 increasing capacity at a rate of 30 per cent a year. Since the 1990s, Chinese share of world capacity has increased more than two times, to 25 per cent in 2006, and Chinese producers have become the world's third largest exporter just behind Japan and Russia.

Substitutes

Steel is a nineteenth-century technology, increasingly substituted for by other materials such as aluminium in cars, plastics and aluminium in packaging and ceramics and composites in many high-tech applications. Steel's own technological advances sometimes work to reduce need: thus steel cans have become about one-third thinner over the last few decades.

Buyer power

Key buyers for steel include the global car manufacturers, such as Ford, Toyota and Volkswagen, and leading can producers such as Crown Holdings, which makes one-third of all food cans produced in North America and Europe. Such companies buy in volume, coordinating purchases around the world. Car manufacturers are sophisticated users, often leading in the technological development of their materials.

Supplier power

The key raw material for steel producers is iron ore. The big three ore producers – CVRD, Rio Tinto and BHP Billiton – control 70 per cent of the international market. In 2005, iron ore producers exploited surging demand by increasing prices by 72 per cent; in 2006 they increased prices by 19 per cent.

Competitive rivalry

The industry has traditionally been very fragmented: in 2000, the world's top five producers accounted for only 14 per cent of production. Most steel is sold on a commodity basis, by the tonne. Prices are highly cyclical, as stocks do not deteriorate and tend to flood the market when demand slows. In the late twentieth century demand growth averaged a moderate 2 per cent per annum. The start of the twenty-first century saw a boom in demand, driven particularly by Chinese growth. Between 2003 and 2005, prices of sheet steel for cars and fridges trebled to \$600 (£336; €480) a tonne. Companies such as Nucor in the USA, Thyssen-Krupp in Germany as well as Mittal and Tata responded by buying up weaker players internationally. New steel giant Mittal accounted for about 10 per cent of world production in 2007. Mittal actually reduced capacity in some of its Western production centres.

Questions

1. In recent years, which of the five forces has become more positive for steel producers, which less so?
2. Explain the acquisition strategies of players such as Mittal, Tata and Nucor.
3. In the future, what might change to make the steel industry less attractive or more attractive?

to use the framework for more than simply listing the forces. The bottom-line is an assessment of the attractiveness of the industry. The analysis should conclude with a judgement about whether the industry is a good one to compete in or not.

The analysis should next prompt investigation of the *implications* of these forces, for example:

- *Which industries to enter (or leave)?* The fundamental purpose of the five forces model is to identify the relative attractiveness of different industries: industries are attractive when the forces are weak. Managers should invest in industries where the five forces work in their favour and avoid or disinvest from markets where they are strongly against.
- *What influence can be exerted?* Industry structures are not necessarily fixed, but can be influenced by deliberate managerial strategies. For example, organisations can build barriers to entry by increasing advertising spend to improve customer loyalty. They can buy up competitors to reduce rivalry and increase power over suppliers or buyers. Influencing industry structure involves many issues relating to *competitive strategy* and will be a major concern of Chapter 6.
- *How are competitors differently affected?* Not all competitors will be affected equally by changes in industry structure, deliberate or spontaneous. If barriers are rising because of increased R&D or advertising spending, smaller players in the industry may not be able to keep up with the larger players, and be squeezed out. Similarly, growing buyer power is likely to hurt small competitors most. Strategic group analysis is helpful here (see 2.4.1)

Although originating in the private sector, five forces analysis can have important implications for organisations in the public sector too. For example, the forces can be used to adjust the service offer or focus on key issues. Thus it might be worth switching managerial initiative from an arena with many crowded and overlapping services (for example, social work, probation services and education) to one that is less rivalrous and where the organisation can do something more distinctive. Similarly, strategies could be launched to reduce dependence on particularly powerful and expensive suppliers, for example energy sources or high shortage skills.

2.3.3 Key issues in using the five forces framework

The five forces framework has to be used carefully and is not necessarily complete, even at the industry level. When using this framework, it is important to bear the following three issues in mind:

- *Defining the 'right' industry.* Most industries can be analysed at different levels. For example, the airline industry has several different segments such as domestic and long haul and different customer groups such as leisure, business and freight (see 2.4.2 below). The competitive forces are likely to be different for each of these segments and can be analysed separately. It is often useful to conduct industry analysis at a disaggregated level, for each distinct segment. The overall picture for the industry as a whole can then be assembled.

Convergence is where previously separate industries begin to overlap in terms of activities, technologies, products and customers

- *Converging industries*. Industry definition is often difficult too because industry boundaries are continuously changing. For example, many industries, especially in high-tech arenas, are undergoing **convergence**, where previously separate industries begin to overlap or merge in terms of activities, technologies, products and customers.[6] Technological change has brought convergence between the telephone and photographic industries, for example, as mobile phones increasingly include camera and video functions. For a camera company like Kodak, phones are increasingly a substitute and the prospect of facing Nokia or Samsung as direct competitors is not remote.

Complementors are products or services for which customers are prepared to pay more if together than if they stand alone

- *Complementary products*. Some analysts argue for a 'sixth force', organisations supplying complementary products or services. These **complementors** are players from whom customers buy complementary products that are worth more together than separately. Thus Dell and Microsoft are complementors in so far as computers and software are complementary products for buyers. Microsoft needs Dell to produce powerful machines to run its latest generation software. Dell needs Microsoft to work its machines. Likewise, television programme makers and television guide producers are complements. Complementors raise two issues. The first is that complementors have opportunities for *cooperation*. It makes sense for Dell and Microsoft to keep each other in touch with their technological developments, for example. This implies a significant shift in perspective. While Porter's five forces sees organisations as battling against each other for share of industry value, complementors may cooperate to increase the value of the whole cake.[7] The second issue, however, is the potential for some complementors to demand a high share of the available value for themselves. Microsoft has been much more profitable than the manufacturers of complementary computer products and its high margins may have depressed the sales and margins available to companies like Dell. The potential for cooperation or antagonism with such a complementary 'sixth force' needs to be included in industry analyses.[8]

2.3.4 The industry life cycle

The power of the five forces typically varies with the stages of the industry life cycle. The industry life cycle concept proposes that industries start small in their development stage, then go through period of rapid growth (the equivalent to 'adolescence' in the human life cycle), culminating in a period of 'shakeout'. The final two stages are first a period of slow or even zero growth ('maturity'), before the final stage of decline ('old age'). Each of these stages has implications for the five forces.[9]

The *development stage* is an experimental one, typically with few players exercising little direct rivalry and highly differentiated products. The five forces are likely to be weak, therefore, though profits may actually be scarce because of high investment requirements. The next stage is one of high growth, with rivalry low as there is plenty of market opportunity for everybody. Buyers may be keen to secure supplies and lack sophistication about what they are buying, so diminishing their power. One downside of the growth stage is that barriers to entry may be low, as existing competitors have not built up much scale, experience or customer loyalty. Another potential downside is the power of suppliers if there is a shortage of components or materials that fast growing businesses need for expansion. The *shake-out stage* begins as the growth rate starts to decline, so that increased rivalry forces the weakest of the new entrants out of the business. In the *maturity stage*, barriers to entry tend to increase, as control over distribution is established and economies of scale and experience curve benefits come into play. Products or service tend to standardise. Buyers may become more powerful as they become less avid for the industry's products or services and more confident in switching between suppliers. For major players, market share is typically key to survival, providing leverage against buyers and competitive advantage in terms of cost. Finally, the *decline stage* can be a period of extreme rivalry, especially where there are high exit barriers, as falling sales force remaining competitors into dog-eat-dog competition. Exhibit 2.3 summarises some of the conditions that can be expected at different stages in the life cycle.

It is important to avoid putting too much faith in the inevitability of life-cycle stages. One stage does not follow predictably after another: industries vary widely in the length of their growth stages, and others can rapidly 'de-mature' through radical innovation. The telephony industry, based for nearly a century on fixed-line telephones, de-matured rapidly with the introduction of mobile and Internet telephony. Anita McGahan warns of the 'maturity mindset', which can leave many managers complacent and slow to respond to new competition.[10] Managing in mature industries is not necessarily just about waiting for decline. Although steady progress through the stages is not inevitable, the life cycle concept does none the less remind managers that conditions will change over time. Especially in fast-moving industries, five forces analyses need to be reviewed quite regularly.

Comparative industry structure analyses

The industry life cycle notion underlines the need to make industry structure analysis dynamic. One effective means of doing this is to compare the five forces over time in a simple 'radar plot'.

Exhibit 2.4 provides a framework for summarising the power of each of the five forces on five axes. Power diminishes as the axes go outwards. Where the

Exhibit 2.3 The industry life cycle

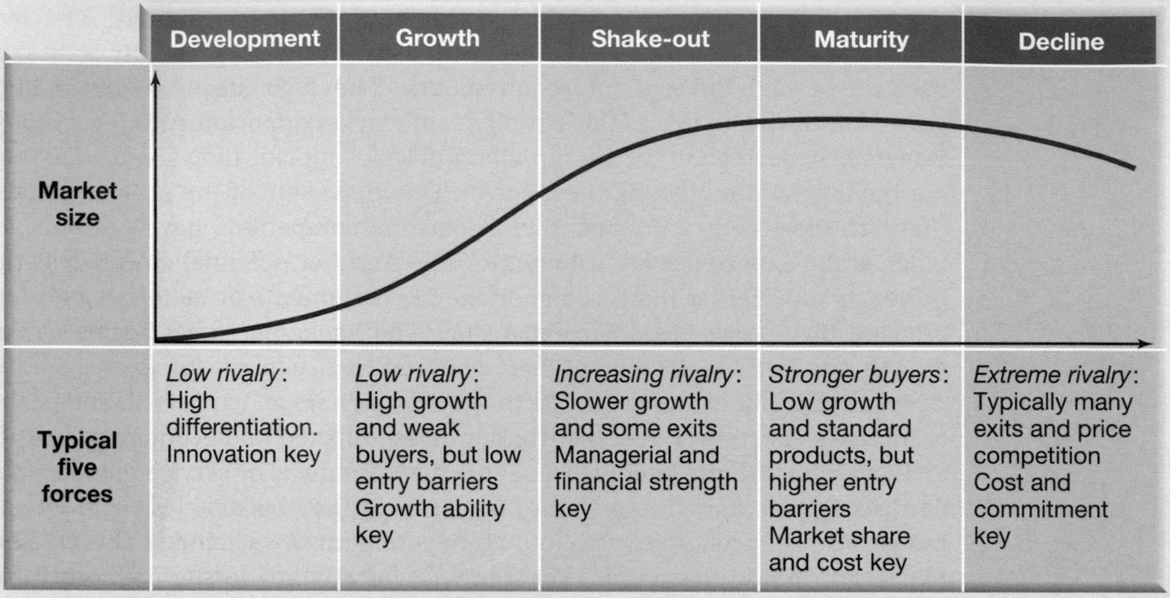
Development
Growth
Shake-out
Maturity
Decline
Market size
Typical five forces
Low rivalry: High differentiation. Innovation key
Low rivalry: High growth and weak buyers, but low entry barriers Growth ability key
Increasing rivalry: Slower growth and some exits Managerial and financial strength key
Stronger buyers: Low growth and standard products, but higher entry barriers Market share and cost key
Extreme rivalry: Typically many exits and price competition Cost and commitment key

Exhibit 2.4 Comparative industry structure analysis

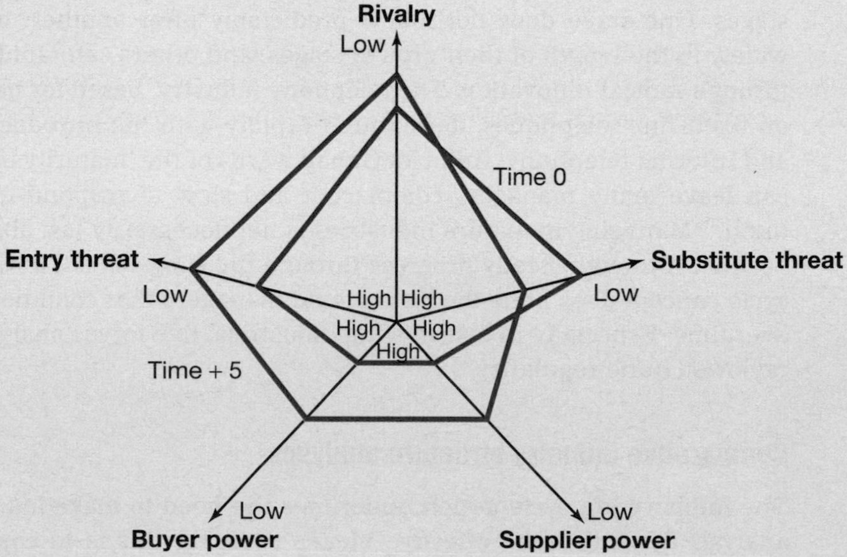

Source: Based on V. Lerville-Anger, F. Fréry, A. Gazengel and A. Ollivier, *Conduire le diagnostic global d'une unité industrielle*, Editions d'Organisation, Paris, 2001.

forces are low, the total area enclosed by the lines between the axes is large; where the forces are high, the total area enclosed by the lines is small. The larger the enclosed area, therefore, the greater is the profit potential. In Exhibit 2.4, the industry at Time 0 (represented by the bright blue lines) has relatively low rivalry (just a few competitors) and faces low substitution threats. The threat of entry is moderate, but both buyer power and supplier power are relatively high. Overall, this looks only a moderately attractive industry to invest in.

However, given the dynamic nature of industries, managers need to look forward, here five years represented by the dark blue lines in Exhibit 2.4.[11] Managers are predicting in this case some rise in the threat of substitutes (perhaps new technologies will be developed). On the other hand, they predict a falling entry threat, while both buyer power and supplier power will be easing. Rivalry will still further reduce. This looks like a classic case of an industry in which a few players emerge with overall dominance. The area enclosed by the dark blue lines is large, suggesting a relatively attractive industry. For a firm confident of becoming one of the dominant players, this might be an industry well worth investing in.

Comparing the five forces over time on a radar plot thus helps to give industry structure analysis a dynamic aspect. Similar plots can be made to aid diversification decisions (see Chapter 7), where possible new industries to enter can be compared in terms of attractiveness. The lines are only approximate, of course, because they aggregate the many individual elements that make up each of the forces into a simple composite measure. Notice too that if one of the forces is very adverse, then this might nullify positive assessments on the other four axes: for example, an industry with low rivalry, low substitution, low entry barriers and low supplier power might still be unattractive if powerful buyers were able to demand by highly discounted prices. With these warnings in mind, such radar plots can none the less be both a useful device for initial analysis and an effective summary of a final, more refined analysis.

2.4 COMPETITORS AND MARKETS

An industry or sector may be too high a level to provide for a detailed understanding of competition. The five forces can impact differently on different kinds of players. To return to the earlier example, Ford and Porsche may be in the same broad industry (automobiles), but they are positioned differently: they face different kinds of buyer power and supplier power at the very least. It is often useful to disaggregate. Many industries contain a range of companies, each of which has different capabilities and competes on different bases. These competitor differences are captured by the concept of *strategic groups*. Customers too can differ significantly. Such customer differences can be captured by distinguishing between *strategic customers* and ultimate consumers and between different *market segments*. Underpinning strategic groups and market segments is recognition of what *customers value* and *critical success factors*. These various concepts will now be discussed.

2.4.1 Strategic groups[12]

Strategic groups are organisations within an industry with similar strategic characteristics, following similar strategies or competing on similar bases

www.pearsoned.co.uk/fos KEY CONCEPT Strategic groups

Strategic groups are organisations within an industry or sector with similar strategic characteristics, following similar strategies or competing on similar bases. These characteristics are different from those in other strategic groups in the same industry or sector. For example, in the grocery retailing industry, supermarkets, convenience stores and corner shops each form different strategic groups. There are many different characteristics that distinguish between strategic groups but these can be grouped into two major categories (see Exhibit 2.5).[13] First, the *scope* of an organisation's activities (such as product range, geographical coverage and range of distribution channels used).

Exhibit 2.5 Some characteristics for identifying strategic groups

It is useful to consider the extent to which organisations *differ* in terms of **characteristics** such as:

Scope of activities

- Extent of product (or service) diversity
- Extent of geographical coverage
- Number of market segments served
- Distribution channels used

Resource commitment

- Extent (number) of **branding**
- **Marketing effort** (e.g. advertising spread, size of salesforce)
- Extent of **vertical integration**
- Product or service **quality**
- **Technological leadership** (a leader or follower)
- **Size** of organisation

Sources: Based on M.E. Porter, *Competitive Strategy*, Free Press, 1980; and J. McGee and H. Thomas, 'Strategic groups: theory, research and taxonomy', *Strategic Management Journal*, vol. 7, no. 2 (1986), pp. 141–160.

Second, the *resource commitment* (such as brands, marketing spend and extent of vertical integration). Which of these characteristics are especially relevant in terms of a given industry needs to be understood in terms of the history and development of that industry and the forces at work in the environment.

Strategic groups can be mapped on to two dimensional charts – for example, one axis might be the extent of product range and the other axis the size of marketing spend. One method for establishing key dimensions by which to map strategic groups is to identify top performers (by growth or profitability) in an industry and to compare them with low performers. Characteristics that are shared by top performers, but not by low performers, are likely to be particularly relevant for mapping strategic groups. For example, the most profitable firms in an industry might all be narrow in terms of product range, and lavish in terms of marketing spend, while the less profitable firms might be more widely spread in terms of products and restrained in their marketing. Here the two dimensions for mapping would be product range and marketing spend. A potential recommendation for the less profitable firms would be to cut back their product range and boost their marketing. In Illustration 2.4, Figure 1 shows a strategic group map of the major providers of MBAs in The Netherlands in 2007.

This strategic group concept is useful in at least three ways:

- *Understanding competition*. Managers can focus on their direct competitors within their particular strategic group, rather than the whole industry. They can also establish the dimensions that distinguish them most from other groups, and which might be the basis for relative success or failure. These dimensions can then become the focus of their action.
- *Analysis of strategic opportunities*. Strategic group maps can identify the most attractive 'strategic spaces' within an industry. Some spaces on the map may be 'white spaces', relatively under-occupied. In the Dutch MBA market, for instance, examples are vocational degrees for the international market and semi-academic education for the regional in-company training market. Such white spaces might be unexploited opportunities. On the other hand, they could turn out to be 'black holes', impossible to exploit and likely to damage any entrant. A strategic group map is only the first stage of the analysis. White spaces need to tested carefully; not all are true strategic spaces.
- *Analysis of mobility barriers*. Of course, moving across the map to take advantage of opportunities is not costless. Often it will require difficult decisions and rare resources. Strategic groups are therefore characterised by 'mobility barriers', obstacles to movement from one strategic group to another. These are similar to barriers to entry in five forces analysis. In Illustration 2.4, Figure 2 shows examples of mobility barriers for the groupings identified in the industry. These may be substantial: to enter the international academic strategic group, a regional, vocational competitor would have to establish the appropriate image, mobilise networks, change its teaching methods and improve its remuneration levels. As with barriers to

Illustration 2.4

Strategic groups in Dutch MBA education

Mapping of strategic groups can provide insights into the competitive structures of industries or sectors and the opportunities and constraints for development.

In the mid-2000s there were three kinds of institutions offering MBA courses in The Netherlands: traditional universities, for-profit business schools (FPBSs) and polytechnics:

- Traditional universities offered a wide range of subjects, carried out research, and attracted students both nationally and internationally. Their programmes were more academic than vocational. A university degree was generally valued more highly than that of a polytechnic.
- FPBSs were relatively new, and provided MBA degrees only. Some of the FPBS now offer a DBA course as well. Usually they were located close to the centre or capital of the country. MBA education at FPBSs was generally more of the action learning type, which made it attractive for practising managers. Many students already had diplomas from a university or polytechnic. Several of these schools received accreditation from the Dutch Validation Council. In 2005 the Dutch minister of education and culture recognised NIMBAS, an FPBS, as an official 'universiteit'. NIMBAS later merged with TIAS, the business school of Universiteit Tilburg.
- Polytechnics (in The Netherlands named HogeScholen) often attracted students from the region and provided education aimed more at application of theory than at developing conceptual thinking. Some of the polytechnics provided MBA degrees, in some cases in cooperation with universities in the UK.

Figure 1 gives an indication of how these three types of institution were positioned in terms of geographical coverage and 'orientation'. Figure 2 shows the barriers confronting organisations who wished to move from one group to another (they show the barriers *into* a group). For example, if the FPBSs tried to 'enter' the strategic group of traditional universities they would need to build up a reputation in research or innovation. They may not be interested in doing research, since there would be high costs and little pay-off for their effort. In reverse, for traditional universities to move in the direction of the FPBSs may be difficult since the faculty may not have skills in action learning and may be inexperienced at working with older students.

Figure 3 shows where 'strategic space' might exist. These spaces are created by changes in the macro-environment – particularly globalisation and information technology. This could provide opportunities for Dutch

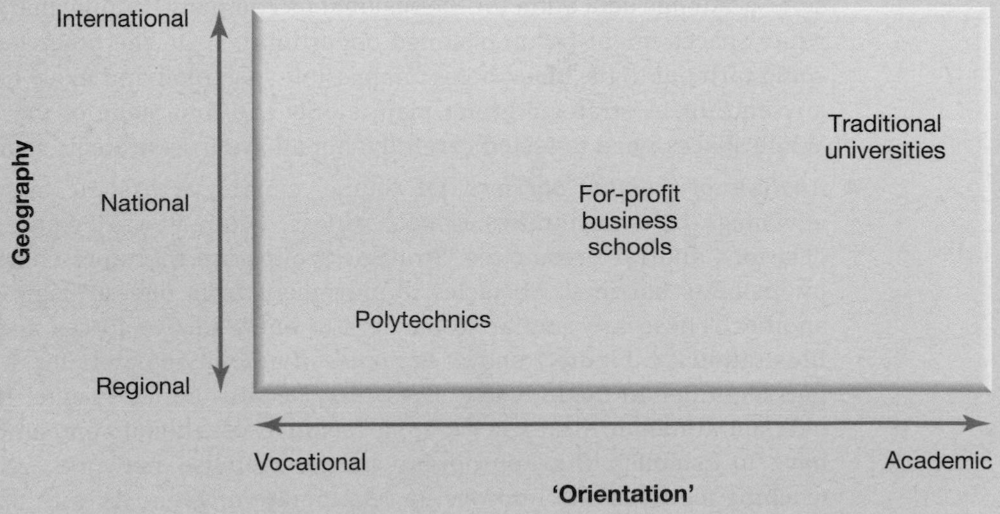

Figure 1 Strategic groups in MBA education in The Netherlands

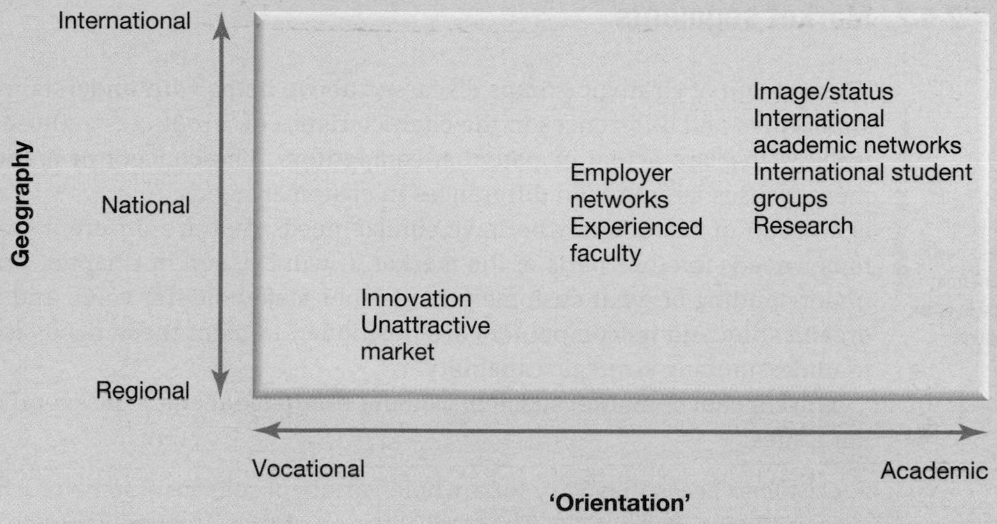

Figure 2 Mobility barriers

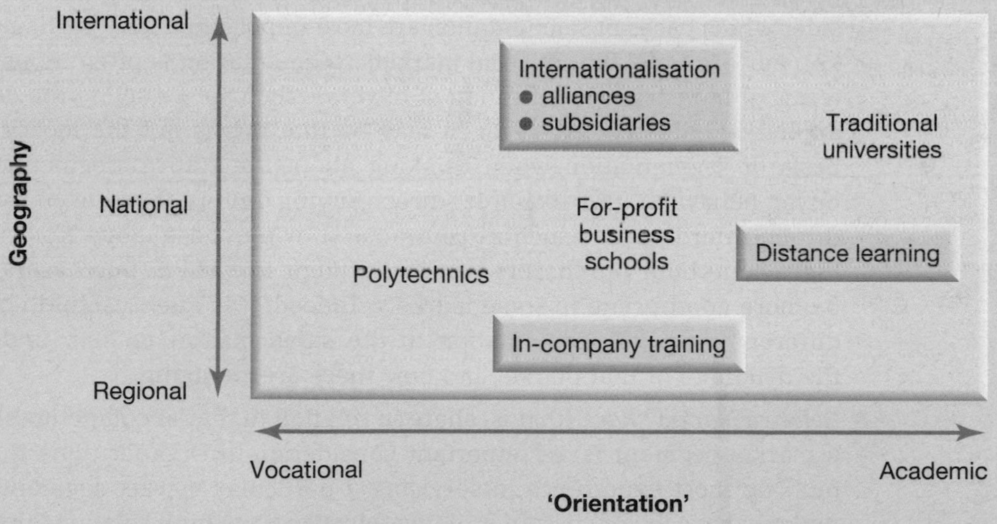

Figure 3 Strategic space

business schools to seek more international business. However, the reverse threat of international competitors entering the Dutch market was a major concern. Information and communication technology helps students study at their own place of work or at home, and also enables them to tap into an international network. So an American or British school could provide content over the Internet and local student support through partnerships with Dutch institutions. Indeed the University of Phoenix had already made efforts to do just this.

Source: This is an updated version of D.J. Eppink and S. de Waal, 'Global influences on the public sector', in G. Johnson and K. Scholes (eds), *Exploring Public Sector Strategy*, FT/Prentice Hall, 2001, chapter 3.

Question

How might this analysis influence the next strategic moves by each of the three types of institution?

entry, it is good to be in a successful strategic group for which there are strong mobility barriers, to impede imitation.

2.4.2 Market segments

A market segment is a group of customers who have similar needs that are different from customer needs in other parts of the market

The concept of strategic groups discussed above helps with understanding the similarities and differences in the characteristics of 'producers' – those organisations that are actual or potential competitors. The concept of market segment focuses attention on differences in customer needs. A **market segment**[14] is a group of customers who have similar needs that are different from customer needs in other parts of the market. It will be seen in Chapter 3 that this understanding of what customers (and other stakeholders) value and how an organisation and its competitors are positioned to meet these needs is critical to understanding strategic capability.

The concept of market segments should remind managers of several important issues:

- *Customer needs* may vary for a whole variety of reasons – some of which are identified in Exhibit 2.6. Theoretically, any of these factors could be used to identify market segments. However, in practical terms it is important to consider which bases of segmentation are most important in any particular market. For example, in industrial markets, segmentation is often thought of in terms of industrial classification of buyers – such as 'we sell to the domestic appliance industry'. However, it may be that this is not the most relevant basis of segmentation when thinking about the future. Segmentation by buyer behaviour (for example, direct buying versus those users who buy through third parties such as contractors) or purchase value (for example, high-value bulk purchasers versus frequent low-value purchasers) might be more appropriate in some markets. Indeed, it is often useful to consider different bases of segmentation in the same market to help understand the dynamics of that market and how these are changing.
- *Relative market share* (that is, share in relation to that of competitors) within a market segment is an important consideration. Organisations that have built up most experience in servicing a particular market segment should not only have lower costs in so doing, but also have built relationships which may be difficult for others to break down. What customers value will vary by market segment and therefore 'producers' are likely to achieve advantage in segments that are especially suited to their particular strengths. They may find it very difficult to compete on a broader basis. For example, a small local brewery competing against the big brands on the basis of its low prices underpinned by low costs of distribution and marketing is confined to that segment of the local market that values low price.
- How market segments can be *identified and 'serviced'*[15] is influenced by a number of trends in the business environment already discussed in this

Exhibit 2.6 Some bases of market segmentation

Type of factor	Consumer markets	Industrial/ organisational markets
Characteristics of people/ organisations	Age, sex, race Income Family size Life-cycle stage Location Lifestyle	Industry Location Size Technology Profitability Management
Purchase/use situation	Size of purchase Brand loyalty Purpose of use Purchasing behaviour Importance of purchase Choice criteria	Application Importance of purchase Volume Frequency of purchase Purchasing procedure Choice criteria Distribution channel
Users' needs and preferences for product characteristics	Product similarity Price preference Brand preferences Desired features Quality	Performance requirements Assistance from suppliers Brand preferences Desired features Quality Service requirements

chapter. For example, the wide availability of consumer data and the ability to process it electronically combined with increased flexibility of companies' operations allow segmentation to be undertaken at a micro-level – even down to individual consumers (so-called 'markets of one'). So Internet shopping selectively targets consumers with special offers based on their past purchasing patterns. The emergence of more affluent, mobile consumers means that geographical segmentation may be much less effective than lifestyle segmentation (across national boundaries).

2.4.3 Identifying the strategic customer

The **strategic customer** is the person(s) at whom the strategy is primarily addressed because they have the most influence over which goods or services are purchased

Bringing goods and services to market usually involves a range of organisations performing different roles. In Chapter 3 this will be discussed in more detail through the concept of the value network. For example, most consumers purchase goods through retail outlets. So the manufacturers must attend to two sorts of customers: the shops, their direct customers; and the shops' customers, the ultimate consumers of the product. Although both customers influence demand, usually one of these will be more influential than the others – this is the strategic customer. The **strategic customer** is the person(s) at whom the strategy is primarily addressed because they have the most influence over which goods or services are purchased. Unless there is clarity on who the strategic customer is, managers can end up analysing and targeting the wrong people. It is the desires of the strategic customer that provide the starting point for strategy. The requirements of the other customers are not unimportant – they have to be met – but the requirements of the strategic customer are paramount. Returning to the example, it should be clear that for many consumer goods the retail outlet is the strategic customer as the way it displays, promotes and supports products in store is hugely influential on the final consumer's preferences. In the public sector the strategic customer is very often the 'body' who controls the funds or authorises use rather than the user of the service. So family doctors are the strategic customers of pharmaceutical companies and so on.

2.4.4 Understanding what customers value – critical success factors

Although the concept of market segments is useful, managers may fail to be realistic about how markets are segmented and the strategic implications of that segmentation. It will be seen in the next chapter that an understanding of customer needs and how they differ between segments is crucial to developing the appropriate strategic capability in an organisation. However, customers will value many product/service features to a greater or lesser degree. From the potential providers' viewpoint it is valuable to understand which features are of particular importance to a group of customers (market segment). These are known as the critical success factors. **Critical success factors** (CSFs) are those product features that are particularly valued by a group of customers and, therefore, where the organisation must excel to outperform competition.

Critical success factors (CSFs) are those product features that are particularly valued by a group of customers and, therefore, where the organisation must excel to outperform competition

The extent to which the offerings of different providers address the factors valued by customers can be visualised by creating a strategy canvas[16] (see Exhibit 2.7). The canvas is a simple but useful way of comparing competitors' positions in a market and potential in different segments. The exhibit relates to the electrical engineering equipment market and illustrates the following:

- Five *critical success factors* are identified in Exhibit 2.7 as particularly important to customers on average (in rank order, the producer's reputation, after-sales service, delivery reliability, testing facilities and technical quality). These are *average* ranks for the five factors determining customer choices, given similar prices; note that individual customers vary.
- Three *competitor profiles* are drawn on the canvas against these factors. It is clear that the relative strengths that company A possesses are not the factors *most* valued by the average customer, whereas B's strengths appear to have a better match. But nobody is doing particularly well with regard to testing and technical quality, which may be very important to some customers.

Exhibit 2.7 **A strategy canvas – perceived value by customers in the electrical engineering equipment market**

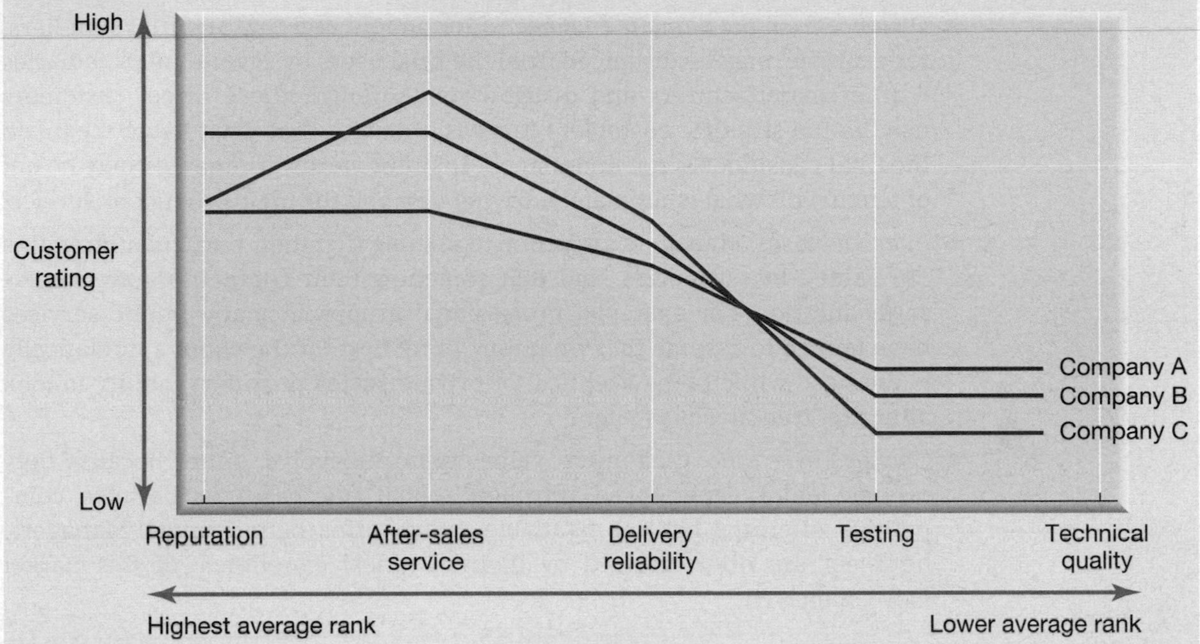

Sources: Reprinted by permission of *Harvard Business Review*. Exhibit adapted from 'Charting your company's future' by C. Kim and R. Mauborgne, Vol. 80, No. 6. Copyright © 2002 by the Harvard Business School Publishing Corporation; all rights reserved.

- *Segment choice* is the next issue. Company A could try to improve on the highest average rank factors. But companies B and C are already strong there, and their customers are highly satisfied. An alternative for company A is to focus on a particular market segment, those for whom testing and quality happen to be much more important than for the average customer. There is less competition there and greater room for improvement. This segment might be relatively small, but targeting this specifically could be much more profitable than tackling companies B and C head-on in their areas of strength. Company A might focus on raising its profile at the right-hand end of the canvas.

The key messages from this example are that it is important to see value through the eyes of the customer and to be clear about *relative* strengths. Although this might appear self-evident, a customer viewpoint and clarity about strengths may not be easy to achieve for several reasons:

- *Sense-making*. Managers may not be able to *make sense* of the complex and varied behaviours they experience in their markets. Often they will have vast amounts of raw data about customer preferences and competitor moves, but they lack the capability to draw useful conclusions from these data (for example, to spot trends or connections). Market researchers and marketing consultants may be able to supply a clearer view from outside.

- *Distance from the ultimate customer*. Component and raw material suppliers, for example, may be distanced from the final users by several intermediaries – other manufacturers and distributors. Although these direct customers may be the strategic customers there is a danger that what value means to the final consumer is not understood. In other words, companies may be out of touch with what is ultimately driving demand for their product or service.
- *Internal biases*. Managers are prone to assume that their particular strengths are valued by customers, and that somehow their competitors are necessarily inferior. For example, professional groups in many public services have tended to assume that what they think best for the client automatically is the best, while being skeptical of private sector providers' ability to look after the 'true' needs of clients.
- *Changes over time*. Customers' values typically evolve, either because they become more experienced (through repeat purchase) or because competitive offerings become available which offer better value. Managers, however, are often trapped by their historical experience of the market (see Chapter 5).

2.5 OPPORTUNITIES AND THREATS

The concepts and frameworks discussed above should be helpful in understanding the factors in the macro-, industry and competitor/market environments of an organisation. However, the critical issue is the *implications* that are drawn from this understanding in guiding strategic decisions and choices. The crucial next stage, therefore, is to draw from the environmental analysis specific strategic opportunities and threats for the organisation. Identifying these opportunities and threats is extremely valuable when thinking about strategic choices for the future (the subject of Chapters 6 to 8). Opportunities and threats forms one half of the Strengths, Weaknesses, Opportunities and Threats (SWOT) analyses that shape many companies strategy formulation (see Section 3.5.3).[17] In responding strategically to the environment, the goal is to reduce identified threats and take advantage of the best opportunities.

A **strategic gap** is an opportunity in the competitive environment that is not being fully exploited by competitors

Taking advantage of a **strategic gap** is an effective way of managing threats and opportunities. W. Chan Kim and Renée Mauborgne have argued that if organisations simply concentrate on competing head-to-head with competitive rivals this will lead to competitive convergence where all 'players' find the environment tough and threatening.[18] They describe this as a 'red ocean' strategy – red because of the bloodiness of the competition and the red ink caused by financial losses. They urge instead that managers attempt 'blue ocean' strategies – searching for, or creating, wide open spaces, free from existing competition. Blue oceans are strategic gaps in the market, opportunities that are not being fully exploited by competitors. One such blue ocean strategy was the creation by the Australian wine producers of fun, easy-to-understand and easy-to-drink wines. A red ocean strategy would have been to compete against the established French producers with fancy labels, wine jargon and complex tastes.

Strategic gaps can be identified with the help of the techniques in this chapter. In terms of the Porter five forces, strategic gaps are where rivalry is low. In terms of strategic group maps, gaps typically lie in the underoccupied 'white spaces'. In term of the strategy canvas, potential strategic gaps are where a big difference can be established with the position of most companies on the various factors valued by customers.

SUMMARY

www.pearsoned.co.uk/kos AUDIO SUMMARY

- Environmental influences can be thought of as layers around an organisation, with the outer layer making up the *macro-environment*, the middle layer making up the *industry or sector* and the inner layer *strategic groups* and *market segments*.
- The macro-environment can be analysed in terms of the *PESTEL factors*, from which *key drivers of change* can be identified. Alternative *scenarios* about the future can be constructed according to how the key drivers develop.
- Industries and sectors can be analysed in terms of *Porter Five Forces* – barriers to entry, substitutes, buyer power, supplier power and rivalry. Together, these determine industry or sector attractiveness, and are influential for overall performance.
- In the inner layer of the environment, *strategic group* analysis, *market segment* analysis and the *strategy canvas* can help identify strategic gaps or opportunities.
- *Blue ocean* strategies characterised by low rivalry are likely to be better opportunities than *red ocean* strategies with many rivals.

Recommended key readings

- The classic book on the analysis of industries is M.E. Porter, *Competitive Strategy*, Free Press, 1980. An updated view is available in M.E. Porter, 'Strategy and the Internet', *Harvard Business Review*, March (2001), pp. 2–19. An influential adaptation of Porter's basic ideas is W.C. Kim and R. Mauborgne, *Blue Ocean Strategy: How to Create Uncontested Market Space and Make Competition Irrelevant*, Harvard Business School Press, 2005.

- For approaches to how environments change, see K. van der Heijden, *Scenarios: the art of strategic conversation*, 2nd edition, Wiley, 2005, and the work of Michael Porter's colleague, A. McGahan, *How Industries Evolve*, Harvard Business School Press, 2004.
- A collection of academic articles on the latest views on PEST, scenarios and similar is the special issue of *International Studies of Management and Organization*, vol. 36, no. 3 (2006), edited by Peter McKiernan.

References

1. PESTEL is an extension of PEST (Politics, Economics, Social and Technology) analysis, taking more account of environmental ('green') and legal issues. For an application of PEST analysis to the world of business schools, relevant also to PESTEL, see H. Thomas, 'An analysis of the environment and competitive dynamics of management education', *Journal of Management Development*, vol. 26, no. 1 (2007), pp. 9–21.
2. For a discussion of scenario planning in practice, see K. van der Heijden, *Scenarios: the art of strategic conversation*, 2nd edition, Wiley, 2005. For how scenario planning fits with other forms of environmental analysis such as PESTEL, see P. Walsh, 'Dealing with the uncertainties of environmental change by adding scenario planning to the strategy reformulation equation', *Management Decision*, no. 43, vol. 1 (2005), pp. 113–122; and G. Burt, G. Wright, R. Bradfield and K. van der Heijden, 'The Role of Scenario Planning in Exploring the Environment in view of the limitations of PEST and its derivatives', *International Studies of Management and Organization*, vol. 36, no. 3 (2006), pp. 50–76.
3. D. Rutherford, *Routledge Dictionary of Economics*, 2nd edition, Routledge, 1995.
4. See M.E. Porter, *Competitive Strategy: Techniques for analysing industries and competitors*, Free Press, 1980, p. 5.
5. Porter, reference 4, Chapter 1. C. Christensen, 'The past and future of competitive advantage', *Sloan Management Review*, vol. 42, no. 2 (2001), pp. 105–109 provides an interesting critique and update of some of the factors underlying Porter's five forces.
6. See L. Van den Berghe and K. Verweire, 'Convergence in the financial services industry', *Geneva papers on Risk and Insurance*, vol. 25, no. 2 (2000), pp. 262–272; and A. Malhotra and A. Gupta, 'An investigation of firms' responses to industry convergence', *Academy of Management Proceedings*, 2001, pp. G1–6.
7. For discussions of the need for a collaborative as well as Porterian competitive approach to industry analysis, see J. Burton, 'Composite strategy: the combination of collaboration and competition', *Journal of General Management*, vol. 21, no. 1 (1995), pp. 3–28 and R. ul-Haq, *Alliances and Co-evolution: insights from the Banking Sector*, Palgrave Macmillan (2005).
8. The classic discussion is A. Brandenburger and B. Nalebuff, 'The right game: use game theory to shape strategy', *Harvard Business Review*, vol. 73, no. 4 (1995), pp. 57–71. On the dangers of 'complementors', see D. Yoffie and M. Kwak, 'With friends like these', *Harvard Business Review*, vol. 84, no. 9 (2006), pp. 88–98.
9. A classic academic overview of the industry life cycle is S. Klepper, 'Industry life cycles', *Industrial and Corporate Change*, vol. 6, no. 1, (1996), pp. 119–143. See also A. McGahan, 'How industries evolve', *Business Strategy Review*, vol. 11, no. 3 (2000), pp. 1–16.
10. A. McGahan, 'How industries evolve', *Business Strategy Review*, vol. 11, no. 3 (2000), pp. 1–16.
11. For a detailed exposition of this technique, see V. Lerville-Anger, F. Fréry, A. Gazengel and A. Ollivier, *Conduire le diagnostic global d'une unité industrielle*, Éditions d'Organisation, Paris, 2001.
12. For a review of the research on strategic groups see: J. McGee, H. Thomas and M. Pruett, 'Strategic groups and the analysis of market structure and industry dynamics', *British Journal of Management*, vol. 6, no. 4 (1995), pp. 257–270. For an example of the use of strategic group analysis see J. Pandian, J. Rajendran, H. Thomas and O. Furrer, 'Performance differences across

strategic groups: an examination of financial market-based performance measures', *Strategic Change*, vol. 15, no. 7/8 (2006), pp. 373–383.

13. These characteristics are based on Porter, reference 4.
14. A useful discussion of segmentation in relation to competitive strategy is provided in M.E. Porter, *Competitive Advantage*, Free Press, 1985, Chapter 7. For a more detailed review of segmentation methods see M. Wedel and W. Kamakura, *Market Segmentation: Conceptual and methodological foundations*, 2nd edition, Kluwer Academic, 1999.
15. M. Wedel, 'Is segmentation history?', *Marketing Research*, vol. 13, no. 4 (2001), pp. 26–29.
16. The term strategy canvas was introduced by C. Kim and R. Mauborgne, 'Charting your company's future', *Harvard Business Review*, vol. 80, no. 6 (2002), pp. 76–82. There is similar discussion in G. Johnson, C. Bowman and P. Rudd's chapter, 'Competitor analysis', in V. Ambrosini with G. Johnson and K. Scholes (eds), *Exploring Techniques of Analysis and Evaluation in Strategic Management*, Prentice Hall, 1998.
17. See also T. Jacobs, J. Shepherd and G. Johnson's chapter on SWOT analysis in V. Ambrosini with G. Johnson and K. Scholes (see reference 16); and E. Valentin, 'SWOT analysis from a resource-based view', *Journal of Marketing Theory and Practice*, vol. 9, no. 2 (2001), pp. 54–69. SWOT will be discussed more fully in Section 3.5.3 and Illustration 3.4.
18. W.C. Kim and R. Mauborgne, 'Value innovation: a leap into the blue ocean', *Journal of Business Strategy*, vol. 26, no. 4 (2005), pp. 22–28, and W.C. Kim and R. Mauborgne, *Blue Ocean Strategy: How to Create Uncontested Market Space and Make Competition Irrelevant*, Harvard Business School Press (2005).

CASE EXAMPLE

Global forces and the European brewing industry

Mike Blee and Richard Whittington

This case is centred on the European brewing industry and examines how the increasingly competitive pressure of operating within global markets is causing consolidation through acquisitions, alliances and closures within the industry. This has resulted in the growth of the brewers' reliance upon super brands.

In the first decade of the twenty-first century, European brewers faced a surprising paradox. The traditional centre of the beer industry worldwide, and still the largest regional market, Europe, was turning off beer. Beer consumption was falling in the largest markets of Germany and the United Kingdom, while burgeoning in emerging markets around the world. China, with 7 per cent annual growth, had become the largest single market by volume, while Brazilian volumes had overtaken Germany in 2005 (Euromonitor, 2006).

Table 1 details the overall decline of European beer consumption. Decline in traditional key markets is due to several factors. Governments are campaigning strongly against drunken driving, affecting the propensity to drink beer in restaurants, pubs and bars. There is increasing awareness of the effects of alcohol on health and fitness. Particularly In the United Kingdom, there is growing hostility towards so-called 'binge drinking', excessive alcohol consumption in pubs and clubs. Wines have also become increasingly popular in Northern European markets. However, beer consumption per capita varies widely between countries, being four times higher in Germany than in Italy, for example. Some traditionally low-consumption European markets have been showing good growth.

The drive against drunken driving and binge drinking has helped shift sales from the 'on-trade' (beer consumed on the premises, as in pubs or restaurants) to the off-trade (retail). Worldwide, the off-trade increased from 63 per cent of volume in 2000 to 66 per cent in 2005. The off-trade is increasingly dominated by large supermarket chains such as Tesco or Carrefour, which often use cut-price offers on beer in order to lure people into their shops. More than one-fifth of beer volume is now sold through supermarkets. German retailers such as Aldi and Lidl have had considerable success with

Photo: © Picturesbyrob/Alamy

their own 'private-label' (rather than brewery-branded) beers. However, although on-trade volumes are falling in Europe, the sales values are rising, as brewers introduce higher-priced premium products such as extra-cold lagers or fruit-flavoured beers. On the other hand, a good deal of this increasing demand for premium products is being satisfied by the import of apparently exotic beers from overseas (see Table 2).

Brewers' main purchasing costs are packaging (accounting for around half of non-labour costs), raw material such as barley, and energy. The European packaging industry is highly concentrated, dominated by international companies such as Crown in cans and Owens-Illinois in glass bottles. During 2006, Dutch brewer Heineken complained of an 11 per cent rise in packaging costs.

Table 1 European beer consumption by country and year (000 hectolitres)

Country	1980	2000	2001	2002	2003	2004	2005
Austria	7651	8762	8627	8734	8979	8881	8970
Belgium	12945	10064	9986	9901	9935	9703	N/A
Denmark	6698	5452	5282	5202	5181	4862	N/A
Finland	2738	4024	4085	4136	4179	4370	N/A
France	23745	21420	21331	20629	21168	20200	N/A
Germany†	89820	103105	100904	100385	97107	95639	94994
Greece	N/A	4288	4181	4247	3905	N/A	N/A
Ireland	4174	5594	5625	5536	5315	5206	N/A
Italy	9539	16289	16694	16340	17452	17194	17340
Luxembourg	417	472	445	440	373	N/A	N/A
Netherlands	12213	13129	12922	11985	12771	12687	12747
Norway*	7651	2327	2290	2420	2270	2490	N/A
Portugal	3534	6453	6276	5948	6008	6266	6224
Spain	20065	29151	31126	30715	33451	N/A	N/A
Sweden	3935	5011	4932	4998	4969	4635	4566
Switzerland*	4433	4194	4141	4127	4334	4262	N/A
UK	65490	57007	58234	59384	60302	59195	N/A

* Non-EU countries; † 1980 excludes GDR. Figures adjusted.

Source: www.brewersofeurope.org.

Table 2 Imports of beer by country

Country	Imports 2002 (% of consumption or production*)	Imports 2004 (% of consumption or production)
Austria	5.1	6.4
Belgium	4.74	10.2
Denmark	2.6	N/A
Finland	2.3	7.3
France	23	31
Germany	3.1	4
Greece	4.1	N/A
Ireland	N/A	N/A
Italy	27.15	37
Luxembourg	N/A	38.4
Netherlands	3.2	14.4
Norway	5.4	N/A
Portugal	1.1	N/A
Spain	11.7	N/A
Sweden	N/A	18
Switzerland	15.4	15.6
UK	10.9	12.3

* Import figures do not include beers brewed under licence in home country; countries vary in measuring % of production or consumption.

Source: www.brewersofeurope.org.

Acquisition, licensing and strategic alliances have all occurred as the leading brewers battle to control the market. There are global pressures for consolidation due to overcapacity within the industry, the need to contain costs and benefits of leveraging strong brands. For example, Belgian brewer Interbrew purchased parts of the old Bass Empire, Becks and Whitbread in 2001 and in 2004 announced a merger with Am Bev, the Brazilian brewery group, to create the largest brewer in the world, InBev. The second largest brewer, the American Anheuser-Busch, has been investing in China, Mexico and Europe. In 2002, South African Breweries acquired the Miller Group (USA) and Pilsner Urquell in the Czech Republic, becoming SABMiller. Smaller players in fast-growing Chinese and South American markets are being snapped up by the large international brewers too. Medium-sized Australian brewer Fosters is withdrawing from direct participation in many international markets, for example selling its European brand-rights to Scottish & Newcastle. Table 3 lists the world's top 10 brewing companies, which accounted for around half of world beer volumes. There remain many small specialist and regional brewers, such as the Dutch company Grolsch

Table 3 The world's top 10 brewery companies by volume: 2005

Company	Share global volume (%)	Country of origin
InBev	10.8	Brazil–Belgium
Anheuser-Busch	9.4	USA
SABMiller	7.3	South Africa (relocated to UK)
Heineken	5.7	Netherlands
Morelo	2.9	Mexico
Carlsberg	2.9	Denmark
Coors	2.6	USA
TsingTao	2.4	China
Baltic Brewery Holdings	2.2	Denmark/UK
Asahi	2.1	Japan

Source: Euromonitor International, *The World Brewing Industry*.

(see below) or the British Cobra Beer, originating in the Indian restaurant market.

Four brewing companies

Heineken (The Netherlands)

Heineken is the biggest of the European brewery businesses, and has three-quarters of its sales in the region. Total sales in 2006 were €11.8bn (£8bn). About 5 per cent of sales are in Asia–Pacific and 17 per cent of sales are in the Americas. The company's biggest brands are Heineken itself and Amstel. The company remains a family-controlled business, which it claims gives it the stability and independence to pursue steady growth internationally.

Heineken's strategy overseas is to use locally acquired companies as a means of introducing the Heineken brand to new markets. It aims to strengthen local companies by transferring expertise and technology. The result is to create economies of scale for both the local beers and Heineken. Heineken's four priorities for action are to accelerate revenue growth, to improve efficiency and cost reduction, to speed up strategy implementation and to focus on those markets where the company believes it can win.

Grolsch (The Netherlands)

Royal Grolsch NV is a medium-size international brewing group, established in 1615. With overall sales in 2005 of €313m, it is less than a twentieth of the size of Heineken. Its key products include Grolsch premium lager and new flavoured beers (Grolsch lemon and Grolsch pink grapefruit). In The Netherlands Grolsch holds the rights for the sale and distribution of the valued US Miller brand. About half its sales are obtained overseas, either through export or licensing of production: the United Kingdom is its second largest market. In 2005, Grolsch centralised its own production on a single new Dutch brewery to increase efficiency and volume, and opened a small additional 'trial' brewery in order to support innovation.

Innovation and branding are core to the company's strategy. The company believes that its strong and distinctive beers can succeed in a market of increased homogenisation. Its brand is reinforced by its striking green bottles and its unique swing-tops.

InBev (Belgium/Brazil)

InBev was created in 2004 from the merger of Belgian InterBrew and Brazilian AmBev. With a turnover of €13.3bn in 2006, it is the largest brewer in the world, holding number one or number two positions in 20 different countries. Its well-known international brands include Beck's and Stella Artois. Through a series of acquisitions, InBev has become the second largest brewer in China.

The company is frank about its strategy: to transform itself from the biggest brewing company in the world to the best. It aims to do this by building strong global brands and increasing efficiency. Efficiency gains will come from more central coordination of purchasing, including media and IT; from the optimisation of its inherited network of breweries; and from the sharing of best practice across sites internationally. Although acquisitions continue, InBev is now emphasising organic growth and improved margins from its existing businesses.

Scottish and Newcastle (UK)

Scottish and Newcastle is a European-focused brewing group based in Edinburgh. In 2005, its turnover was £3.9bn (€5.5bn). Its key brands include John Smiths, Kronenbourg, Kanterbrau, Baltika and (in Europe) Fosters. It is the fourth largest brewer in Europe in volume terms, and market leader in the UK, France and Russia. The company has made many acquisitions in the UK (including Bulmer's cider), France, Greece and

Finland. The group's 50 per cent investment in Baltic Beverages has given it exposure to the fast-growing markets of Russia, Ukraine and the Baltic countries. In China, Scottish and Newcastle has a 20 per cent stake in CBC, the country's fifth largest brewery. In India, the company's United Breweries is the country's largest brewer, with the Kingfisher brand. In the USA, Scottish and Newcastle is the second largest importer of foreign beers. The company emphasises the development of innovative and premium beers, and is closing down its more inefficient breweries.

Questions

1 Using the data from the case (and any other sources available), carry out for the European brewing industry (i) a PESTEL analysis and (ii) a five forces analysis. What do you conclude?

2 For the four breweries outlined above (or breweries of your own choice) explain:

(a) how these trends will impact differently on these different companies; and

(b) the relative strengths and weaknesses of each company.

3

Strategic Capability

LEARNING OUTCOMES

After reading this chapter you should be able to:

→ Distinguish elements of strategic capability in organisations: resources, competences, core competences and dynamic capabilities.

→ Recognise the role of continual improvement in cost efficiency as a strategic capability.

→ Analyse how strategic capabilities might provide sustainable competitive advantage on the basis of their value, rarity, inimitability and non-substitutability.

→ Diagnose strategic capability by means of value chain analysis, benchmarking and SWOT analysis.

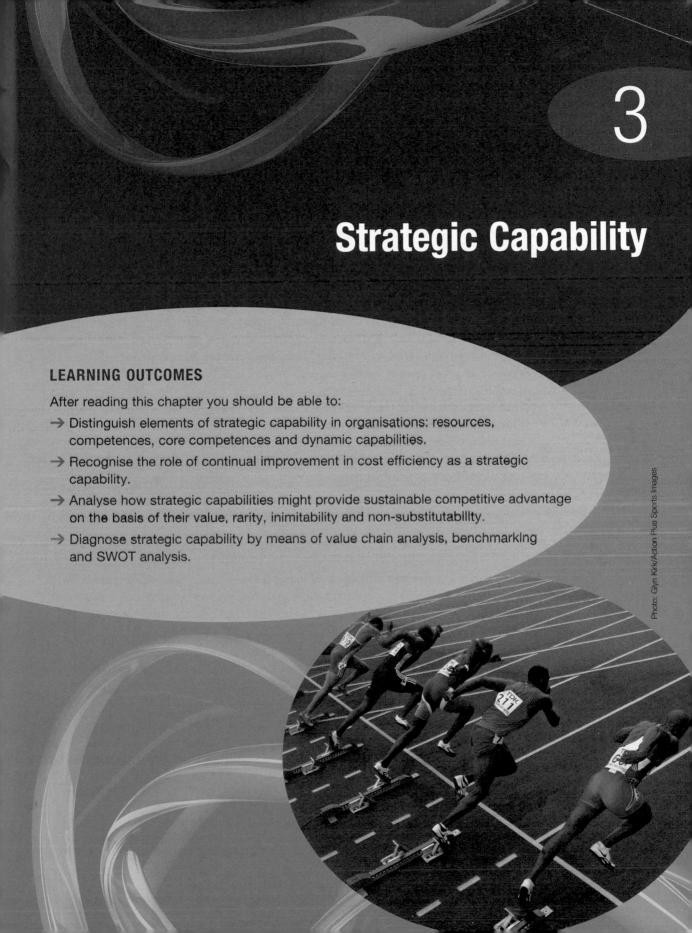

Photo: Glyn Kirk/Action Plus Sports Images

3.1 INTRODUCTION

Chapter 2 outlined how the external environment of an organisation can create both strategic opportunities and threats. However, Tesco, Sainsbury and Asda all compete in the same environment, yet Tesco is a superior performer. It is not the environment that distinguishes between them but their internal *strategic capabilities*. The importance of strategic capability is the focus of this chapter. There are three key concepts that underpin the discussion. The first is that organisations are not identical, but have different capabilities. The second is that it can be difficult for one organisation to obtain or copy the capabilities of another. For example, Sainsbury cannot readily obtain the whole of Tesco's retail sites, its management or its experience. The third arises from these: if an organisation is to achieve competitive advantage, it will do so on the basis of capabilities that its rivals do not have or have difficulty in obtaining. In turn this helps explain how some organisations are able to achieve superior performance compared with others. They have capabilities that permit them to produce at lower cost or generate a superior product or service at standard cost in relation to other organisations with inferior capabilities. These concepts underlie what has become known as the **resource-based view** of strategy[1] (though it might more appropriately be labeled the 'capabilities view'): that the competitive advantage and superior performance of an organisation is explained by the distinctiveness of its capabilities.

The resource-based view of strategy: the competitive advantage and superior performance of an organisation is explained by the distinctiveness of its capabilities

The chapter has four sections:

- Section 3.2 discusses the *foundations of strategic capability* and considers the distinction between *resources* and *competences*.
- Section 3.3 is concerned with a vital basis of strategic capability of any organisation: namely the ability to achieve and continually improve *cost efficiency*.
- Section 3.4 considers what sort of capabilities allow organisations to *sustain* competitive advantage over time (in a public sector context the equivalent concern might be how some organisations sustain relative superior performance over time).
- Section 3.5 moves on to consider different ways strategic capability might be analysed. These include *value chain and value network* analyses, and *benchmarking*. The section concludes by explaining the use of *SWOT* analysis as a basis for pulling together the insights from the analyses of the environment (explained in Chapter 2) and of strategic capability in this chapter.

3.2 FOUNDATIONS OF STRATEGIC CAPABILITY

Different writers, managers and consultants use different terms and concepts in explaining the importance of strategic capability. Given such differences, it

Exhibit 3.1 Strategic capabilities and competitive advantage

	Resources	Competences
Threshold capabilities	**Threshold resources** • Tangible • Intangible	**Threshold competences**
Capabilities for competitive advantage	**Unique resources** • Tangible • Intangible	**Core competences**

Strategic capability is the resources and competences of an organisation needed for it to survive and prosper

is important to understand how the terms are used here. Overall, **strategic capability** can be defined as the resources and competences of an organisation needed for it to survive and prosper. Exhibit 3.1 shows the elements of strategic capability that are employed in the chapter to explain the concept.

3.2.1 Resources and competences

Tangible resources are the physical assets of an organisation such as plant, labour and finance

Intangible resources are non-physical assets such as information, reputation and knowledge

Perhaps the most basic concept is that of *resources*. **Tangible resources** are the physical assets of an organisation such as plant, people and finance. **Intangible resources** are non-physical assets such as information, reputation and knowledge. Typically, an organisation's resources can be considered under the following four broad categories:

- *Physical resources* – such as the machines, buildings or the production capacity of the organisation. The nature of these resources, such as the age, condition, capacity and location of each resource, will determine the usefulness of such resources.
- *Financial resources* – such as capital, cash, debtors and creditors, and suppliers of money (shareholders, bankers, etc.).
- *Human resources* – including the mix (e.g. demographic profile), skills and knowledge of employees and other people in an organisation's networks.
- *Intellectual capital* as an intangible resource includes patents, brands, business systems and customer databases. An indication of the value of these is

Exhibit 3.2 Strategic capability: the terminology

Term	Definition	Example (athletics)
Strategic capability	The ability to perform at the level required to survive and prosper. It is underpinned by the resources and competences of the organisation	Equipment and athletic ability suited to a chosen event
Threshold resources	The resources needed to meet customers' minimum requirements and therefore to continue to exist	A healthy body (for individuals) Medical facilities and practitioners Training venues and equipment Food supplements
Threshold competences	Activities and processes needed to meet customers' minimum requirements and therefore to continue to exist	Individual training regimes Physiotherapy/injury management Diet planning
Unique resources	Resources that underpin competitive advantage and are difficult for competitors to imitate or obtain	Exceptional heart and lungs Height or weight World-class coach
Core competences	Activities that underpin competitive advantage and are difficult for competitors to imitate or obtain	A combination of dedication, tenacity, time to train, demanding levels of competition and a will to win

that when businesses are sold, part of the value is 'goodwill'. In a knowledge-based economy intellectual capital is likely to be a major asset of many organisations.

Such resources are certainly important; but what an organisation does – how it employs and deploys these resources – matters at least as much as what resources it has. There would be no point in having state-of-the-art equipment or valuable knowledge or a valuable brand if they were not used effectively. The efficiency and effectiveness of physical or financial resources, or the people in an organisation, depends not only on their existence but also on how they are managed, the cooperation between people, their adaptability, their innovatory capacity, the relationship with customers and suppliers and the experience and learning about what works well and what does not. These are all **competences**, by which is meant the skills and abilities by which resources are deployed effectively through an organisation's activities and processes.

Competences are the skills and abilities by which resources are deployed effectively through an organisation's activities and processes

Within these broad definitions, other terms are commonly used. As the explanation proceeds, it might be useful to refer to the two examples provided in Exhibit 3.2: one relating the concepts to a business and the other to sport.

3.2.2 Threshold capabilities

Threshold capabilities are those capabilities needed for an organisation to meet the necessary requirements to compete in a given market

A distinction needs to be made between capabilities (resources or competences) that are at a threshold level and those that might help the organisation achieve competitive advantage and superior performance. **Threshold capabilities** are those needed for an organisation to meet the necessary requirements to compete in a given market. These could be *threshold resources* required to meet minimum customer requirements: for example, modern multiple retailers demand that their suppliers possess quite sophisticated IT infrastructure simply to stand a chance of meeting retailer requirements. Or they could be the *threshold competences* required to deploy resources so as to meet customers' requirements and support particular strategies. Retailers do not simply expect suppliers to have the required IT infrastructure, but to be able to use it effectively so as to guarantee the required level of service.

Identifying and managing threshold capabilities raises at least two significant challenges:

- *Threshold levels of capability will change* as critical success factors change (see section 2.4.4) or through the activities of competitors and new entrants. To continue the example, suppliers to major retailers did not require the same level of IT and logistics support a decade ago. But the retailers' drive to reduce costs, improve efficiency and ensure availability of merchandise to their customers means that their expectations of their suppliers has increased markedly in that time and continues to do so. So there is a need for those suppliers continuously to review and improve their logistics resource and competence base just to stay in business.
- *Trade-offs* may need to be made to achieve the threshold capability required for different sorts of customers. For example, businesses have found it difficult to compete in market segments that require large quantities of standard product as well as market segments that require added value specialist products. Typically, the first requires high-capacity, fast-throughput plant, standardised highly efficient systems and a low-cost labour force: the second a skilled labour force, flexible plant and a more innovative capacity. The danger is that an organisation fails to achieve the threshold capabilities required for either segment.

3.2.3 Unique resources and core competences

Unique resources are those resources that critically underpin competitive advantage and that others cannot easily imitate or obtain

While threshold capabilities are important, they do not of themselves create competitive advantage or the basis of superior performance. These are dependent on an organisation having distinctive or unique capabilities that competitors will find difficult to imitate. This could be because the organisation has **unique resources** that critically underpin competitive advantage and that others cannot imitate or obtain – a long-established brand, for example. It is,

Illustration 3.1

Strategic capabilities

Executives emphasise different strategic capabilities in different organisations.

Freeport-McMoRan Copper and Gold, Inc. is an international mining company in North America. It claims a leading position in the mining industry on the basis of 'large, long lived, geographically diverse assets and significant proven and probable reserves of copper, gold and molybdenum'. More specifically, in terms of its Indonesian operation it points to a 'principal asset' as the 'world class Grasberg mine discovered in 1988' which has 'the world's largest single copper reserve and world's largest single gold reserve'.

Source: Annual Report 2006.

Daniel Bouton, Chairman and CEO of **Société Générale**, in response to the question: *How do you maintain your competitive advantage in equity derivatives?*

The barrier to entry is high, because of two significant costs. The first is IT. The systems you need to perform well cost at least €200 million a year, and it's not something you can buy from Dell or SAP. The second is the sheer number of people you need to work on managing your risk. Before you launch a product, you need to have the front office guys that propose, calculate and write the first model. Then you need the IT guy that creates the IT system in order to be able to calculate risks every 10 seconds. And you need a good validating team in order to verify all the hypotheses. After that, you need high-quality middle and back office people.

Source: Interviewed by Clive Horwood in *Euromoney*, vol. 27, no. 447 (July 2006), pp. 84–89.

Tony Hall, Chief Executive of the **Royal Opera House**:

'world-class' is neither an idle nor boastful claim. In the context of the Royal Opera House the term refers to the quality of our people, the standards of our productions and the diversity of our work and initiatives. Unique? Unashamedly so. We shy away from labels such as 'elite', because of the obvious negative connotations of exclusiveness. But I want people to take away from here the fact that we are elite in the sense that we have the best singers, dancers, directors, designers, orchestra, chorus, backstage crew and administrative staff. We are also amongst the best in our ability to reach out to as wide and diverse a community as possible.

Source: Annual Review 2005/6, p. 11.

Dave Swift, President of **Whirlpool** North America:

Executing our strategy requires a unique toolkit of competencies that we continue to build for our people globally. The starting point of building new competencies is what we call 'Customer Excellence' – our ability to proactively understand and anticipate the needs of customers. Customer Excellence is a collection of tools that allows our people to analytically assess and prioritize the needs and desires of customers along all aspects of the purchase cycle – from when they first might investigate an appliance on a web site, to the in-store experience on a retailer's floor, to the features and aesthetics of the product, to the installation and service experience, and ultimately to their need to repeat this cycle. With these consumer insights in-hand, we then turn them into customer solutions through our innovation tools. As a result, our innovation capability has produced a robust pipeline of products, achieving a steady-state estimated value of over $3 billion. . . . Our knowledge of customers, coupled with our innovative customer solutions, is driving the attractiveness of our brands and creating greater value for our shareholders.

Source: Whirlpool Corporation 2005 Annual Report.

Questions

1. Categorise the range of capabilities highlighted by the executives in terms of section 3.2 and Exhibit 3.2.
2. With reference to section 3.4, which of the capabilities might be especially important in terms of achieving competitive advantage and why?
3. For an organisation of your choice undertake the same exercise as in questions 1 and 2 above.

however, more likely that an organisation achieves competitive advantage because it has distinctive, or core, competences. The concept of core competences was developed, most notably by Gary Hamel and C.K. Prahalad. While various definitions exist, here **core competences**[2] are taken to mean the skills and abilities by which resources are deployed through an organisations's activities and processes such as to achieve competitive advantage in ways that others cannot imitate or obtain. For example, a supplier that achieves competitive advantage in a retail market might have done so on the basis of a unique resource such as a powerful brand, or by finding ways of providing service or building relationships with that retailer in ways that its competitors find difficult to imitate – a core competence. Section 3.4 discusses in more depth the role played by unique resources and core competences in contributing to long-term competitive advantage.

Core competences are the skills and abilities by which resources are deployed through an organisation's activities and processes such as to achieve competitive advantage in ways that others cannot imitate or obtain

www.pearsoned.co.uk/fos
KEY CONCEPT
Core competences

Putting these concepts together, the summary argument is this. To survive and prosper an organisation needs to address the challenges of the environment that it faces discussed in Chapter 2. In particular it must be capable of performing in terms of the critical success factors that arise from demands and needs of its customers, discussed in section 2.4.4. The strategic capability to do so is dependent on the resources and the competences it has. These must reach a threshold level in order for the organisation to survive. The further challenge is to achieve competitive advantage. This requires it to have strategic capabilities that its competitors find difficult to imitate or obtain. These could be unique resources but are more likely to be the core competences of the organisation. Illustration 3.1 shows how executives of different organisations describe the strategic capabilities of their organisations.

3.3 COST EFFICIENCY

Managers often refer to the management of costs as a key strategic capability. So it is. Moreover, understanding the management of cost efficiency as a strategic capability illustrates some of the points made in section 3.2.

Customers can benefit from cost efficiencies in terms of lower prices or more product features for the same price. The management of the cost base of an organisation could also be a basis for achieving competitive advantage (see sections 6.2.1 and 6.3.1). However, for many organisations the management of costs is becoming a threshold strategic capability for two reasons:

- *Customers do not value product features at any price*. If the price rises too high they will sacrifice value and opt for lower price. So the challenge is to ensure that an appropriate level of value is offered at an acceptable price. This means that everyone is forced to keep costs as low as possible, consistent with the value to be provided. Not to do so invites customers to switch products or invites competition.

- *Competitive rivalry* will continually require the driving down of costs because competitors will be trying to reduce their cost so as to underprice their rivals while offering similar value.

If cost is to be managed effectively, attention has to be paid to key *cost drivers* as follows:

- *Economies of scale* may be especially important in manufacturing organisations, since the high capital costs of plant need to be recovered over a high volume of output. Traditionally manufacturing sectors where this has been especially important have been motor vehicles, chemicals and metals. In other industries, such as drinks and tobacco and food, scale economies are important in distribution or marketing.
- *Supply costs* can be important. Location may influence supply costs, which is why, historically, steel and glass manufacturing were close to raw material or energy sources. In some instances, ownership of raw materials was a unique resource, giving cost advantage. Supply costs are of particular importance to organisations that act as intermediaries, where the value added through their own activities is low and the need to identify and manage input costs is critically important to success. For example, retailers pay a great deal of attention to trying to achieve lower costs of supply than their competitors.
- *Product/process design* also influences cost. Efficiency gains in production processes have been achieved by many organisations through improvements in *capacity-fill, labour productivity, yield* (from materials) or *working capital* utilisation. Understanding the relative importance of each of these to maintaining a competitive position is important. For example, in terms of managing capacity-fill: an unfilled seat in a plane, train or theatre cannot be 'stocked' for later sale. So marketing special offers (while protecting the core business) and having the IT systems to analyse and optimise revenue are important capabilities. Product design will also influence costs in other parts of the value system – for example, in distribution or after-sales service. For example in the photocopier market Canon eroded Xerox's advantage (which was built on service and a support network) by designing a copier that needed far less servicing.
- *Experience*[3] can be a key source of cost efficiency and there is evidence it may provide competitive advantage in particular in terms of the relationship between the cumulative experience gained by an organisation and its unit costs – described as the *experience curve*. See Exhibit 3.3. The experience curve suggests that an organisation undertaking any activity develops competences in this activity over time and therefore does it more efficiently. Since companies with higher market share have more 'cumulative experience' – simply because high share gives them greater volumes of production or service – it follows that it is important to gain and hold market share, as discussed in Chapter 2. It is important to remember that it is the *relative market share* in definable market segments that matters. There are

Exhibit 3.3 The experience curve

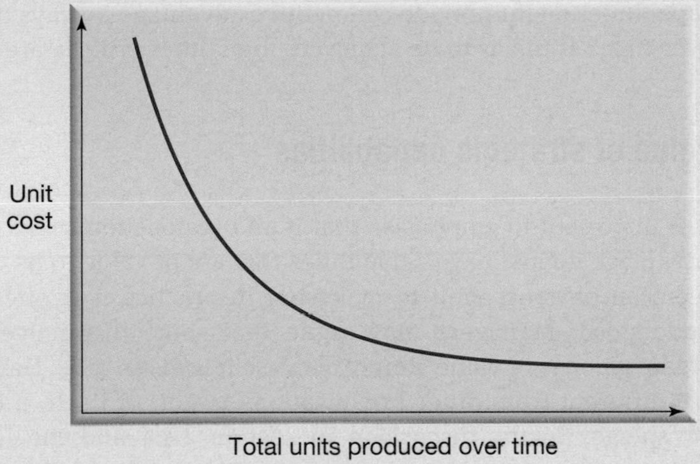

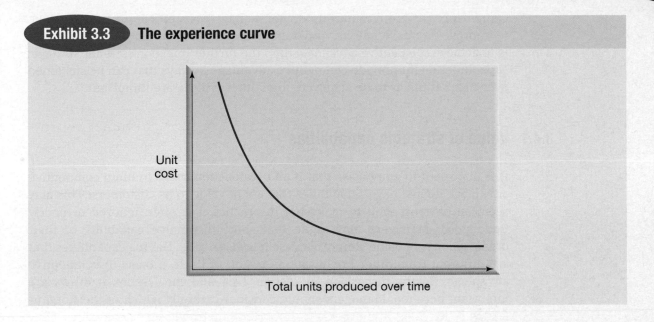

important implications of the experience curve concept that could influence an organisation's competitive position:

- *Growth is not optional* in many markets. If an organisation chooses to grow more slowly than the competition, it should expect the competitors to gain cost advantage in the longer term – through experience.
- *Unit costs should decline year on year* as a result of cumulative experience. In high-growth industries this will happen quickly, but even in mature industries this decline in costs should occur. Organisations that fail to achieve this are likely to suffer at the hands of competitors who do. The implication of this is that *continual reduction in costs is a necessity* for organisations in competitive markets. Even if it is not able to provide competitive advantage, it is a threshold competence for survival.
- *First-mover advantage* can be important. The organisation that moves down the experience curve by getting into a market first should be able to reduce its cost base because of the accumulated experience it builds up over its rivals by being first.

3.4 CAPABILITIES FOR ACHIEVING AND SUSTAINING COMPETITIVE ADVANTAGE

The lessons of sections 3.2 and 3.3 are these: if the capabilities of an organisation do not meet customer needs, at least to a threshold level, the organisation cannot survive; and if managers do not manage costs efficiently and continue to improve on this, it will be vulnerable to those who can. However, if the aim is to achieve *competitive advantage* then the further question is: what strategic capabilities might provide competitive advantage in ways that can be sustained over time? If this is to be achieved, then other criteria are important.[4]

3.4.1 Value of strategic capabilities

It is important to emphasise that if an organisation seeks to build competitive advantage it must have capabilities that are of value to its customers. This may seem an obvious point to make but in practice it is often ignored or poorly understood. Managers may argue that some distinctive capability of their organisation is of value simply because it is distinctive. Having capabilities that are different from other organisations is not, of itself, a basis of competitive advantage. So the discussion in section 2.4.4 and the lessons it draws are important here too. Managers should consider carefully which of their organisation's activities are especially important in providing such value. They should also consider which are less valued. Value chain analysis explained in section 3.5.1 can help here.

3.4.2 Rarity of strategic capabilities

Competitive advantage might be achieved if a competitor possesses a unique or rare capability. This could take the form of *unique resources*. For example, some libraries have unique collections of books unavailable elsewhere; a company may have a powerful brand; retail stores may have prime locations. Some organisations have patented products or services that give them advantage – resources that may need to be defended by a willingness to bring litigation against illegal imitators. For service organisations unique resources may be intellectual capital – particularly talented individuals.

Competitive advantage could also be based on rare competences; for example, unique skills developed over time. However, there are three important points to bear in mind about the extent to which rarity of competences might provide sustainable competitive advantage:

- *Ease of transferability*. Rarity may depend on who owns the competence and how easily transferable it is. For example, the competitive advantage of some professional service organisations is built around the competence of specific individuals – such as a doctor in 'leading-edge' medicine, individual fund managers, the manager of a top sports team or the CEO of a business. But since these individuals may leave or join competitors, this resource may be a fragile basis of advantage. More durable advantage *may* be found in competences that exist for recruiting, training, motivating and rewarding such individuals or be embedded in the culture that attracts them to the organisation – so ensuring that they do not defect to 'competitors'.

- *Sustainability*. It may be dangerous to assume that competences that are rare will remain so. *Rarity could be temporary*. If an organisation is successful on the basis of a unique set of competences, then competitors will seek to imitate or obtain those competences. So it may be necessary to consider other bases of sustainability.
- *Core rigidities*. Another danger is that of redundancy. Rare capabilities may come to be what Dorothy Leonard-Barton refers to as *'core rigidities'*,[5] difficult to change and therefore damaging to the organisation. Managers may be so wedded to these bases of success that they perceive them as strengths of the organisation and 'invent' customer values around them.

3.4.3 Inimitable strategic capabilities

It should be clear by now that the search for strategic capability that provides sustainable competitive advantage is not straightforward. It involves identifying capabilities that are likely to be durable and which competitors find difficult to imitate or obtain.

At the risk of over-generalisation, it is unusual for competitive advantage to be explainable by differences in the tangible resources of organisations, since over time these can usually be imitated or traded. Advantage is more likely to be determined by the way in which resources are deployed to create competences in the organisation's activities. For example, as suggested earlier, an IT system itself will not improve an organisation's competitive standing: it is how it is used that matters. Indeed, what will probably make most difference is how the system is used to bring together customer needs with activities and knowledge both inside and outside the organisation. It is therefore to do with linking sets of competences. So, extending the earlier definition, *core competences* are likely to be the skills and abilities to *link* activities or processes through which resources are deployed so as to achieve competitive advantage. In order to achieve this advantage, core competences therefore need to fulfil the following criteria:

- They must relate to an activity or process that underpins the value in the product or service features – as seen through the eyes of the customer (or other powerful stakeholder). This is the value criterion discussed earlier.
- The competences must lead to levels of performance that are significantly better than competitors (or similar organisations in the public sector).
- The competences must be difficult for competitors to imitate – or inimitable.

With regard to this third requirement of inimitability, Exhibit 3.4 summarises how this might be achieved and Illustration 3.2 also gives an example. The three main reasons are:

Exhibit 3.4 Criteria for inimitability of strategic capabilities

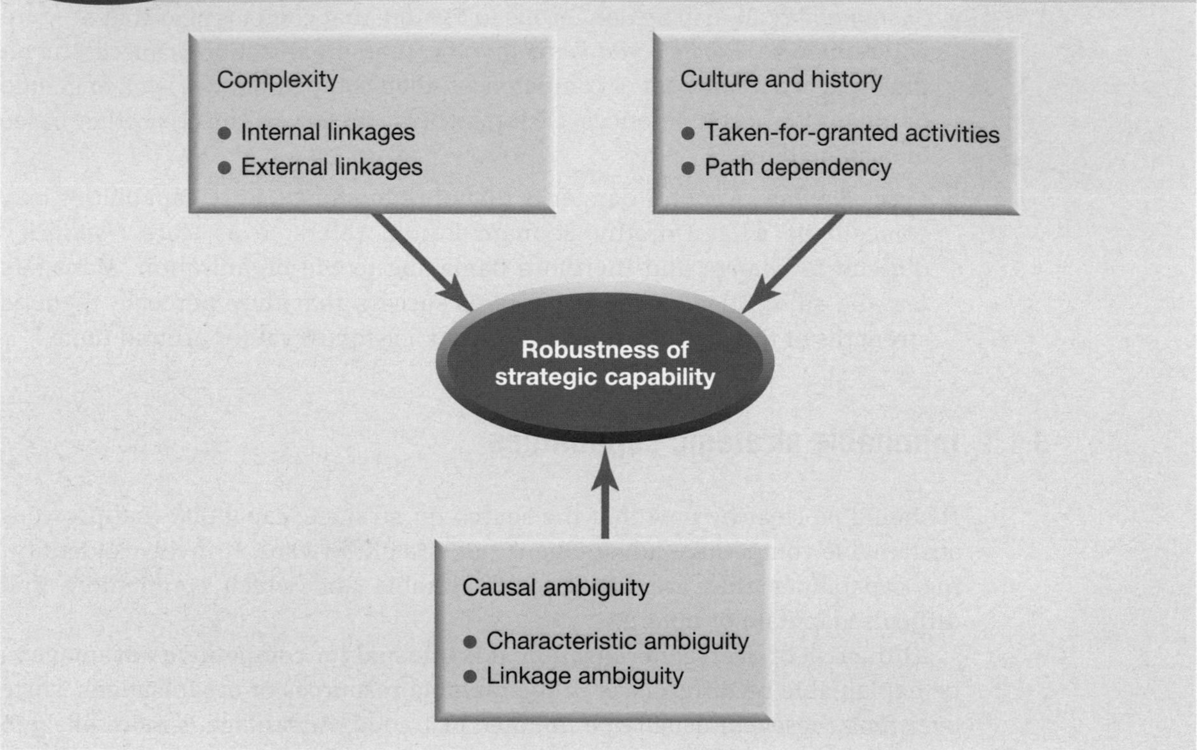

Complexity

The core competences of an organisation may be difficult to imitate because they are complex. This may be for two main reasons.

- *Internal linkages*. It may be the ability to link activities and processes that, together, deliver customer value. The managers in Plasco (see Illustration 3.2) talked about 'flexibility' and 'innovation'; but 'flexibility' or 'innovation' are themselves made up of and dependent on sets of related activities as Illustration 3.2 shows.
- *External interconnectedness*. Organisations can make it difficult for others to imitate or obtain their bases of competitive advantage by developing activities together with the customer on which the customer is dependent on them. This is sometimes referred to as *co-specialisation*. For example, an industrial lubricants business moved away from just selling its products to customers by coming to agreements with them to manage the applications of lubricants within the customers' sites against agreed targets on cost savings. The more efficient the use of lubricants, the more both parties benefited. Similarly software businesses can achieve advantage by developing computer programs that are distinctively beneficial to specific customer needs.

Illustration 3.2

Strategic capability for Plasco

Strategic capability underpinning competitive success may be based on complex linkages rooted in the history and culture of an organisation.

Plasco, a manufacturer of plastics goods, had won several major retail accounts from competitors. Managers were keen to understand the bases of these successes as a way of understanding strategic capabilities better. To do this they undertook an analysis of customer value (as explained in section 2.4.4 in Chapter 2). From this they identified that the major retailers with whom it had been successful particularly valued a powerful brand, a good product range, innovation, good service and reliable delivery. In particular, Plasco was outperforming competitors when it came to delivery, service and product range.

They then undertook a detailed analysis of the competencies of Plasco to identify the processes and activities within the business that delivered this value to customers. Some of what emerged from this the senior management knew about; but they were not aware of some of the other explanations for success that emerged.

When they analysed the bases of reliable delivery, they could not find reasons why they were outperforming competitors. The logistics of the company were no different from other companies. They were essential but not unique – threshold resources and competences.

When they examined the activities that gave rise to the good service they provided, however, they found other explanations. They were readily able to identify that much was down to their having a more flexible approach than their competitors, the main one of which was a major US multinational. But the explanations for this flexibility were less obvious. The flexibility took form, for example, in the ability to amend the requirements of the retailers' orders at short notice; or when the buyers in the retailers had made an error, to 'bale them out' by taking back stock that had been delivered. What was much less obvious were the activities underpinning this flexibility. The mapping surfaced some explanations:

- The junior manager and staff within the firm were 'bending the rules' to take back goods from the major retailers when, strictly speaking, the policies and systems of the business did not allow it.
- Plant utilisation was relatively lower and less automated than competitors, so it was easier to change production runs at short notice. Company policy, on the other hand, was to improve productivity through increased utilisation and to begin to automate the plants. Lower levels of production management were not anxious to do this, knowing that if they did, it would reduce the flexibility and therefore diminish their ability to provide the service customers wanted.

Much of this was down to the knowledge of quite junior managers, sales representatives and staff in the factory as to 'how to work the system' and how to work together to solve the retailers' problems. This was not a matter of company policy or formal training, but custom and practice that had built up over the years. The result was a relationship between sales personnel and retail buyers in which buyers were encouraged to 'ask the impossible' of the company when difficulties arose.

Sound logistics and good-quality products were vital, but the core competences which underpinned their success were the result of linked sets of activities built up over the years which it was difficult, not only for competitors but also for people in the organisation, to identify clearly.

Questions

1. Why might it be difficult for a large, automated US plastics manufacturer to deal with retailers in the same way as Plasco?
2. How should Plasco senior managers respond to the explanations of strategic capability surfaced by the mapping?
3. What could erode the bases of competitive advantage that Plasco has?

Culture and history

Core competences may become embedded in an organisation's culture. Indeed, managers within an organisation may not understand them *explicitly* themselves. So coordination between various activities occurs 'naturally' because people know their part in the wider picture or it is simply 'taken for granted' that activities are done in particular ways. For example, in Plasco the experience in rapid changes in production runs and the close links between sales personnel, production and despatch were not planned or formalised: they were the way the firm had come to operate over the years.

Linked to this cultural embeddedness, therefore, is the likelihood that such competences have developed over time and in a way specific to an organisation that can be difficult for others to imitate. Again, however, it should be noted that there is a danger that culturally embedded competences built up over time become so embedded that they are difficult to change; that they become core rigidities.

Causal ambiguity[6]

Another reason why competences might be difficult to imitate is that competitors find it difficult to discern the causes and effects underpinning an organisation's advantage. This is called *causal ambiguity*. This could relate to any or all of the aspects of strategic capability discussed in the preceding sections of this chapter. Causal ambiguity may exist in two different forms:[7]

- *Characteristic ambiguity*. Where the significance of the characteristic itself is difficult to discern or comprehend, perhaps because it is based on tacit knowledge or rooted in the organisation's culture. For example, it is quite possible that the 'rule bending' in Plasco would have been counter-cultural for its US rival and therefore not readily identified or seen as relevant or significant.
- *Linkage ambiguity*. Where competitors cannot discern which activities and processes are dependent on which others to form linkages that create core competences. It would be difficult for competitors to understand the cause and effect linkages in Plasco given that the management of Plasco did not fully comprehend them themselves.

3.4.4 Non-substitutability of strategic capabilities

Providing value to customers and possessing competences that are complex, culturally embedded and causally ambiguous may mean that it is very difficult for organisations to copy them. However, the organisation may still be at risk from substitution. Substitution could take two different forms:

- *Product or service substitution*. As already discussed in Chapter 2 in relation to the five forces model of competition, a product or service as a whole might be a victim of substitution. For example, increasingly e-mail systems have substituted for postal systems. No matter how complex and culturally embedded were the competences of the postal service, it could not avoid this sort of substitution.

- *Competence substitution*. Substitution might, however, not be at the product or service level but at the competence level. For example, task-based industries have often suffered because of an over-reliance on the competences of skilled craftsmen that have been replaced by expert systems and mechanisation.

In summary and from a resource-based view of organisations, managers need to consider whether their organisation has strategic capabilities to achieve and sustain competitive advantage. To do so they need to consider how and to what extent it has capabilities which are (a) valuable to buyers, (b) rare, (c) inimitable, and (d) non-substitutable. If such capabilities for competitive advantage do not exist, then managers need to consider if they can be developed.

3.4.5 Dynamic capabilities

The discussion so far has tended to assume that strategic capabilities can provide sustainable competitive advantage over time: that they are durable. However, managers often claim that their competitive environment is changing ever more rapidly. Moreover that technology is giving rise to innovation at a faster rate and therefore greater capacity for imitation and substitution of existing products and services. Nonetheless, even in such circumstances, some firms do achieve competitive advantage over others. To explain this, more emphasis has to be placed on the organisation's capability to change, innovate, to be flexible and to learn how to adapt to a rapidly changing environment.

Dynamic capabilities are an organisation's abilities to renew and recreate its strategic capabilities to meet the needs of changing environments

David Teece argued that the strategic capabilities that achieve competitive advantage in such dynamic conditions are **dynamic capabilities**, by which he means an organisation's ability to *renew and recreate its strategic capabilities* to meet the needs of changing environments.[8] Dynamic capabilities may be relatively formal, such as systems for new product development or procedures for agreement for capital expenditure. They may take the form of major strategic moves, such as acquisitions or alliances by which new skills are learned by the organisation. Or they may be more informal, such as the way in which decisions get taken faster than usual when fast response is needed. They could also take the form of embedded 'organisational knowledge' about how to deal with particular circumstances the organisation faces, or how to innovate. Indeed, dynamic capabilities are likely to have both formal and informal, visible and invisible, characteristics associated with them. For example, Kathy Eisenhardt[9] has shown that successful acquisition processes that bring in new knowledge to organisations depend on high-quality pre- and post-acquisition analysis of how the acquisition can be integrated into the new organisation so as to capture synergies and bases of learning from that acquisition. However, hand-in-hand with these formal procedures will be more informal ways of doing things in the acquisition process built on infomal personal relationships and the exchange of knowledge in more informal ways.

In summary, whereas in more stable conditions competitive advantage might be achieved by building capabilities that may be durable over time, in more dynamic conditions competitive advantage requires the building of capacity to change, innovate and learn – to build dynamic capabilities.

3.5 DIAGNOSING STRATEGIC CAPABILITY

So far this chapter has been concerned with explaining strategic capability and associated concepts. This section now provides some ways in which strategic capabilities can be diagnosed.

3.5.1 The value chain and value network

If organisations are to achieve competitive advantage by delivering value to customers, managers need to understand which activities they undertake are especially important in creating that value and which are not. Value chain and value network concepts can be helpful in understanding this.

The value chain

A **value chain** describes the categories of activities within and around an organisation, which together create a product or service

Primary activities are directly concerned with the creation or delivery of a product or service

www.pearsoned.co.uk/fos KEY CONCEPT Value chain and value network

The **value chain** describes the categories of activities within and around an organisation, which together create a product or service. The concept was developed in relation to competitive strategy by Michael Porter.[10] Exhibit 3.5 is a representation of a value chain. **Primary activities** are *directly* concerned with the creation or delivery of a product or service. For example, for a manufacturing business:

- *Inbound logistics* are activities concerned with receiving, storing and distributing inputs to the product or service including materials handling, stock control, transport, etc.
- *Operations* transform these inputs into the final product or service: machining, packaging, assembly, testing, etc.
- *Outbound logistics* collect, store and distribute the product to customers; for example warehousing, materials handling, distribution, etc.
- *Marketing and sales* provide the means whereby consumers/users are made aware of the product or service and are able to purchase it. This includes sales administration, advertising and selling.

Exhibit 3.5 The value chain within an organisation

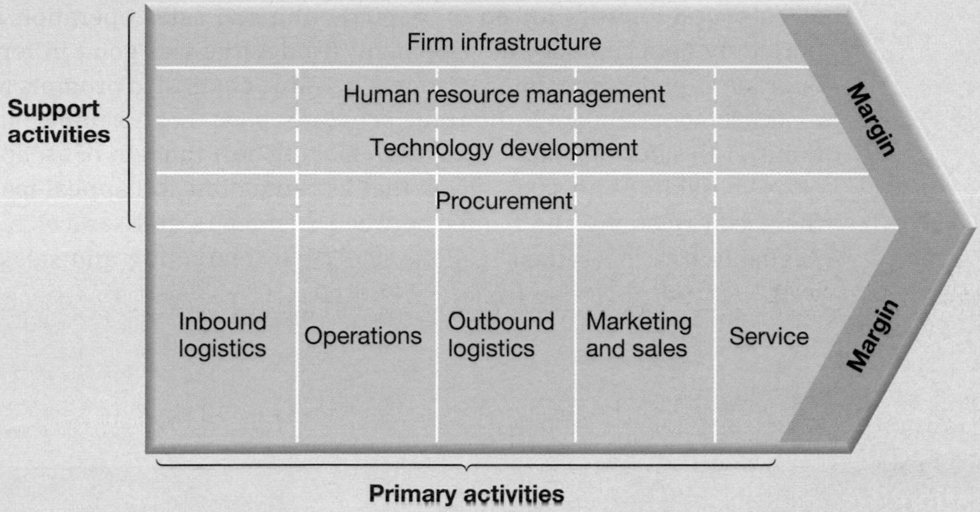

Source: Reprinted with the permission of The Free Press, a Division of Simon & Schuster Adult Publishing Group, from *Competitive Advantage: Creating and Sustaining Superior Performance* by Michael E. Porter. Copyright © 1985, 1998 by Michael E. Porter. All rights reserved.

- *Service* includes those activities that enhance or maintain the value of a product or service, such as installation, repair, training and spares.

Support activities help to improve the effectiveness or efficiency of primary activities

Each of these groups of primary activities is linked to support activities. **Support activities** help to improve the effectiveness or efficiency of primary activities:

- *Procurement*. The *processes* that occur in many parts of the organisation for acquiring the various resource inputs to the primary activities.
- *Technology development*. All value activities have a 'technology', even if it is just know-how. Technologies may be concerned directly with a product (for example, R&D, product design) or with processes (for example, process development) or with a particular resource (for example, raw materials improvements).
- *Human resource management*. This transcends all primary activities. It is concerned with those activities involved in recruiting, managing, training, developing and rewarding people within the organisation.
- *Infrastructure*. The formal systems of planning, finance, quality control, information management, and the structures and routines that are part of an organisation's culture (see section 5.3).

The value chain can help with the analysis of the strategic position of an organisation in two different ways.

- As *generic descriptions of activities* that can help managers understand if there is a cluster of activities providing benefit to customers located within particular areas of the value chain. Perhaps a business is especially good at outbound logistics linked to its marketing and sales operation and supported by its technology development. It might be less good in terms of its operations and its inbound logistics. The value chain also prompts managers to think about the role different activities play. For example, in a local family-run sandwich bar, is sandwich making best thought of as 'operations' or as 'marketing and sales', given that its reputation and appeal may rely on the social relations and banter between customers and sandwich makers? Arguably it is 'operations' if done badly but 'marketing and sales' if done well.

Illustration 3.3

A value chain for Ugandan chilled fish fillet exports

Even small enterprises can be part of an international value chain. Analysing it can provide strategic benefits.

A fish factory in Uganda barely made any profit. Fish were caught from small motorboats owned by poor fishermen from local villages. Just before they set out they would collect ice and plastic fish boxes from the agents who bought the catch on their return. The boxes were imported, along with tackle and boat parts. All supplies had to be paid for in cash in advance by the agents. Sometimes ice and supplies were not available in time. Fish landed with insufficient ice achieved half of the price of iced fish, and sometimes could not be sold to the agents at all. The fish factory had always processed the fillets in the same way – disposing of the waste back into the lake. Once a week, some foreign traders would come and buy the better fillets; they didn't say who they sold them to, and sometimes they didn't buy very much.

By mapping the value chain it was clear that there were opportunities for capturing more value along the chain and reducing losses. Together with outside specialists, the fish factory and the fishing community developed a strategy to improve their capabilities, as indicated in the figure, until they became a flourishing international business, The Lake Victoria Fish Company, with regular air-freight exports around the world. You can see more of their current operations at http://www.ufpea.co.ug/, and find out more about the type of analytical process applied at www.justreturn.ch.

(The approximate costs and prices given represent the situation before improvements were implemented.)

Questions

1 Draw up a value chain for another business in terms of the activities within its component parts.

2 Estimate the relative costs and/or assets associated with these activities.

3 What are the strategic implications of your analysis?

- In terms of the *cost and value of activities*.[11] Illustration 3.3 shows this in relation to fish farming. Value chain analysis was used by Ugandan fish farmers as a way of identifying what they should focus on in developing a more profitable business model.

The value network

The **value network** is the set of interorganisational links and relationships that are necessary to create a product or service

A single organisation rarely undertakes in-house all of the value activities from design through to the delivery of the final product or service to the final consumer. There is usually specialisation of role so any one organisation is part of a wider *value network*. The **value network** is the set of interorganisational links and relationships that are necessary to create a product or service (see

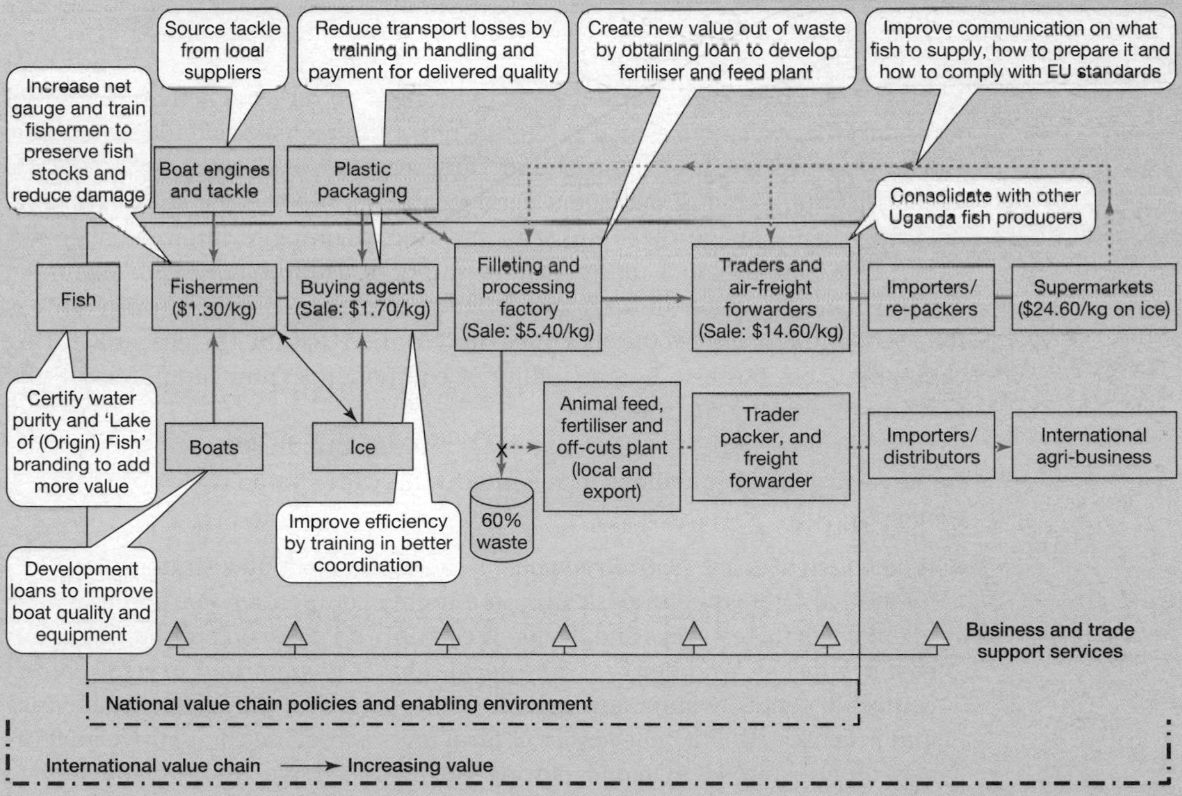

Source: Ian Sayers, Senior Adviser for the Private Sector, Division of Trade Support Services, International Trade Centre, Geneva. E-mail: sayers@intracen.org.

Exhibit 3.6 The value network

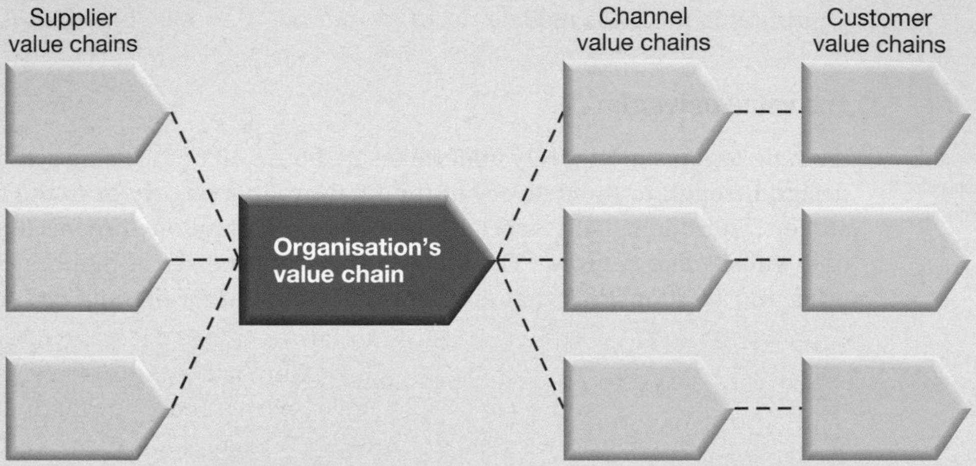

Source: Reprinted with the permission of The Free Press, a Division of Simon & Schuster Adult Publishing Group, from *Competitive Advantage: Creating and Sustaining Superior Performance* by Michael E. Porter. Copyright © 1985, 1998 by Michael E. Porter. All rights reserved.

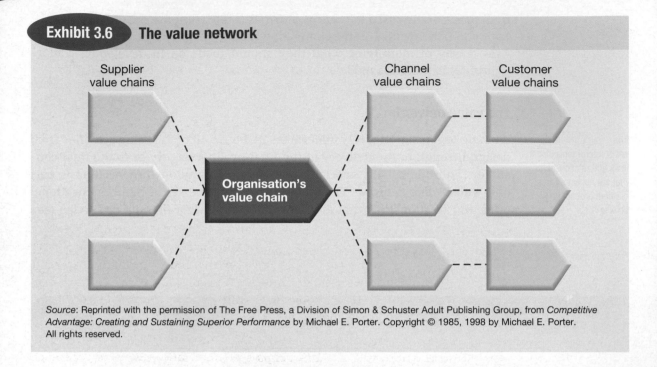

Exhibit 3.6). So an organisation needs to be clear about what activities it ought to undertake itself and which it should not and, perhaps, should outsource. However, since much of the cost and value creation will occur in the supply and distribution chains, managers need to understand this whole process and how they can manage these linkages and relationships to improve customer value. It is not sufficient to look within the organisation alone. For example, the quality of a cooker or a television when it reaches the final purchaser is not only influenced by the activities undertaken within the manufacturing company itself, but also by the quality of components from suppliers and the performance of the distributors.

It is therefore important that managers understand the bases of their organisation's strategic capabilities in relation to the wider value network. Four key issues are:

- *Which activities are centrally important* to an organisation's strategic capability and which less central? A firm in a highly competitive market may have to cut costs in key areas and decide it can only do so by outsourcing to lower cost producers. Another firm may decide that it is important to retain direct control of centrally important capabilities, especially if they relate to activities and processes that it believes are central to its achieving competitive advantage. For example, diamond cutting businesses have traditionally had to source rough diamonds from the giant De Beers. However, in a revolutionary move the Lev Leviev Group decided to invest in its own diamond mining operations, arguing: 'Nothing is stable unless you own your own mine.'[12]

Profit pools refer to the different levels of profit available at different parts of the value network

- *Where are the profit pools?*[13] **Profit pools** refer to the different levels of profit available at different parts of the value network. Some parts of a value network may be inherently more profitable than others because of the differences in competitive intensity. For example, in the computer industry microprocessors and software have historically been more profitable than hardware manufacture. The strategic question becomes whether it is possible to focus on the areas of greatest profit potential? Care has to be exercised here. It is one thing to identify such potential; it is another to be successful in it given the capabilities the organisation has. For example, in the 1990s many car manufacturers recognised that greater profit potential lay in services such as car hire and financing rather than manufacturing but they did not have the relevant competences to succeed in such sectors.
- *The 'make or buy'* decision for a particular activity or component is therefore critical. This is the *outsourcing* decision. There are businesses that now offer the benefits of outsourcing. Of course, the more an organisation outsources, the more its ability to influence the performance of other organisations in the value network may become a critically important competence in itself and even a source of competitive advantage.
- *Partnering*: who might be the best partners in the parts of the value network? And what kind of *relationships* are important to develop with each partner? For example, should they be regarded as suppliers or should they be regarded as alliance partners (see section 9.2.3)? Some businesses have benefited from closer relationships with suppliers such that they increasingly cooperate on such things as market intelligence, product design, and research and development.

3.5.2 Benchmarking

Benchmarking can be used as a way of understanding how an organisation's strategic capability, in terms of internal processes, compare with those of other organisations.

There are different approaches to benchmarking:

- *Historical benchmarking*. Organisations may consider their performance in relation to previous years in order to identify any significant changes. The danger is that this can lead to complacency since it is the rate of improvement compared with that of competitors that is really important.
- *Industry/sector benchmarking*. Insights about performance standards can be gleaned by looking at the comparative performance of other organisations in the same industry sector or between similar service providers against a set of performance indicators. Some public sector organisations have, in effect, acknowledged the existence of strategic groups by benchmarking against similar organisations rather than against everybody: for example, local

government services and police treat 'urban' differently from 'rural' in their benchmarking and league tables. An overriding danger of industry norm comparisons (whether in the private or public sector) is, however, that the whole industry may be performing badly and losing out competitively to other industries that can satisfy customers' needs in different ways. Another danger with benchmarking within an industry is that the boundaries of industries are blurring through competitive activity and industry convergence. For example, supermarkets are (incrementally) entering retail banking and their benchmarking needs to reflect this (as does the benchmarking of the traditional retail banks).

- *Best-in-class benchmarking.* Best-in-class benchmarking compares an organisation's performance against 'best in class' performance – wherever that is found – and therefore seeks to overcome the limitations of other approaches. It may also help challenge managers' mindsets that acceptable improvements in performance will result from incremental changes in resources or competences. It can therefore encourage a more fundamental reconsideration of how to improve organisational competences. For example, British Airways improved aircraft maintenance, refuelling and turnround time by studying the processes surrounding Formula One Grand Prix motor racing pit stops. A police force wishing to improve the way in which it responded to emergency telephone calls studied call centre operations in the banking and IT sectors.

The importance of benchmarking is, then, not so much in the detailed 'mechanics' of comparison but in the impact that these comparisons might have on behaviours. It can be usefully regarded as a process for gaining momentum for improvement and change. But it has dangers too:

- *Measurement distortion*: Benchmarking can lead to a situation where *you get what you measure* and this may not be what is intended strategically. It can therefore result in changes in behaviour that are unintended or dysfunctional. For example, the university sector in the UK has been subjected to rankings in league tables on research output, teaching quality and the success of graduating students in terms of employment and starting salaries. This has resulted in academics being 'forced' to orientate their published research to certain types of academic journals that may have little to do directly with the quality of the education in universities.
- *Surface comparisons*: Benchmarking compares inputs (resources), outputs or outcomes; it does not identify the reasons for the good or poor performance of organisations since the process does not compare competences directly. For example, it may demonstrate that one organisation is poorer at customer service than another but not show the underlying reasons. However, if well directed it could encourage managers to seek out these reasons and hence understand how competences could be improved.

3.5.3 SWOT[14]

The key 'strategic messages' from both the business environment (Chapter 2) and this chapter can be summarised in the form of an analysis of strengths, weaknesses, opportunities and threats (SWOT). **SWOT** summarises the key issues from the business environment and the strategic capability of an organisation that are most likely to impact on strategy development. This can also be useful as a basis against which to generate strategic options and assess future courses of action.

A **SWOT** summarises the key issues from the business environment and the strategic capability of an organisation that are most likely to impact on strategy development

www.pearsoned.co.uk/fos
KEY CONCEPT
SWOT

The aim is to identify the extent to which strengths and weaknesses are relevant to, or capable of dealing with, the changes taking place in the business environment. However, in the context of this chapter, if the strategic capability of an organisation is to be understood, it must be remembered it is not absolute but relative to its competitors. So SWOT analysis is really only useful if it is comparative – if it examines strengths, weaknesses, opportunities and threats in relation to competitors. Illustration 3.4 takes the example of a pharmaceuticals firm (Pharmcare). It assumes that key environmental impacts have been identified from analyses explained in Chapter 2 and that major strengths and weaknesses have been identified using the analytic tools explained in this chapter. A scoring mechanism (plus 5 to minus 5) is used as a means of getting managers to assess the interrelationship between the environmental impacts and the strengths and weaknesses of the firm. A positive (+) denotes that the strength of the company would help it take advantage of, or counteract, a problem arising from an environmental change or that a weakness would be offset by that change. A negative (–) score denotes that the strength would be reduced or that a weakness would prevent the organisation from overcoming problems associated with that change.

Pharmcare's share price had been declining because investors were concerned that its strong market position was under threat. This had not been improved by a merger that was proving problematic. The pharmaceutical market was changing with new ways of doing business, driven by new technology, the quest to provide medicines at lower cost and politicians seeking ways to cope with soaring healthcare costs and an ever more informed patient. But was Pharmcare keeping pace? The strategic review of the firm's position (Illustration 3.4a) confirmed its strengths of a flexible salesforce, well-known brand name and new healthcare department. However, there were major weakness, namely relative failure on low cost drugs, competence in information and communication technology (ICT) and a failure to get to grips with increasingly well-informed users. When the impact of environmental forces on competitors was analysed (Illustration 3.4b), it showed that Pharmcare was still outperforming its traditional competitor (Company W), but potentially vulnerable to changing dynamics in the general industry structure courtesy of niche players (X and Y).

Illustration 3.4

SWOT analysis of Pharmcare

A SWOT analysis explores the relationship between the environmental influences and the strategic capabilities of an organisation compared with its competitors.

(a) SWOT analysis for Pharmcare

	Environmental change (opportunities and threats)					
	Health care rationing	**Complex and changing buying structures**	**Increased integration of health care**	**Informed patients**	**+**	**–**
Strengths						
Flexible salesforce	+3	+5	+2	+2	12	0
Economies of scale	0	0	+3	+3	+6	0
Strong brand name	+2	+1	0	–1	3	–1
Health care education department	+4	+3	+4	+5	+16	0
Weaknesses						
Limited competences in biotechnology and genetics	0	0	–4	–3	0	–7
Ever lower R&D productivity	–3	–2	–1	–2	0	–8
Weak ICT competences	–2	–2	–5	–5	0	–14
Over-reliance on leading product	–1	–1	–3	–1	0	–6
Environmental impact scores	+9 –6	+9 –5	+9 –14	+10 –12		

(b) Competitor SWOT analyses

	Environmental change (opportunities and threats)				
	Health care rationing	**Complex and changing buying structures**	**Increased integration of health care**	**Informed and passionate patients**	**Overall impact**
Pharmcare *Big global player suffering fall in share price, low research productivity and post mega-merger bureaucracy*	–3 Struggling to prove cost-effectiveness of new drugs to new regulators of health care rationing	+6 Well-known brand, a flexible salesforce combined with a new health care education department creates positive synergy	–3 Weak ICT and lack of integration following mergers means sales, research and admin. are all underperforming	–2 Have yet to get into the groove of patient power fuelled by the Internet	–2 Declining performance over time worsened after merger
Company W *Big pharma with patchy response to change, losing ground in new areas of competition*	–4 Focus is on old-style promotional selling rather than helping doctors control costs through drugs	–4 Traditional salesforce not helped by marketing which can be unaccommodating of national differences	+0 Alliances with equipment manufacturers but little work done across alliance to show dual use of drugs and new surgical techniques	+4 New recruits in the ICT department have worked cross-functionally to involve patients like never before	–4 Needs to modernise across the whole company
Organisation X *Partnership between a charity managed by people with venture capital experience and top hospital geneticists*	+3 Potentially able to deliver rapid advances in genetic-based illnesses	+2 Able possibly to bypass these with innovative cost effective drug(s)	+2 Innovative drugs can help integrate health care through enabling patients to stay at home	+3 Patients will fight for advances in treatment areas where little recent progress has been made	+10 Could be the basis of a new business model for drug discovery – but all to prove as yet
Company Y *Only develops drugs for less common diseases*	+3 Partnering with big pharma allows the development of drugs discovered by big pharma but not economical for them to develop	0 Focus on small market segments so not as vulnerable to overall market structure, but innovative approach might be risky	+2 Innovative use of web to show why products still worthwhile developing even for less common illnesses	+1 Toll-free call centres for sufferers of less common illnesses Company, like patients, is passionate about its mission	+6 Novel approach can be considered either risky or a winner, or both!

Questions

1 What does the SWOT analysis tell us about the competitive position of Pharmcare with the industry as a whole?

2 How readily do you think executives of Pharmacare identify the strengths and weaknesses of competitors?

3 Identify the benefits and dangers (other than those identified in the text) of a SWOT analysis such as that in the illustration.

Prepared by Jill Shepherd, Segal Graduate School of Business, Simon Fraser University, Vancouver, Canada.

A SWOT analysis should help focus discussion on future choices and the extent to which an organisation is capable of supporting these strategies. There are, however, two main dangers:

- A SWOT exercise can generate very *long lists* of apparent strengths, weaknesses, opportunities and threats. Whereas, what matters is to be clear about what is really important and what is less important.
- There is a danger of *overgeneralisation*. Remember the lessons of section 3.4.3. Identifying a very general explanation of strategic capability does not explain the underlying reasons for that capability. SWOT analysis is not a substitute for more rigorous, insightful analysis, by using the techniques and concepts explained in Chapter 2 and this chapter.

SUMMARY

www.pearsoned.co.uk/fos AUDIO SUMMARY

- *Strategic capability* is concerned with the adequacy and suitability of resources and competences required for an organisation to survive and prosper. Strategic capabilities comprise resources and competences, which are the way such resources are used and deployed.
- If organisations are to achieve *competitive advantage*, they require resources and competences which are both valuable to customers and difficult for competitors to imitate (such competences are known as *core competences*).
- The continual improvement of *cost efficiency* is a vital strategic capability if an organisation is to continue to prosper.
- The sustainability of competitive advantage is likely to depend on strategic capabilities being of *value to customers, rare, inimitable* or *non substitutable*.
- In dynamic conditions, it is unlikely that such strategic capabilities will remain stable. In such circumstances *dynamic capabilities* are important, i.e. the ability to continually change strategic capabilities.
- Ways of *diagnosing organisational capabilities* include:
  - Analysing an organisation's *value chain and value network* as a basis of understanding how value to a customer is created and can be developed.
  - *Benchmarking* as means of understanding the relative performance of organisations and challenging the assumptions managers have about the performance of their organisation.
  - *SWOT analysis* as a way of drawing together an understanding of strengths, weaknesses, opportunities and threats an organisation faces.

Recommended key readings

- For an understanding of the resource based view of the firm, an early and much cited paper is by Jay Barney: 'Firm Resources and Sustained Competitive Advantage', *Journal of Management*, vol. 17 (1991), pp. 99–120.
- The concept of Dynamic Capabilities is reviewed in C.L. Wang and P.K. Ahmed, 'Dynamic Capabilities: a review and research Agenda', *International Journal of Management Reviews*, vol. 9, no. 1 (2007), 31–52.
- Michael Porter explains how mapping what he calls 'activity systems' can be important in considering competitive strategy in his article 'What is Strategy?', *Harvard Business Review*, November–December (1996).
- For a critical discussion of the use and misuse of SWOT analysis see T. Hill and R. Westbrook, 'SWOT Analysis: Its Time for a Product Recall', *Long Range Planning*, vol. 30, no. 1 (1997), pp. 46–52.

References

1. The concept of resource-based strategies was introduced by B. Wernerfelt, 'A resource-based view of the firm', *Strategic Management Journal*, vol. 5, no. 2 (1984), pp. 171–180. A much cited paper is by Jay Barney, 'Firm resources and sustained competitive advantage', *Journal of Management*, vol. 17, no. 1 (1991), pp. 99–120.
2. Gary Hamel and C.K. Prahalad were the academics who promoted the idea of core competences. For example: G. Hamel and C.K. Prahalad, 'The core competence of the corporation', *Harvard Business Review*, vol. 68, no. 3 (1990), pp. 79–91. The idea of driving strategy development from the resources and competences of an organisation is discussed in G. Hamel and C.K. Prahalad, 'Strategic intent', *Harvard Business Review*, vol. 67, no. 3 (1989), pp. 63–76 and G. Hamel and C.K. Prahalad, 'Strategy as stretch and leverage', *Harvard Business Review*, vol. 71, no. 2 (1993), pp. 75–84. Also see G. Hamel and A. Heene (eds), *Competence-based Competition*, Wiley, 1994.
3. P. Conley, *Experience Curves as a Planning Tool*, available as a pamphlet from the Boston Consulting Group. See also A.C. Hax and N.S. Majluf, in R.G. Dyson (ed.), *Strategic Planning: Models and analytical techniques*, Wiley, 1990.
4. The headings used in this chapter are those used most commonly by writers in academic papers on RBV. These are sometimes referred to as VRIN. This stands for Valuable, Rare, Difficult to Imitate and Non-substitutable and were first identified by Jay Barney, 'Firm resources and sustained competitive advantage', *Journal of Management*, vol. 17, no. 1 (1991), pp. 99–120.
5. For a full explanation of 'core rigidities' see D. Leonard-Barton, 'Core capabilities and core rigidities: a paradox in managing new product development', *Strategic Management Journal*, vol. 13 (Summer 1992), pp. 111–125.
6. The seminal paper on causal ambiguity is S. Lippman and R. Rumelt, 'Uncertain imitability: an analysis of interfirm differences in efficiency under competition', *Bell Journal of Economics*, vol. 13 (1982), pp. 418–438.
7. The distinction between and importance of characteristic and linkage ambiguity is explained in detail by A.W. King, and C.P. Zeithaml in 'Competencies and firm performance: examining the causal ambiguity paradox', *Strategic Management Journal*, vol. 22, no. 1 (2001), pp. 75–99.
8. For a summary paper on dynamic capabilities see C.L. Wang and P.K. Ahmed, 'Dynamic Capabilities: a review and research agenda', *International Journal of Management Reviews*, vol. 9, no. 1 (2007), pp. 31–52.
9. See K.M. Eisenhardt and J.A. Martin, 'Dynamic Capabilities; What Are They?', *Strategic Management Journal*, vol. 21 (2000), pp. 1105–1121.

10. An extensive discussion of the value chain concept and its application can be found in M.E. Porter, *Competitive Advantage*, Free Press, 1985.

11. For an extended example of value chain analysis see 'Understanding and using value chain analysis' by Andrew Shepherd in *Exploring Techniques of Analysis and Evaluation in Strategic Management* edited by Veronique Ambrosini, Prentice Hall, 1998.

12. This quote is attributed to Lev Leviev in the *Financial Times*, 14 December 2006, p. 10.

13. The importance of profit pools is discussed by O. Gadiesh and J.L. Gilbert in 'Profit pools: a fresh look at strategy', *Harvard Business Review*, vol. 76, no. 3 (May–June 1998), pp. 139–147.

14. The idea of SWOT as a commonsense checklist has been used for many years: for example, S. Tilles, 'Making strategy explicit', in I. Ansoff (ed.), *Business Strategy*, Penguin, 1968. See also T. Jacobs, J. Shepherd and G. Johnson's chapter on SWOT analysis in V. Ambrosini (ed.), *Exploring Techniques of Strategy Analysis and Evaluation*, Prentice Hall, 1998. For a critical discussion of the (mis)use of SWOT, see T. Hill and R. Westbrook, 'SWOT Analysis: It's time for a product recall', *Long Range Planning*, vol. 30, no. 1 (1997), pp. 46–52.

CASE EXAMPLE

Making eBay work

Jill Shepherd, Segal Graduate School of Business
Simon Fraser University, Canada

In 2006, there were over 200 million eBayers worldwide. For around 750,000 people, eBay (http://www.ebay.com/) was their primary source of income. A survivor of the dot.com bust of the late 1990s, eBay represents a new business model courtesy of the Internet. Whatever statistics you choose – from most expensive item sold to number of auctions in any one day – the numbers amaze. 'This is a whole new way of doing business,' says Meg Whitman, the CEO and President since 1998. 'We're creating something that didn't exist before.'

Photo: © Claro Cortes IV/Reuters/Corbis

eBay's business model

Value in eBay is created by providing a virtual worldwide market for buyers and sellers and collecting a tax on transactions as they happen. The business model of eBay relies on its customers being the organisation's product development team, sales- and marketing force, merchandising department and the security department. It is arguably the first web 2.0 company.

According to eBay managers, of key importance is listening to customers: keeping up with what they want to sell, buy and how they want to do it. If customers speak, eBay listens. Technology allows every move of every potential customer to be traced, yielding rich information. Conventional companies might spend big money on getting to know their customers and persuading them to provide feedback; for eBay such feedback is often free and offered without the need for enticement. Even so some of the company's most effective ways of getting user input do not rely on the net and do not come free. eBay organises Voice of the Customer groups which involve flying in a new group of about 10 sellers and buyers from around the country to its offices every few months to discuss the company in depth. Teleconferences are held for new features and policies, however small a change they involve. Even workshops and classes are held to teach people how to make the most of the site. Participants tend to double their selling activity on eBay after taking a class. Others run their own websites offering advice on how to sell on eBay. Rumours have it that buyers have devised computer programs that place bids in the last moment. Sellers that leave the site unable to compete any more are known to write blogs on what went wrong to help others.

The company is governed from both outside and within. The eBay system has a source of automatic control in the form of buyers and sellers rating each other on each transaction, creating rules and norms. Both buyers and sellers build up reputations which are valuable, in turn encouraging further good behaviour in themselves and others. Sales of illegal products are dealt with by withdrawing what is on sale and invariably banning the seller.

eBay's management

Meg Whitman's style and past have heavily influenced the management of eBay. When she joined the company in 1998, it was more of a collection of geeks, handpicked by the pony-tailed founder Pierre Omidyar, than a blue-chip, something which underpinned Omidyar's recruitment of Meg. Meg, an ex-consultant, filled many of the senior management roles including the head of the US business, head of international operations and vice president of consumer marketing with consultants. The result: eBay has become data and metric driven. 'If you can't measure it, you can't control it', Meg says. Whereas in the early days you could touch and feel the way the organisation worked, its current size means it needs to be measured. Category managers, reminiscent of Meg's days in Procter and Gamble, are expected to spend their days measuring and acting upon data within their fiefdom.

However, unlike their counterparts in Procter and Gamble, category managers in eBay can only indirectly control their products. They have no stock to reorder once levels of toothpaste or washing-up liquid run low on the supermarket shelves. They provide tools to buy and sell more effectively:

> What they can do is endlessly try to eke out small wins in their categories – say, a slight jump in scrap-metal listings or new bidders for comic books. To get there, they use marketing and merchandising schemes such as enhancing the presentation of their users' products and giving them tools to buy and sell better.

Over and above this unusual existence, the work environment can be tough and ultra competitive, say ex-eBayers. Changes often come only after PowerPoint slides are exchanged and refined at a low level, eventually presented at a senior level and after the change has been approved in a sign-off procedure which includes every department.

In time eBay has upgraded its ability to ensure the technology does not rule. Until the late 1990s, the site was plagued with outages, including one in 1999 which shut the site down for 22 hours courtesy of software problems and no backup systems. Former Gateway Inc. Chief Information Officer Maynard Webb, who joined as president of eBay's technology unit, quickly took action to upgrade systems. Its use of technology is upgraded constantly. In 2005, Chris Corrado was appointed Senior Vice President and Chief Technology Officer. In eBay's press release COO Maynard Webb said:

> Chris is one of the leading technology platform experts in the corporate world, and we are thrilled that he is joining us. It is testament to the tremendous reputation of the eBay technology organization that we were able to bring Chris to the team.

Meg is a leader who buys into the company in more ways than one. Having auctioned some $35,000 (€28,000; £19,500) worth of furnishings in her ski condo in Colorado to understand the selling experience, she became a top seller among the company's employees and ensured that her learning from the experience was listened to by fellow top execs. Meg is also known for listening carefully to her employees and expects her managers to do the same. As the business is as much, if not more, its customers, any false move can cause revolts within the community that is eBay.

Most of all, eBay tries to stay aware and flexible. Nearly all of its fastest-growing new categories emerged from registering seller activity in the area and quietly giving it a nudge at the right moment. For example, after noticing a few car sales, eBay created a separate site called eBay Motors in 1999, with special features such as vehicle inspections and shipping. Some four years later, eBay expects to gross some $1 billion worth of autos and parts, many of which are sold by professional dealers.

The democratic underpinning of eBay, whilst easily embraced by customers, can, however, take some getting used too. New managers take time to understand the ethos. 'Some of the terms you learn in business school – drive, force, commit – don't apply,' says former PepsiCo Inc. exec William C. Cobb, now President eBay North America, with a background in restaurants and PepsiCo, 'We're over here listening, adapting, enabling.'

Competition and cooperation

As the Internet has become a more competitive arena eBay has not stood still. In 2005 it bought Skype, the Internet telephony organisation (http://www.skype.com/), surrounded by much debate in the press as to the logic of the $2.6bn deal. With Skype, eBay argues it can create an unparalleled e-commerce engine, pointing to the 2002 purchase of online payment system PayPal (http://www.paypal.com/) that spurred on the business at that time. All three benefit from so-called network effects – the more members, the more valuable the company – and eBay has to be a world leader in managing network effects.

In 2006 it also announced a deal with Google. eBay is one of Google's biggest advert customers. Google in turn is attracted to eBay's Skype customers for click-to-call adverts. This deal was after eBay signed an advertising deal with Yahoo! which made some think eBay was teaming up with Yahoo! against Google's dominance. But in the interconnected world of the Internet, defining competition and cooperation is a new game. eBay also formed a partnership between Baidu Inc., a Chinese web portal and eBay EachNet. Baidu promotes PayPal Beibao as the preferred payment method on Baidu whilst EachNet uses Baidu as its exclusive search provider. The development of a co-branded toolbar is set to cement the partnership. So whilst in the West Yahoo! and eBay are partnering against Google, in the East Yahoo! is a rival.

Despite eBay being the Internet auction phenomenon, it does not do as well in the East as the West. It pulled out of Japan, is suffering in Taiwan and lags behind a rival in China. In Korea, GMarket, partly owned by Yahoo!, is more or less equal in size to eBay's Internet Auction. GMarket offers less emphasis on open auctions than eBay, although eBay now does have eBay Express where new products from multiple sellers can be purchased in one transaction backed as ever by customer support including live chat. Innovative marketing that makes the experience fun for shoppers and helps sellers improve their performance is perhaps another way GMarket differentiates itself from eBay. GMarket has itself attracted imitators.

Once a web 2.0 company always a web 2.0 company? Although the news did not produce much reaction when announced during an eBay Live! Session, in 2006 eBay created eBay Wiki (http://www.ebaywiki.com/), hosted by Jotspot, allowing people to contribute their knowledge of eBay to others, along with eBay blogs (http://blogs.ebay.com/). But eBay has always been about community so perhaps they will catch on in time.

Questions

1. Analyse eBay's strategic capability using an analytical framework(s) from the chapter.
2. What are the capabilities that have provided eBay with competitive advantage and why?
3. Using the concepts of sustainability and dynamic capabilities, how would you manage this capability (create new resources and competences, invest/divest in others, extend others), given:
   (a) New entrants in the marketplace?
   (b) The changing nature of eBay?

4

Strategic Purpose

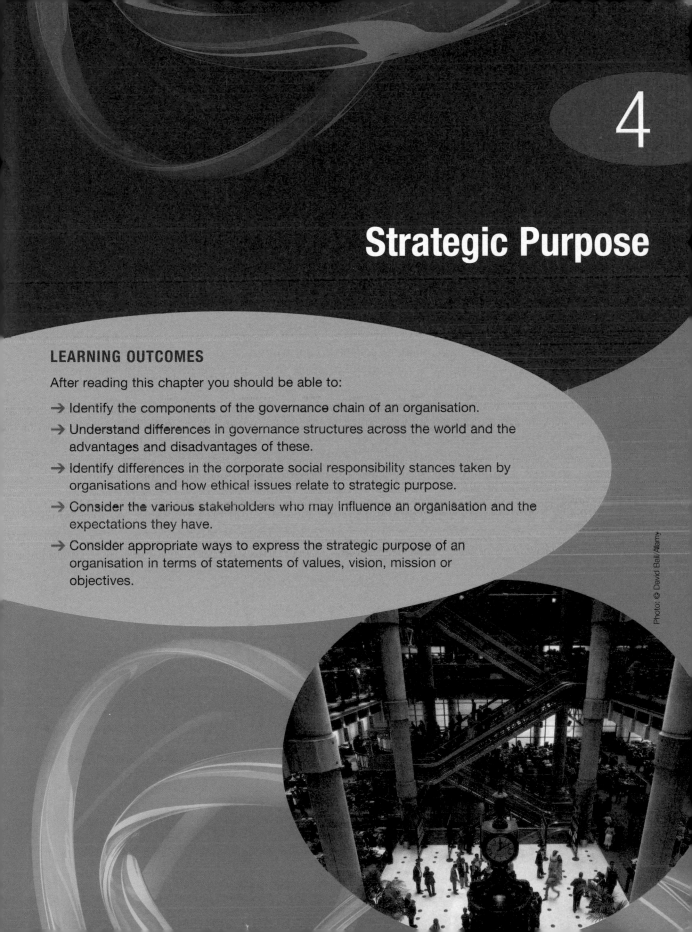

LEARNING OUTCOMES

After reading this chapter you should be able to:

- → Identify the components of the governance chain of an organisation.
- → Understand differences in governance structures across the world and the advantages and disadvantages of these.
- → Identify differences in the corporate social responsibility stances taken by organisations and how ethical issues relate to strategic purpose.
- → Consider the various stakeholders who may influence an organisation and the expectations they have.
- → Consider appropriate ways to express the strategic purpose of an organisation in terms of statements of values, vision, mission or objectives.

Photo: © David Ball/Alamy

4.1 INTRODUCTION

Stakeholders are those individuals or groups who depend on an organisation to fulfil their own goals and on whom, in turn, the organisation depends

The previous two chapters have looked respectively at the influence of the environment and capabilities on an organisation's strategic position. However, a fundamental decision that has to be taken concerns the *purpose* of the strategy that is to be followed. This is the focus of this chapter, together with the influences on such purpose by expectations of *stakeholders* of an organisation. **Stakeholders** are those individuals or groups who depend on an organisation to fulfil their own goals and on whom, in turn, the organisation depends. An underlying issue raised by this chapter is whether the strategic purpose of the organisation should be determined in response to a particular stakeholder, for example, shareholders in the case of a commercial enterprise, or to broader stakeholder interests – at the extreme society and the social good. This theme is considered in relation to a number of key issues.

- Section 4.2 considers *corporate governance* and the *regulatory framework* within which organisations operate. Here the concern is with the way in which formally constituted bodies such as investors or boards influence strategic purpose through the formalised processes of supervising executive decisions and actions. In turn this raises issues of *accountability*: who are strategists accountable to? There are significant differences in the approach to corporate governance internationally, broadly relating to either shareholder or wider stakeholder orientations and these are also discussed.

Exhibit 4.1 Influences on strategic purpose

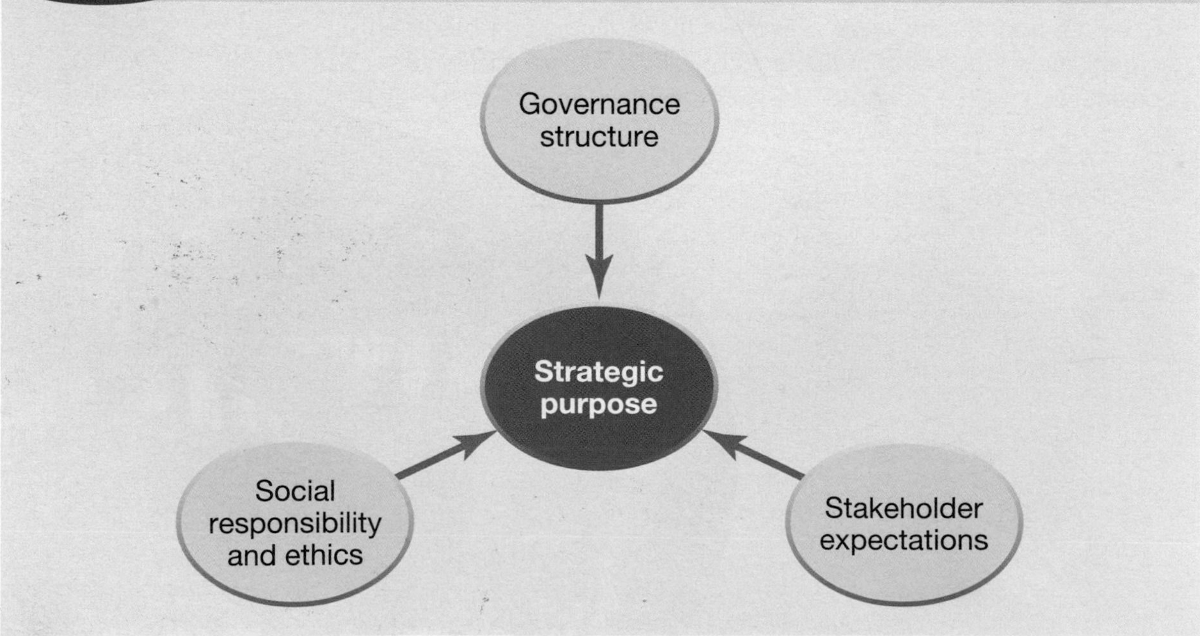

- Section 4.3 is concerned with issues of *social responsibility and ethics*. Here the question is which purposes an organisation *should* fulfil. How should managers respond to the expectations society has of their organisations, both in terms of *corporate social responsibility*?
- In all this it is, then, important to understand *different stakeholder expectations* and their relative influence on strategic purpose. This requires an understanding of both the *power* and *interest* of different stakeholder groups. This is addressed through *stakeholder analysis*.
- The chapter concludes by considering different ways in which organisations *express strategic purpose*. This may include statements of *values, vision, mission* or *objectives*.

Exhibit 4.1 summarises these different influences on strategic purpose discussed in the chapter.

4.2 CORPORATE GOVERNANCE

Corporate governance is concerned with the structures and systems of control by which managers are held accountable to those who have a legitimate stake in an organisation

Corporate governance is concerned with the structures and systems of control by which managers are held accountable to those who have a legitimate stake in an organisation.[1] It has become an increasingly important issue for organisations for three main reasons.

- *The separation of ownership and management control* of organisations (which is now the norm except with very small businesses) means that most organisations operate within a hierarchy, or chain, of governance. This chain represents those groups that influence an organisation through their involvement in either ownership or management of an organisation.
- *Corporate scandals* since the late 1990s have increased public debate about how different parties in the governance chain should interact and influence each other. Most notable here is the relationship between shareholders and the boards of businesses; but an equivalent issue in the public sector is the relationship between government or public funding bodies and public sector organisations.
- *Increased accountability to wider stakeholder interests* has also come to be increasingly advocated; in particular the argument that corporations need to be more visibly accountable and/or responsive, not only to 'owners' and 'managers' in the governance chain but to wider social interest.

4.2.1 The governance chain

The governance chain illuminates the roles and relationships of different groups involved in the governance of an organisation. In a small family business,

Exhibit 4.2 The chain of corporate governance: typical reporting structures

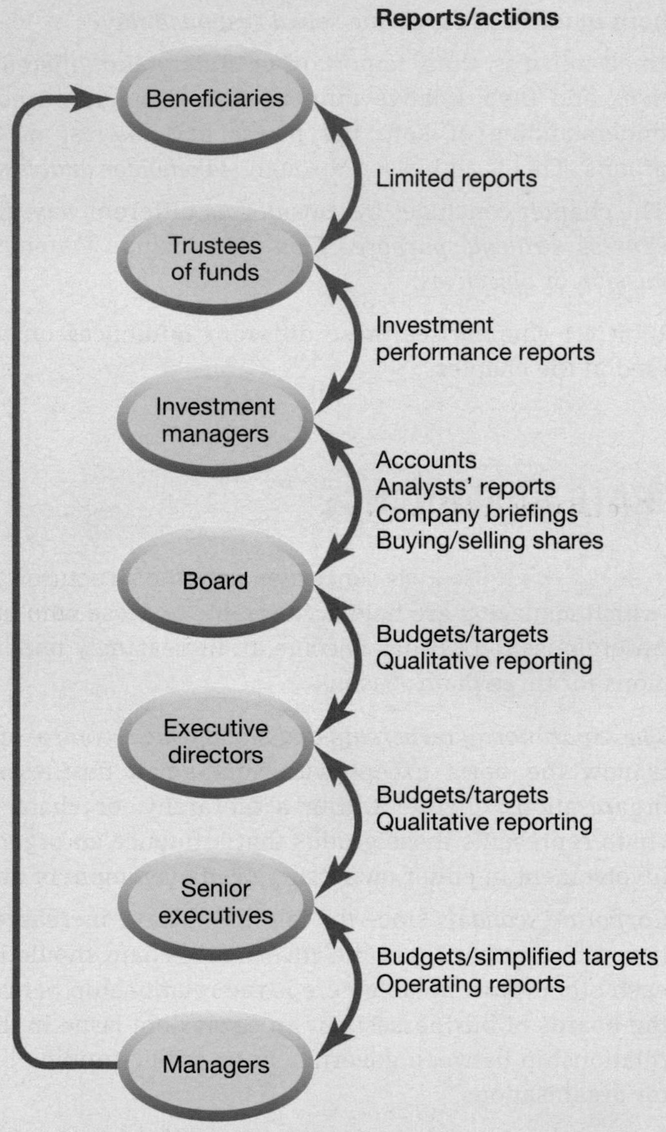

Source: Adapted from David Pitt-Watson, Hermes.

www.pearsoned.co.uk/fos KEY CONCEPT Governance chain

the governance chain is quite simple: there are family shareholders; there is a board, with some family members; and there are managers, some of whom may be family too. Here there are just three layers in the chain. However, Exhibit 4.2 shows a governance chain for a typical large, publicly quoted organisation. Here the size of the organisation means that there are extra layers of management internally, while being publicly quoted introduces more investor layers as well. Individual investors (the ultimate beneficiaries) often invest in public companies through collective funds, for example, unit trusts or pensions funds, which then invest in a range of companies on their behalf. Such finds are of growing importance. In 2006, they owned 50 per cent of the equity of American corporations (19 per cent in 1970) and over 70 per cent in the UK (25 per cent in 1963). Funds are typically controlled by trustees, with day-to-day investment activity undertaken by investment managers. So the ultimate beneficiaries may not even know which companies they have a financial stake in and have little power to influence the companies' boards directly.

The relationships in such governance chains can be understood in terms of the *principal–agent model*.[2] Here 'principals' pay 'agents' to act on their behalf, just as home-owners employ estate agents to sell their homes. In Exhibit 4.2, the beneficiaries are the ultimate principals and fund trustees are their agents in terms of achieving good returns on their investments. Further down the chain, company boards are principals too, with senior executives their agents in managing the company. There are many layers of agents between ultimate principals and the managers at the bottom, with the reporting mechanisms between each layer liable to be imperfect.

Principal–agent theory assumes that agents will not work diligently for principals unless incentives are carefully and appropriately aligned. However, it can be seen from Exhibit 4.2 that in large companies board members and other managers driving strategy are likely to be very remote from the ultimate beneficiaries of the company's performance. In such circumstances, the danger is twofold:

- *Misalignment of incentives and control*. As influence passes down the governance chain, the expectations of one group are not passed on to the next appropriately. For example, ultimate beneficiaries may be mainly concerned with the long-term security of their pension fund, but the investment managers and analysts or the boards with whom they interact may be place a greater emphasis on short-term growth.
- *Self interest*. Any agent in the chain may act out of self interest. Managers will be striving for promotion and/or increased earnings, investment managers will be seeking to increase their bonuses and so on.

The result may be that decisions are taken that are not in the best interests of the final beneficiary. This is just what has happened in the case of many of the corporate scandals of recent years, the most notorious of which was probably Enron (see Illustration 4.1).

In this context, the governance chain helps highlight important issues that affects the management of strategy.

- *Responsibility to whom?* A fundamental question in large corporations is whether executives should regard themselves as *solely* responsible to shareholders, or as 'trustees of the assets of the corporation' acting on behalf of a wider range of stakeholders? Even in terms of formal governance structures this varies across the world, as section 4.2.2 shows.

Illustration 4.1

The Enron corporate scandal

Executive decisions may not always be in the interest of shareholders; sometimes disastrously so.

Enron was one of the world's leading electricity, natural gas, pulp, paper and communications companies, based in Houston, Texas. It employed around 21,000 people with claimed revenues of $101bn (€80bn) in 2000. However at the end of 2001 it was revealed that its reported financial condition was sustained mostly by systematic and creative accounting fraud. When Enron sought Chapter 11 protection in the USA in late 2001, it was the biggest bankruptcy in US history and cost 4,000 employees their jobs. The scandal also caused the dissolution of Arthur Andersen, a Big Five accounting firm.

Many of Enron's recorded assets and profits were inflated, fraudulent and non-existent. Enron had put debts and losses into 'offshore' companies not included in the company's financial statements and used sophisticated financial transactions with related companies known as 'special purposes entities' (SPEs) to take unprofitable transactions off the company's books. Later investigations revealed that some executives at Enron knew about the offshore accounts that were hiding losses for the company. Chief Financial Officer Andrew Fastow led the team which created the off-books companies and manipulated the deals to provide himself, his family and friends with hundreds of millions of dollars in guaranteed revenue, at the expense of the stockholders. As the scandal unfolded, Enron shares dropped from over $90.00 to $0.30.

US Congressional hearings revealed that a group of Enron employees had been expressing concerns as early as 1998. Growing apprehension led to an all-employee meeting in mid-2001, where other related issues were discussed. Following the meeting, Sherron Watkins, Vice President, met with the then CEO, the late Ken Lay, handing him a memo detailing her concerns. She especially highlighted the roles of Vinson & Elkins, LLP, a large and reputable US law firm, and Arthur Andersen, LLP, as complicit with dubious deals. Top management asked Vinson & Elkins to investigate the concerns. However, the law firm reported that apart from some 'bad cosmetics', and 'aggressive and creative accounting', they found no problem with the SPEs. Arthur Andersen in turn confirmed that it was comfortable with the accounting.

Late in October 2002, the Securities and Exchange Commission opened a formal inquiry into Enron, which also started a devastating trail of events at Arthur Andersen. By the time Andersen received notice from the SEC in mid-November, a large number of Enron-related audit documents had been destroyed. This subsequently led to Andersen's indictment in June 2002. The trial of Arthur Andersen also exposed its accounting fraud at WorldCom, setting off a wave of other accounting scandals.

J.P. Morgan Chase, Citigroup, Merrill Lynch, Credit Suisse First Boston, Canadian Imperial Bank of Commerce (CIBC), Bank America, Barclays Bank, Deutsche Bank; and Lehman Brothers were also named as players in the series of fraudulent transactions that ultimately cost shareholders more than $25bn. Two law firms were identified as involved in the fraud: Vinson & Elkins and Chicago-based Kirkland & Ellis, which Enron used to represent a number of SPEs.

By mid-2006, 16 of Enron's top executives, including Ken Lay, Jeff Skilling (CEO), David Delainey (Head of Enron's Energy Trading Unit), Richard Causey (Chief Accounting Officer), Andrew Fastow (Chief Financial Officer) and Mark Koenig (Head of Investor Relations), pleaded guilty or were convicted and in the process of being sentenced.

Prepared by Rajshree Prakash, University of Lancaster Management School.

Questions

1 What mechanisms in the governance chain should (or could) have prevented what happened at Enron?

2 What changes in corporate governance are required to prevent similar occurrences?

- *Who are the shareholders?* If managers do see themselves as primarily responsible to shareholders, what does this mean in terms of the governance chain? As explained above, the final beneficiaries are far removed from the managers, so for many managers responsibility to them is notional. In practical terms, directors of a firm are likely to engage most frequently with institutional representatives of those shareholders – an investment manager or analyst from a pension fund or insurance company perhaps. The principal–agent problem arises here too. The final beneficiaries are also distant for investment managers and analysts, who may also be pursuing their own self-interest. Strategists within a firm therefore face a difficult choice, even if they espouse primary responsibility to shareholders. Do they develop strategies they believe to be in the best interest of a highly fragmented group of unknown shareholders? Or to meet the needs and aspirations of the investment managers? A similar problem exists for public sector managers. They may see themselves as developing strategies in the public good; but they may face direct scrutiny from an agency acting on behalf of the government. Is the strategy to be designed for the general public good, or to meet the scrutiny of the agency? For example, health service managers and doctors in the UK health service are dedicated to the wellbeing of their patients. But increasingly how they manage their services is governed by the targets placed upon them by a government department, who themselves presumably also believe they are acting in the public good.

- *The role of institutional investors.* The role institutional investors with regard to the strategy of firms differs according to governance structures around the world (see section 4.2.2). However, a common issue is the extent to which they do or should actively seek to influence strategy. Historically economies like those of the UK or USA investors have exerted their influence on firms simply through the buying and selling of shares rather than through an in-depth engagement with the company on strategic issues. The stock market becomes the judge of their actions through share price movements. There are signs, however, that investors are becoming more actively involved in the strategies of the firms in which they invest.[3] Such involvement varies a good deal but has grown, and there is evidence that institutional investors that seek to work proactively with boards to develop strategy do better for beneficiaries than those who do not.

- *Scrutiny and control.* Given the concerns about governance that have grown in the last decade, there have been increasing attempts to build means of scrutinising and controlling the activities of 'agents' in the chain to safeguard the interests of the final beneficiaries. Exhibit 4.2 indicates the information typically available to each 'player' in the chain to judge the performance of others in that chain. There are increasing statutory requirements as well as voluntary codes placed upon boards to disclose information publicly and regulate their activities. Nonetheless managers are still left with a great deal of discretion as to what information to provide to whom and, indeed, what information to require of those who report to them. For example, what information should be presented to investment analysts who will influence a firm's share price? How specific should a chief executive be in explaining future strategy to shareholders in public statements such as annual reports? There are also issues of internal reporting that have to be resolved. What are the appropriate targets and measures to incentivise and control management within a firm? Should these primarily be concerned with the achievement of shareholder value? Or is a more balanced scorecard approach appropriate to meet the needs of various stakeholders (see section 10.3.4)? Are the typical accountancy methods (such as return on capital employed) the most appropriate measures or should measures be specifically designed to fit the needs of particular strategies or particular stakeholder/shareholder expectations? There are no categoric answers to these questions. How managers answer them will depend on what they decide the strategic purpose of the organisation is, which itself will be influenced by their view on to whom they see themselves responsible.

4.2.2 Different governance structures

The governing body of an organisation is typically a board of directors. The primary statutory responsibility of a board is to ensure that an organisation fulfils the wishes and purposes of the primary stakeholders. However, who these stakeholders are varies. In the private sector in some parts of the world it is shareholders, but in other parts of the world it is a broader or different stakeholder base. In the public sector, the governing body is accountable to the political arm of government – possibly through some intermediate 'agency' such as a funding body. These differences lead to differences in the way firms operate, how the purposes of an organisation are shaped and how strategies are developed as well as the role and composition of boards.

At the most general level there are two governance structures: the shareholder model and the stakeholder model. These are more or less common in different parts of the world.

A shareholder model of governance

Here shareholders have the legitimate primacy in relation to the wealth generated by the corporations, though proponents argue that maximising shareholder value benefits other stakeholders too. There is dispersed shareholding, though a large proportion of shares is held by financial institutions. At least in principle, the trading of shares provides a regulatory mechanism for maximising shareholder value, given that dissatisfied shareholders may sell their shares, the result being a drop in share price and the threat of takeovers for underperforming firms. The shareholder model is epitomised by the economies of US and the UK.

There are arguments for and against the shareholder model. The *argued advantages* include:

- *Benefits for investors*. Relative to the stakeholder model the investor gets a higher rate of return. Shareholders can also reduce risk through diversifying their holdings in an equity market where shares can be readily traded.
- *Benefits to the economy*. Since the system facilitates higher risk taking by investors, there is a higher likelihood of the encouragement of economic growth and of entrepreneurship. It is also argued that one reason why the UK gets more than its 'fair share' of inward investment to the EU is because the ownership structures are more open to new investors than elsewhere.
- *Benefits for management*. Arguably the separation of ownership and management makes strategic decisions more objectively related to the potentially different demands and constraints of financial, labour and customer markets. A diversified shareholding also means that no one shareholder is likely to control management decisions, provided the firm performs well.

The *argued disadvantages* include:

- *Disadvantages for investors:* dispersed shareholdings prevent close monitoring of the management. This may result in the managers sacrificing shareholder value to pursue their own agendas. For example, CEOs may further their own egos at the expense of the shareholders with mergers that add no value.
- *Disadvantages for the economy: the risk of short termism*. Lack of control of management may lead to them taking decisions to benefit their own careers (for example, to gain promotion). This, combined with the threat of takeovers, may encourage managers to focus on short-term gains at the expense of long-term projects.
- *Corporate reputation and top management greed:* the lack of management control allows for the huge compensations the managers reward themselves in the form of salary, bonuses and stock options. In the US CEOs have 531 times more compensation than their employees in comparison to Japan where the comparable figure is closer to a multiple of 10.

The stakeholder model of governance

An alternative model of governance pursued in various forms is the stakeholder model. This is founded on the principle that wealth is created, captured and distributed by a variety of stakeholders. This may include shareholders but could include other investors, such as banks, as well as employees or their union representatives. As such, management need to be responsive to multiple stakeholders who, themselves, may be formally represented on boards.

However, stakeholder models are also sometimes known as the *block holder system of governance*. One or two large group of investors come to dominate ownership. For example, in Germany just less than three-quarters of all the

German listed companies have a majority owner. In addition, in countries like Germany and Sweden banks play a dominant role and Japanese banks tend to have shareholdings in organisations, as against simply providing loan capital. There is also likely to be a complex web of cross-shareholdings between companies.

Germany and Japan are often cited as examples of the stakeholder model. In Germany there is a two-tier board system. The supervisory board (Aufsichtsrat), mandatory for companies having more than 500 employees, and the management board (Vorstand). The supervisory board is a forum where the interest of various groups is represented, including shareholders and employees but also typically bankers, lawyers, and stock exchange experts. Strategic planning and operational control are vested with the management board, but major decisions like mergers and acquisitions require approval of the supervisory board. In other European countries, notably the Netherlands and France, two-tier boards also exist.

In Japan, profit maximisation or shareholder value is not viewed as the ultimate goal of business enterprises, so much as long-term growth and security of the company. There is concentrated ownership of firms, with a small group of shareholders owning a large percentage of the company, and a system of cross-shareholding, where large companies own shares of other companies and banks finance the same sub-group. Japanese firms have a single-tier board system.

There are *argued advantages* for the stakeholder model of governance:

- *Advantages for stakeholders*. Apart from the argument that the wider interests of stakeholders are taken into account, it is also argued that employee influence in particular is a deterrent to high-risk decisions and investments.
- *Advantages for investors*. Perhaps ironically it is argued that it is block investments that provide economic benefits in several ways. There may be a closer level of monitoring of management, with investors having greater access to information from within the firm. Given that power may reside with relatively few block investors, intervention may also be easier in case of management failure.
- *Long-term horizons*. It is argued that the major investors – banks or other companies, for example – are likely to regard their investments as long-term, thus reducing the pressure for short-term results as against longer-term performance.

There are also *argued disadvantages* of the stakeholder model of governance:

- *Disadvantages for management*. Close monitoring could lead to interference, slowing down of decision processes and the loss of management objectivity when critical decisions have to be made.
- *Disadvantages for investors*. Due to lack of pressure from shareholders, long-term investments are made on projects where the returns may be below market expectations.

- *Disadvantage for the economy*. There are fewer alternatives for raising finance, thus limiting the possibilities of growth and entrepreneurial activity.

It is also worth noting that there are implications with regard to the financing of businesses. In the shareholder model, equity is the dominant form of long-term finance and commercial banks provide debt capital, so relationships with bankers are essentially contractual. There are significant implications. Managers need to limit gearing to a prudent level, so more equity is needed for major strategy developments. It also means that the company itself has a higher degree of influence over strategic decisions since the banks are not seeking a strategic involvement with the company. However, if strategies start to fail, the organisation can become increasingly dependent on the bank as a key stakeholder. This often happens in family-owned small businesses. In the extreme banks may exercise their power through *exit* (i.e. withdrawing funds), even if this liquidates the company. In contrast, in some stakeholder systems (notably Japan and to a lesser extent Germany), banks often have significant equity stakes or be part of the same parent company. They are less likely to adopt an arms-length relationship and more likely to seek active strategic involvement.

Governance structures in transition

There are pressures for change to traditional governance models. Some of these have already been discussed in relation to the governance chain in section 4.2.1. There are, nonetheless, suggestions that there is a convergence around the world on the shareholder model of governance. This is because of the many of the advantages explained above, in particular the view that there is mutual advantage to both shareholders and wider stakeholders. It is also because of the increasing role of institutional investors acting on behalf of a growing mass shareholder class and increasing globalisation and cross-country mergers and acquisitions.

So, for example, in Japan, institutional and foreign investors are gaining influence, and deregulation and liberalisation are increasing the pressure to changer governance structures. In Germany, too, it is argued that if companies are to remain globally competitive, employee representation on boards needs to be reviewed in order to reduce costs and speed decision making. In Sweden, historically, firms were privately owned or in the hands of family-controlled foundations, holding companies and investment companies. However, Sweden's entry into the European Union (EU) has reduced restrictions on capital inflow and increasingly companies are becoming foreign-owned, though most companies still have a majority owner that gives them a controlling position akin to the stakeholder model.

In India there was a high level of state protectionism till the 1980s, with major industries like airlines and banks nationalised and restrictions on inward foreign investment. However, since 1991 there has been radical change.

Import licensing has been abolished, and import tariffs reduced. Restrictions on foreign equity have been relaxed in certain industries, some public sector enterprises have been disinvested and firms allowed to register on the international stock exchanges. India is still characterised by family firms, but with increasing separation of ownership and management. The codes of governance being proposed indicate a move towards a shareholder model of governance with a single board and between 30–50 per cent non-executive directors.

In China the major stakeholders in firms are the state or quasi-state institutions and senior managers have usually started their careers in government positions. China has a two-tier board model. The supervisory board has a minimum of one third of employees as members, but with limited influence on organisational activities, which is the responsibility of operating boards. However, boards are required to have non-executive directors who have recently been required to be independent.

4.3 CORPORATE SOCIAL RESPONSIBILITY

Corporate social responsibility is concerned with the ways in which an organisation exceeds its minimum obligations to stakeholders specified through regulation

The regulatory environment and the corporate governance arrangements for an organisation determine its minimum obligations towards its stakeholders. **Corporate social responsibility** (CSR) is concerned with the ways in which an organisation exceeds its minimum obligations to stakeholders specified through regulation. However, the legal and regulatory frameworks under which businesses operate pay uneven attention to the rights of different stakeholders. For example *contractual stakeholders* – such as customers, suppliers or employees – have a legal relationship with an organisation, and *community stakeholders* – such as local communities, consumers (in general) and pressure groups – do not have the protection of the law. CSR policies of companies will be particularly important to these community stakeholders.

Different organisations take very different stances on social responsibility. The discussion that follows also explains what such stances typically involve in terms of the ways companies act.[4]

4.3.1 *Laissez-faire*

The *laissez-faire* view (literally 'let do' in French) represents an extreme stance where organisations take the view that the only responsibility of business is the short-term interests of shareholders and to 'make a profit, pay taxes and provide jobs'.[5] It is for government to prescribe, through legislation and regulation, the constraints which society chooses to impose on businesses in their pursuit of economic efficiency. The organisation will meet these minimum obligations but no more. Expecting companies to exercise social duties beyond this can, in extreme cases, undermine the authority of government.

This stance may be taken by executives who are persuaded of it ideologically or by smaller businesses that do not have the resources to do other than minimally comply with regulations. In so far as social good is pursued, this is justified in terms of improving profitability. This might occur, for example, if social obligations were imposed as a requirement for gaining contracts (for example, if equal opportunities employment practices were required from suppliers to public sector customers) or to defend their reputation.

4.3.2 Enlightened self-interest

Enlightened self-interest is tempered with recognition of the *long-term financial benefit to the shareholder* of well-managed relationships with other stakeholders. The justification for social action is that it makes good business sense. An organisation's *reputation*[6] is important to its long-term financial success and there is a business case to be made for a more proactive stance on social issues in order to recruit and retain staff, for example. So corporate philanthropy[7] or welfare provision might be regarded as sensible expenditure like any other form of investment or promotion expenditure. The sponsorship of major sporting or arts events by companies is an example. The avoidance of 'shady' marketing practices is also necessary to prevent the need for yet more legislation in that area. Managers here would take the view that organisations not only have responsibility to their shareholders but also a responsibility for *relationships with* other stakeholders (as against *responsibilities to* other stakeholders) and communication with stakeholder groups is likely to be more interactive than for *laissez-faire* type organisations. They may well also set up systems and policies to ensure compliance with best practice (for example, ISO 14000 certification, the protection of human rights in overseas operations) and begin to monitor their social responsibility performance. Top management may also play more of a part, at least in so far as they support the firm taking a more proactive social role.

4.3.3 A forum for stakeholder interaction

A *forum for stakeholder interaction*[8] explicitly incorporates multiple stakeholder interests and expectations rather than just shareholders as influences on organisational purposes and strategies. Here the argument is that the performance of an organisation should be measured in a more pluralistic way than just through the financial bottom line. Companies in this category might retain uneconomic units to preserve jobs, avoid manufacturing or selling 'anti-social' products, and be prepared to bear reductions in profitability for the social good. Some financial service organisations have also chosen to offer socially responsible investment (SRI) 'products' to investors. These only include holdings in organisations that meet high standards of social responsibility in their activities.

However, here there are difficult issues of balance between the interests of different stakeholders. For example, many public sector organisations are, rightly, positioned within this group as they are subject to a wide diversity of expectations, and unitary measures of performance are often inadequate in reflecting this diversity. There are also many family-owned small firms that are in this category through the way that they operate. They will balance their own self-interest with that of their employees and local communities even where this might constrain the strategic choices they make (for example, overseas sourcing vs. local production). Organisations in this category inevitably take longer over the development of new strategies as they are committed to wide consultation with stakeholders and with managing the difficult political trade-offs between conflicting stakeholders' expectations as discussed in section 4.3.

BP claim to have embraced the logic of 'multi stakeholder capitalism', believing that its long-term survival is not just dependent on its economic performance but on its social and environmental performance. Organisations such as BP may elevate corporate social responsibility to Board level appointments and set up structures for monitoring social performance across their global operations. Targets, often through balanced scorecards, may be built into operational aspects of business and issues of social responsibility managed proactively and in a coordinated fashion. The expectation is that such a corporate stance will, in turn, be reflected in the ethical behaviour of individuals within the firm. Organisations that take this position do, of course, suffer if they are not seen to be meeting the standards of performance they espouse. Indeed, BP found this in 2006 when it suffered both in the US courts and worldwide in the press for its shortcomings in health and safety procedures that led to a fatal explosion at its refinery in Texas City (see Illustration 4.2).

4.3.4 Shapers of society

Shapers of society regard financial considerations as of secondary importance or a constraint. These are activists, seeking to change society and social norms. The firm may have been founded for this purpose, as in the case of the Body Shop. The social role is, then the *raison d'être* of the business. They may see their strategic purpose as 'changing the rules of the game' through which they may benefit but by which they wish to assure that society benefits. In this role it is unlikely that they will be operating on their own: rather they are likely to be partnering with other organisations, commercial and otherwise, to achieve their purposes.

The extent to which this is a viable ethical stance depends upon issues of regulation, corporate governance and accountability. It is easier for a privately

Illustration 4.2

BP, 'Beyond Petroleum' and the Texas City disaster

Companies have increasingly been explicit about their stance on social responsibility. But in so doing they can increase their vulnerability when things go wrong.

The global energy company BP under the leadership of John Browne has been applauded for developing an explicit code of social responsibility emphasising efficient and sustainable energy, energy diversity, concern for climate change, local development where it operates and high levels of safety. This stance was publicised in an advertising campaign promoting the slogan 'Beyond Petroleum'. Further, as John Browne stated (*Business Strategy Review*, vol. 17, no. 3 (2006), pp. 53–56), 'Our commitment to responsibility has to be expressed not in words, but in the actions of the business, day in and day out, in every piece of activity and every aspect of behaviour.'

It was, therefore, a major disaster, not only to the local community and its families, but also to BP when, in 2005, an explosion at BP's Texas City oil refinery killed 15 workers. In September 2005 BP was given a £12m (€17m) fine by the US Department of Labor for 300 safety violations at the Texas City plant.

The press were unremitting in their criticism. The disaster had happened in the same year as BP profits soared and Browne, himself, was given pay and share remuneration in 2005 estimated at £6.5m. BPs top management were aware of 'significant safety problems' not only at the Texas City refinery but at 34 other locations around the world. They emphasised cost cutting over safety. They didn't listen to people lower down in the organisation; they reported a staff survey that rated 'making money' as the top priority and 'people' as the lowest. Too many jobs have been outsourced to cheaper contractors, and so it went on.

In January 2007 John Browne announced that he would be quitting BP 18 months early to be succeeded by Tony Haywood who had been in charge of BP's exploration and production division. Passed over was John Manzoni, the board director in charge of refining, with the responsibility of refineries.

In 2005 BP had asked James Baker, former US Secretary of State, to undertake an independent investigation. In January 2007, Baker reported:

> BP has not provided effective process safety leadership and has not adequately established process safety as a core value across all its five U.S. refineries. . . . BP tended to have a short-term focus and its decentralized management system and entrepreneurial culture have delegated substantial discretion to U.S. refinery plant managers without clearly defining process safety expectations, responsibilities or accountabilities. . . . The company did not always insure that adequate resources were effectively allocated to support or sustain a high level of process safety performance.

The company relied excessively on monitoring injury rates which 'significantly hindered its perception of process risk'. Incidents and near misses were probably under-reported and, when spotted, root causes often not identified correctly.

BP responded that it planned 'significant external recruitment . . . to increase underlying capability in operations and engineering' and that modern process control systems would be installed at its refineries. But the company's social responsibility stance had taken a battering.

Questions

1. Why do you think BP took its highly publicised stance on social responsibility?
2. Can top management effectively manage social responsibility at local level? How?
3. Will the negative publicity around the Texas City disaster affect BP's strategy?

owned organisation to operate in this way, since it is not accountable to external shareholders. Some would argue that the great historical achievements of the public services in transforming the quality of life for millions of people were largely because they were 'mission-driven' in this way, supported by a political framework in which they operated. However, in many countries there have been challenges to the legitimacy of this mission-driven stance of public services and demands for citizens (as taxpayers) to expect demonstrable best value from them. Charitable organisations face similar dilemmas. It is fundamental to their existence that they have zeal to improve the interests of particular groups in society; but they also need to remain financially viable, which can lead to them being seen as over-commercial and spending too much on administration or promotional activities.

On the face of it, shapers of society represent the other end of the spectrum from *laissez-faire* firms. However, it is worth noting that some large firms that espouse a *laissez-faire* approach, such as NewsCorp or Haliburton (arguably), are actively engaged in trying to shape society, albeit towards their view of the social role of business.

Increasingly there is a view by managers themselves that the *laissez-faire* position is not acceptable[9] and that businesses need to take a socially responsible position. This is not solely for ethical reasons but because there is a belief that there are advantages to businesses in so doing and dangers if they do not. Being socially responsible reduces the risk of negative stakeholder (not least customer) reactions and can help retain loyal, motivated employees. Social responsibility is therefore justified in terms of the 'triple bottom line' – social and environmental benefits as well as increased profits. Indeed it is argued that socially responsible strategies should be followed because they can provide a basis of gaining competitive advantage. The need is to seek 'win-win' situations to optimise the economic return on environmental investments: 'The essential test . . . is not whether a cause is worthy but whether it presents an opportunity to create shared value – that is meaningful benefit for society that is also valuable to the business'.[10] Fighting the AIDS pandemic in Africa is not just a matter of 'good works' for a pharmaceutical company or an African mining company, it is central to their own interests.

Social auditing[11] is a way of ensuring that issues of corporate social responsibility are systematically reviewed and has been championed by a number of progressive organisations. This takes several forms, ranging from social audits undertaken by independent external bodies, through aspects of the social agenda that are now mandatory in company reporting (for example, some environmental issues) to voluntary social accounting by organisations themselves.

4.4 STAKEHOLDER EXPECTATIONS

www.pearsoned.co.uk/fos
KEY CONCEPT
Stakeholders

It should be clear from the preceding sections that the decisions managers have to make about the purpose and strategy of their organisation are influenced by the expectations of stakeholders. This poses a challenge because there are likely to be many stakeholders, especially for a large organisation (see Exhibit 4.3), with different, perhaps conflicting expectations. This means that managers need to take a view on (a) which stakeholders will have the greatest influence, therefore (b) which expectations they need to pay most attention to and (c) to what extent the expectations and influence of different stakeholders vary.

External stakeholders can be usefully divided into three types in terms of the nature of their relationship with the organisation and, therefore, how they might affect the success or failure of a strategy:[12]

Exhibit 4.3 Stakeholders of a large organisation

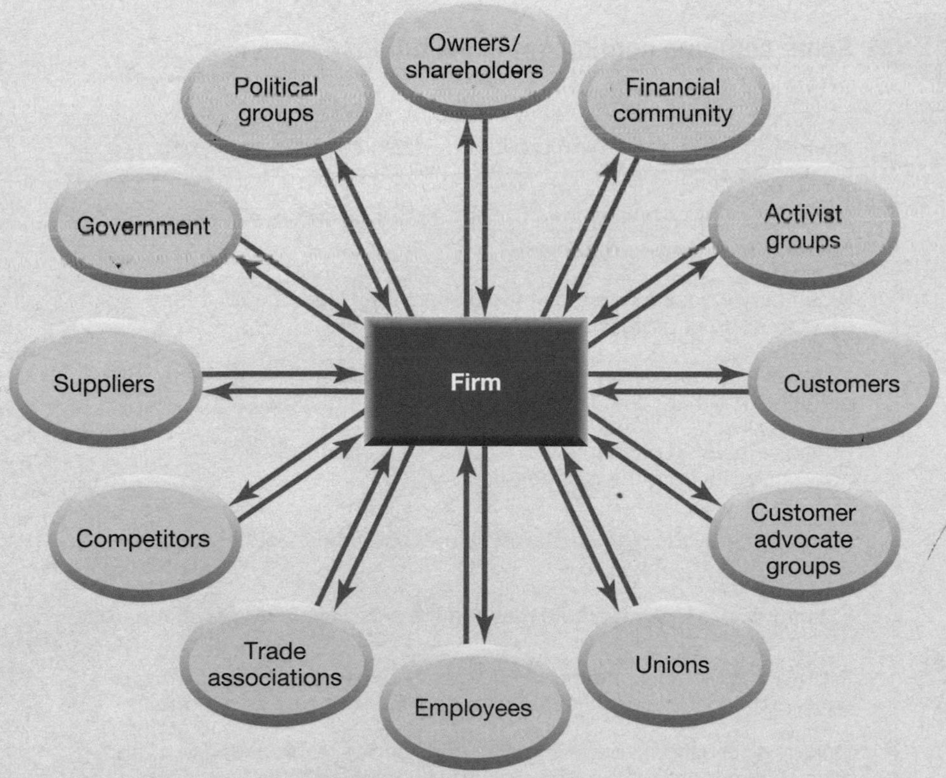

Source: R.E. Freeman, *Strategic Management: A Stakeholder Approach*, pub. Pitman 1984. Copyright 1984 by R. Edward Freeman.

- *Economic stakeholders*, including suppliers, competitors, distributors (whose influence can be identified using the five-forces framework from Chapter 2 (Exhibit 2.2) and shareholders (whose influence can be considered in terms of the governance chain discussed in section 4.2.1 above).
- *Socio/political stakeholders*, such as policy makers, regulators and government agencies who will influence the 'social legitimacy' of the strategy.
- *Technological stakeholders*, such as key adopters, standards agencies and owners of competitive technologies who will influence the diffusion of new technologies and the adoption of industry standards.

The influence of these different types of stakeholders is likely to vary in different situations. For example, the 'technological group' will be crucial for strategies of new product introduction whilst the 'social/political' group is usually particularly influential in the public sector context.

There are also stakeholder groups internal to an organisation, which may be departments, geographical locations or different levels in the hierarchy. Individuals may belong to more than one stakeholder group, and such groups may 'line up' differently depending on the issue or strategy in hand. Of course,

Exhibit 4.4 Some common conflicts of expectations

- In order to grow, short-term profitability, cash flow and pay levels may need to be sacrificed.
- 'Short-termism' may suit managerial career aspirations but preclude investment in long-term projects.
- When family businesses grow, the owners may lose control if they need to appoint professional managers.
- New developments may require additional funding through share issue or loans. In either case, financial independence may be sacrificed.
- Public ownership of shares will require more openness and accountability from the management.
- Cost efficiency through capital investment can mean job losses.
- Extending into mass markets may require a decline in quality standards.
- In public services, a common conflict is between mass provision and specialist services (e.g. preventative dentistry or heart transplants).
- In large multinational organisations, conflict can result because of a division's responsibilities to the company and also to its host country.

external stakeholders may seek to influence an organisation's strategy through their links with internal stakeholders. For example, customers may exert pressure on sales managers to represent their interests within the company.

Since the expectations of stakeholder groups will differ, it is normal for conflict to exist regarding the importance or desirability of many aspects of strategy. In most situations, a compromise will need to be reached. Exhibit 4.4 shows some of the typical stakeholder expectations that exist and how they might conflict. Global organisations may have added complications as they are operating in multiple arenas. For example, an overseas division is part of the parent company, with all that implies in terms of expectations about behaviour and performance, but is also part of a local community, which has different expectations. These two 'worlds' may not sit comfortably alongside each other.

For these reasons, the stakeholder concept is valuable when trying to understand the political context within which strategic developments take place. Indeed, taking stakeholder expectations and influence into account is an important aspect of strategic choice, as will be seen in Chapter 9.

4.4.1 Stakeholder mapping[13]

Stakeholder mapping identifies stakeholder expectations and power and helps in understanding political priorities

There are different ways in which stakeholder mapping can be used to gain an understanding of stakeholder influence. The approach to **stakeholder mapping** here identifies stakeholder expectations and power and helps in understanding political priorities. It underlines the importance of two issues:

- How *interested* each stakeholder group is in impressing its expectations on the organisation's purposes and choice of strategies.
- Whether stakeholders have the *power* to do so.

Power/interest matrix

The power/interest matrix can be seen in Exhibit 4.5. It describes the context within which a strategy might be pursued by classifying stakeholders in relation to the power they hold and the extent to which they are likely to show interest in supporting or opposing a particular strategy. The matrix helps in thinking through stakeholder influences on the development of strategy. However, it must be emphasised that how managers handle relationships will depend on the governance structures under which they operate (see section 4.2 above) and the stance taken on corporate responsibility (section 4.3 above). For example, in some countries unions may be very weak but in others they may be represented on supervisory boards; banks may take an 'arm's length' relationship with regard to strategy in some countries, but be part of the governance structures in others. A *laissez-faire* type business may take the view that it will only pay attention to stakeholders with the most powerful economic influence (for example, investors), whereas shapers of society might go out of

Exhibit 4.5 **Stakeholder mapping: the power/interest matrix**

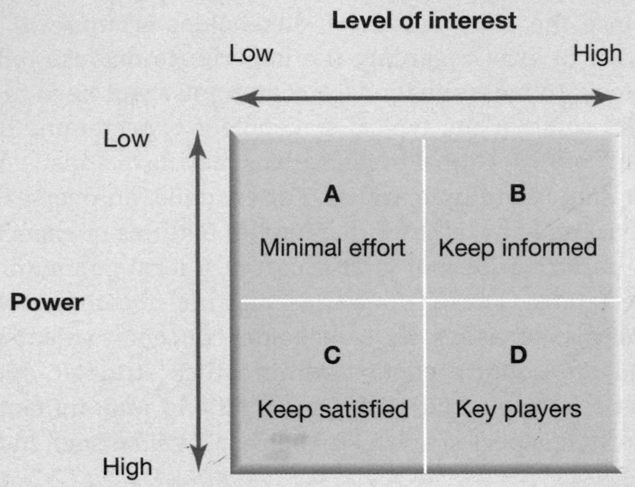

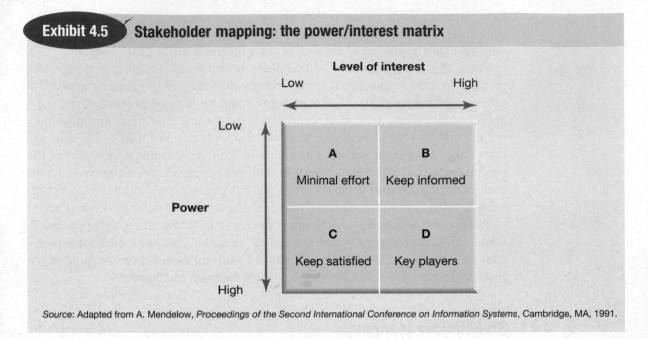

Source: Adapted from A. Mendelow, *Proceedings of the Second International Conference on Information Systems*, Cambridge, MA, 1991.

their way to engage with and influence the expectations and involvement of stakeholders who would not typically see themselves as influential.

In order to show the way in which the matrix may be used, the discussion here takes the perspective of a business where managers see themselves as formulating strategy by trying to ensure the compliance of stakeholders to their own assessment of strategic imperatives. In this context the matrix indicates the type of relationship that such an organisation might typically establish with stakeholder groups in the different quadrants. Clearly, the acceptability of strategies to *key players* (segment D) is of major importance. It could be that these are major investors, but it could also be particular individuals or agencies with a lot of power – for example, a major shareholder in a family firm or a government funding agency in a public sector organisation. Often the most difficult issues relate to stakeholders in segment C. Although these might, in general, be relatively passive, a disastrous situation can arise when their level of interest is underrated and they suddenly *reposition* to segment D and frustrate the adoption of a new strategy. Institutional shareholders such as pension funds or insurance firms can fall into this category. They may show little interest unless share prices start to dip, but may then demand to be heard by senior management.

Similarly, organisations might address the expectations of stakeholders in segment B, for example community groups, through information provision. It may be important not to alienate such stakeholders because they can be crucially important 'allies' in influencing the attitudes of more powerful stakeholders: for example, through *lobbying*.

Stakeholder mapping might help in understanding better some of the following issues:

- In *determining purpose and strategy*, which stakeholder expectations need to be most considered?
- Whether the *actual levels of interest and power* of stakeholders properly reflect the corporate governance framework within which the organisation is operating, as in the examples above (institutional investors, community groups).
- Who the key *blockers* and *facilitators* of a strategy are likely to be and how this could be responded to – for example, in terms of education or persuasion.
- Whether *repositioning* of certain stakeholders is desirable and/or feasible. This could be to lessen the influence of a key player or, in certain instances, to ensure that there are more key players who will champion the strategy (this is often critical in the public sector context).
- *Maintaining* the level of interest or power of some key stakeholders may be essential. For example, public 'endorsement' by powerful suppliers or customers may be critical to the success of a strategy. Equally, it may be necessary to discourage some stakeholders from repositioning themselves. This is what is meant by *keep satisfied* in relation to stakeholders in segment C, and to a lesser extent *keep informed* for those in segment B. The use of *side payments* to stakeholders as a means of securing the acceptance of new strategies can be a key maintenance activity. For example, a 'deal' may be done with another department to support them on one of *their* strategies if they agree not to oppose *this* strategy.

These questions can raise difficult ethical issues for managers in deciding the role they should play in the political activity surrounding stakeholder management. This takes the debate back to the considerations of governance and ethics discussed earlier in the chapter. For example, are managers really the honest brokers who weigh the conflicting expectations of stakeholder groups? Or should they be answerable to one stakeholder – such as shareholders – and hence is their role to ensure the acceptability of their strategies to other stakeholders? Or are they, as many authors suggest, the real power themselves, constructing strategies to suit their own purposes and managing stakeholder expectations to ensure acceptance of these strategies?

Illustration 4.3 shows some of the practical issues of using stakeholder mapping to understand the political context surrounding a new strategy and to establish political priorities. The example relates to a German bank with headquarters in Frankfurt (Germany) and providing corporate banking services from head office and a regional office in Toulouse (France). It is considering the closure of its Toulouse office and providing all corporate banking services from Frankfurt.

The example illustrates two further issues.

- Stakeholder groups are *not usually 'homogeneous'* but contain a variety of subgroups with different expectations and power. In the illustration, *customers* are shown divided into those who are largely supportive of the strategy (customer X), those who are actively hostile (customer Y) and those who are indifferent (customer Z). So when using stakeholder mapping, there is clearly a balance to be struck between describing stakeholders too generically – hence hiding important issues of diversity – and too much subdivision, making the situation confusing and difficult to interpret.

- The *role and the individual* currently undertaking that role need to be distinguished. It is useful to know if a new individual in that role would shift the positioning. Serious misjudgements can be made if care is not paid to this point. In the example, it has been concluded that the German minister (segment C) is largely indifferent to the new development – it is low in her

Illustration 4.3

Stakeholder mapping at Tallman GmbH

Stakeholder mapping can be a useful tool for determining the political priorities for specific strategic developments or changes.

Tallman GmbH was a German bank providing both retail and corporate banking services throughout Germany, Benelux and France. There were concerns about its loss in market share in the corporate sector which was serviced from two centres – Frankfurt (for Germany and Benelux) and Toulouse (for France). It was considering closing the Toulouse operation and servicing all corporate clients from Frankfurt. This would result in significant job losses in Toulouse, some of which would be replaced in Frankfurt alongside vastly improved IT systems.

Two power/interest maps were drawn up by the company officials to establish likely stakeholder reactions to the proposed closure of the Toulouse operation. Map A represents the likely situation and map B the preferred situation – where support for the proposal would be sufficient to proceed.

Referring to map A, it can be seen that, with the exception of customer X and IT supplier A, the stakeholders in box B are currently opposed to the closure of the Toulouse operation. If Tallman was to have any chance of convincing these stakeholders to change their stance to a more supportive one, the company must address their questions and, where possible, alleviate their fears. If such fears were overcome, these people might become important allies in influencing the more powerful stakeholders in boxes C and D. The supportive attitude of customer X could

Map A: The likely situation

A	Shareholder M (–) Toulouse office (–) Customer X (+) French minister (–) Marketing (–) IT supplier A (+) B
Customer Z German minister C	Customer Y (+) Frankfurt office (+) Corporate finance (+) D

Map B: The preferred situation

French minister A	Shareholder M (–) Toulouse office (–) Marketing (–) IT supplier A (+) B
Customer Z German minister C	Customer X (+) Customer Y (+) Frankfurt office (+) Corporate finance (+) D

priorities. However, a change of minister might change this situation. Although it will be impossible for the bank to remove such uncertainties entirely, there are implications for the political priorities. For example, those permanent officials who are advising the minister need to be kept satisfied, since they will outlive individual ministers and provide a continuity which can diminish uncertainty. It is also possible, of course, that the German minister's level of interest will be raised by lobbying from her French counterpart. This would have implications for how the company handles the situation in France.

be usefully harnessed in this quest. Customer X was a multinational with operations throughout Europe. It had shown dissatisfaction with the inconsistent treatment that it received from Frankfurt and Toulouse.

The relationships Tallman had with the stakeholders in box C were the most difficult to manage since, whilst they were considered to be relatively passive, largely due to their indifference to the proposed strategy, a disastrous situation could arise if their level of interest was underrated. For example, if the German minister were replaced, her successor might be opposed to the strategy and actively seek to stop the changes. In this case they would shift to box D.

The acceptability of the proposed strategy to the current players in box D was a key consideration. Of particular concern was customer Y (a major French manufacturer who operated only in France – accounting for 20 per cent of Toulouse corporate banking income). Customer Y was opposed to the closure of the Toulouse operation and could have the power to prevent it from happening, for example by the withdrawal of its business. The company clearly needed to have open discussions with this stakeholder.

By comparing the position of stakeholders in map A and map B, and identifying any changes and mismatches, Tallman could establish a number of tactics to change the stance of certain stakeholders to a more positive one and to increase the power of certain stakeholders. For example, customer X could be encouraged to champion the proposed strategy and assist Tallman by providing media access, or even convincing customer Y that the change could be beneficial.

Tallman could also seek to dissuade or prevent powerful stakeholders from changing their stance to a negative one: for example, unless direct action were taken, lobbying from her French counterpart may well raise the German minister's level of interest. This has implications for how the company handles the situation in France. Time could be spent talking the strategy through with the French minister and also customer Y to try to shift them away from opposition at least to neutrality, if not support.

Question

To ensure that you are clear about how to undertake stakeholder mapping, produce your own complete analysis for Tallman GmbH against a different strategy, that is *to service all corporate clients from Toulouse*. Ensure that you go through the following steps:

1. Plot the most likely situation (map A) – remembering to be careful to *reassess* interest and power for each stakeholder in relation to this *new* strategy.
2. Map the preferred situation (map B).
3. Identify the mismatches – and hence the political priorities. Remember to include the need to *maintain* a stakeholder in its 'opening' position (if relevant).
4. Finish off by listing the actions you would propose to take and give a final view of the degree of political risk in pursuing this new strategy.

4.5 VALUES, MISSION, VISION AND OBJECTIVES

The previous sections have looked at factors that influence the overall purpose of an organisation. However, it is managers who will need to form a view on this purpose and find a way of expressing it. It may be that an explicit statement of such a purpose is a formal requirement of corporate governance or expected of the organisation by one or more stakeholders. Or it may be that managers themselves decide such a statement is useful. This section will look at the different ways in which such purpose may be expressed explicitly through statements of *corporate values, vision, mission* and *objectives*.

4.5.1 Corporate values

Core values are the underlying principles that guide an organisation's strategy

Increasingly organisations have been keen to develop and communicate a set of corporate values that define the way that the organisation operates.[14] Of particular importance are an organisation's **core values** – these are the underlying 'principles' that guide an organisation's strategy. For example, emergency services such as ambulance and fire fighters have an overriding commitment to saving life that employees are committed to the extent that they will break strike action or risk their own lives to attend emergencies when life is threatened. Jim Collins and Jerry Porras have argued that the long-run success of many US corporates – such as Disney, General Electric or 3M – can be attributed (at least in part) to strong core values.[15] There are again, however, potential downsides to public statements of corporate values if an organisation demonstrably fails to live them out in practice (see Illustration 4.2). It is also important to distinguish between the *core values* expressing the way the organisation *is*, as distinct from those to which the organisation wishes to *aspire*. Unless this distinction is clear there is room for considerable misunderstanding and cynicism about statements of corporate values..

4.5.2 Mission and vision statements

A **mission statement** aims to provide employees and stakeholders with clarity about the overall purpose and raison d'être of the organisation

A **vision statement** is concerned with what the organisation aspires to be

Whereas corporate values may be a backcloth and set boundaries within which strategies are developed, a **mission statement** and a **vision statement** are typically more explicitly concerned with the purpose of an organisation in terms of its strategic direction. Illustration 4.4 shows examples of mission, vision and value statements. In practice the distinction between mission and vision statements can be hazy but they are intended to be different as follows:

- *A mission statement* aims to provide employees and stakeholders with clarity about the overall purpose and raison d'être of the organisation. It is

Illustration 4.4

Mission, vision and values statements

Can well-crafted statements of mission, vision or values be an important means of motivating an organisation's stakeholders?

Tata Steel

Mission 2007
Consistent with the vision and values of the founder Jamsetji Tata, Tata Steel strives to strengthen India's industrial base through the effective utilisation of staff and materials. The means envisaged to achieve this are high technology and productivity, consistent with modern management practices.

Tata Steel recognises that while honesty and integrity are the essential ingredients of a strong and stable enterprise, profitability provides the main spark for economic activity.

Overall, the company seeks to scale the heights of excellence in all that it does in an atmosphere free from fear, and thereby reaffirms its faith in democratic values.

Vision 2007
To seize the opportunities of tomorrow and create a future that will make us an EVA positive company.

To continue to improve the quality of life of our employees and the communities we serve.

To revitalise the core business for a sustainable future.

To venture into new businesses that will own a share of our future.

To uphold the spirit and values of Tatas towards nation building.

The Metropolitan Police

Mission and values

Our mission: Working together for a safer London.

Our values: Working together with all our citizens, all our partners, all our colleagues:

We will have pride in delivering quality policing. There is no greater priority.

We will build trust by listening and responding.

We will respect and support each other and work as a team.

We will learn from experience and find ways to be even better.

We are one team – we all have a duty to play our part in making London safer.

Villeroy & Boch

Company vision
To be the leading European lifestyle brand with high competence and trend-setting style for high-end design and living.

Five values – one philosophy

I. *Customers*. Our success is measured by the enthusiasm our customers show for our products and services. A constant challenge is to satisfy the high expectations architects, retailers, the trade and end consumers have of the 'Villeroy & Boch' brand. We convince them with competence and experience.

II. *Employees*. In the long run a strong market position can only be achieved by having innovative and committed employees. Our priority task is to motivate them and cultivate their team spirit, encouraging them to achieve personal and joint goals.

III: *Innovation*. If we lay claim to a leading position on the international markets it is not enough to follow trends. Those who want to secure their competitive edge worldwide must recognise and shape trends early on.

IV: *Earning power*. An important concern for us is to maintain the independence of the company and achieve long-term success. The fundamentals for this are a balanced portfolio, earnings-oriented growth, high and constant rates of return and appropriate dividends.

V: *Responsibility*. Not many companies have made regional economic history as well as European cultural and social history. Villeroy & Boch is one of them, and thus bears many responsibilities. We feel obligated not only to our employees, shareholders and customers, but also to the environment and society.

Questions

1 Which of these statements do you think are likely to motivate which stakeholders? Why?

2 Could any of them have been improved? How?

3 Identify other statements of mission, vision, purpose or values that you think are especially well crafted and explain why.

www.pearsoned.co.uk/fos KEY CONCEPT Mission and vision

therefore to do with building understanding and confidence about how the strategy of the organisation relates to that purpose.

- *A vision statement* is concerned with what the organisation aspires to be. Its purpose is to set out a view of the future so as to enthuse, gain commitment and stretch performance.

Although both mission and vision statements became widely adopted by the early 2000s, many critics regard them as bland and wide-ranging. However, arguably if there is substantial disagreement within the organisation or with stakeholders as to its mission (or vision), it may well give rise to real problems in resolving the strategic direction of the organisation. So, given the political nature of strategic management, they can be a useful means of focusing debate on the fundamentals of the organisation.

4.5.3 Objectives

Objectives are statements of specific outcomes that are to be achieved

Objectives are statements of specific outcomes that are to be achieved. Objectives – both at the corporate and business unit level – are often expressed in financial terms. They could be the expression of desired sales or profit levels, rates of growth, dividend levels or share valuations. However, organisations may also have market-based objectives, many of which are quantified as targets – such as market share, customer service, repeat business and so on.

There are two related issues that managers need to consider with regard to setting objectives.

- *Objectives and measurement.* Objectives are typically quantified. Indeed, some argue that objectives are not helpful unless their achievement can be measured. However, this does raise the question as to how many objectives expressed in such ways are useful? Certainly there are times when specific quantified objectives are required, for example when urgent action is needed and it becomes essential for management to focus attention on a limited number of priority requirements – as in a *turnaround* situation. If the choice is between going out of business and surviving, there is no room for latitude through vaguely stated requirements. However, it may be that in other circumstances – for example, in trying to raise the aspirations of people in the organisation – more attention needs to be paid to qualitative statements of purpose such as mission or vision statements.
- *Objectives and control.* A recurring problem with objectives is that managers and employees 'lower down' in the hierarchy are unclear as to how their day-to-day work contributes to the achievement of higher level of objectives. This could, in principle, be addressed by a 'cascade' of objectives – defining a set of detailed objectives at each level in the hierarchy. Many organisations attempt to do this to some extent. Here consideration needs to be given to a trade-off: how to achieve required levels of clarity on strategy without being over restrictive in terms of the latitude people have. There is evidence, for

example, that innovation is stymied by over-restrictive target setting and measurement.[16]

An underlying theme in this chapter has been that strategists have to consider the overall strategic purpose of their organisations. However, a central question that arises is what stakeholder expectations they should respond to in so doing.

SUMMARY

www.pearsoned.co.uk/fos AUDIO SUMMARY

- The purpose of an organisation will be influenced by the expectations of its *stakeholders*.
- The influence of some key stakeholders will be represented formally within the *governance structure* of an organisation. This can be represented in terms of a *governance chain*, showing the links between ultimate beneficiaries and the managers of an organisation.
- There are two generic governance structures systems: the *shareholder model* and the *stakeholder model*. There are variations of these internationally, but some signs that there is convergence towards a shareholder model.
- There are also ethical dimensions to the purpose of an organisation. At an organisational level, this takes form of its stance on *corporate social responsibility*.
- Different stakeholders exercise different influence on organisational purpose and strategy, dependent on the extent of their power and interest.
- An important managerial task is to decide how the organisation should express its strategic purpose through statements of *values, vision, mission* or *objectives*.

Recommended key readings

- For books providing a fuller explanation of corporate governance: R. Monks and N. Minow (eds), *Corporate Governance*, 3rd edition, Blackwell, 2003; and J. Solomon, *Corporate Governance and Accountability*, 2nd edition, Wiley, 2007. For a provocative critique and proposals for the future of corporate governance linked to issues of social responsibility see S. Davies, J. Lukomnik and D. Pitt-Watson, *The New Capitalists*, Harvard Business School Press, 2006.
- For a review of different stances on corporate social responsibility see P. Mirvis and B. Googins, 'Stages of corporate citizenship', *California Management Review*, vol. 48, no. 2 (2006), pp. 104–126.
- The case for the importance of clarity of strategic values and vision is especially strongly made by J. Collins and J. Porras, *Built to Last: Successful habits of visionary companies*, Harper Business, 2002 (in particular see chapter 11).

References

1. This definition is based on, but adapted from, that in S. Jacoby, 'Corporate governance and society', *Challenge*, vol. 48, no. 4 (2005), pp. 69–87.
2. The principal–agency model is part of agency theory which developed within organisational economics but is now widely used in the management field as described here. Two useful references are: K. Eisenhardt, 'Agency theory: an assessment and review', *Academy of Management Review*, vol. 14, no. 1 (1989), pp. 57–74; J.-J. Laffont and D. Martimort, *The Theory of Incentives: The Principal–Agent Model*, Princeton University Press, 2002.
3. For a strong advocacy of this position see S. Davies, J. Lukomnik and D. Pitt-Watson, *The New Capitalists*, Harvard Business School Press, 2006.
4. Based on research undertaken at the Center for Corporate Citizenship at the Boston College, reported in P. Mirvis and B. Googins, 'Stages of corporate citizenship', *California Management Review*, vol. 48, no. 2 (2006), pp. 104–126.
5. Often quoted as a summary of Milton Friedman's argument is: Milton Friedman: 'The social responsibility of business is to increase its profits', *The New York Times Magazine*, 13 September 1970.
6. See S. Macleod, 'Why worry about CSR?', *Strategic Communication Management*, Aug/Sept (2001), pp. 8–9.
7. See M. Porter and M. Kramer, 'The competitive advantage of corporate philanthropy', *Harvard Business Review*, vol. 80, no. 12 (2002), pp. 56–68.
8. H. Hummels, 'Organizing ethics: a stakeholder debate', *Journal of Business Ethics*, vol. 17, no. 13 (1998), pp. 1403–1419.
9. D. Vogel, 'Is there a market for virtue? The business case for corporate social responsibility', *California Management Review*, vol. 47, no. 4 (2005), pp. 19–45.
10. This quote is from Porter and Kramer, (7 above p. 80).
11. For a discussion of the range of performance measures being used in relation to CSR and their effectiveness, see A. Chatterji and D. Levine, 'Breaking down the wall of codes: evaluating non-financial performance measures', *California Management Review*, vol. 48, no. 2 (2006), pp. 29–51.
12. Details of how these three groups interact with organisations in detail can be found in: J. Cummings and J. Doh, 'Identifying who matters: mapping key players in multiple environments', *California Management Review*, vol. 42, no. 2 (2000), pp. 83–104.
13. This approach to stakeholder mapping has been adapted from A. Mendelow, *Proceedings of the 2nd International Conference on Information Systems*, Cambridge, MA, 1991. See also K. Scholes' chapter, 'Stakeholder analysis' in V. Ambrosini with G. Johnson and K. Scholes (eds), *Exploring Techniques of Analysis and Evaluation in Strategic Management*, Prentice Hall, 1998. For a public sector explanation, see K. Scholes, 'Stakeholder mapping: a practical tool for public sector managers', in G. Johnson and K. Scholes (eds), *Exploring Public Sector Strategy*, Financial Times/Prentice Hall, 2001, chapter 9.
14. P. Lencioni, 'Make your values mean something', *Harvard Business Review*, vol. 80, no. 7 (2002), pp. 113–117.
15. See J. Collins and J. Porras, *Built to Last: Successful habits of visionary companies*, Harper Business, 2002.
16. See A. Neely, 'Measuring performance in innovative firms', chapter 6 in *The Exceptional Manager*, by R. Delbridge, L. Grattan and G. Johnson, Oxford University Press, 2006.

CASE EXAMPLE

(PRODUCT) RED and Gap

(RED) was created by Bono and Bobby Shriver, Chairman of DATA, to raise awareness and money for The Global Fund by teaming up with the world's most iconic brands to produce (PRODUCT) RED-branded products. A percentage of each (PRODUCT) RED product sold is given to The Global Fund. The money helps women and children with HIV/AIDS in Africa.[1]

The (RED) initiative was set up in early 2006, with Rwanda selected as the initial country to benefit from sales of the (RED) products. The first products launched in the UK were the (PRODUCT) RED American Express card and a (PRODUCT) RED vintage T-shirt from Gap launched in March 2006. Other companies joining the scheme included Motorola, Converse, Apple (introducing a (PRODUCT) RED iPod) and Emporio Armani. There was also a special (PRODUCT) RED edition of the *Independent*, guest edited by Bono.

THE (RED)™ MANIFESTO

ALL THINGS BEING EQUAL, THEY ARE NOT.

AS FIRST WORLD CONSUMERS, WE HAVE TREMENDOUS POWER. WHAT WE COLLECTIVELY CHOOSE TO BUY, OR NOT TO BUY, CAN CHANGE THE COURSE OF LIFE AND HISTORY ON THIS PLANET.

(RED) IS THAT SIMPLE AN IDEA. AND THAT POWERFUL. NOW, YOU HAVE A CHOICE. THERE ARE (RED) CREDIT CARDS, (RED) PHONES, (RED) SHOES, (RED) FASHION BRANDS. AND NO, THIS DOES NOT MEAN THEY ARE ALL RED IN COLOR. ALTHOUGH SOME ARE.

IF YOU BUY A (RED) PRODUCT OR SIGN UP FOR A (RED) SERVICE, AT NO COST TO YOU, A (RED) COMPANY WILL GIVE SOME OF ITS PROFITS TO BUY AND DISTRIBUTE ANTI-RETROVIRAL MEDICINE TO OUR BROTHERS AND SISTERS DYING OF AIDS IN AFRICA.

WE BELIEVE THAT WHEN CONSUMERS ARE OFFERED THIS CHOICE, AND THE PRODUCTS MEET THEIR NEEDS, THEY WILL CHOOSE (RED). AND WHEN THEY CHOOSE (RED) OVER NON-(RED), THEN MORE BRANDS WILL CHOOSE TO BECOME (RED) BECAUSE IT WILL MAKE GOOD BUSINESS SENSE TO DO SO. AND MORE LIVES WILL BE SAVED.

(RED) IS NOT A CHARITY. IT IS SIMPLY A BUSINESS MODEL. YOU BUY (RED) STUFF. WE GET THE MONEY, BUY THE PILLS AND DISTRIBUTE THEM. THEY TAKE THE PILLS, STAY ALIVE, AND CONTINUE TO TAKE CARE OF THEIR FAMILIES AND CONTRIBUTE SOCIALLY AND ECONOMICALLY IN THEIR COMMUNITIES.

IF THEY DON'T GET THE PILLS, THEY DIE. WE DON'T WANT THEM TO DIE. WE WANT TO GIVE THEM THE PILLS. AND WE CAN. AND YOU CAN. AND IT'S EASY.

ALL YOU HAVE TO DO IS UPGRADE YOUR CHOICE.

Source: http://www.joinred.com/manifesto.asp.

Support for the (RED) campaign has come from Bill Gates, interviewed in *Advertising Age*: 'Red is about saving lives . . . if there's not enough money to buy drugs, people die, and so we can say, "Hey, let's just let that happen," or we can take all the avenues available to us.' He acknowledged that this included governments being more generous, but also believed that consumers wanted 'to associate themselves with saving lives' and that what Gap or Armani were doing through (PRODUCT) RED provided this opportunity.

Other commentators were not so positive. Another article in *Advertising Age*[2] claimed that the campaign had raised only $18m (€15m; £10m) in a year despite a marketing outlay by companies involved in the scheme (including Gap) of $100m. Gap was the biggest spender here with an advertising budget of $7.8m. A spokeswoman for (RED) claimed that the *Ad Age* figure of 100 million was merely a 'phantom number pulled out of thin air'.

An article in the *Independent* went on to do its own mathematics, concluding that the figure raised was $25 million in six months and that, on an advertising investment of $40 million, this was a 'staggeringly good rate of return'.

They went on to argue:[3]

> what the RED initiative has set out to do – and with some success if $25 million in six months is half the profits RED products would have made – is create a stream of revenue for the fight against AIDS in Africa which will far exceed one-off payments from corporate philanthropy budgets. It looks set to create a major source of cash for the global fund, and one which is sustainable. It is an entirely new model for fund raising.

But wouldn't it be better if people simply gave the money that they spend on the products directly to charity? 'If only that were the choice. But most people wouldn't give the cost of a new ipod to the global fund.' They continued:

> The money RED has raised means that some 160,000 Africans will be put on life saving anti-retrovirals in the coming months, orphans are being fed and kept in school in Swaziland and a national HIV treatment and prevention programme has begun in Rwanda.

(RED) Gap

On their website Gap's Senior Vice President for Social Responsibility, Dan Henkle, explained Gap's commitment in relation to its work in Lesotho. Lesotho has a population of 1.8 million, with almost one-third HIV positive. Gap has invested significantly in the manufacture of T-shirts in that country, as well as in community initiatives, for example in HIV testing and treatment to garment workers. It has also promoted forums to encourage the growth of the garment industry in that country.

The British pressure group, Labour Behind the Label, which campaigns to improve the working conditions of garment workers around the world, expressed its support for efforts being made by Gap to move towards more responsible sourcing of products. By deciding to manufacture the (PRODUCT) RED T-shirts in Lesotho, Gap had helped to safeguard workers' livelihoods there at a time when other companies were increasingly sourcing garments from China and India:

> While GAP, like all clothing companies, is a long way from resolving all workers' rights issues in its supply chain, it has come further than many. Whilst we would like to see initiatives like RED being more comprehensive in their attitude towards combining charity and political change, so far indications suggest that the way the RED T-shirt has been put together could be a positive step for the African garment industry as well as for the fight against AIDS.[4]

Others were less supportive. A parodying website, mirroring the Gap advertising, was set up by protesters in San Francisco. It urged people to support causes directly, rather than via shopping. Its message: 'Shopping is not a solution. Buy (Less). Give More. Join us in rejecting the ti(red) notion that shopping is a reasonable response to human suffering.'

And in October 2006 there was a lengthy critique in *The Times*:[5]

> GAP, America's still-trendy mass-market clothing retailer, is winning plaudits over here for its new campaign . . . designed to generate awareness and money to alleviate suffering in Africa. . . . It is pledging to give half of the profits from its iconic red T-shirts and leather jackets to Aids/HIV relief. The campaign was launched here last week, with the always crucial imprimatur of Hollywood. It features stars such as Steven Spielberg and Penelope Cruz in red T-shirts with one-word messages that say, with a modesty that doesn't fit quite as well as the clothes, INSPI(RED) and ADMI(RED). The message is that, by buying these products, ordinary mortals such as you and I (well, all right, you) can look like Hollywood stars and save lives in Africa too. You can almost taste the pity and charity oozing from Ms Cruz's pouted lips, the love pouring from Mr Spielberg's dewy eyes.
>
> Sorry to play the curmudgeon here. But this latest concession to the galloping forces of corporate social responsibility, far from helping the benighted of the world, is actually going to make things worse. I am sick and TI(RED) of companies trying to demonstrate to me how seriously they take their supposed duty to bring joy to and remove pain from the world. They can take their charge card (S, CREWnecks and mobile phones and ask THEMSELVES) whether this is really the sort of thing they should be doing with their shareholders' money.
>
> Now I don't here intend to demean the charitable spirit or the work of good people such as Bono or Bob Geldof, nor the perfectly decent motivation of millions in the wealthy

Photo: M. Spencer Green/AP/PA Photos

Bono and Oprah promoting Gap

world who genuinely want to help to improve the wretched lives of those less fortunate than themselves. Don't get me wrong; charity remains one of the finest of virtues and should, in almost all instances, be encouraged.

Nor am I going to point out the nauseating conspicuousness of the consumption represented by the RED campaign ('Look,' it says, 'I not only look good. I AM good!'). Nor am I even going to dwell on the fact, though I could, that for all the aid Africa has received over the past 50 years, the continent remains poorer than ever, and certainly poorer than parts of the world that have received little in the way of charity in that time.

My problem here is with what this does for the very idea of capitalism, for companies pursuing their real and entirely wholesome responsibility of making money. Free market capitalism, untrammelled by marketing people in alliance with special interest groups on a mission to save the world, has done more to alleviate poverty than any well-intentioned anti-poverty campaign in the history of the globe.

By concentrating on selling quality, low-priced goods, some of them made with labour that would otherwise lie idle (and dying) in the developing world, Gap saves lives. By helping to keep prices down and generating profits, Gap ploughs money back into the pockets of people in the US, the UK and elsewhere. Which creates the demand for imports of products from the developing world. Which keeps the poor of those countries from suffering even more than they do now.

In a complex world, we all operate in a division of labour. Companies make profits. It is what they are designed to do. It is what they do best. When they depart from that mission, they lead their employees and their shareholders down a long, slow route to perdition.

You think that is over the top? What is most troubling about campaigns such as Product Red is that they represent an accommodation with groups who think the business of capitalism is fundamentally evil. By appeasing people who regard globalisation as a process of exploitation, companies such as Gap are making the world much worse for all of us. They are implicitly acknowledging that their main business – selling things that people want for a profit – is inherently immoral and needs to be expiated by an occasional show of real goodness.

Rather than resisting it, they are nurturing and feeding an anti-business sentiment that will impoverish us all. What's more, this encroachment by companies is fundamentally undemocratic. Companies should not collude with interest groups and non-governmental organisations to decide on public priorities. That is for free people, through their elected governments, to do.

None of this is to say companies – or the people who run them – should not behave morally. They should observe not only the law, but the highest ethical standards, which means honesty, straight dealing and openness. It might even at times be in their corporate interests (ie, longer-term profitability) to contribute to political or charitable causes – in those cases shareholders can and should vote on the appropriation of funds for such purposes.

But shareholders – all of us – should be concerned when managements decide, for whatever reason, to make common cause with those who oppose the very principles on which their business is conducted. That represents a case of misguided corporate BULLS(HIT) TING the wrong target.

Notes

1. *Source*: (PRODUCT) RED website http://joinred.blogspot.com/.
2. M. Frazier, 'Costly Red Campaign reaps meager $18m', *Advertising Age*, vol. 78, no. 10 (5 March 2007).
3. P. Vallely, 'The Big Question: Does the RED campaign help big Western brands more than Africa', *Independent*, p. 50, 9 March (2007). Copyright The Independent, 9.3.07.
4. *Source*: http://www.labourbehindthelabel.org/content/view/67/51/.
5. Gerard Baker, 'Mind the Gap – with this attack on globalisation', *The Times*, 24 October (2006). © Gerard Baker/N.I. Syndication Limited, 24.10.06.

Questions

1 What is the rationale of:
   (a) The founders of (PRODUCT) RED?
   (b) Dan Henkle and Gap?
   (c) The author of the article in *The Times*?

2 What views might shareholders of Gap have of its involvement in (PRODUCT) RED?

3 In your view is (PRODUCT) RED an appropriate corporate activity?

4 If you were a shareholder of a company and wished to persuade top management to join the (PRODUCT) RED initiative, how might you do this? (Use stakeholder analysis as a means of considering this.)

5

Culture and Strategy

LEARNING OUTCOMES

When you have read this chapter you should be able to:

- → Identify organisations that have experienced strategic drift and recognise the symptoms of strategic drift.
- → Analyse the influence of an organisation's culture on its strategy using the cultural web.
- → Recognise the importance of strategists questioning the taken-for-granted aspects of a culture.

Photo: Grant Pritchard/Britain on View

5.1 INTRODUCTION

Chapters 2, 3 and 4 have considered the important influences of the environment, organisational capabilities and stakeholder expectations on the development of strategy.

A cultural perspective can also help an understanding of both opportunities and constraints that organisations face, many of which are also discussed in other chapters of this book. In particular the capabilities of an organisation (Chapter 3), especially those that provide organisations with competitive advantage, may have built up over time. In so doing, such capabilities may become part of the culture of an organization – the taken-for-granted way of doing things – therefore difficult for other organisations to copy. However, they may also be difficult to change. So understanding the cultural basis of such capabilities also informs the challenges of strategic change (see Chapter 10). The powers and influence of different stakeholders are also likely to have historical origins that are important to understand. The theme of this chapter is,

Exhibit 5.1 Chapter themes

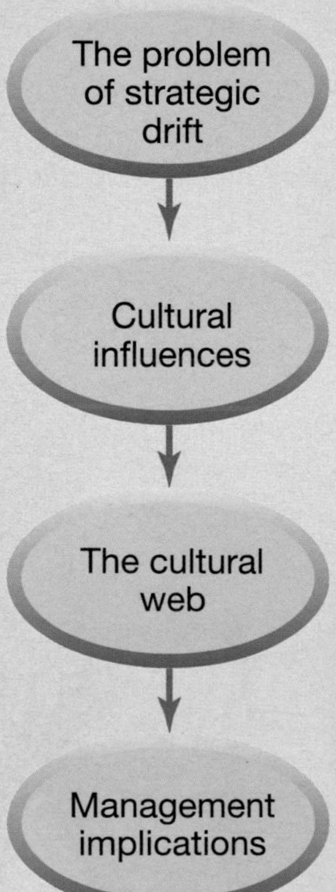

then, that the strategic position of an organisation has cultural roots and that understanding those roots helps managers develop the future strategy of their organisations.

The chapter begins by explaining the phenomenon of strategic drift that highlights the importance of culture in relation to strategy development and identifies important challenges managers face in managing that development. Section 5.3 then explains what is meant by culture and how cultural influences at the national, institutional and organisational levels influence current and future strategy. It then suggests how a culture can be analysed and its influence on strategy understood. Exhibit 5.1 summarises the chapter themes.

5.2 STRATEGIC DRIFT

Strategic drift is the tendency for strategies to develop incrementally on the basis of historical and cultural influences but which fail to keep pace with a changing environment

Historical studies of organisations have shown a pattern that is represented in Exhibit 5.2. **Strategic drift**[1] is the tendency for strategies to develop incrementally on the basis of historical and cultural influences, but which fail to keep pace with a changing environment. An example of strategic drift is given in Illustration 5.1. The reasons and consequences of strategic drift are important to understand, not only because it is common, but because it helps explain why organisations often 'run out of steam'. It also highlights some significant challenges for managers which, in turn, points to some important lessons.

Exhibit 5.2 Strategic drift

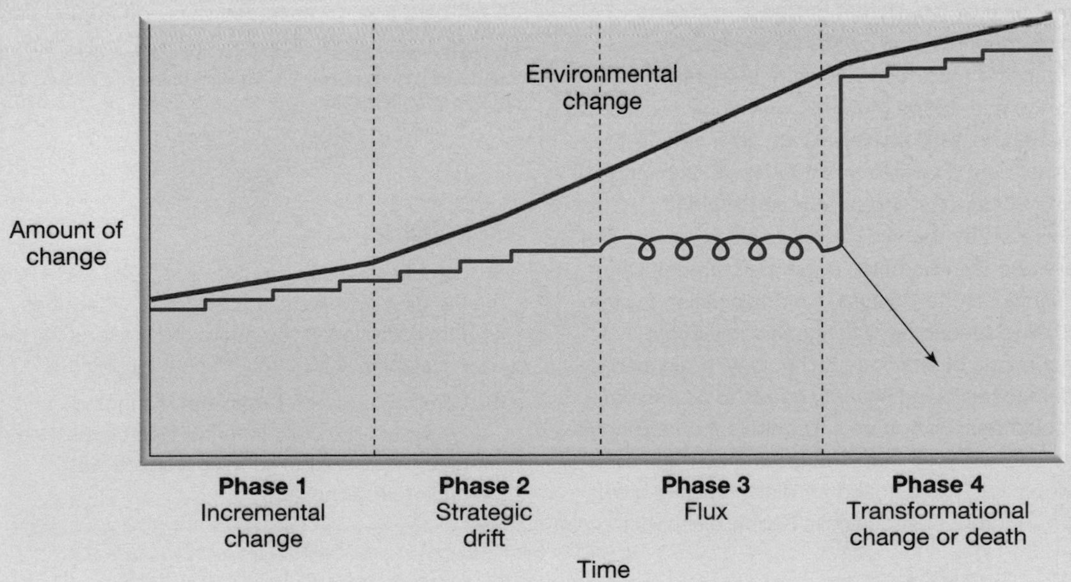

Illustration 5.1

Motorola: an analogue history facing a digital revolution

The bases of a firm's success may in turn be a cause of strategic drift.

In 1994 Motorola had 60 per cent of the US mobile telephone market. Founded in 1928, it was known for its technological innovation. It introduced the two-way walkie-talkie radio device commonly used in the Second World War, it marketed the first television to sell for under $200 in 1948. By the 1950s it had developed capabilities in printed circuit, ceramic substrate technology and electronic system design. By the 1970s it was a leading producer of microprocessors and was regarded as a world leader in technology.

However, even in the early days it was evident that the emphasis was on technology, rather than the market. Critics suggested that the firm put technology before consumers.

Mobile phones had been developed by Bell Labs in the 1970s. By the mid-1980s Motorola was the leading producer of cell phones using analogue technology, but none the less a logical progression from its military walkie-talkie systems using the post-war technology it had developed. However, these devices were bulky and expensive, targeted at business managers who were on the move and could not use landlines. The phones were not widely known or available.

By the mid-1990s Motorola was highly successful. From 1992 to 1995 sales revenue grew at an average of 27 per cent a year to reach $27bn (€22bn) and net income 58 per cent a year to reach $1.8bn.

However, by the mid-1990s digital technology for mobile phones was being developed through what was known as the Personal Communication System (PCS). This technology overcame some of the shortcomings of analogue technology. It reduced interference, allowed security codes to be encrypted and could deal with more subscribers than analogue. It was a technology that supported mass market development. The demand for digital phones grew rapidly, not amongst business people alone, but amongst a wider consumer market. These consumers were much less concerned about functionality and much more concerned about ease of use and aesthetic appeal.

According to a Motorola chief executive of the time, Robert Galvin, the company 'was at the forefront of the development of digital technology'. However, it chose to stay with analogue technology for many years, licensing its digital to Nokia and Ericsson through which it earned increasing royalties. Indeed Motorola launched a new analogue phone, Star-TAC, and embarked on an aggressive marketing campaign to promote it.

Not only was it clear from the growing royalties that digital phones were taking off, wireless carrier customers were lobbying Motorola to develop digital phones: 'They told us we didn't know what we were talking about. . . . These were not friendly conversations. But Motorola didn't do it. Instead we launched with Ericsson, then Nokia.'

By 1998 Motorola's market share had dropped to 34 per cent and it was forced to lay off 20,000 people.

Source: Adapted from S. Finkelstein, 'Why smart executives fail: four case histories of how people learn the wrong lessons from history', *Business History*, vol. 48, no. 2 (2006), pp. 153–170.

Questions

1 Identify on a timeline between 1928 and 1998 the major events identified here. What does this analysis tell you about the reasons for the resistance of Motorola to new technology?

2 Given that Motorola had the technology and knew that the digital market was developing, give reasons as to why it persisted with analogue technology.

5.2.1 Strategies change incrementally

www.pearsoned.co.uk/fos
KEY CONCEPT
Strategic drift

Strategies of organisations tend to change gradually, developing on the basis of what the organisation has done in the past – especially if that has been successful. For example Sainsbury's was one of the most successful retailers in the world for decades till the early 1990s, with its formula of selling food of a higher quality than competitors at reasonable prices. Always under the patriarchal guidance of a Sainsbury family chief executive it gradually extended its product lines, enlarged its stores and its geographical coverage, but it did not deviate from its tried and tested ways of doing business. This is shown in phase 1 of Exhibit 5.2. In most successful businesses there are usually long periods of relative *continuity* during which established strategy remains largely unchanged or changes very *incrementally*. There are three main reasons for this.

- *Alignment with environmental change*. It could well be that the environment, particularly the market, is changing gradually and the organisation is keeping in line with those changes by such incremental change. It would make no sense for the strategy to change dramatically when the market is not doing so.
- *The success of the past*. There may be a natural unwillingness by managers to change a strategy significantly if it has been successful in the past, especially if it is built on capabilities that have been shown to be the basis of competitive advantage (see Chapters 3 and 6) or of innovation.
- *Experimentation around a theme*. Indeed managers may have learned how to build variations around their successful formula; in effect experimenting without moving too far from their capability base.

This poses challenges for managers however. For how long and to what extent can they rely on incremental change building on the past being sufficient? When should they make more fundamental strategic changes? How are they to detect when this is necessary?

5.2.2 The tendency towards strategic drift

Whilst an organisation's strategy may continue to change incrementally, it may not change in line with the environment. This does not necessarily mean that there has to be dramatic environmental changes; phase 2 of Exhibit 5.2 shows environmental change accelerating, but it is not sudden. For Sainsbury's there was the growing share of its rival, Tesco, accompanied by the growth of larger size stores, with wider ranges of goods (for example, non-food) and changes in distribution logistics of competitors. These changes, however, had been taking place for many years. The problem that gives rise to strategic drift is that, as with many organisations, Sainsbury's strategy was not keeping pace with these changes. There are at least five reasons for this:

- *The problem of hindsight*. Chapter 2 has provided ways of analysing the environment and such analyses may yield insights. But how are managers to be sure of the direction and significance of such changes? Or changes may be seen as temporary. Managers may be understandably wary of changing what they are likely to see as a winning strategy on the basis of what might only be a fad in the market, or a temporary downturn in demand. It may be easy to see major changes with hindsight, but it may not be so easy to see their significance as they are happening.
- *Building on the familiar*. Managers may see changes in the environment about which they are uncertain or which they do not entirely understand. In these circumstances they may try to minimise the extent to which they are faced with such uncertainty by looking for answers that are familiar, which they understand and which have served them well in the past. This will lead to a bias towards continued incremental strategic change. For example, Sainsbury managers clung to the belief that they had loyal customers who valued the superior quality of Sainsbury goods. Tesco had been a cheaper retailer with what they saw as inferior goods. Surely the superior quality of Sainsbury would continue to be recognised.
- *Core rigidities*. As Chapter 3 explains, success in the past may well have been based on capabilities that are unique to an organisation and difficult for others to copy. However the capabilities that have been bases of advantage can become difficult to change; in effect *core rigidities*. There are two reasons. First, over time, the ways of doing things that have delivered past success may become taken for granted. This may well have been an advantage in the past because it was difficult for competitors to imitate them. However, taken for granted core competences rarely get questioned and therefore tend to persist beyond their usefulness. Second, ways of doing things develop over time and become more and more embedded in organisational routines that reinforce and rely on each other and are difficult to unravel.
- *Relationships become shackles*.[2] Success has probably been built on the basis of excellent relationships with customers, suppliers and employees. Maintaining these may very likely be seen as fundamental to the long-term health of the organisation. Yet these relationships may make it difficult to make fundamental changes to strategy that could entail changing routes to market or the customer base, developing products requiring different suppliers or changing the skill base of the organisation with the risk of disrupting relationships with the workforce.
- *Lagged performance effects*. The effects of such drift may not be easy to see in terms of the performance of the organisation. Financial performance may continue to hold up in the early stages of strategic drift. Customers may be loyal and the organisation, by becoming more efficient, cutting costs or simply trying harder, may continue to hold up its performance. So there may not be internal signals of the need for change or pressures from managers or, indeed, external observers to make major changes.

However over time, if strategic drift continues, there will be symptoms that become evident: a downturn in financial performance; a loss in market share to competitors perhaps; a decline in the share price. Indeed such a downturn may happen quite rapidly once external observers, not least competitors and financial analysts, have identified that such drift has occurred. Even the most successful companies may drift in this way. They become captured by the formula that has delivered that success.

5.2.3 A period of flux

The next phase (phase 3) may be a period of *flux* triggered by the downturn in performance. Strategies may change but in no very clear direction. There may also be management changes, often at the very top as the organisation comes under pressure to make changes from its stakeholders, not least shareholders in the case of a public company. There may be internal rivalry as to which strategy to follow, quite likely based on differences of opinion as to whether future strategy should be based on historic capabilities or whether those capabilities are becoming redundant. Indeed, there have been highly publicised boardroom rows when this has happened. All this may result in a further deterioration of confidence in the organisation: perhaps a further drop in performance or share price, a difficulty in recruiting high-quality management, or a further loss of customers' loyalty.

5.2.4 Transformational change or death

As things get worse it is likely that the outcome (phase 4) will be one of three possibilities: (i) the organisation may die (in the case of a commercial organisation it may go into receivership, for example); (ii) it may get taken over by another organisation; or (iii) it may go through a period of *transformational change*. Such change could take form in multiple changes related to the organisation's strategy. For example, a change in products, markets or market focus, changes of capabilities on which the strategy is based, changes in the top management of the organisation and perhaps the way the organisation is structured.

Transformational change does not take place frequently in organisations and is usually the result of a major downturn in performance. Often it is transformational changes that are heralded as the success stories of top executives; this is where they most visibly make a difference. The problem is that, from the point of view of market position, shareholder wealth and jobs, it may be rather too late. Competitive position may have been lost, shareholder value has probably already been destroyed and, very likely, many jobs will have been lost too. The time when 'making a difference' really matters most is in stage 2 in Exhibit 5.1, when the organisation is beginning to drift. The problem is that, very likely, such drift is not easy to see before performance suffers. So in understanding the strategic position of an organisation so as to avoid the damaging effects of strategic drift, it is vital to take seriously the extent to which historical tendencies in strategy development tend to persist in the cultural fabric of organisations. The rest of this chapter focuses on this.

5.3 WHAT IS CULTURE AND WHY IS IT IMPORTANT?

Organisational culture is the 'basic *assumptions and beliefs* that are shared by members of an organisation, that operate unconsciously and define in a basic taken-for-granted fashion an organisation's view of itself and its environment'

Edgar Schein defines **organisational culture** as the 'basic *assumptions and beliefs* that are shared by members of an organisation, that operate unconsciously and define in a basic taken-for-granted fashion an organisation's view of itself and its environment'.[3] Related to this are taken-for-granted ways of doing things, the routines, that accumulate over time. In other words, culture is about that which is taken for granted but nonetheless contributes to how groups of people respond and behave in relation to issues they face. It therefore has important influences on the development and change of organisational strategy.

In fact cultural influences exist at multiple levels as Exhibit 5.3 shows. The sections that follow will identify the important factors and issues in terms

Exhibit 5.3 Cultural frames of reference

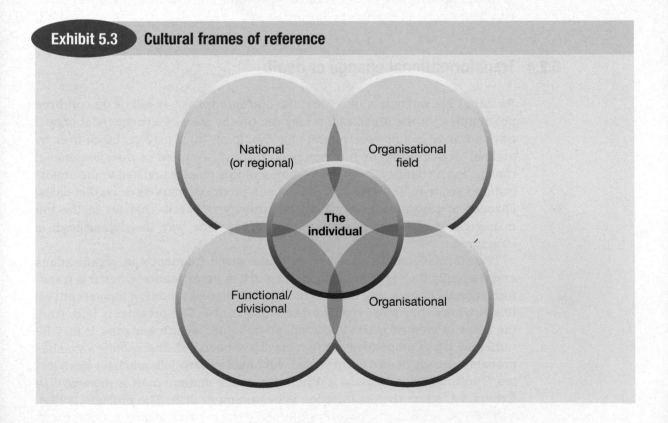

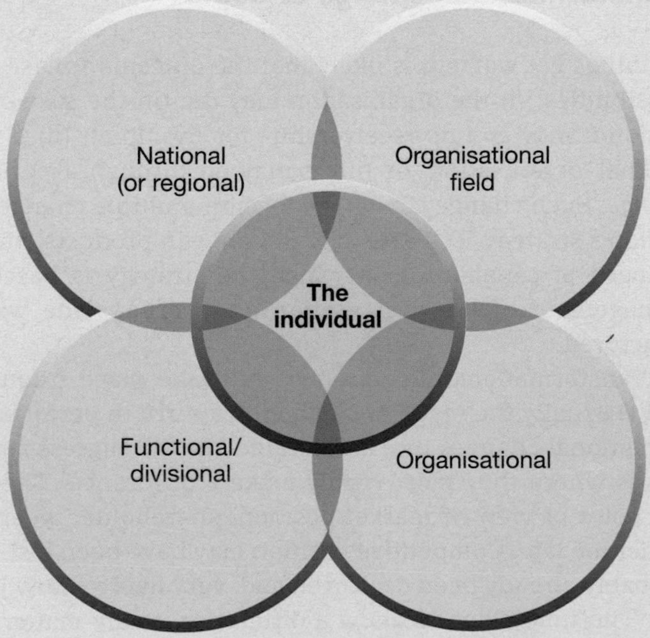

www.pearsoned.co.uk/fos
KEY CONCEPT
Organisational culture and cultural web

of different cultural frames of reference and then show how organisational culture can be analysed and characterised as a means of understanding the influences of culture on both current and future organisational purposes and strategies.

5.3.1 National and regional cultures

Many writers, perhaps the most well known of which is Geert Hofstede,[4] have shown how attitudes to work, authority, equality and other important factors differ from one country to another. Such differences have been shaped by powerful cultural forces concerned with history, religion and even climate over many centuries. Organisations that operate internationally need to understand and cope with such differences that can manifest themselves in terms of different standards, values and expectations in the various countries in which they operate.[5] For example, Euro Disney's attempt to replicate the success of the Disney theme parks in the US was termed 'cultural imperialism' in the French media and has experienced difficulties. There was a decline in visitors of 0.3 per cent a year between 1999 and 2005. Illustration 5.2 also shows how cultural differences can pose challenges for managers seeking to develop markets in China.

Although they are not shown separately in Exhibit 5.3 (for reasons of simplification), it may also be important to understand *subnational* (usually regional) cultures. For example, attitudes to some aspects of employment and supplier relationships may differ at a regional level even in a relatively small and cohesive country like the UK, and quite markedly elsewhere in Europe (for example, between northern and southern Italy). There may also be differences between urban and rural locations.

5.3.2 Organisational culture

The culture of an organisation is often conceived as consisting of four layers (see Exhibit 5.4).

- *Values* may be easy to identify in an organisation, and are often written down as statements about an organisation's mission, objectives or strategies (see section 4.5). However, they can be vague, such as 'service to the community' or 'honouring equal employment opportunities'.
- *Beliefs* are more specific, but may not be written down, rather discerned in how people talk about issues the organisation faces; for example a belief that the company should not trade with particular countries, or that professional staff should not have their professional actions appraised by managers.

Both with regard to values and beliefs it is important to remember that in relation to culture, the concern is with the collective rather than individuals'

Illustration 5.2

When in China . . .

As Western firms move into China, understanding Chinese ways of doing business becomes crucial.

David Hands has operated in Beijing for real estate firm Jones Lang Lasalle (JLL), where he had to develop the business in China. *Management Today* reported an interview with him:

> There are a huge number of opportunities in China but it's crucial to sort the wheat from the chaff and you need to work on efficiency to do that. For example, we had problems with time management in the early stages. Imagine trying to set up a meeting where everybody is turning up at different times, and where nobody has thought to specify an agenda for the meeting. Or there will be three multi-hour meetings for a client who barely gives us any business. It was tough to make people understand the importance of breaking down costs versus benefits.

It took time to get the Chinese to value the advice that JLL could provide because, whilst they are accustomed to paying for goods, paying for services came as a culture shock:

> You have to learn to go step by step and give a little. You can't turn up at someone's office and say: 'Pay me a large amount of money in advance'. And you have to really show them where you can add value to their operations.

There are also problems of understanding hierarchy:

> You may think you are dealing with the top guy and he is asking you for a discount. You give him one. But then you meet up with another five managers in gradually ascending order and they all ask for discounts. So beware!

The symbols of hierarchy are not the same either. Unlike in some Western countries where status symbols such as car and clothing brands may signify status, in China senior management are likely to dress 'more drably':

> Cheap clothing is important in a culture plagued by corruption: dressing down diverts attention from any ill-gotten gains, but the head honcho still wants to assert his authority and one way he does that is by having an entourage of flunkies. . . . I learnt early on that if I didn't reciprocate by going to meetings with one or more assistants, people would just take me less seriously.

To the Westerner there may also seem to be a lack of courtesy: 'They basically think they own you, in the same way as they own a car or luxury watch after they have paid for them.'

Staff relationships to the boss are also more important than staff relationships to the company: 'That's why you'll find staff cleaning their boss' cars on the weekend. We have to teach staff that this will not earn them promotion . . .'.

Another interviewee had experience of Chinese bureaucracy:

> When you are negotiating with the government you need to find somebody who feels you can help him personally benefit from the deal. Once your interests are aligned, he can then guide you through the maze. . . . It's not a matter of getting somebody's name card and going out for a drink. In China you have to earn that person's gratitude and trust and you do that by doing them favours. The bigger the favour, the more they will help you professionally as well as privately.

Source: D. Slater, 'When in China . . .', *Management Today*, May (2006). Reproduced from *Management Today* magazine with the permission of the copyright owner, Haymarket Business Publications Limited.

Questions

1. On the evidence of these interviews identify how the cultural norms and taken-for-granted assumptions of Chinese managers differ from those of Western managers.
2. If you are seeking to operate in a country with a very different culture, other than talking with people experienced in that market, how else would you set about trying to understand the culture and its underlying assumptions?

Exhibit 5.4 Culture in four layers

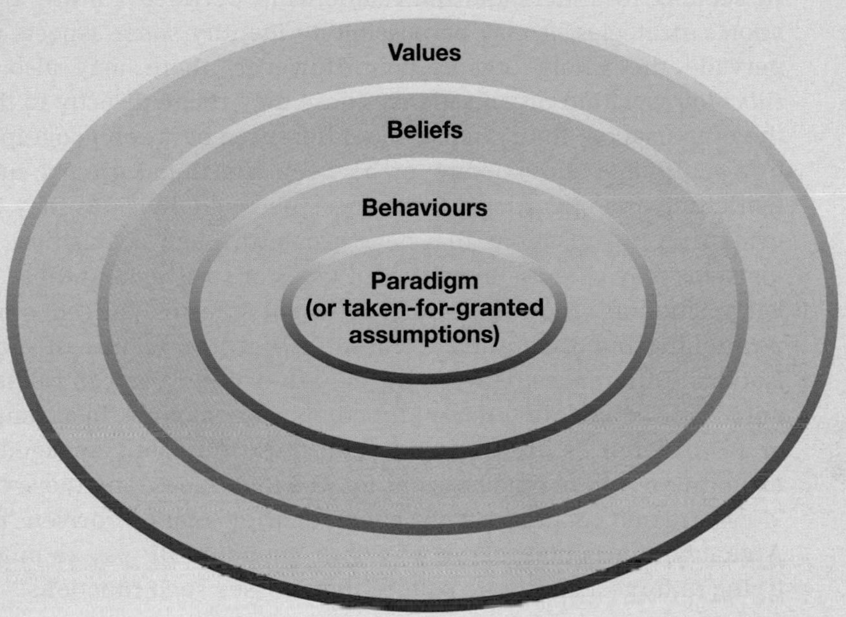

values and beliefs. Indeed it may be that individuals in organisations have values and beliefs that at times run counter to their organisations, which can give rise to ethical tensions and problems.

- *Behaviours* are the day-to-day way in which an organisation operates and can be seen by people both inside and outside the organisation. This includes the work routines, how the organisation is structured and controlled and 'softer' issues around symbolic behaviours.
- *Taken-for-granted assumptions* are the core of an organisation's culture. They are the aspects of organisational life which people find difficult to identify and explain. Here they are referred to as the organisational paradigm. The **paradigm** is the set of assumptions held in common and taken for granted in an organisation. For an organisation to operate effectively there is bound to be such a generally accepted set of assumptions. As mentioned above, these assumptions represent *collective experience* without which people would have to 'reinvent their world' for different circumstances that they face. The paradigm can underpin successful strategies by providing a basis of common understanding in an organisation, but can also be a major problem, for example when major strategic change is needed, or when organisations try to merge and find they are incompatible. The importance of the paradigm is discussed further in section 5.3.5.

A **paradigm** is the set of assumptions held relatively in common and taken for granted in an organisation

5.3.3 Organisational subcultures

In seeking to understand the relationship between culture and an organisation's strategies, it may be possible to identify some aspects of culture that pervade the whole organisation. However, there may also be important *subcultures* within organisations. These may relate directly to the structure of the organisation: for example, the differences between geographical divisions in a multinational company, or between functional groups such as finance, marketing and operations. Differences between divisions may be particularly evident in organisations that have grown through acquisition. Also different divisions may be pursuing different types of strategy and these different market positionings require or foster different cultures. Indeed, aligning strategic positioning and organisational culture is a critical feature of successful organisations. Differences between business functions also can relate to the different nature of work in different functions. For example, in a company like Shell or BP differences are likely between those functions engaged in 'upstream' exploration, where time horizons may be in decades, and those concerned with 'downstream' retailing, with much shorter market driven time horizons. Arguably, this is one reason why both Shell and BP pay so much attention to trying to forge a corporate culture that crosses such functions.

5.3.4 Culture's influence on strategy

The taken for granted nature of culture is what makes it centrally important in relation to strategy and the management of strategy. There are two primary reasons for this.

- *Managing culture*. Because it is difficult to observe, identify and control that which is taken for granted, it is difficult to manage. This is why having a way to analyse culture so as to make it more evident is important – the subject of the next section.
- *Culture as a driver of strategy*. Organisations can be 'captured' by their culture and find it very difficult to change their strategy outside the bounds of that culture. Managers, faced with a changing business environment, are more likely to attempt to deal with the situation by searching for what they can understand and cope with in terms of the existing culture. The result is likely to be the incremental strategic change with the risk of eventual strategic drift explained in section 5.2. Culture is, in effect, an unintended driver of strategy.

The effect of culture on strategy is shown in Exhibit 5.5.[6] Faced with a stimulus for action, such as declining performance, managers first try to improve the implementation of existing strategy. This might be through trying to lower cost, improve efficiency, tighten controls or improve accepted way of doing things.

Exhibit 5.5 Culture's influence on strategy development

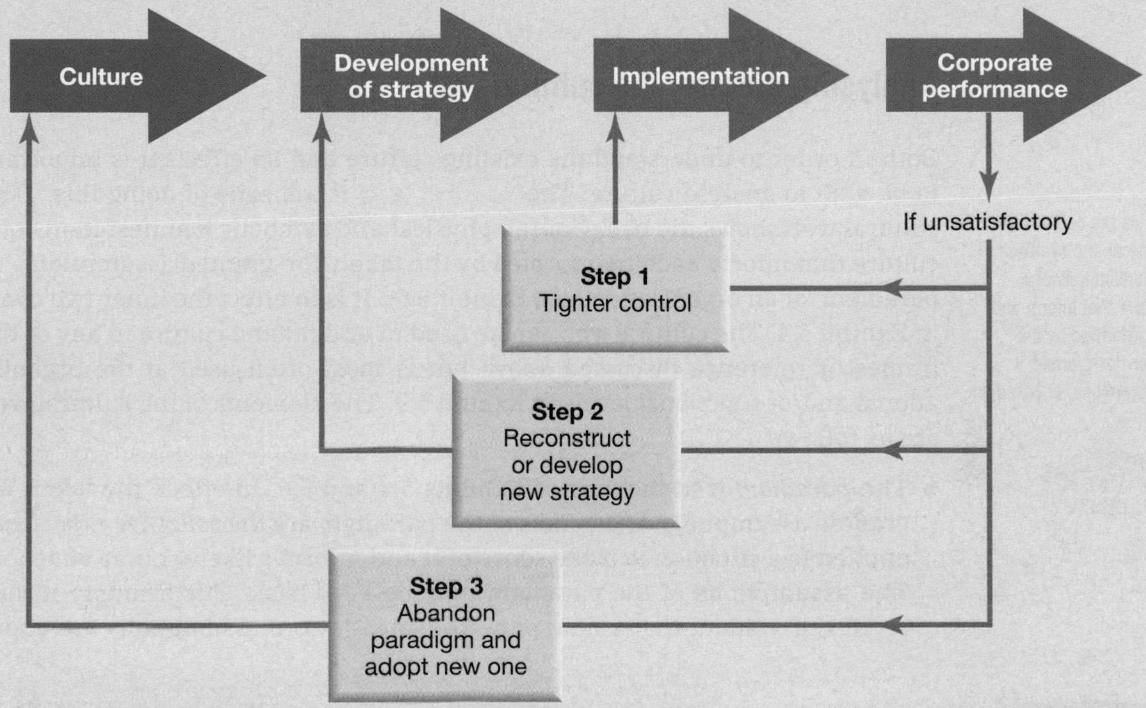

Source: Adapted from P. Grinyer and J.-C. Spender, *Turnaround: Managerial Recipes for Strategic Success*, Associated Business Press, 1979, p. 203.

If this is not effective, a change of strategy may occur, but in line with the existing culture. For example, managers may seek to extend the market for their business, but assume that it will be similar to their existing market, and therefore set about managing the new venture in much the same way as they have been used to. Alternatively, even where managers know intellectually that they need to change, indeed know technologically how to do so, they find themselves constrained by taken-for-granted organisational routines and assumptions or political processes, as seems likely in Illustration 5.1. This often happens, for example, when there are attempts to change highly bureaucratic organisations to be customer oriented. Even if people who accept intellectually the need to change a culture's emphasis on the importance of conforming to established rules, routines and reporting relationships, they do not readily do so. The notion that reasoned argument necessarily changes deeply embedded assumptions rooted in collective experience built up over long periods of time is flawed. Readers need only think of their own experience in trying to persuade others to rethink their religious beliefs or, indeed, allegiances to sports teams, to realise this. What occurs is the predominant application of the familiar and the attempt to avoid or reduce uncertainty or ambiguity. This is likely to continue until there is, perhaps, dramatic evidence of the redundancy of the culture, quite likely as the result of the organisation entering phases 3 or 4 of strategic drift (see Exhibit 5.2).

5.3.5 Analysing culture: the cultural web

The **cultural web** shows the behavioural, physical and symbolic manifestations of a culture that inform and are informed by the taken-for-granted assumptions, or paradigm

www.pearsoned.co.uk/fos KEY CONCEPT Organisational culture and cultural web

Both in order to understand the existing culture and its effects it is important to be able to analyse culture. The **cultural web** is a means of doing this.[7] The cultural web shows the behavioural, physical and symbolic manifestations of a culture that inform and are informed by the taken-for-granted assumptions, or paradigm, of an organisation (see Exhibit 5.6). It is in effect the inner two ovals in Exhibit 5.4. The cultural web can be used to understand culture in any of the frames of reference discussed above but is most often used at the organisational and/or functional levels in Exhibit 5.3. The elements of the cultural web are as follows:

- The *paradigm* is at the core of Exhibits 5.4 and 5.6. In effect, the taken for granted assumptions and beliefs of the paradigm are the *collective experience* applied to a situation to make sense of it and inform a likely course of action. The assumptions of the paradigm may be very basic. For example it may seem self-evident that a newspaper business's core assumptions are about

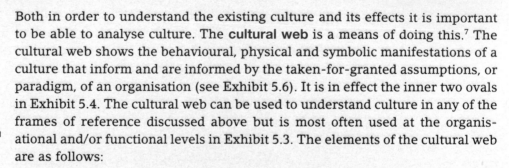

Exhibit 5.6 The cultural web of an organisation

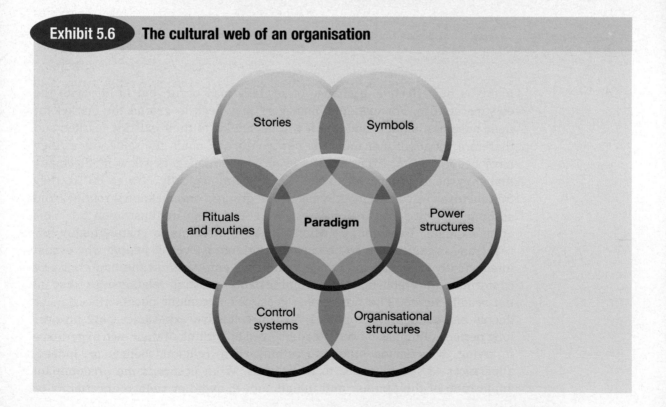

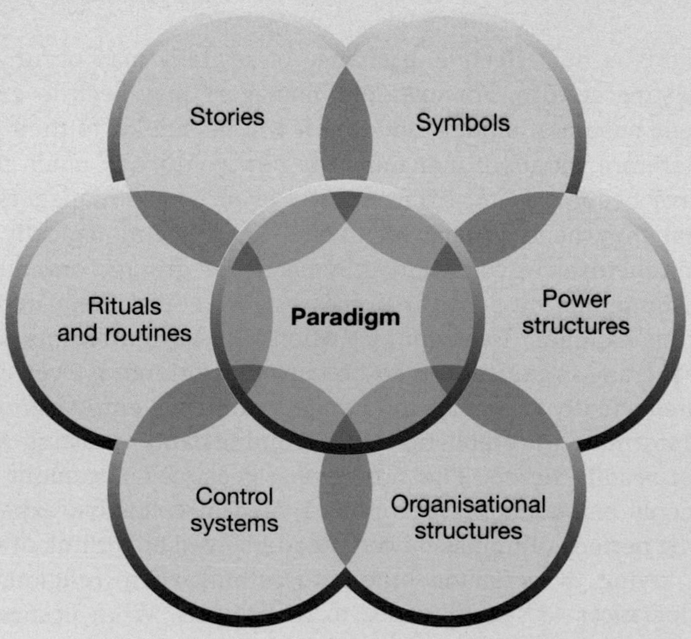

the centrality of news coverage and reporting. However, from a strategic point of view, increasingly newspapers' revenues are reliant on advertising income and the strategy may need to be directed to this. The paradigm of a charity may be about doing good works for the needy: but this cannot be achieved if it is not run effectively for the purpose of raising money. So understanding what the paradigm is and how it informs debate on strategy matters. The problem is that, since it is unlikely to be talked about, trying to identify it can be difficult, especially if you are part of that organisation. Outside observers may find it relatively easy to identify simply by listening to what people say and watching what they do and emphasise, but this may not be so easy for insiders who are part of the culture. One way of 'insiders' getting to see the assumptions they take for granted is to focus initially on other aspects of the cultural web because these are to do with more visible manifestations of culture. Moreover these other aspects are likely to act to reinforce the assumptions within that paradigm.

Routines are 'the way we do things around here on a day-to-day basis'

- **Routines** are 'the way we do things around here' on a day-to-day basis. These may have a long history and may well be common across organisations. At their best, these lubricate the working of the organisation, and may provide a distinctive organisational competence. However, they can also represent a taken-for-grantedness about how things should happen which, again, can be difficult to change.

Rituals are activities or events that emphasise, highlight or reinforce what is especially important in the culture

- **Rituals** of organisational life are activities or events that emphasise, highlight or reinforce what is especially important in the culture. Examples include training programmes, interview panels, promotion and assessment procedures, sales conferences and so on. An extreme example, of course, is the ritualistic training of army recruits to prepare them for the discipline required in conflict. However, rituals can also be informal activities such as drinks in the pub after work or gossiping around photocopying machines.
- The *stories*[8] told by members of an organisation to each other, to outsiders, to new recruits and so on, may act to embed the present in its organisational history and also flag up important events and personalities. They typically have to do with successes, disasters, heroes, villains and mavericks (who deviate from the norm). They can be a way of letting people know what is important in an organisation.

Symbols are objects, events, acts or people that convey, maintain or create meaning over and above their functional purpose

- **Symbols**[9] are objects, events, acts or people that convey, maintain or create meaning over and above their functional purpose. For example offices and office layout, cars and titles have a functional purpose, but are also typically signals about status and hierarchy. Particular people, may come to represent specially important aspects of an organisation or historic turning points. The form of language used in an organisation can also be particularly revealing, especially with regard to customers or clients. For example, the head of a consumer protection agency in Australia described his clients as 'complainers'. In a major teaching hospital in the UK, consultants described patients as 'clinical material'. Whilst such examples might be amusing, they reveal an underlying assumption about customers (or patients) that might play a significant role in influencing the strategy of an organisation. Although symbols are shown separately in the cultural web, it should be remembered that many elements of the web are symbolic. So, routines, control and reward systems and structures are not only functional but also symbolic.

- *Power structures*. The most powerful groupings within an organisation are likely to be closely associated with the core assumptions and beliefs. For example, in firms that experience strategic drift, it is not unusual to find powerful executives who have long association with long established ways of doing things. In analysing power the guidance given in section 4.4.1 is useful.
- *Organisational structure* is likely to reflect power and show important roles and relationships. Formal hierarchical, mechanistic structures may emphasise that strategy is the province of top managers and everyone else is 'working to orders'. Highly devolved structures may signify that collaboration is less important than competition and so on.
- *Control systems*, measurements and reward systems emphasise what is important to monitor in the organisation. For example, public service organisations have often been accused of being concerned more with stewardship of funds than with quality of service. This is reflected in their procedures, which are more about accounting for spending rather than with quality of service. Individually based bonus schemes related to volume is likely to signal a culture of individuality, internal competition and an emphasis on sales volume rather than teamwork and an emphasis on quality.

Illustration 5.3 shows a cultural web drawn up by managers and staff in the Forestry Commission of the UK as part of a strategy development programme, together with a commentary on the significance of its elements. The key point to emerge was that at a time when this public body was charged with changing strategy towards opening up forests to the public, they saw themselves as technical experts and the public as a nuisance. Similar problems can often emerge through such an analysis. A cultural web analysis for an accountancy firm espousing closeness to clients as central to their strategy revealed a culture of 'partner care and centrality', rather than clients. Perhaps most significant, politicians and managers of the British Labour Party undertook a cultural web analysis in the mid-1990s prior to their election victory of 1997. It revealed a party culturally 'built to oppose', as it had done with every government in power through its history – including Labour governments! Not surprisingly, Tony Blair, who became Prime Minister, saw culture change of the party as a major necessity.

5.3.6 Undertaking cultural analysis

If an analysis of the culture of an organisation is to be undertaken, there are some important issues to bear in mind:

Illustration 5.3

The cultural web of the UK Forestry Commission

The cultural web can be used to identify the behaviours and taken-for-granted assumptions of an organisation.

This is an adapted version of a cultural web produced by managers and staff of the UK Forestry Commission. The Forestry Commission (FC) was a public sector organisation charged with managing the forests of the UK.

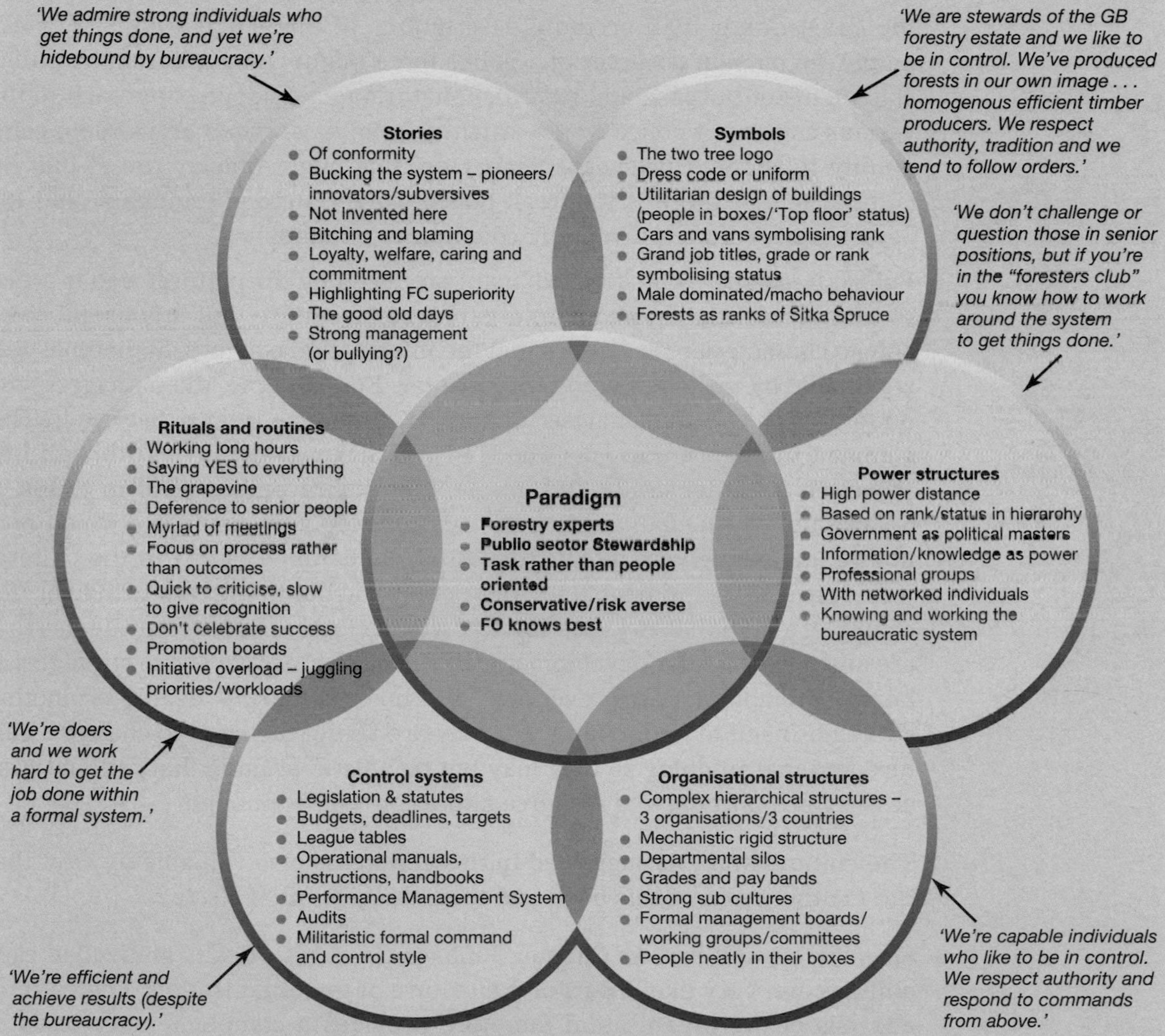

Source: Adapted from The Forestry Commission case study by Anne McCann.

Questions

1 How would you characterise the dominant culture here?

2 What are the strategic implications?

- *The questions to ask*. Exhibit 5.7 outlines some of the questions that might help build up an understanding of culture using the cultural web.
- *Statements of cultural values*. As organisations increasingly make visible often carefully considered public statements of their values, beliefs and purposes – for example, in annual reports, mission or values statements and business plans – there is a danger that these are seen as useful and accurate descriptions of the organisational culture. But this is likely to be at best only partially true, and at worst misleading. This is not to suggest that there is any organised deception. It is simply that the statements of values and beliefs are often statements of the aspirations of a particular stakeholder (such as the CEO) rather than accurate descriptions of the actual culture. For example, an outside observer of a police force might conclude from its public statements of purpose and priorities that it had a balanced approach to the various aspects of police work – catching criminals, crime prevention, community relations. However, a deeper probing might quickly reveal that (in cultural terms) there is the 'real' police work (catching criminals) and the 'lesser work' (crime prevention, community relations).
- *Pulling it together*. The detailed 'map' produced by the cultural web is a rich source of information about an organisation's culture, but it is useful to be able to characterise the culture that the information conveys. Sometimes this is possible by means of graphic descriptor. For example, the managers who undertook a cultural analysis in the UK National Health Service (NHS) summed up their culture as 'The National Sickness Service'. Although this approach is rather crude and unscientific, it can be powerful in terms of organisational members seeing the organisation as it really is – which may not be immediately apparent from all of the detailed points in the cultural web. It can also help people to understand that culture drives strategies; for example, a 'national sickness service' would clearly prioritise strategies that are about spectacular developments in curing sick people above strategies of health promotion and prevention. So those favouring health promotion strategies need to understand that they are facing the need to change a culture and that in doing so they may not be able to assume that rational processes like planning and resource allocation will be enough.

The cultural analysis suggested in this chapter is also valuable in ways that relate to other parts of this book and the management of strategy:

- *Strategic capabilities*. As Chapter 3 makes clear, historically embedded capabilities are, very likely, part of the culture of the organisation. The cultural analysis of the organisation therefore provides a complementary basis of analysis to an examination of strategic capabilities (see Chapter 3). In effect, such an analysis of capabilities should end up digging into the culture of the organisation, especially in terms of its routines, control systems and the everyday way in which the organisation runs, very likely on a 'taken-for-granted' basis.

Exhibit 5.7 The cultural web: some useful questions

Stories
- What core beliefs do stories reflect?
- How pervasive are these beliefs (through levels)?
- Do stories relate to:
  - strengths or weaknesses?
  - successes or failures?
  - conformity or mavericks?
- Who are the heroes and villains?
- What norms do the mavericks deviate from?

Symbols
- Are there particular symbols which denote the organisation?
- What status symbols are there?
- What does the language and jargon signify?
- What aspects of strategy are highlighted in publicity?

Routines and rituals
- Which routines are emphasised?
- Which are embedded in history?
- What behaviour do routines encourage?
- What are the key rituals?
- What core beliefs do they reflect?
- What do training programmes emphasise?
- How easy are rituals/routines to change?

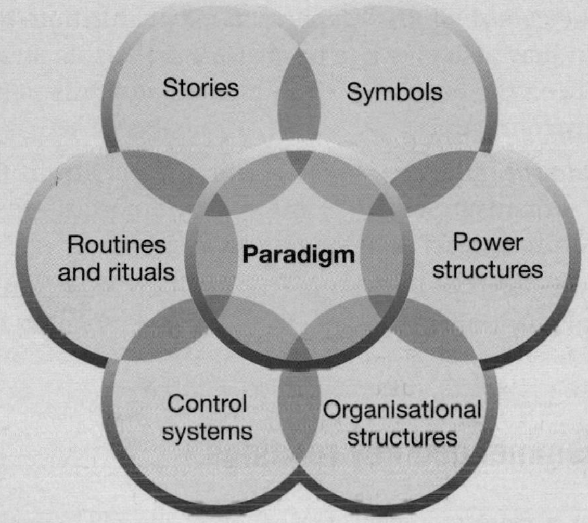

Power structures
- How is power distributed in the organisation?
- What are the core assumptions and beliefs of the leadership?
- How strongly held are these beliefs (idealists or pragmatists)?
- Where are the main power blockages to change?

Control systems
- What is most closely monitored/controlled?
- Is emphasis on reward or punishment?
- Are controls related to history or current strategies?
- Are there many/few controls?

Organisational structures
- How mechanistic/organic are the structures?
- How flat/hierarchical are the structures?
- How formal/informal are the structures?
- Do structures encourage collaboration or competition?
- What types of power structure do they support?

Overall
- What do the answers to these questions suggest are the (four) fundamental assumptions that are the paradigm?
- How would you characterise the dominant culture?
- How easy is this to change?

- *Strategy development*. An understanding of organisational culture sensitises managers to the way in which historical and cultural influences will likely affect future strategy for good or ill.
- *Managing strategic change*. An analysis of the culture also provides a basis for the management of strategic change, since it provides a picture of the existing culture that can be set against a desired strategy so as to give insights as to what may constrain the development of that strategy or what needs to be changed in order to achieve it (see section 10.4).

SUMMARY

www.pearsoned.co.uk/fos AUDIO SUMMARY

- The *culture* of an organisation may contribute to its strategic capabilities, but may also give rise to *strategic drift* as its strategy develops incrementally on the basis of such influences and fails to keep pace with a changing environment.
- *Cultural influences* both inform and constrain the strategic development of organisations. It is therefore important to understand organisation culture as part of managing strategy.
- An understanding of the culture of an organisation and its relationship to organisational strategy can be gained by using the *cultural web*.

Recommended key readings

- For a more thorough explanation of the phenomenon of strategic drift see Gerry Johnson, 'Re-Thinking Incrementalism', *Strategic Management Journal*, vol. 9 (1988), pp. 75–91; and 'Managing Strategic Change – Strategy, Culture and Action', *Long Range Planning*, vol. 25, no. 1 (1992), pp. 28–36. (These papers also explain the cultural web). Also see Donald S. Sull, 'Why Good Companies Go Bad', *Harvard Business Review*, July/Aug (1999), pp. 42–52.
- For a comprehensive and critical explanation of organisational culture see Mats Alvesson, *Understanding Organizational Culture*, Sage, 2002.

References

1. For an explanation of strategic drift see G. Johnson, 'Re-Thinking Incrementalism', *Strategic Management Journal*, vol. 9 (1988), pp. 75–91; and 'Managing Strategic Change – Strategy, Culture and Action', *Long Range Planning*, vol. 25, no. 1 (1992), pp. 28–36. Also see E. Romanelli and M.L. Tushman, 'Organizational Transformation as Punctuated Equilibrium: an Empirical Test', *Academy of Management Journal*, vol. 7, no. 5 (1994), pp. 1141–1166. They explain the tendency of strategies to develop very incrementally with periodic transformational change.
2. This is a term used by Donald S. Sull in accounting for the decline of high performing firms (see 'Why Good Companies Go Bad', *Harvard Business Review*, July/Aug (1999), pp. 42–52).
3. This definition of culture is taken from E. Schein, *Organisational Culture and Leadership*, 2nd edition, Jossey-Bass, 1997, p. 6.

4. See G. Hofstede, *Culture's Consequences*, 2nd edition, Sage, 2001. For a critique of Hofstede's work see B. McSweeney, 'Hofstede's model of national cultural differences and their consequences: A triumph of faith – a failure of analysis', *Human Relations*, vol. 55, no. 1 (2002), pp. 89–118.

5. On cross-cultural management also see R. Lewis, *When Cultures Collide: Managing successfully across cultures*, 2nd edition, Brealey, 2000, a practical guide for managers. It offers an insight into different national cultures, business conventions and leadership styles. Also S. Schneider and J.-L. Barsoux, *Managing Across Cultures*, 2nd edition, Financial Times/Prentice Hall, 2003.

6. Exhibit 5.3 is adapted from the original in P. Grinyer and J.-C. Spender, *Turnaround: Managerial Recipes for Strategic Success*, Associated British Press, 1979, p. 203.

7. A fuller explanation of the cultural web can be found in G. Johnson, *Strategic Change and the Management Process*, 1987; and G. Johnson, 'Managing strategic change: strategy, culture and action', *Long Range Planning*, vol. 25, no. 1 (1992), pp. 28–36.

8. See A.L. Wilkins, 'Organisational Stories as Symbols which Control the Organisation', in L.R. Pondy, P.J. Frost, G. Morgan and T.C. Dandridge (eds), *Organisational Symbolism*, JAI Press, 1983.

9. The significance of organisational symbolism is explained in G. Johnson, 'Managing strategic change: the role of symbolic action', *British Journal of Management*, vol. 1, no. 4 (1990), pp. 183–200.

CASE EXAMPLE

Marks & Spencer (A)

Nardine Collier

The M&S formula for success

Photo: Charles Hewitt/Picture Post/Getty Images

Michael Marks began his penny bazaars in the late 1880s. He soon decided he needed a partner to help run the growing firm and Tom Spencer, a cashier of Marks' supplier, was recommended. From this partnership Marks & Spencer (M&S) steadily grew. Simon Marks took over the running of M&S from his father, turning the penny bazaars into stores, establishing a simple pricing policy and introducing the 'St Michael' logo as a sign of quality. There was a feeling of camaraderie and a close-knit family atmosphere within the stores, with staff employed whom the managers believed would 'fit in' and become part of that family. The staff were also treated better and paid more than in other companies. The family nature of this firm dominated top management too: until the late 1970s the board was made up of family members only.

Marks was renowned for his personal, top-down, autocratic management style and his attention to detail. This also manifested itself in the way he dealt with suppliers. He always used the same UK-based suppliers and meticulously ensured that goods were exactly to specification, a relationship designed to build reliance of the suppliers and ensure high and consistent quality.

Until the late 1990s M&S was hugely successful in terms of profit and market share, running its operations according to a set of fundamental principles; namely to:

- offer customers high-quality, well-designed and attractive merchandise at reasonable prices under the brand name St Michael;
- encourage suppliers to use the most modern and efficient production techniques;
- work with suppliers to ensure the highest standards of quality control;
- provide friendly, helpful service and greater shopping comfort and convenience to customers;
- improve the efficiency of the business, by simplifying operating procedures;
- foster good human relations with customers, suppliers and staff and in the communities in which M&S trade.

Its specialist buyers operated from a central buying office from which goods were allocated to the stores. The store managers followed central direction on merchandising, layout, store design and training. Every M&S store was identical in the procedures it followed, leading to a consistency of image and a guarantee of M&S standards. However, it also meant store managers were severely restricted in how they could respond to the local needs of customers.

This is an abridged version of the full 'A' case (which can be found in the classic case collection). A 'B' case can be found in the Text and Cases version of the 8th edition of *Exploring Corporate Strategy*.

This case was prepared by Nardine Collier, Cranfield School of Management. It is intended as a basis for class discussion and not as an illustration of either good or bad management practice.

During M&S's growth there were few changes to its methods of operation or strategies. Its reputation for good-quality clothing was built on basics, the essentials which every customer needed and would outlast the current fashion and trends seen in other high street retailers. As it did not have fitting rooms till the 1990s, all assistants carried tape measures and M&S would give a 'no quibble' refund to any customer who was unhappy with the product he or she had purchased. As its products remained in the stores all year round for most of its history it never held sales.

The success of M&S continued into the 1990s. Richard Greenbury, the CEO from 1991, explained this success:

> we followed absolutely and totally the principles of the business with which I was embued. . . . I ran the business with the aid of my colleagues based upon the very long standing, and proven ways of running it. (Radio 4, August 2000)

Successive chief executives were renowned for their attention to detail in terms of supplier control, merchandise and store layout; and it seemed to work. M&S's success under Marks was often attributed to his understanding of customer preferences and trends. However, because of this, it could also mean that buyers tended to select merchandise which they knew chief executives would approve of. For example, since it was known Greenbury did not want M&S to be at the cutting edge of fashion, buyers concentrated on the types of product they knew he would like – 'classic, wearable fashions'.

There were other problems of centralised authority. On one occasion Greenbury had decided that to control costs there would be less full-time sales assistants. Although this led to an inability in stores to meet the service levels required by M&S, when Greenbury visited, all available employees were brought in so that it appeared the stores were giving levels of service that, at other times, they were not. It also meant there was little disagreement with directives from the top, so policies and decisions remained unchallenged even when executives or store managers were concerned about negative effects. Customer satisfaction surveys that showed decreasing satisfaction throughout the late 1990s were kept from Greenbury by senior executives who felt he might be annoyed by the results.

A hitch in the formula

M&S's problems began to hit the headlines in October 1998 when it halted its expansion programme in Europe and America and in November announced a 23 per cent decline in first-half profits, causing its shares to fall drastically. Greenbury blamed a turbulent competitive environment, saying that M&S had lost sales and market share to its competitors from both the top and bottom ends of the retail market. Competitors at the top end of the market, such as the Gap, Oasis and Next, offered similarly priced goods, but more design focused with up-to-date fashions. At the bottom end, Matalan and supermarkets ranges such as the 'George' range at Asda offered basic clothing at significantly lower prices. Moreover, Tesco and Sainsbury's were now offering added value foods which had been pioneered by M&S.

Commentators suggested that M&S no longer understood or reacted to its customers' needs. It misread its target market, and could not understand that customers who purchased food or underwear might not want products from its home furnishings range. It had continued too long with its traditional formula and ignored changes in the marketplace. Greenbury was too focused on the day-to-day operations of the firm rather than long-term strategy. M&S was tied to a generalised view of the market, instead of trying to understand and tailor offerings to the various market segments. It had no loyalty card at a time when almost every other retailer did. Although a large proportion of M&S customers were women and much of the merchandise was womenswear, top management were dominated by men. Almost all managers and executives were promoted internally, starting at the bottom of the organisation and becoming immersed in its routines and traditions. It had an inward-looking culture strongly reinforced by Greenbury and his autocratic approach.

In November 1998, Greenbury announced that he would be stepping down. There followed a series of heavily publicised arguments between Keith Oates, Greenbury's deputy, and Peter Salsbury, another director, whom the media suggested was Greenbury's favoured successor. It was Salsbury who was eventually appointed as CEO. Oates elected to take early retirement. Analysts commented that, as Salsbury had only worked in womenswear, one of the worst-performing units in M&S, it might have been wiser to bring in an outsider.

During this period of boardroom scuffles, M&S's problems were compounded by its £192m (€270m) purchase of 19 Littlewoods department stores. These required refurbishment at a cost of £100m at the same time as existing M&S stores were being refurbished. The disruption had a far worse effect on customers than M&S had expected, leading Greenbury to describe the clothing section as a 'bloodbath'. In January 1999 M&S announced its second profits warning. It had been a bad Christmas trading period made worse by M&S overestimating sales and buying £250m worth of stock that then had to be heavily discounted.

New tactics . . . but more problems

In an attempt to regain confidence, Salsbury implemented a restructuring strategy, splitting the company into three: UK retail business, overseas business and financial services. He also established a company-wide marketing department to break down the power of the traditional buying fiefdoms established around product lines. The marketing department would adopt a customer-focused approach, rather than allowing buyers to dictate what the stores should stock. There were new clothing and food ranges, reinforced by a large-scale promotional campaign, to attempt to restore its image as an innovative retailer offering unique, quality products. Explaining that he wanted to move away from a bureaucratic culture by creating a decision-making environment that was unencumbered by hierarchy, Salsbury stripped away of layers of hierarchy and established a property division so that rents were charged to stores to make store managers more accountable for branch performance.

In June Greenbury retired a year early, a decision which came just before the board entered a three-day meeting to discuss 'a few hundred pages of its new strategy'. Salsbury commented:

> What we are doing has moved away from his [Greenbury's] methodology and thought processes . . . decisions were reached without him being able to have an input. (*Financial Times*, 23 June 1999)

In September M&S stated that it was in the process of overseas sourcing while severing links with some UK suppliers, streamlining international operations, diversifying into home and Internet shopping, and creating a department dedicated to identifying new business opportunities. However, customers continued to voice their concerns regarding the clothing range:

> There are so many items here to find and they don't tend to segregate it out, so there's something I might like next to something my granny might like. (*Financial Times*, 28 September 1999)

By November M&S had more bad news for its shareholders when it revealed its shares had fallen to the lowest price since 1991. There followed reports of Tesco, American pension fund companies and Philip Green, the retail entrepreneur, being interested in acquiring M&S. To counteract these rumours M&S implemented another management restructuring to become more customer focused, establishing seven business units: lingerie, womenswear, menswear, childrenswear, food, home, and beauty. Executives were appointed at just below board level to head the units, reporting directly to Salsbury who believed the flatter structure allowed M&S to be more responsive to market changes and customer needs.

A new horizon

In January 2000 Luc Vandevelde was appointed chairman. Belgian-born Vandevelde had left his managing director role at Promodés, the French food retailer, where he had achieved a sixfold increase in stock value. This was the first time anyone from outside M&S had been appointed to the position of chairman.

In the next two years there followed more changes. He unveiled an exclusive clothes collection from haute couture designers. Purchasing of the clothing range was shifted to almost 100 per cent Asian sources. M&S stopped using its famous green carrier bags, and relegated the St Michael logo to inside clothing. Stores were grouped on the basis of demographic characteristics and lifestyle patterns, instead of operating with the old system which allocated merchandise dependent on floor space. Still the fortunes of the company declined. In May 2000 M&S announced a fall in profit of £71.2m.

There was another restructuring into five operating divisions: UK retail; international retail; financial services; property; and ventures. Within the UK retail division seven customer business units were established, and to ensure customer focus each unit would have dedicated buying and selling teams. There was further store modernisation; more customer advisers on the shop floor; and the opening of three prototype stores where all new initiatives and concepts would be tested. M&S disclosed plans to offer clothes at a discounted price in factory outlet malls. Early in 2001 it announced its plans to withdraw from its stores in Europe and Brooks Brothers in America and franchise those in Hong Kong. In the midst of this, in September 2000, Salsbury retired.

Discussing the still disappointing end-of-year results, Vandevelde scaled back on the promises he had made on his arrival for recovery within two years. However, he was confident that he had the right recipe for recovery, it was just a matter of time.

There followed the decision to move out of its headquarters in Baker Street, London, and into a new building in Paddington. For those who had worked in M&S's headquarters, the grey and imposing building symbolised much that had gone wrong with the retailer. Its endless corridors were described as Kremlin-like, and the small individual offices reflected the status of the occupant by the thickness of the carpet. Former managers described the building as 'oppressive', with facilities that were not conducive to modern working practices, few casual meeting rooms, and a highly structured hierarchy for the 4,000 employees who worked there. Commentators were delighted with the move; they felt it showed M&S was at last tackling the problems at its core, not just altering merchandise and store layout.

It was not till the end of November 2001 that there were signs of an upturn in trading performance. This followed the arrival of Yasmin Yousef, a new creative designer, and the much heralded collaboration with George Davies, founder of Next and the creator of the 'George' clothing range at Asda. Davies introduced the Per Uno women's range targeted at 25–35 fashion-conscious customers to compete with brands like Mango and Kookai. Davies had secured a deal whereby he owned Per Una, and retained the profits from supplying M&S. To operate so autonomously he had invested £21m of his own money. He was therefore designing, manufacturing and distributing the clothes independently of M&S.

In 2001 Vandevelde also head-hunted Roger Holmes to be Head of UK Retailing. Holmes started his career as a consultant for McKinsey, moving to become Financial Director of DIY chain B&Q, Managing Director of retailers Woolworths, and finally Chief of Electricals for the Kingfisher group. Was a new era for M&S beginning?

Sources:

BBC2, 'Sparks at Marks', *The Money Programme*, 1 November (2000).

BBC2, 'Marks and Spencer', *Trouble at the Top*, 6 December (2001).

G. Beaver, 'Competitive advantage and corporate governance: shop soiled and needing attention, the case of Marks and Spencer plc', *Strategic Change*, vol. 8 (1999), pp. 325–334.

J. Bevan, *The rise and fall of Marks and Spencer*, Profile Books, (2001).

Channel 4, 'Inside Marks and Spencer', 25 February (2001).

Radio 4, Interview with Sir Richard Greenbury, 22 August (2000).

G. Rees, *St Michael: A history of Marks and Spencer*, Weidenfeld and Nicolson, (1969).

K. Tse, *Marks and Spencer: Anatomy of Britain's most efficiently managed company*, Pergamon, (1985).

Questions

1. Analyse the organisational culture of M&S in the 1990s.
2. Why was M&S so successful for so long?
3. Why did it suffer the downturn in the 1990s?
4. Why did the changes made from 1998 to 2001 fail to overcome the problems?

6

Business-Level Strategy

LEARNING OUTCOMES

After reading this chapter you should be able to:

- → Explain bases of achieving competitive advantage in terms of 'routes' on the strategy clock.
- → Assess the extent to which these are likely to provide sustainable competitive advantage.
- → Explain the relationship between competition and collaboration.

Photo: © BAA Ltd. www.baa.com/photolibrary

6.1 INTRODUCTION

This chapter is about a fundamental strategic choice: what competitive strategy to adopt in order to gain competitive advantage in a market at the business unit level. For example, faced with increasing competition from low price airlines, should British Airways seek to compete on price or maintain and improve their strategy of differentiation? Exhibit 6.1 shows the main themes that provide the structure for the rest of the chapter:

- First, *bases of competitive strategy* are considered. These include price-based strategies, differentiation strategies, hybrid and focus strategies.
- Section 6.3 considers *ways of sustaining competitive advantage* over time.
- The final section (6.4) considers the question of when *collaborative strategies* may be advantageous rather than direct competition.

Exhibit 6.1 Business level strategies

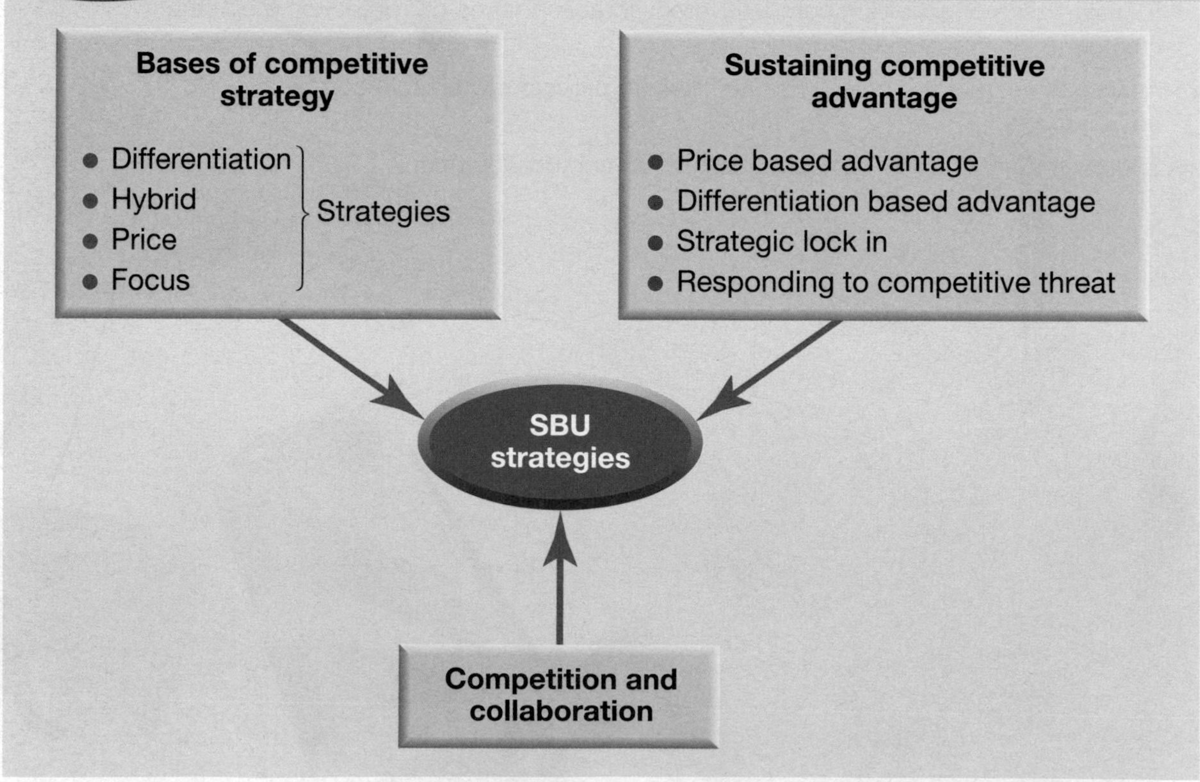

6.2 BASES OF COMPETITIVE ADVANTAGE: THE 'STRATEGY CLOCK'

Competitive strategy is concerned with the basis on which a business unit might achieve competitive advantage in its market

www.pearsoned.co.uk/fos KEY CONCEPT Strategy clock

This section reviews different ways of thinking about **competitive strategy**, the bases on which a business unit might achieve competitive advantage in its market. For public service organisations, the equivalent concern is the bases on which the organisation chooses to achieve superior quality of services in competition with others for funding, i.e. how it provides 'best value'.

This book employs 'market-facing' generic strategies similar to those used by Bowman and D'Aveni.[1] These are based on the principle that competitive advantage is achieved by providing customers with what they want, or need, better or more effectively than competitors. Building on this proposition, Michael Porter's[2] categories of differentiation and focus alongside price can be represented in the strategy clock (see Exhibit 6.2) – as discussed in the sections below.

In a competitive situation, customers make choices on the basis of their perception of value-for-money, the combination of price and perceived product/service benefits. The 'strategy clock' represents different positions in a market where customers (or potential customers) have different 'requirements' in terms of value-for-money. These positions also represent a set of generic strategies for achieving competitive advantage. Illustration 6.1 shows examples of different competitive strategies followed by firms in terms of these different positions on the strategy clock. The discussion of each of these strategies that follows also acknowledges the importance of an organisation's costs – particularly relative to competitors. But it will be seen that cost is a strategic consideration for all strategies on the clock – not just those where the lead edge is low price.

Since these strategies are 'market-facing' it is important to understand the critical success factors for each position on the clock. Customers at positions 1 and 2 are primarily concerned with price, but only if the product/service benefits meet their threshold requirements. This usually means that customers emphasise functionality over service or aspects such as design or packaging. In contrast, customers at position 5 require a customised product or service for which they are prepared to pay a price premium. The volume of demand in a market is unlikely to be evenly spread across the positions on the clock. In commodity-like markets demand is substantially weighted towards positions 1 and 2. Many public services are of this type too. Other markets have significant demand in positions 4 and 5. Historically professional services were of this type. However, markets change over time. Commodity-like markets develop value-added niches which grow as disposable incomes rise. For example, this has occurred in the drinks market with premium and speciality beers. And customised markets may become more commodity-like particularly where IT can demystify and routinise the professional content of the product – as in financial services.

Exhibit 6.2 The strategy clock: competitive strategy options

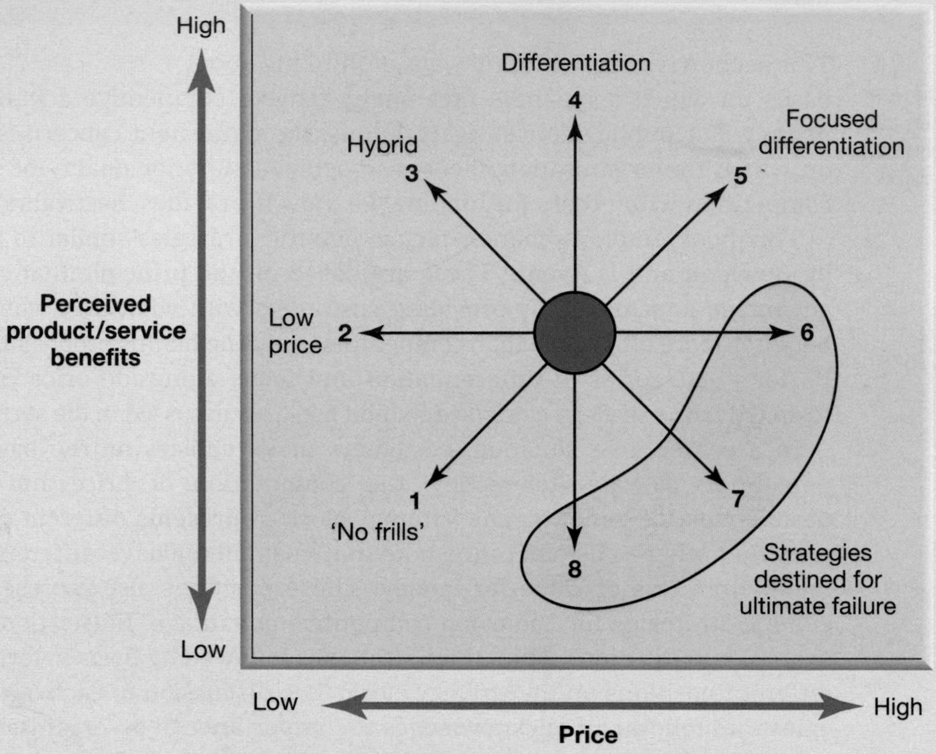

		Needs/risks	
1	'No frills'	Likely to be segment specific	
2	Low price	Risk of price war and low margins; need to be cost leader	
3	Hybrid	Low cost base and reinvestment in low price and differentiation	Differentiation
4	Differentiation		Differentiation
	(a) Without price premium	Perceived added value by user, yielding market share benefits	Differentiation
	(b) With price premium	Perceive added value sufficient to bear price premium	Differentiation
5	Focused differentiation	Perceived added value to a particular segment, warranting price premium	Differentiation
6	Increased price/standard value	Higher margins if competitors do not follow; risk of losing market share	Likely failure
7	Increased price/low value	Only feasible in monopoly situation	Likely failure
8	Low value/standard price	Loss of market share	Likely failure

Note: The strategy clock is adapted from the work of Cliff Bowman (see D. Faulkner and C. Bowman, *The Essence of Competitive Strategy*, Prentice Hall, 1995). However, Bowman uses the dimension 'Perceived Use Value'.

Illustration 6.1

Competitive strategies on the strategy clock

The competitive strategies of UK grocery retailers have shifted in the last three decades.

The supermarket retail revolution in the UK began in the late 1960s and 1970s as, initially, Sainsbury's began to open up supermarkets. Since the dominant form of retailing at that time was the corner grocery shop, Sainsbury's supermarkets were, in effect, a hybrid strategy: very clearly differentiated in terms of the physical layout and size of the stores as well as the quality of the merchandise, but also lower priced than many of the corner shop competitors.

As more and more retailers opened up supermarkets a pattern emerged. Sainsbury's was the dominant differentiated supermarket retailer. Tesco grew as a 'pile it high, sell it cheap' no frills operator. Competing in between as lower priced, but also lower quality than Sainsbury's, were a number of other supermarket retailers.

The mid-1990s saw a major change. Under the leadership of Ian Maclaurin, Tesco made a dramatic shift in strategy. It significantly increased the size and number of its stores, dropped the 'pile it high, sell it cheap' stance and began offering a much wider range of merchandise. Still not perceived as equal to Sainsbury's on quality, it none the less grew its market share at the expense of the other retailers and began to challenge Sainsbury's dominance. However the big breakthrough came for Tesco when it also shifted to higher-quality merchandise but still at perceived lower prices than Sainsbury's. In effect it was now adopting a hybrid strategy. In so doing it gained massive market share. By early 2007 this stood at over 30 per cent of the retail grocery market in the UK. In turn Sainsbury's had seen its share eroded to just 16 per cent, as it sought to find a way to resurrect its differentiated image of quality in the face of this competition.

In the meantime, other competitive strategy positions had consolidated. The low-price strategy was being followed by Asda (Wal-Mart) which also had a 16 per cent share of the market and Morrison's (with 11 per cent). In the no-frills segment was Netto, Lidl and Aldi, all retail formats that arrived in the 1990s from European neighbours and with a combined share of around 6 per cent.

The strategy of differentiation no longer really existed in a pure form. The closest was Waitrose (almost 4 per cent) emphasising a higher-quality image, but targeting a more select, upper-middle-class, market in selected locations. The focused differentiated stance remained the domain of the specialists: delicatessens and, of course in a London context, Harrods Food Hall.

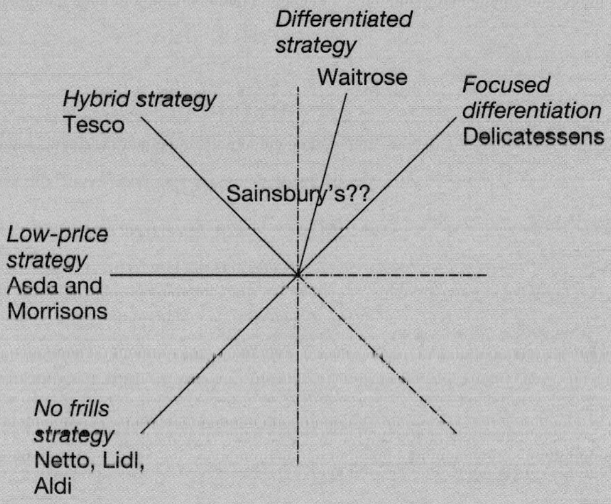

Questions

1. Who is 'stuck in the middle' here? Why?
2. Is a differentiated strategy or a low-price strategy defensible if there is a successful hybrid strategy, similar to that being followed by Tesco?
3. What might prevent other competitors following the Tesco strategy and competing successfully with them? (That is, does Tesco have strategic capabilities that provide sustainable competitive advantage?)
4. For another market of your choice, map out the strategic positions of the competitors in that market in terms of the strategy clock.

(Tesco is the case example in Chapter 9.)

So the strategy clock can help managers understand the changing requirements of their markets and the choices they can make about positioning and competitive advantage. Each position on the clock will now be discussed.

6.2.1 Price-based strategies (routes 1 and 2)

A **'no frills' strategy** combines a low price, low perceived product/service benefits and a focus on a price-sensitive market segment

Route 1 is the **'no frills' strategy**, which combines a low price with low perceived product/service benefits and a focus on a price-sensitive market segment. These segments might exist because of the following:

- The existence of *commodity markets*. These are markets where customers do not value or discern differences in the offering of different suppliers, so price becomes the key competitive issue. Basic foodstuffs – particularly in developing economies – are an example.
- There may be *price-sensitive customers*, who cannot afford, or choose not, to buy better-quality goods. This market segment may be unattractive to major providers but offer an opportunity to others (Aldi, Lidl and Netto in Illustration 6.1 for example). In the public services funders with tight budgets may decide to support only basic-level provision (for example, in subsidised spectacles or dentistry).
- Buyers have *high power and/or low switching costs* so there is little choice – for example in situations of tendering for government contracts.
- It offers an opportunity to *avoid major competitors*: Where major providers compete on other bases, a low-price segment may be an opportunity for smaller players or a new entrant to carve out a niche or to use route 1 as a bridgehead to build volume before moving on to other strategies.

A **low-price strategy** seeks to achieve a lower price than competitors whilst trying to maintain similar perceived product or service benefits to those offered by competitors

Route 2, the **low-price strategy**, seeks to achieve a lower price than competitors whilst maintaining similar perceived product or service benefits to those offered by competitors. Increasingly this has been the competitive strategy chosen by Asda (owned by Wal-mart) and Morrisons in the UK supermarket sector (see Illustration 6.1). In the public sector, since the 'price' of a service to the provider of funds (usually government) is the unit costs of the organisation receiving the budget, the equivalent is year-on-year efficiency gains achieved without loss of perceived benefits.

Competitive advantage through a low-price strategy might be achieved by focusing on a market segment that is unattractive to competitors and so avoiding competitive pressures eroding price. However, a more common and more challenging situation is where there is competition on the basis of price, for example in the public sector and in commodity-like markets. There are two pitfalls when competing on price:

- *Margin reductions for all.* Although tactical advantage might be gained by reducing price this is likely to be followed by competitors, squeezing profit margins for everyone.

- An *inability to reinvest*. Low margins reduce the resources available to develop products or services and result in a loss of perceived benefit of the product.

So, in the long run, both a 'no frills' strategy and a low-price strategy cannot be pursued without a *low-cost base*. However, low cost in itself is not a basis for advantage. Managers often pursue low-cost that does not give them competitive advantage. The challenge is how costs can be reduced in ways which others cannot match such that a low-price strategy might give sustainable advantage. This is difficult but possible ways are discussed in section 6.3.1 below. Illustration 6.2 also shows how easyJet has sought to reduce costs to pursue its 'no frills' strategy.

6.2.2 (Broad) differentiation strategies (route 4)

A **differentiation strategy** seeks to provide products or services benefits that are different from those of competitors and that are widely valued by buyers

The next option is a broad **differentiation strategy** providing products or services that offer benefits different from those of competitors and that are widely valued by buyers.[3] The aim is to achieve competitive advantage by offering better products or services at the same price or enhancing margins by pricing slightly higher. In public services, the equivalent is the achievement of a 'centre of excellence' status, attracting higher funding from government (for example, universities try to show that they are better at research or teaching than other universities).

The success of a differentiation approach is likely to be dependent on two key factors:

- *Identifying and understanding the strategic customer*. The concept of the strategic customer is helpful because it focuses consideration on who the strategy is targeting. However, this is not always straightforward, as discussed in section 2.4.3. For example, for a newspaper business, is the customer the reader of the newspaper, the advertiser, or both? They are likely to have different needs and be looking for different benefits. For a branded food manufacturer is it the end consumer or the retailer? It may be important that public sector organisations offer perceived benefits, but to whom? Is it the service user or the provider of funds? However *what is valued* by the strategic customer can also be dangerously taken for granted by managers, a reminder of the importance of identifying critical success factors (section 2.4.4).
- *Identifying key competitors*. Who is the organisation competing against? For example, in the brewing industry there are now just a few major global competitors, but there are also many local or regional brewers. Players in each strategic group (see section 2.4.1) need to decide who they regard as competitors and, given that, which bases of differentiation might be considered. Heineken appear to have decided that it is the other global competitors – Carlsberg and Anheuser Busch for example. SABMiller built their global reach on the basis of acquiring and developing national brands and competing

Illustration 6.2

easyJet's 'no frills' strategy

Multiple bases for keeping costs down can provide a basis for a successful 'no frills' strategy.

Launched in 1995, easyJet was seen as the brash young upstart of the European airline industry and widely tipped to fail. But by the mid-2000s this Luton-based airline had done more than survive. From a starting point of six hired aircraft working one route, by 2006 it had 122 aircraft flying 262 routes to 74 airports and carrying over 33 million passengers per annum and impressive financial results: £129m profit on £1,619m revenue (≈ €187m on ≈ €2,348m).

The principles of its strategy and its business model were laid down in annual reports year by year. For example, in 2006:

- The internet is used to reduce distribution costs . . . now over 95% of all seats are sold online, making easyJet one of Europe's biggest internet retailers;
- Maximizing the utilization of substantial assets. We fly our aircraft intensively, with swift turnaround times each time we land. This gives us a very low unit cost;
- Ticket-less travel. Passengers receive booking details via an email rather than paper. This helps to significantly reduce the cost of issuing, distributing, processing and reconciling millions of transactions each year;
- No 'free lunch'. We eliminate unnecessary services, which are complex to manage such as free catering, pre-assigned seats, interline connections and cargo services. This allows us to keep our total costs of production low;
- Efficient use of airports. easyJet flies to main destination airports throughout Europe, but gains efficiencies compared to traditional carriers with rapid turnaround times, and progressive landing charge agreements with airports. [It might have added here that since it does not operate a hub system, passengers have to check in and offload their luggage at each stage. This means that aircraft are not held up whilst luggage is transferred between flights.]

It might also have added that other factors contributed to low costs:

- A focus on the Airbus A319 aircraft, and the retirement of 'old generation' Boeing 737 aircraft, meant 'a young fleet of modern aircraft secured at very competitive rates' benefiting maintenance costs. And, since an increasing proportion of these were owned by easyJet, financing costs were being reduced.
- A persistent focus on reducing ground handling costs.
- In the face of rising fuel costs, hedging on future buying of fuel.

In addition to all the factors above the 2006 annual report stated that easyJet's customer proposition is defined by

> low cost with care and convenience. . . . We fly to main European destinations from convenient local airports and provide friendly onboard service. People are a key point of difference at easyJet and are integral to our success. This allows us to attract the widest range of customers to use our services – both business and leisure.

Source: easyJet annual report 2006.

Questions

1. Read sections 6.2.1 and 6.3.1 and identify the bases of easyJet's 'no frills' strategy.
2. How easy would it be for larger airlines such as BA to imitate the strategy?
3. On what bases could other low-price airlines compete with easyJet?

on the basis of local tastes and traditions, but have more recently also acquired Miller to compete globally.

The competitor analysis explained in section 2.4.4 (and Exhibit 2.7) can help in both of these regards.

- The *difficulty of imitation*. The success of a strategy of differentiation must depend on how easily it can be imitated by competitors. This highlights the importance of non-imitable strategic capabilities discussed in section 3.4.3.
- The extent of *vulnerability to price based competition*. In some markets customers are more price sensitive than others. So it may be that bases of differentiation are just not sufficient in the face of lower prices. Managers often complain, for example, that customers do not seem to value the superior levels of service they offer. Or, to take the example of UK grocery retailing (see Illustration 6.1), Sainsbury could once claim to be the broad differentiator on the basis of quality but customers now perceive that Tesco is comparable and seen to offer lower prices.

6.2.3 The hybrid strategy (route 3)

A **hybrid strategy** seeks simultaneously to achieve differentiation and a price lower than that of competitors

A **hybrid strategy** seeks simultaneously to achieve differentiation and low price relative to competitors. The success of this strategy depends on the ability to deliver enhanced benefits to customers together with low prices whilst achieving sufficient margins for reinvestment to maintain and develop bases of differentiation. It is, in effect the strategy Tesco is seeking to follow. It might be argued that, if differentiation can be achieved, there should be no need to have a lower price, since it should be possible to obtain prices at least equal to competition, if not higher. Indeed, there is a good deal of debate as to whether a hybrid strategy can be a successful competitive strategy rather than a suboptimal compromise between low price and differentiation. If it is the latter very likely it will be ineffective. However, the hybrid strategy could be advantageous when:

- Much *greater volumes* can be achieved than competitors so that margins may still be better because of a low cost base, much as Tesco is achieving given its market share in the UK.
- *Cost reductions are available outside its differentiated activities*. For example IKEA concentrates on building differentiation on the basis of its marketing, product range, logistics and store operations but low customer expectations on service levels allow cost reduction because customers are prepared to transport and build its products.
- Used as an *entry strategy* in a market with established competitors. For example, in developing a global strategy a business may target a poorly run operation in a competitor's portfolio of businesses in a geographical area of the world and enter that market with a superior product at a lower price to establish a foothold from which it can move further.

6.2.4 Focused differentiation (route 5)

A focused differentiation strategy seeks to provide high perceived product/service benefits justifying a substantial price premium, usually to a selected market segment (niche)

A **focused differentiation** strategy provides high perceived product/service benefits, typically justifying a substantial price premium, usually to a selected market segment (or niche). These could be premium products and heavily branded, for example. Manufacturers of premium beers, single malt whiskies and wines from particular chateaux all seek to convince customers who value or see themselves as discerning of quality that their product is sufficiently differentiated from competitors' to justify significantly higher prices. In the public services centres of excellence (such as a specialist museum) achieve levels of funding significantly higher than more generalist providers. However, focused differentiation raises some important issues:

- A *choice* may have to be made between a focus strategy (position 5) and broad differentiation (position 4). A firm following a strategy of international growth may have to choose between building competitive advantage on the basis of a common global product and brand (route 4) or tailoring their offering to specific markets (route 5).
- *Tensions between a focus strategy and other strategies.* For example broad-based car manufacturers, such as Ford, acquired premier marques, such as Jaguar and Aston Martin, but learned that trying to manage these in the same way as mass market cars was not possible. By 2007 Ford had divested Aston Martin and were seeking to divest others. Such tensions limit the degree of diversity of strategic positioning that an organisation can sustain, an important issue for corporate-level strategy discussed in Chapter 7.
- *Possible conflict with stakeholder expectations.* For example, a public library service might be more cost-efficient if it concentrated its development efforts on IT-based online information services. However, this would very likely conflict with its purpose of social inclusion since it would exclude people who were not IT literate.
- *Dynamics of growth for new ventures.* New ventures often start in very focused ways – offering innovative products or services to meet particular needs. It may, however, be difficult to find ways to grow such new ventures. Moving from route 5 to route 4 means a lowering of price and therefore cost, whilst maintaining differentiation features.
- *Market changes may erode differences between segments,* leaving the organisation open to much wider competition. Customers may become unwilling to pay a price premium as the features of 'regular' offerings improve. Or the market may be further segmented by even more differentiated offerings from competitors. For example, 'up-market' restaurants have been hit by rising standards elsewhere and by the advent of 'niche' restaurants that specialise in particular types of food.

6.3 SUSTAINING COMPETITIVE ADVANTAGE

Organisations that try to achieve competitive advantage hope to preserve it over time and much of what is written about competitive strategy takes the need for sustainability as a central expectation. This section builds on the discussion in section 3.2 relating to strategic capability to consider how sustainability might be possible.

6.3.1 Sustaining price-based advantage

An organisation pursuing competitive advantage through low prices might be able to sustain this in a number of ways:

- *Operating with lower margins* may be possible for a firm either because it has much greater sales volume than competitors or can cross-subsidise a business unit from elsewhere in its portfolio (see section 7.5 for further discussion of portfolio strategies).
- *A unique cost structure*. Some firms may have unique access to low-cost distribution channels, be able to obtain raw materials at lower prices than competitors or be located in an area where labour cost is low.
- *Organisationally specific capabilities* may exist for a firm such that it is able to drive down cost throughout its value chain. Indeed Porter defines cost leadership as '*the* low-cost producer in its industry . . . [who] must find and exploit all sources of cost advantage'.[4] (see section 3.3 and Exhibit 3.3).

Of course, if either of these last two approaches is to be followed it matters that the operational areas of low cost do truly deliver cost advantages to support real price advantages over competition. It is also important that competitors find these advantages difficult to imitate as discussed in Chapter 3. This requires a mindset where innovation in cost reduction is regarded as essential to survival. An example of this is RyanAir in the low price 'no frills' airline sector who, in 2006, declared it was their ambition to be able to eventually offer passengers flights for free.

- *Focusing on market segments* where low price is particularly valued by customers but other features are not. An example is the success of dedicated producers of own-brand grocery products for supermarkets. They can hold prices low because they avoid the high overhead and marketing costs of major branded manufacturers. However, they can only do so provided they focus on that product and market segment.

There are however dangers with trying to pursue low-price strategies:

- *Competitors may be able to do the same*. There is no point in trying to achieve advantage through low price on the basis of cost reduction if competitors can do it too.

Illustration 6.3

The strategy battle in the wine industry: Australia vs. France

The benefits of successful differentiation may be difficult to sustain.

For centuries French wines were regarded as superior. Building on the Appellation d'Origine Contrôlée (AOC) system, with its separate label requirements and controls for nearly 450 wine-growing regions, the emphasis was on the distinct regionality of the wines and the chateau-based branding. In the AOC system the individual wine-grower is a custodian of the *terroir* and its traditions. The quality of the wines and the distinct local differences are down to the differences in soil and climate as well as the skills of the growers, often on the basis of decades of local experience.

However, by 2001 the traditional dominance of French wines in the UK seemed to have ended, with sales of Australian wine outstripping them for the first time. This went hand in hand with huge growth in wine consumption as it became more widely available in supermarkets, where Australian wine was especially succesful. The success of Australian wines with retailers was for several reasons. The quality was consistent, compared with French wines that could differ by year and location. Whilst the French had always highlighted the importance of the local area of origin of the wine, in effect Australia 'branded' the country as a wine region and then concentrated on the variety of grape – a Shiraz or a Chardonnay, for example. This avoided the confusing details of the location of vineyards and the names of chateaux that many customers found difficult about French wines. The New World approach to the production of wine in terms of style, quality and taste was also based around consumer demand, not local production conditions. Grapes were sourced from wherever necessary to create a reliable product. French wines could be unpredictable – charming to the connoisseur, but infuriating to the dinner-party host, who expects to get what he or she paid for.

Between 1994 and 2003 France lost 84,000 growers. There was so much concern that in 2001, the French government appointed a committee to study the problem. The committee's proposals were that France should both improve the quality of its appellation wine and also create an entirely new range of quality, generic wines, so-called 'vins de cepage' (wines based on a grape variety). A company called OVS planned to market the Chamarré brand – French for 'bursting with colours', to sell between £5 and £7 (€7.25 and €10.15), the price range where New World wines have made the biggest inroads. OVS President Pascal Renaudat, who has had 20 years in the wine business, explained:

> We have to simplify our product and reject an arrogant approach that was perhaps natural to us. It is important to produce wine that corresponds to what people want to drink and at a good price. . . . This is not wine for connoisseurs. It is for pleasure.

'It's time to get rid of the stuffy pretentiousness that surrounds French wine,' said Renaud Rosari, Chamarré's master wine-maker. 'Chamarré is about bringing our wines to life for the consumers – the brand is lively, uncomplicated and approachable and means consistently high quality wines, with the fresh easy drinking style customers are looking for.'

There was qualified optimism: Jamie Goode of wineanorak.com saw it as a brave commercial decision. However: 'The trouble is that everybody is doing it. . . . Access to market is key. You need to get into the supermarkets, but you need to have a strong brand with which to negotiate or else they will savage you on price.'

Sources: Adapted from *Financial Times*, 11 February and 3/4 March (2001); *Independent*, 4 August (2003); *Sunday Times*, 5 February (2006); Guardian Unlimited, 7 February (2006).

Questions

1. Explain the high and distinct reputation of French wines of the past in terms of the bases of sustainable differentiation explained in sections 3.4 and 6.3.2.
2. What were the reasons for the success of Australian wines? Are these as sustainable?
3. What competitive strategy is Chamarré adopting to respond to the challenge of Australian (and other 'New World') wines?

- Customers start to *associate low price with low product/service benefits* and an intended route 2 strategy slips to route 1 by default.
- Cost reductions may result in an *inability to pursue a differentiation strategy*. For example, outsourcing IT systems for reasons of cost efficiency may mean that no one takes a strategic view of how competitive advantage might be achieved through IT.

6.3.2 Sustaining differentiation-based advantage

There is little point in striving to be different if competitors can imitate readily; there is a need for sustainability of the basis of advantage. For example, many firms that try to gain advantage through launching new products or services find them copied rapidly by competitors. Illustration 6.3 shows how wine producers in France and Australia have been seeking bases of differentiation over each other over the years.

Ways of attempting to sustain advantage through differentiation include the following:

- *Create difficulties of imitation*. Section 3.4.3 discussed the factors that can make strategies difficult to imitate.
- *Imperfect mobility* such that the capabilities that sustain differentiation cannot be *traded*. For example, a pharmaceutical firm may gain great benefits from having top research scientists, or a football club from its star players, but they may be poached by competitors: they are tradable. On the other hand, some bases of advantage are very difficult to trade. For example:
  - *Intangible assets* such as brand, image, or reputation that are intangible or competences rooted in an organisation's culture are difficult for a competitor to imitate or obtain. Indeed even if the competitor acquires the company to gain these, they may not readily transfer given new ownership.
  - There may be *switching costs*. The actual or perceived cost for a buyer of changing the source of supply of a product or service may be high. Or the buyer might be dependent on the supplier for particular components, services or skills. Or the benefits of switching may simply not be worth the cost or risk.
  - *Co-specialisation*. If one organisation's resources or competences are intimately linked with the buyers' operations. For example, a whole element of the value chain for one organisation, perhaps distribution or manufacturing, may be undertaken by another.
- A *lower cost position* than competitors can allow an organisation to sustain better margins that can be reinvested to achieve and maintain differentiation. For example, Kellogg's or Mars may well be the lowest cost in their markets, but they reinvest their profits into branding and product and service differentiation not low prices.

6.3.3 Strategic lock-in

Strategic lock-in is where an organisation achieves a proprietary position in its industry; it becomes an industry standard

Another approach to sustainability, whether for price based or differentiation strategies is the creation of **strategic lock in**.[5] This is where an organisation achieves a proprietary position in its industry; it becomes an industry standard. For example, Microsoft became an industry standard. Many argue that technically the Apple Macintosh had a better operating system, but Microsoft Windows became the industry standard by working to ensure that the 'architecture' of the industry was built around them. Other businesses had to conform or relate to that standard in order to prosper.

The achievement of lock-in is likely to be dependent on:

- *Size or market dominance*. It is unlikely that others will seek to conform to such standards unless they perceive the organisation that promotes it as dominant in its market.
- *First mover dominance*. Such standards are likely to be set *early in life cycles of markets*. In the volatility of growth markets it is more likely that the single-minded pursuit of lock-in by the *first movers* will be successful than when the market is mature. For example Sky, with the financial support of the News Corporation, was able to undercut competitors and invest heavily in technology and fast market share growth, sustaining substantial losses over many years, in order to achieve dominance.
- *Self-reinforcing commitment*. When one or more firms support the standard more come on board, then others are obliged to, and so on.
- *Insistence on the preservation* of the lock-in position. Insistence on conformity to the standard is strict so rivals will be seen off fiercely. This can of course lead to problems, as Microsoft found in the American courts when it was deemed to be operating against the interests of the market.

6.3.4 Responding to competitive threat[6]

The preservation of competitive advantage in the face of competitors who attack by targeting customers on the basis of a different competitive strategy can be a serious threat. One of the most common is low price competitors entering markets dominated by firms that have built a strong position through differentiation. For example low price airlines have taken substantial share from most of the leading airlines throughout the world. An equivalent situation in the public sector arises given the insistence by funding providers on year-on-year 'efficiency gains'. It is an opportunity for new entrants to undercut existing service providers, or indeed it may be that those providers find themselves being forced to undercut themselves.

Exhibit 6.3 suggests the series of questions that might be asked and the appropriate responses and there are some general guidelines. First, *if a strategy*

Exhibit 6.3 A framework for responding to low-cost rivals

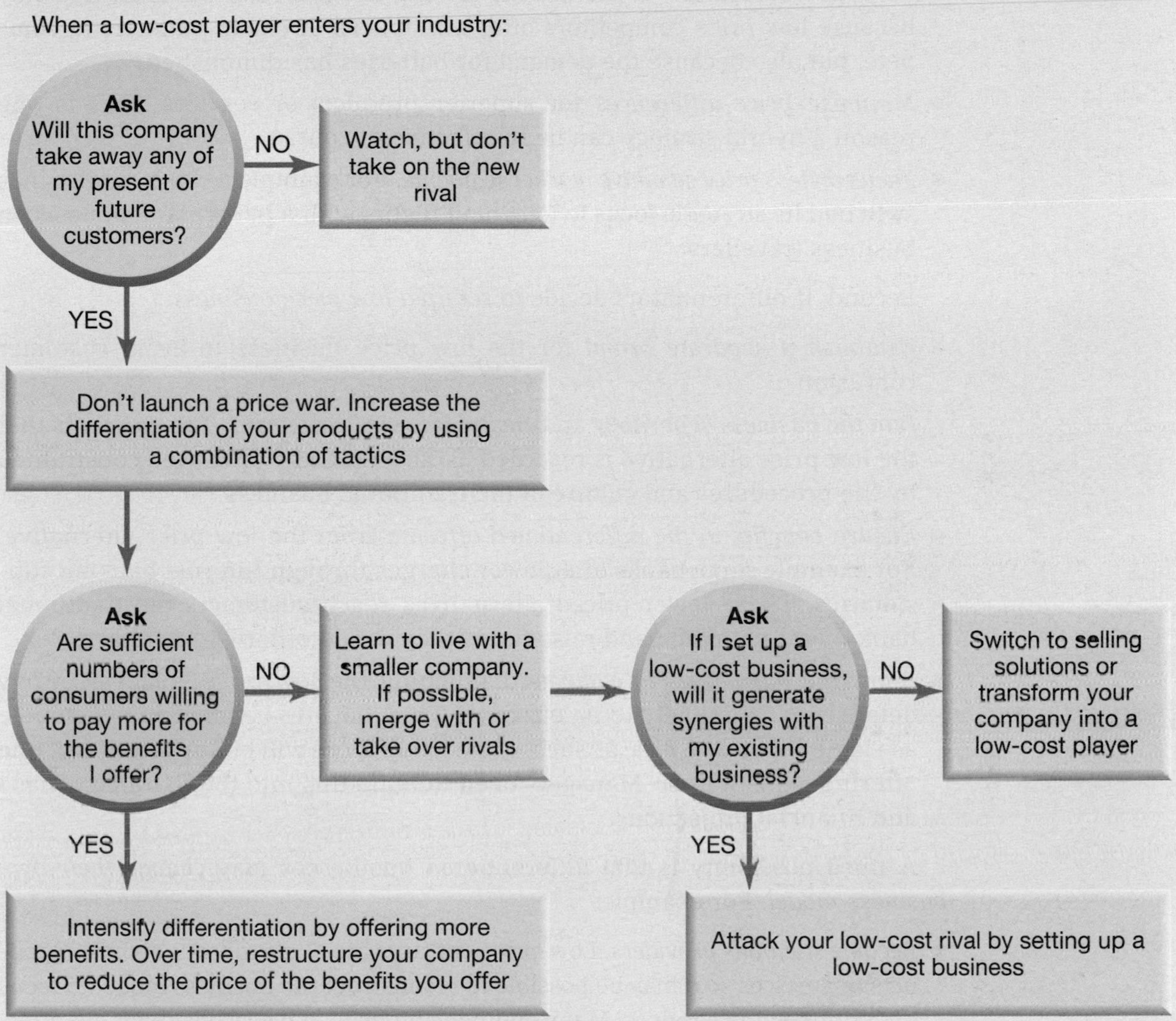

Source: Reprinted by permission of *Harvard Business Review*. Exhibit from 'Strategies to fight low-cost rivals' by N. Kumar, Vol. 84, Issue 12, December 2006.

of differentiation is retained as the basis of retaliation (or in the public sector if the decision is to maintain a 'centre of excellence' status):

- *Build multiple bases of differentiation*. There is more likelihood of highlighting relative benefits if they are multiple: for example, Bang and Olufsen's design of hi-fi systems linked to product innovation and their relationships with retailers to ensure they present their products distinctly in stores.

- *Ensure a meaningful basis of differentiation*. Customers need to be able to discern a meaningful benefit. For example Gillette has found it difficult to persuade customers of the benefit of long life Duracell batteries not only because low price competitors offer multipacks of cheap batteries to compete, but also because the demand for batteries has diminished.
- *Minimise price differences* for superior products or services. This is one reason a hybrid strategy can be so effective of course.
- *Focus on less price sensitive market segments*. For example, British Airways has switched its strategic focus to long haul flights with a particular emphasis on business travellers.

Second, if differentiators decide to *set up a low price business*:

- *Establish a separate brand* for the low price business to avoid customer confusion.
- *Run the business separately* and *ensure it is well resourced*: The danger is that the low price alternative is regarded as 'second class' or is over-constrained by the procedures and culture of the traditional business.
- *Ensure benefits to the differentiated offering* from the low price alternative. For example some banks offer lower charges through Internet banking subsidiaries. These lower priced alternatives reach customers the traditional bank might not reach and raise funds they would otherwise not have.
- *Allow the businesses to compete*. Launching the low price business purely defensively is unlikely to be effective. They have to be allowed to compete as viable separate SBUs; as such, quite likely there will be substitution of one offering with another. Managers need to build this into their strategic plans and financial projections.

A third possibility is that differentiated businesses may *change their own business model*. For example:

- *Become solutions providers*. Low-price entrants are likely to focus on basic products or services so it may be possible to reconstruct the business model to focus on higher-value services. Many engineering firms have realised, for example, the higher-value potential of design and consultancy services rather than labour-based engineering operations that are easily undercut in price.
- *Become a low-price provider*. The most radical response would be to abandon the reliance on differentiation and learn to compete head on with the low-price competitor.[7] Perhaps not surprisingly, there is not much evidence of the success of such a response, not least because it would mean competing on the basis of competences better understood by the incumbent.

6.4 COMPETITION AND COLLABORATION[8]

So far the emphasis has been on competition and competitive advantage. However, advantage may not always be achieved by competing. Collaboration between organisations may be a way of achieving advantage or avoiding competition. Collaboration between potential competitors or between buyers and sellers is likely to be advantageous when the combined costs of purchase and buying transactions (such as negotiating and contracting) are lower through collaboration than the cost of operating alone. Collaboration also helps build switching costs. This can be shown by returning to the five forces framework from section 2.3.1 (also see Exhibit 6.4):

- *Collaboration to increase selling power*. In the aerospace industry component manufacturers might seek to build close links with customers. Achieving accredited supplier status can be tough, but may significantly increase seller power once achieved. It may also help in research and development activities, in reducing stock and in joint planning to design new products.
- *Collaboration to increase buying power*. Historically, the power and profitability of pharmaceutical companies were aided by the fragmented nature of their buyers – individual doctors and hospitals. But many governments have promoted, or required, collaboration between buyers of pharmaceuticals

Exhibit 6.4 Competition and collaboration

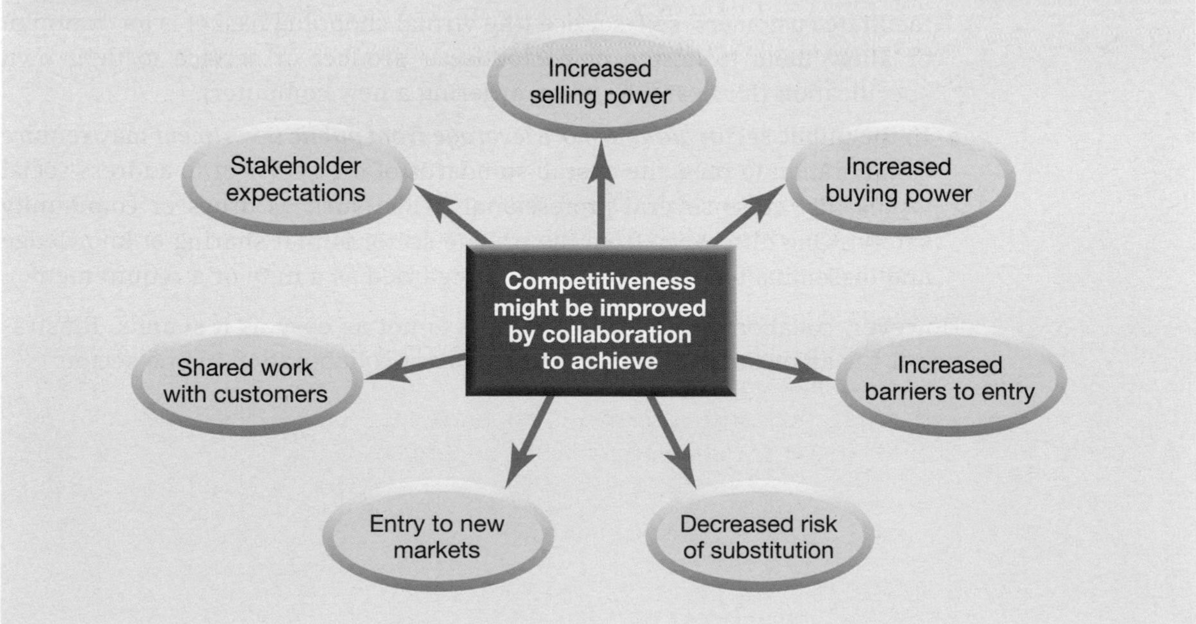

and centralised government drug-specifying agencies, the result of which has been more coordinated buying power.

- *Collaboration to build barriers to entry or avoid substitution*. Faced with threatened entry or substitute products, firms in an industry may collaborate to invest in research and development or marketing. Trade associations may promote an industry's generic features such as safety standards or technical specifications to speed up innovation and pre-empt the possibility of substitution.
- *Collaboration to gain entry and competitive power*. Organisations seeking to develop beyond their traditional boundaries (for example, geographical expansion) may collaborate with others to gain entry into new arenas. Gaining local market knowledge may also require collaboration with local operators. Indeed, in some parts of the world, governments require entrants to collaborate in such ways. Collaboration may also help in developing required infrastructure such as distribution channels, information systems or research and development activities. It may also be needed because buyers may prefer to do business with local rather than expatriate managers. Especially in hi-tech and hypercompetitive situations there is increasing disintegration (or 'unbundling') of value chains because there is innovatory competition at each stage of that chain. In such circumstances there also is likely to be increasing need for co-operative strategies between such competitors to offer coherent solutions for customers.[9]
- *Collaboration to share work with customers*. An important trend in public services is *co-production* with clients, for example, self-assessment of income tax. The motives include cost efficiency, quality/reliability improvement or increased 'ownership/responsibility' from the clients. Websites also facilitate customers' self-service (the virtual shopping basket is an example) or allow them to design or customise a product or service to their own specification (for example, when ordering a new computer).
- In the public sector *gaining more leverage from public investment* may require collaboration to raise the overall standards of the sector or to address social issues that cross several professional fields (such as drugs or community safety). One difference from the private sector is that sharing of knowledge and dissemination of best practice is regarded as a duty or a requirement.

However, collaborating with competitors is not as easy as it sounds. Illustration 6.4 is an example of public/private sector collaboration in one sector.

Illustration 6.4

Business–university collaboration in the creative and cultural industries

Public/private sector collaboration may bring benefits to both parties.

In 2003 the UK government set up a committee (The Lambert Committee) to report on business–university collaboration in the UK and to propose how it might be improved. The first stage was to seek ideas from a wide range of stakeholders. The following is an extract from the Arts and Humanities Research Council (AHRC), which supported work that was fundamental to a range of creative and cultural industries:

We are in the early stages of exploring a range of partnerships and possible strategic interventions (see below). In collaboration with the Department for Culture, Media and Sports (DCMS) and others, a Creative Industries/Higher Education Forum has been established. This group will seek to bring together the supply and demand side of this relationship to foster stronger links and new activities.

Creative and cultural industries: a role for creative clusters

Many universities have developed links with businesses in the creative and cultural industries. . . . However, many of the companies in the creative industries are small (SMEs). . . . An organic development in recent years has been the creation of a number of 'creative clusters' bringing together local or regional HEIs with business for the generation of new ideas, products and processes. Examples exist from around the country, including Scotland, Sheffield, London, Bristol, Nottingham. Such creative clusters supported by business enterprise and support services could provide the basis for supporting small-scale individual entrepreneurship.

Working with Regional Development Agencies (RDAs)

Both the Research Councils and RDAs are channels to their respective communities, and work has already commenced on identifying ways in which jointly they can be both a catalyst for new ideas and a facilitator of knowledge transfer. Such activities might cover individual projects, jointly-sponsored schemes, and facilitation of sector clusters, such as creative clusters.

Embedding practitioners and professionals in HEIs

Many traditional models of the relationship between HEIs and business describe a linear process in which knowledge is passed to industry. However, it can be argued that, increasingly, knowledge transfer is not a process, but an interaction based on access to people, information, data and infrastructure. In the creative and performing arts the concept of portfolio careers is not uncommon. Individuals can hold part-time research or teaching positions alongside other forms of employment or self-employment, including artistic performance. In addition, it is not uncommon for businesses and other non-private sector organisations to provide visiting professorships or lectureships.

Widening the definition of knowledge transfer in a knowledge economy

Increasingly a large number of people are trading their knowledge, expertise and experience through non-conventional employment means. However, in looking for evidence of knowledge transfer from academia to business the focus tends to be on the numbers of patents, spin-outs and companies created. These are undoubtedly important indicators to industrial performance, but a wider evidence base looking at employment patterns and self-employment would give a wider perspective.

Charting this new landscape

It is the role of bodies such as the AHRC to provide an environment that enables the ideas and creativity of the academic community to be unlocked and developed. Working with analogous bodies in other sectors, such as the RDAs, the aspiration is to find ways to improve the links out from academia to the wider society and economy.

Source: AHRC Response from the AHRC to the Lambert Review of Business–University Collaboration, http://www.ahrc.ac.uk.

Questions

1 Look at section 6.4 and then identify the potential benefits from business–university collaboration to a number of the important stakeholders.

2 What are the risks of collaboration to each of these stakeholders (as against 'going it alone')?

SUMMARY

www.pearsoned.co.uk/fos AUDIO SUMMARY

- Competitive strategy is concerned with seeking competitive advantage in markets at the business level, or in the public services, providing best value services.
- Different bases of competitive strategy include:
  - A *'no frills'* strategy, combining low price and low perceived added value.
  - A *low-price* strategy providing lower price than competitors at similar added value of product or service to competitors.
  - A *differentiation* strategy, which seeks to provide products or services which are unique or different from competitors.
  - A *hybrid* strategy, which seeks simultaneously to achieve differentiation and prices lower than competitors.
  - A *focused differentiation* strategy, which seeks to provide high perceived value justifying a substantial price premium.
- Managers need to consider the bases upon which price based or differentiation strategies can be sustained based on strategic capabilities, developing durable relationships with customers or the ability to achieve a 'lock-in' position so becoming the 'industry standard' recognised by suppliers and buyers.
- Strategies of collaboration may offer alternatives to competitive strategies or may run in parallel.

Recommended key readings

- The foundations of the discussions of generic competitive strategies are to be found in the writings of Michael Porter, which include *Competitive Strategy* (1980) and *Competitive Advantage* (1985), both published by Free Press. Both are recommended for readers who wish to understand the background to discussions in sections 6.3 and 6.4 of this chapter on competitive strategy and competitive advantage.
- There is a lively debate about whether sustainable competitive advantage is possible. Two papers offering different evidence on this are R.W. Wiggins and T.W. Ruefli, 'Schumpeter's Ghost: Is Hypercompetition Making the Best of Times Shorter?', *Strategic Management Journal*, vol. 26 (2005), 887–911, which argues there is no evidence for sustainable competitive advantage; and G. McNamara, P.M. Vaaler and C. Devers, 'Same as it Ever Was: the Search for Evidence of Increasing Hypercompetition', *Strategic Management Journal*, vol. 24 (2003), 261–278, which argues that it is.

References

1. See D. Faulkner and C. Bowman, *The Essence of Competitive Strategy*, Prentice Hall, 1995. A similar framework is also used by Richard D'Aveni, *Hypercompetitive Rivalries: Competing in highly dynamic environments*, Free Press, 1995.
2. M. Porter, *Competitive Advantage*, Free Press, 1985.
3. B. Sharp and J. Dawes, 'What is differentiation and how does it work?', *Journal of Marketing Management*, vol. 17, no. 7/8 (2001), pp. 739–759 reviews the relationship between differentiation and profitability.
4. These quotes concerning Porter's three competitive strategies are taken from his book *Competitive Advantage*, Free Press, 1985, pp. 12–15.
5. The Delta Model is explained and illustrated more fully in A.C. Hax and D.L. Wilde II, 'The Delta Model', *Sloan Management Review*, vol. 40, no. 2 (1999), pp. 11–28.
6. This section is based on research by N. Kumar, 'Strategies to Fight Low Cost Rivals', *Harvard Business Review*, vol. 84, no. 12 (2006), 104–113.
7. For a discussion of how to compete in such circumstances, see A. Rao, M. Bergen and S. Davis, 'How to fight a price war', *Harvard Business Review*, vol. 78, no. 2 (2000), pp. 107–115.
8. Useful books on collaborative strategies are Y. Doz and G. Hamel, *Alliance Advantage: The art of creating value through partnering*, Harvard Business School Press, 1998; *Creating Collaborative Advantage*, ed. Chris Huxham, Sage Publications, 1996 and D. Faulkner, *Strategic Alliances: Co-operating to compete*, McGraw-Hill, 1995.
9. This case for cooperation in hi-tech industries is argued and illustrated by V. Kapur, J. Peters and S. Berman, 'High Tech 2005: the Horizontal, Hypercompetitive Future', *Strategy and Leadership*, vol. 31, no. 2 (2003).

CASE EXAMPLE

Madonna: still the reigning queen of pop?

Phyl Johnson, Strategy Explorers

The music industry has always been the backdrop for one-hit wonders and brief careers. Pop stars who have remained at the top for decades are very few. Madonna is one such phenomenon; the question is, after over 25 years at the top, how much longer can it last?

Described by *Billboard Magazine* as the smartest business woman in show business, Madonna, Louise Ciccone, began her music career in 1983 with the hit single 'Holiday' and in 2005–2006 once again enjoyed chart success for her album 'Confessions on a Dance Floor'. In the meantime she had consistent chart success with her singles and albums, multiple sell-out world tours, major roles in six films, picked up 18 music awards, been the style icon behind a range of products from Pepsi and Max Factor to the Gap and H&M, and became a worldwide best-selling children's author.

The foundation of Madonna's business success was her ability to sustain her reign as the 'queen of pop' since 1983. Along with many others, Phil Quattro, the President of Warner Brothers, has argued that 'she always manages to land on the cusp of what we call contemporary music, every established artist faces the dilemma of maintaining their importance and relevance, Madonna never fails to be relevant.' Madonna's chameleon-like ability to change persona, change her music genre with it and yet still achieve major record sales has been the hallmark of her success.

Photo: Roland Weihrauch/DPA/PA Photos

Madonna's early poppy style was targeted at young 'wannabe' girls. The image that she portrayed through hits such as 'Holiday' and 'Lucky Star' in 1983 was picked up by Macy's, the US-based department store. It produced a range of *Madonna lookalike* clothes that mothers were happy to purchase for their daughters. One year later in 1984, Madonna then underwent her first image change and, in doing so, offered the first hint of the smart cookie behind the media image. In the video for her hit 'Material Girl', she deliberately mirrored the glamour-based, sexual pussycat image of Marilyn Monroe whilst simultaneously mocking both the growing materialism of the late 1980s and the men fawning after her. Media analysts Sam and Diana Kirschner commented that with this kind of packaging, Madonna allowed the record companies to keep hold of a saleable 'Marilyn image' for a new cohort of fans, but also allowed her original fan base of now growing up wannabe girls to take the more critical message from the music. The theme of courting controversy but staying marketable enough has been recurrent throughout her career, if not slightly toned down in later years.

Madonna's subsequent image changes were more dramatic. First she took on the Catholic Church in her

1989 video 'Like a Prayer' where, as a red-dressed 'sinner', she kissed a black saint easily interpreted as a Jesus figure. Her image had become increasingly sexual whilst also holding on to a critical social theme: for example, her pointed illustration of white-only imagery in the Catholic Church. At this point in her career, Madonna took full control of her image in the $60m (€48m; £33m) deal with Time-Warner that created her record company Maverick. In 1991, she published a coffee-table soft-porn book entitled *Sex* that exclusively featured pictures of herself in erotic poses. Her image and music also reflected this erotic theme. In her 'Girlie' tour, her singles 'Erotica' and 'Justify my Love' and her fly-on-the-wall movie 'In bed with Madonna' she played out scenes of sadomasochistic and lesbian fantasies. Although allegedly a period of her career she would rather forget, Madonna more than survived it. In fact, she gained a whole new demography of fans who not only respected her artistic courage, but also did not miss the fact that Madonna was consistent in her message: her sexuality was her own and not in need of a male gaze. She used the media's love affair with her, and the *cause célèbre* status gained from having MTV ban the video for 'Justify my Love', to promote the message that women's sexuality and freedom is just as important and acceptable as men's.

Changing gear in 1996, Madonna finally took centre stage in the lead role in the film *Evita* that she had chased for over five years. She beat other heavyweight contenders for the role including Meryl Streep and Elaine Page, both with more acceptable pasts than Madonna. Yet she achieved the image transition from erotica to saint-like persona of Eva Peron and won critical acclaim to boot. Another vote of confidence from the 'establishment' came from Max Factor, who in 1999 signed her up to front its relaunch campaign that was crafted around a glamour theme. Procter and Gamble (owners of the Max Factor make-up range) argued that they saw Madonna as 'the closest thing the 90s has to an old-style Hollywood star . . . she is a real woman'.

With many pre-release leaks, Madonna's keenly awaited album 'Ray of Light' was released in 1998. Radio stations worldwide were desperate to get hold of the album being billed as her most successful musical voyage to date. In a smart move, Madonna had teamed up with techno pioneer William Orbit to write and produce the album. It was a huge success, taking Madonna into the super-trendy techno sphere, not the natural environment for a pop star from the early 1980s. Madonna took up an 'earth mother/spiritual' image and spawned a trend for all things Eastern in fashion and music. This phase may have produced more than just an image as it is the time in Madonna's life which locates the beginning of her continued faith in the Kabbalah tradition of Eastern spiritual worship.

By 2001, her next persona was unveiled with the release of her album 'Music'. Here her style had moved on again to 'acid rock'. With her marriage to British movie director Guy Ritchie, the ultimate 'American Pie' had become a fully fledged Brit babe earning the endearing nick name of 'Madge' in the British press.

By 2003 some commentators were suggesting that an interesting turn of events hinted that perhaps 'the cutting-edge' Madonna, 'the fearless', was starting to think about *being part of* rather than *beating* the establishment when she launched her new Che-Guevara-inspired image. Instead of maximising the potential of this image in terms of its political and social symbolism during the Second Gulf War, in April 2003 she withdrew her militaristic image and video for the album 'American Life'. That action timed with the publication of her children's book *The English Roses*, based on the themes of compassion and friendship, which sparked questions in the press around the theme 'has Madonna gone soft?'.

By late 2003 she had wiped the military image from the West's collective memory with a glitzy high-profile ad campaign for the Gap, the clothing retailer in which she danced around accompanied by rapper Missy Elliot to a retrospective remix of her 1980s' track 'Get into the Groove'. Here Madonna was keeping the 'thirty-somethings', who remembered the track from first time around, happy. They could purchase jeans for themselves and their newly teenage daughters whilst also purchasing the re-released CD (on sale in store) for them to share and a copy of *The English Roses* (also promoted in the Gap stores) for perhaps the youngest member of the family.

Late 2005 saw the release of the 'Confessions on a Dance Floor' album that was marketed as her comeback album after her lowest-selling 'American Life'. It and the linked tour achieved one of the highest-selling peaks of her career. The album broke a world record for solo-female artists when it debuted at number one in 41 countries. By February 2007 it had sold 8 million copies.

Releases	Year	Image	Target audience
Lucky Star	1982	Trashy pop	Young wannabe girls, dovetailing from fading disco to emerging 'club scene'
Like a Virgin *Like a Prayer*	1984	Originally a Marilyn glamour image, then became a saint and sinner	More grown-up rebellious fan base, more critical female audience and male worshippers
Vogue *Erotica* *Bedtime Stories*	1990 1992 1994	Erotic porn star, sadomasochistic, sexual control, more Minelli in *Cabaret* than Monroe	Peculiar mix of target audiences: gay club scene, 1990s' women taking control of their own lives, also pure male titillation
Something to Remember Evita	1995	Softer image, ballads preparing for glamour image of *Evita* film role	Broadest audience target, picking up potential film audiences as well as regular fan base. Most conventional image. Max Factor later used this mixture of Marilyn and Eva Peron to market its glamour image
Ray of Light	1998	Earth mother, Eastern mysticism, dance music fusion	Clubbing generation of the 1990s, new cohort of fans plus original fan base of now 30-somethings desperately staying trendy
Music	2000	Acid rock, tongue in cheek Miss USA/cow girl, cool Britannia	Managing to hit the changing club scene and 30-something Brits
American Life	2003	Militaristic image Che Guevara Anti-consumerism of American dream	Unclear audience reliant on existing base
Confessions on a Dance Floor	2005	Retro-1980s' disco imagery, high-motion dance–pop sound	Strong gay–icon audience, pop–disco audience, dance-based audience

Here Madonna focused on the high-selling principal of *remix*, choosing samples of the gay–iconic disco favourites of Abba and Giorgio Moroder to be at the heart of her symbolic reinvention of herself from artist to DJ. By cross-marketing the album image with Dolce & Gabbana in its men's fashion shows, Madonna cashed in on her regaining the dance–pop crown. Will this, her latest album, stand the musical test of time? Who knows? But for now it seems to have more than met the moment.

Sources: 'Bennett takes the reins at Maverick', *Billboard Magazine*, 7 August (1999); 'Warner Bros expects Madonna to light up international markets', *Billboard Magazine*, 21 February (1998); 'Maverick builds on early success', *Billboard Magazine*, 12 November (1994); A. Jardine 'Max Factor strikes gold with Madonna', *Marketing*, vol. 29 (1999), pp. 14–15; S. Kirschner and D. Kirschner, 'MTV, adolescence and Madonna: a discourse analysis', in *Perspectives on Psychology & the Media*, American Psychological Association, Washington, DC, 1997; 'Warner to buy out maverick co-founder', *Los Angeles Times*, 2 March (1999); 'Why Madonna is back in Vogue', *New Statesman*, 18 September (2000); 'Madonna & Microsoft', *Financial Times*, 28 November (2000).

Questions

1. Describe and explain the strategy being followed by Madonna in terms of the explanation of competitive strategy given in Chapter 6.
2. Why has she experienced sustained success over the past two decades?
3. What might threaten the sustainability of her success?

7

Strategic Directions and Corporate-Level Strategy

LEARNING OUTCOMES

After reading this chapter, you should be able to:

- Identify alternative directions for strategy, including market penetration or consolidation, product development, market development and diversification.
- Recognise when diversification is an effective strategy for growth.
- Distinguish between different diversification strategies (related and unrelated) and identify conditions under which they work best.
- Analyse the ways in which a corporate parent can add or destroy value for its portfolio of business units.
- Analyse portfolios of business units and judge which to invest in and which to divest.

Photo: Dynamic Graphics, Inc.

7.1 INTRODUCTION

Chapter 6 was concerned with choices at the level of single business or organisational units, for instance through pricing strategies or differentiation. This chapter is about choices of *products and markets* for an organisation to enter or exit. Should the organisation be very focused on just a few products and markets? Or should it be much broader in scope, perhaps very diversified in terms of both products (or services) and markets? Many organisations do choose to enter many new product and market areas. For example, the Virgin Group started out in the music business, but is now highly diverse, operating in the holiday, cinema, retail, air travel and rail markets. Sony began by making small radios, but now produces games, music and movies, as well as a host of electronic products. As organisations add new units, their strategies are no longer concerned just with the business-level but with the corporate-level choices involved in having many different businesses or markets.

The chapter begins by introducing Ansoff's matrix, which generates an initial set of alternative strategic directions. The four basic directions are *increased penetration* of existing markets; *market development*, which includes building new markets, perhaps overseas or in new customer segments; *product development*, referring to product improvement and innovation; and *diversification*, involving a significant broadening of an organisation's scope in terms of both markets and products. This chapter gives a particularly hard look at the diversification option, proposing good reasons for doing so and warning of less good reasons: diversification does not always pay. Chapter 8 takes up internationalisation as one form of market development.

The **corporate parent** refers to the levels of management above that of the business units, and therefore without direct interaction with buyers and competitors

Diversification raises the other themes of the chapter. The first theme here is the role of the 'corporate-level' executives that perform a **corporate parent** role with regard to the individual business units that make up diversified organisations' portfolios. Given their detachment from the actual marketplace, how can corporate-level activities, decisions and resources add value to the actual businesses? The second theme is how to achieve a good mix of businesses within the corporate portfolio. Which businesses should corporate parents cultivate and which should they divest? Here *portfolio matrices* help structure corporate-level choices.

The chapter is not just about large commercial businesses. Even small businesses may consist of a number of business units. For example, a local builder may be undertaking contract work for local government, work for industrial buyers and for local homeowners. Not only are these different market segments, but the mode of operation and capabilities required for competitive success are also likely to be different. Moreover, the owner of that business has to take decisions about the extent of investment and activity in each segment. Public sector organisations such as local government or health services also provide different services, which correspond to business units in commercial organisations. Corporate-level strategy is highly relevant to the appropriate

Exhibit 7.1 Strategic directions and corporate-level strategy

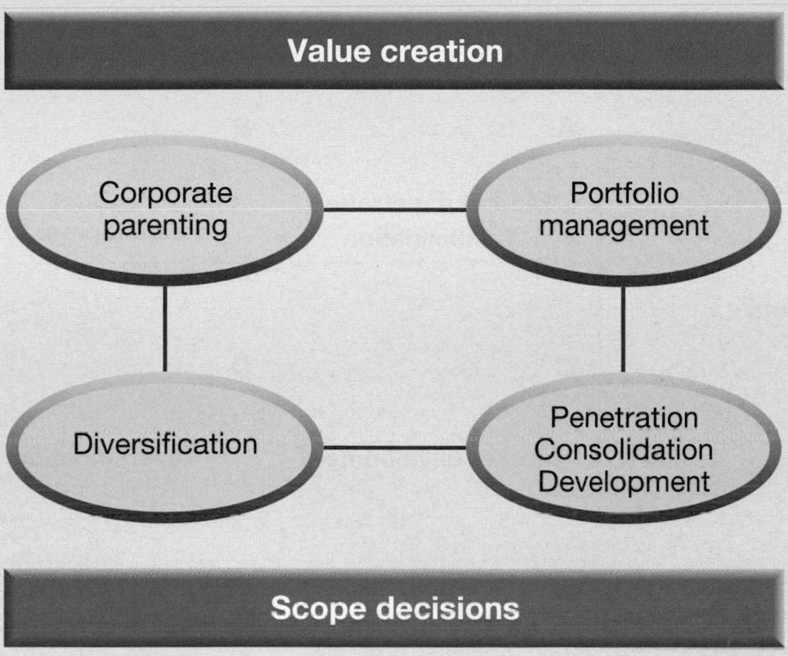

drawing of organisational boundaries in the public sector, and privatisation and outsourcing decisions can be considered as responses to the failure of public sector organisations to add sufficient value by their parenting.

Exhibit 7.1 summarises the key themes of this chapter. After reviewing Ansoff's strategic directions, the chapter focuses specifically on diversification. Diversification in turn raises the two related topics of the role of the corporate parent and the use of business portfolio matrices.

7.2 STRATEGIC DIRECTIONS

www.pearsoned.co.uk/fos
KEY CONCEPT
Strategic directions (Ansoff)

The Ansoff product/market growth matrix[1] provides a simple way of generating four basic alternative directions for strategic development: see Exhibit 7.2. An organisation typically starts in box A, the top left-hand one, with its existing products and existing markets. According to the matrix, the organisation basically has a choice between *penetrating* still further within its existing sphere (staying in box A); moving rightwards by *developing new products* for its existing markets (box B); moving downwards by bringing its *existing products into new markets* (box C); or taking the most radical step of full *diversification*, with altogether new markets and new products (box D).

Exhibit 7.2 Strategic directions (Ansoff matrix)

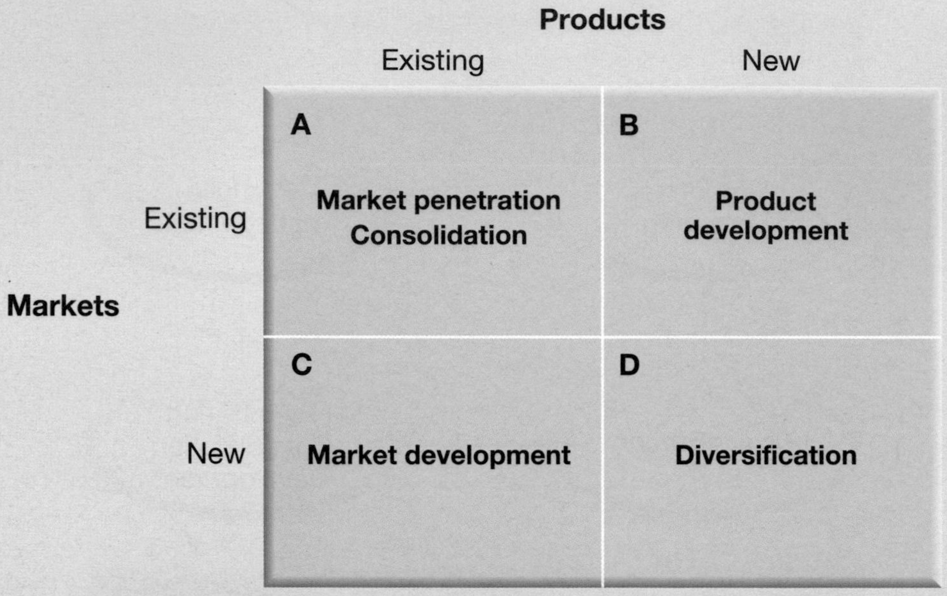

Source: Adapted from H.I. Ansoff, *Corporate Strategy*, Penguin, 1988, Chapter 6. (The Ansoff matrix was later developed – see reference 1.)

The Ansoff matrix explicitly considers growth options. Growth is rarely a good end in itself. Public sector organisations are often accused of growing out-of-control bureaucracies; similarly, some private-sector managers are accused of empire-building at the expense of shareholders. This chapter therefore adds *consolidation* as a fifth option. Consolidation involves protecting existing products and existing markets and therefore belongs in box A. The rest of this section considers the five strategic directions in more detail.

7.2.1 Market penetration

Market penetration is where an organisation gains market share

Further **market penetration**, by which the organisation takes increased share of its existing markets with its existing product range, is on the face of it the most obvious strategic direction. It builds on existing strategic capabilities and does not require the organisation to venture into uncharted territory. The organisation's scope is exactly the same. Moreover, greater market share implies increased power *vis-à-vis* buyers and suppliers (in terms of the five forces), greater economies of scale and experience curve benefits.

However, organisations seeking greater market penetration may face two constraints:

- *Retaliation from competitors.* In terms of the five forces (Section 2.3), increasing market penetration is likely to exacerbate industry rivalry as other competitors in the market defend their share. Increased rivalry might involve price wars or expensive marketing battles, which may cost more than any market share gains are actually worth. The dangers of provoking fierce retaliation are greater in low-growth markets, as any gains in volume will be much more at the expense of other players. Where retaliation is a danger, organisations seeking market penetration need strategic capabilities that give a clear competitive advantage. In low growth or declining markets, it can be more effective simply to acquire competitors. Some companies have grown quickly in this way. For example, in the steel industry the Indian company LNM (Mittal) moved rapidly in the 2000s to become the largest steel producer in the world by acquiring struggling steel companies around the world. Acquisitions can actually reduce rivalry, by taking out independent players and consolidating them under one umbrella: see also the consolidation strategy in 7.2.2 below.
- *Legal constraints.* Greater market penetration can raise concerns from official competition regulators concerning excessive market power. Most countries have regulators with the powers to restrain powerful companies or prevent mergers and acquisitions that would create such excessive power. In the UK, the Competition Commission can investigate any merger or acquisition that would account for more than 25 per cent of the national market, and either halt the deal or propose measures that would reduce market power. The European Commission has an overview of the whole European market and can similarly intervene. For example, when Gaz de France and Suez, two utility companies with dominant positions in France and Belgium, decided to merge in 2006, the European Commission insisted that the two companies reduced their power by divesting some of their subsidiaries and opening up their networks to competition.[2]

7.2.2 Consolidation

Consolidation is where organisations focus defensively on their current markets with current products

Consolidation is where organisations focus defensively on their current markets with current products. Formally, this strategy occupies the same box in the Ansoff matrix as market penetration, but is not orientated to growth. Consolidation can take two forms:

- *Defending market share.* When facing aggressive competitors bent on increasing their market share, organisations have to work hard and often creatively to protect what they already have. Although market share should rarely be an end in itself, it is important to ensure that it is sufficient to sustain the business in the long term. For example, turnover has to be high enough to spread essential fixed costs such as R&D. In defending market share, differentiation strategies in order to build customer loyalty and switching costs are often effective.

- *Downsizing or divestment.* Especially when the size of the market as a whole is declining, reducing the size of the business through closing capacity is often unavoidable. An alternative is divesting (selling) some activities to other businesses. Sometimes downsizing can be dictated by the needs of shareholders, for instance an entrepreneur wishing to simplify their business as they approach retirement. Divesting or closing peripheral businesses can also make it easier to sell the core business to a potential purchaser.

The term consolidation is sometimes also used to describe strategies of *buying up rivals* in a fragmented industry, particularly one in decline. By acquiring weaker competitors, and closing capacity, the consolidating company can gain market power and increase overall efficiency. As this form of consolidation increases market share, it could be seen as a kind of market penetration, but here the motivation is essentially defensive.

Although both consolidation and market penetration strategies are by no means static ones, their limitations often propel managers to consider alternative strategic directions.

7.2.3 Product development

Product development is where organisations deliver modified or new products to existing markets

Product development is where organisations deliver modified or new products (or services) to existing markets. This is a limited extension of organizational scope. In practice, even market penetration will probably require some product development, but here product development implies greater degrees of innovation. For Sony, such product development would include moving the Walkman portable music system from audio tapes, through CDs to MP3-based systems. Effectively the same markets are involved, but the technologies are radically different. In the case of the Walkman, Sony probably had little choice but to make these significant product developments. However, product development can be an expensive and high-risk activity for at least two reasons:

- *New strategic capabilities.* Product development typically involves mastering new technologies that may be unfamiliar to the organisation. For example, many banks entered online banking at the beginning of this century, but suffered many setbacks with technologies so radically different to their traditional high street branch means of delivering banking services. Success frequently depended on a willingness to acquire new technological and marketing capabilities, often with the help of specialised information technology and e-commerce consultancy firms.[3] Thus product development typically involves heavy investments and high risk of project failures.
- *Project management risk.* Even within fairly familiar domains, product development projects are typically subject to the risk of delays and increased costs due to project complexity and changing project specifications over time. A famous recent case was the €11bn (£7.6bn) Airbus A380 double-decker airline project, which suffered two years of delays in the mid-2000s because of

wiring problems. Airbus had managed several new aircraft developments before, but the high degrees of customisation required by each airline customer, and incompatibilities in computer-aided design software, led to greater complexity than the company's project management staff could handle.

7.2.4 Market development

Market development is where existing products are offered in new markets

If product development is risky and expensive, an alternative strategy is market development. **Market development** involves offering existing products to new markets. Again, the extension of scope is limited. Typically, of course, this may entail some product development as well, if only in terms of packaging or service. Market development might take three forms:

- *New segments*. For example in the public services, a college might offer its educational services to older students than its traditional intake, perhaps via evening courses.
- *New users*. Here an example would be aluminium, whose original users packaging and cutlery manufacture are now supplemented by users in aerospace and automobiles.
- *New geographies*. The prime example of this is internationalisation, but the spread of a small retailer into new towns would also be a case.

In all cases, it is essential that market development strategies are based on products or services that meet the *critical success factors* of the new market (see Section 2.4.4). Strategies based on simply off-loading traditional products or services in new markets are likely to fail. Moreover, market development faces similar problems as product development. In terms of strategic capabilities, market developers often lack the right marketing skills and brands to make progress in a market with unfamiliar customers. On the management side, the challenge is coordinating between different segments, users and geographies, which might all have different needs. International market development strategy is considered in Chapter 8.

For a description of the various strategic directions considered by chief executive Mattias Döpfner for the German publisher Axel Springer see Illustration 7.1.

7.2.5 Diversification

Diversification is defined as a strategy that takes an organisation away from both its existing markets and its existing products

Diversification is strictly a strategy that takes the organisation away from both its existing markets and its existing products (i.e. box D in Exhibit 7.2). In this sense, it radically increases the organisation's scope. In fact, much diversification is not as extreme as implied by the closed boxes of the Ansoff growth matrix. Box D tends to imply unrelated or conglomerate diversification

Illustration 7.1

Strategic directions for Axel Springer

This German publishing company has many opportunities, and the money to pursue them.

In 2007, Mathias Döpfner, Chairman and Chief Executive of Axel Springer publishers, had about €2bn (£1.5bn) to invest in new opportunities. The previous year, the competition authorities had prohibited his full takeover of Germany's largest television broadcaster, ProSiebenSat.1. Now Döpfner was looking for alternative directions.

Founded in 1946 by Axel Springer himself, the company was in 2007 already Germany's largest publisher of newspapers and magazines, with more than 10,000 employees and over 150 titles. Famous print titles included *Die Welt*, the *Berliner Morgenpost*, *Bild* and *Hörzu*. Outside Germany, Axel Springer was strongest in Eastern Europe. The company also had a scattering of mostly small investments in German radio and television companies, most notably a continuing 12 per cent stake in ProSiebenSat.1. Axel Springer described its strategic objectives as market leadership in the German-language core business, internationalisaton and digitalisation of the core business.

Further digitalisation of the core newspaper and magazine business was clearly important and would require substantial funding. There were also opportunities for the launch of new print magazine titles in the German market. But Döpfner was considering acquisition opportunities: 'it goes without saying,' he told the *Financial Times*, 'that whenever a large international media company comes on to the market (i.e. is up for sale), we will examine it very closely – whether in print, TV or the online sector'.

Döpfner mentioned several specific kinds of acquisition opportunity. For example, he was still interested in buying a large European television broadcaster, even if it would probably have to be outside Germany. He was also attracted by the possibility of buying undervalued assets in the old media (namely, print), and turning them around in the style of a private equity investor: 'I would love to buy businesses in need of restructuring, where we can add value by introducing our management and sector expertise'. However, Döpfner reassured his shareholders by affirming that he felt no need 'to do a big thing in order to do a big thing'. He was also considering what to do with the 12 per cent minority stake in ProSiebenSat.1.

Main source: Financial Times Deutschland, 2 April (2007).

Questions

1. Referring to Exhibit 7.1, classify the various strategic directions considered by Mattias Döpfner for Axel Springer.
2. Using the Ansoff matrix, what other options could Döpfner pursue?

(see section 7.3.2), but a good deal of diversification in practice involves building on relationships with existing markets or products. Frequently too market penetration and product development entail some diversifying adjustment of products or markets. Diversification is a matter of degree.

Nonetheless, the Ansoff matrix does make clear that the further the organisation moves from its starting point of existing products and existing markets, the more it has to learn to do. Diversification is just one direction for developing the organisation, and needs to be considered alongside its alternatives. The drivers of diversification, its various forms and the ways it is managed are the main topics of this chapter.

7.3 REASONS FOR DIVERSIFICATION

In terms of the Ansoff matrix, diversification is the most radical strategic direction.[4] Diversification might be chosen for a variety of reasons, some more value-creating than others. Three potentially value-creating reasons for diversification are as follows.

Synergy refers to the benefits that are gained where activities or assets complement each other so that their combined effect is greater than the sum of the parts

- *Efficiency gains* can be made by applying the organisation's existing resources or capabilities to new markets and products or services. These are often described as *economies of scope*, by contrast to economies of scale.[5] If an organisation has underutilised resources or competences that it cannot effectively close or sell to other potential users, it can make sense to use these resources or competences by diversification into a new activity. In other words, there are economies to be gained by extending the scope of the organisation's activities. For example, many universities have large resources in terms of halls of residence, which they must have for their students but which are underutilised out of term-time. These halls of residence are more efficiently used if the universities expand the scope of their activities into conferencing and tourism during vacation periods. Economies of scope may apply to both *tangible* resources, such as halls of residence, and *intangible* resources and competences, such as brands or staff skills. Sometimes these scope advantages are referred to as the benefits of **synergy**,[6] by which is meant that activities or assets are more effective together than apart (the famous 2 + 2 = 5 equation). Thus a film company and a music publisher would be synergistic if they were worth more together than separately. Illustration 7.2 shows how a French company, Zodiac, has diversified following this approach.
- *Stretching corporate parenting capabilities* into new markets and products or services can be another source of gain. In a sense, this extends the point above about applying existing competences in new areas. However, this point highlights corporate parenting skills that can otherwise easily be neglected. At the corporate parent level, managers may develop a competence at managing a range of different products and services which can be applied even to businesses which do not share resources at the operationing unit level. Prahalad and Bettis have described this set of corporate parenting skills as the 'dominant general management logic', or 'dominant logic' for short.[7] Thus the French conglomerate LVMH includes a wide range of businesses – from champagne, through fashion and perfumes, to financial media – that share very few operational resources or competences. LVMH creates value for these specialised companies by adding parenting skills – for instance, the

Illustration 7.2

Zodiac: inflatable diversifications

An organisation may seek the benefits of synergies by building a portfolio of businesses through related diversification.

The Zodiac company was founded near Paris, France, in 1896 by Maurice Mallet just after his first hot-air balloon ascent. For 40 years, Zodiac manufactured only dirigible airships. In 1937, the German Zeppelin *Hindenburg* crashed near New York, which abruptly stopped the development of the market for airships. Because of the extinction of its traditional activity, Zodiac decided to leverage its technical expertise and moved from dirigibles to inflatable boats. This diversification proved to be very successful: in 2004, with over 1 million units sold in 50 years, the Zodiac rubber dinghy (priced at approximately €10,000 (£7,000)) was extremely popular worldwide.

However, because of increasing competition, especially from Italian manufacturers, Zodiac diversified its business interests. In 1978, it took over Aerazur, a company specialising in parachutes, but also in life vests and inflatable life rafts. These products had strong market and technical synergies with rubber boats and their main customers were aircraft manufacturers. Zodiac confirmed this move to a new market in 1987 by the takeover of Air Cruisers, a manufacturer of inflatable escape slides for aircraft. As a consequence, Zodiac became a key supplier to Boeing, McDonnell Douglas and Airbus. Zodiac strengthened this position through the takeover of the two leading manufacturers of aircraft seats: Sicma Aero Seats from France and Weber Aircraft from the USA. In 1997, Zodiac also took over, for €150m, MAG Aerospace, the world leader for aircraft vacuum waste systems. Finally, in 1999, Zodiac took over Intertechnique, a leading player in active components for aircraft (fuel circulation, hydraulics, oxygen and life support, electrical power, flight-deck controls and displays, systems monitoring, etc.). By combining these competences with its traditional expertise in inflatable products, Zodiac launched a new business unit: airbags for the automobile industry.

In parallel to these diversifications, Zodiac strengthened its position in inflatable boats by the takeover of several competitors: Bombard-L'Angevinière in 1980, Sevylor in 1981, Hurricane and Metzeler in 1987.

Finally, Zodiac developed a swimming-pool business. The first product line, back in 1981, was based on inflatable structure technology, and Zodiac later moved – again through takeovers – to rigid above-ground pools, modular in-ground pools, pool cleaners and water purification systems, inflatable beach gear and air mattresses.

In 2003, total sales of the Zodiac group reached €1.48bn with a net profit of €115m. Zodiac was a very international company, with a strong presence in the USA. It was listed on the Paris Stock Exchange and rumours of takeovers from powerful US groups were frequent. However, the family of the founder, institutional investors, the management and the employees together held 55 per cent of the stocks.

Far above the marine and the leisure businesses, aircraft products accounted for almost 75 per cent of the total turnover of the group. Zodiac held a 40 per cent market share of the world market for some airline equipment: for instance, the electrical power systems of the new Airbus A380 were Zodiac products. In 2004, Zodiac even reached Mars: NASA Mars probes *Spirit* and *Opportunity* were equipped with Zodiac equipment, developed by its US subsidiary Pioneer Aerospace.

Prepared by Frédéric Fréry, ESCP-EAP European School of Management.

Questions

1. What were the bases of the synergies underlying each of Zodiac's diversifications?
2. What are the advantages and potential dangers of such a basis of diversification?

support of classic brands and the nurturing of highly creative people – that are relevant to all these individual businesses (see section 7.4.1).

- *Increasing market power* can result from having a diverse range of businesses. With many businesses, an organisation can afford to cross-subsidise one business from the surpluses earned by another, in a way that competitors may not be able to. This can give an organisation a competitive advantage for the subsidised business, and the long-run effect may be to drive out other competitors, leaving the organisation with a monopoly from which good profits can then be earned. This was the fear behind the European Commission's refusal to allow General Electric's $43bn (£24bn; €37bn) bid for electronic controls company Honeywell in 2001. General Electric might have bundled its jet engines with Honeywell's aviation electronics in a cheaper package than rival jet engine manufacturers could possibly match. As aircraft manufacturers and airlines increasingly chose the cheaper overall package, rivals could have been driven out of business. General Electric would then have the market power to put up its prices without threat from competition.

There are several other reasons that are often given for diversification, but which are less obviously value-creating and sometimes serve managerial interests more than shareholders' interests.

- *Responding to market decline* is one common but doubtful reason for diversification. It is arguable that Microsoft's diversification into electronic games such as the Xbox – whose launch cost $500m (£280m; €415m) in marketing alone – is a response to slowing growth in its core software businesses. Shareholders might have preferred the Xbox money to have been handed back to shareholders, leaving Sony and Nintendo to make games, while Microsoft gracefully declined. Microsoft itself defends its various diversifications as a necessary response to convergence in electronic and computer media.
- *Spreading risk* across a range of businesses is another common justification for diversification. However, conventional finance theory is very sceptical about risk-spreading by business diversification. It argues that investors can diversify more effectively themselves by investing in a diverse portfolio of quite different companies. While managers might like the security of a diverse range of businesses, investors do not need each of the companies they invest in to be diversified as well – they would prefer managers to concentrate on managing their core business as well as they can. On the other hand, for private businesses, where the owners have a large proportion of their assets tied up in the business, it can make sense to diversify risk across a number of distinct activities, so that if one part is in trouble, the whole business is not pulled down.
- *The expectations of powerful stakeholders*, including top managers, can sometimes drive inappropriate diversification. Under pressure from Wall

Street analysts to deliver continued revenue growth, in the late 1990s the US energy company Enron diversified beyond its original interest in energy trading into trading commodities such as petrochemicals, aluminium and even bandwidth.[8] By satisfying the analysts in the short term, this strategy boosted the share price and allowed top management to stay in place. However, it soon transpired that very little of this diversification had been profitable, and in 2001 Enron collapsed in the largest bankruptcy in history.

In order to decide whether or not such reasons make sense and help organisational performance, it is important to be clear about different forms of diversification, in particular the degree of relatedness (or unrelatedness) of business units in a portfolio. The next sections consider related and unrelated diversification.

7.3.1 Related diversification

Related diversification is corporate development beyond current products and markets, but within the capabilities or value network of the organisation

Related diversification can be defined as corporate development beyond current products and markets, but within the capabilities or the value network of the organisation (see section 3.4). For example, Procter and Gamble and Unilever are diversified corporations, but virtually all of their interests are in fast-moving consumer goods distributed through retailers. Their various businesses benefit therefore from shared capabilities in research and development, consumer marketing, building relationships with powerful retailers and global brand development.

The value network provides one way of thinking about different forms of related diversification is shown in Exhibit 7.3:

Vertical integration is backward or forward integration into adjacent activities in the value network

Backward integration is development into activities concerned with the inputs into the company's current business

Forward integration is development into activities which are concerned with a company's outputs

Horizontal integration is development into activities which are complementary to present activities

- **Vertical integration** describes either backward or forward integration into adjacent activities in the value network. **Backward integration** refers to development into activities concerned with the inputs into the company's current business (i.e. they are further back in the value network). For example, the acquisition by a car manufacturer of a component supplier would be related diversification through backward integration. **Forward integration** refers to development into activities which are concerned with a company's outputs (i.e. are further forward in the value system): for a car manufacturer, this might be distribution, repairs and servicing.
- **Horizontal integration** is development into activities which are complementary or adjacent to present activities. For example, Internet search company Google has spread horizontally into news, images and maps, amongst other services (another example is Zodiac – see Illustration 7.2).

It is important to recognise that capabilities and value links are distinct. A link through the value network does not necessarily imply the existence of capabilities. For example, in the late 1990s some car manufacturers began to integrate forward into repairs and servicing following a value network logic.

Exhibit 7.3 **Related diversification options for a manufacturer**

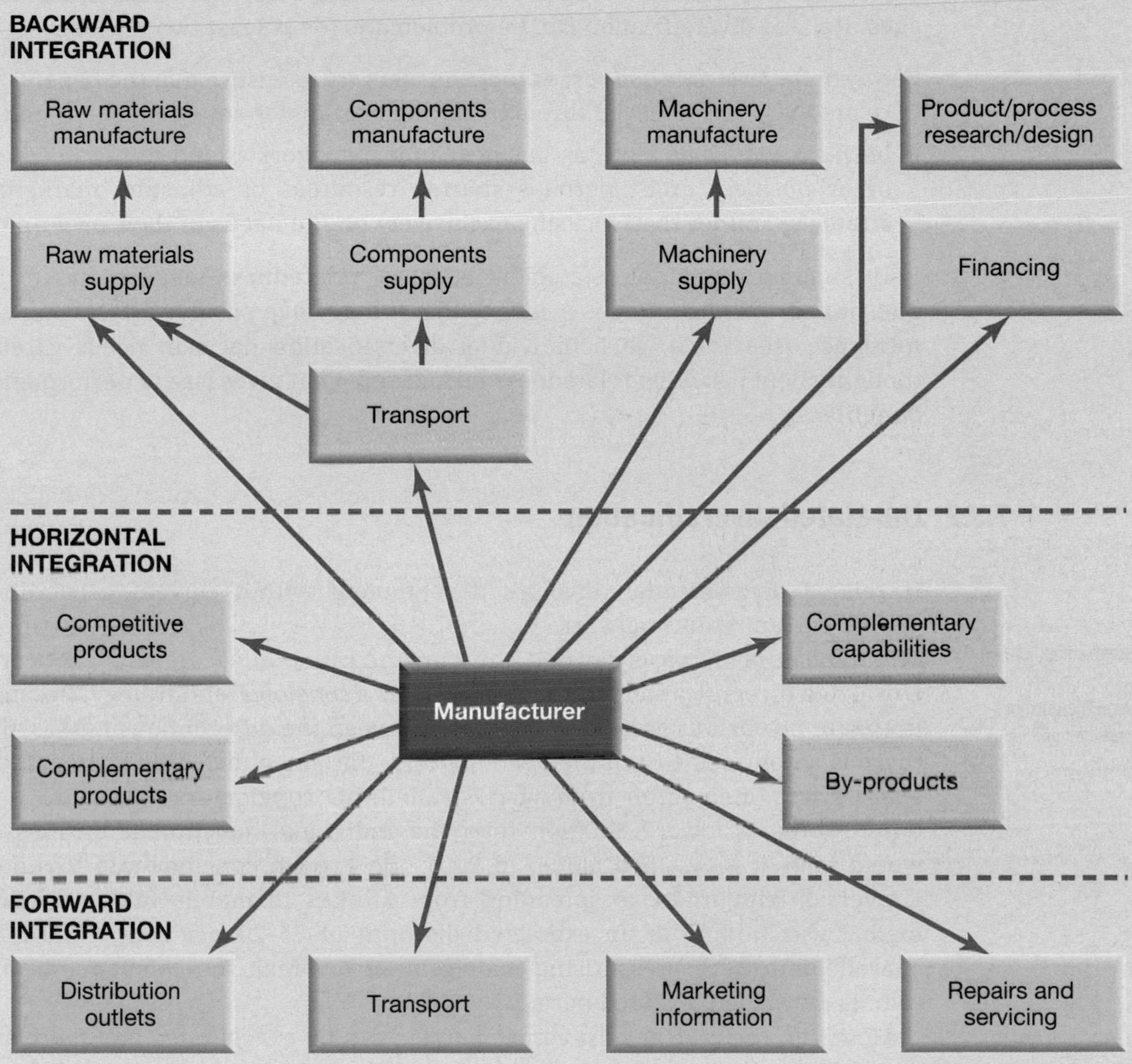

Note: Some companies will manufacture components or semi-finished items. In those cases there will be additional integration opportunities into assembly or finished product manufacture.

The car manufacturers thought they could create value by using forward links to ensure a better overall customer experience with their cars. However, the manufacturers rapidly realised that these new businesses involved quite different capabilities: not manufacturing in large factories, but service in many scattered small units. In the end, the absence of relevant capabilities outweighed the potential from the value-network links, and the car manufacturers generally withdrew from these forward integration initiatives. Synergies are often harder to identify and more costly to extract in practice than managers like to admit.[9]

It is also important to recognise that relationships have potential disadvantages. Related diversification can be problematic for at least two reasons:

- *corporate-level time and cost* as top managers try to ensure that the benefits of relatedness are achieved through sharing or transfer across business units;
- *business unit complexity*, as business unit managers attend to the needs of other business units, perhaps sharing resources or adjusting marketing strategies, rather than focusing exclusively on the needs of their own unit.

In summary, a simple statement such as 'relatedness matters' has to be questioned.[10] Whilst there is evidence that it may have positive effects on performance (see 7.3.3), each individual diversification decision needs careful thought about just what relatedness means and what gives rise to performance benefits.

7.3.2 Unrelated diversification

Unrelated diversification is the development of products or services beyond the current capabilities and value network

If related diversification involves development within current capabilities or the current value network, **unrelated diversification** is the development of products or services beyond the current capabilities or value network. Unrelated diversification is often described as a *conglomerate* strategy. Because there are no obvious economies of scope between the different businesses, but there is an obvious cost of the headquarters, unrelated diversified companies' share prices often suffer from what is called the 'conglomerate discount' – in other words, a lower valuation than the individual constituent businesses would have if they stood alone. In 2003, the French conglomerate Vivendi-Universal, with interests spreading from utilities to mobile telephony and media, was trading at an estimated discount of 15–20 per cent. Naturally, shareholders were pressurising management to break the conglomerate up into its more highly valued parts.

However, the case against conglomerates can be exaggerated and there are certainly potential advantages to unrelated diversification in some conditions:

- *Exploiting dominant logics*, rather than concrete operational relationships, can be a source of conglomerate value creation. As at Berkshire Hathaway (see Illustration 7.3), a skilled investor such as Warren Buffett, the so-called Oracle of Omaha and one of the richest men in the world, may be able to add value to diverse businesses within his dominant logic.[11] Berkshire Hathaway includes businesses in different areas of manufacturing, insurance, distribution and retailing, but Buffett focuses on mature businesses that he can understand and whose managers he can trust. During the e-business boom of the late 1990s, Buffett deliberately avoided buying high-technology businesses because he knew they were outside his dominant logic.

Illustration 7.3

Berkshire Hathaway Inc.

A portfolio manager may seek to manage a highly diverse set of business units on behalf of its shareholders.

Berkshire Hathaway's Chairman is Warren Buffett, one of the world's richest men, and Charles Munger is Vice Chairman. The businesses in the portfolio are highly diverse. There are insurance businesses, including GEICO, the sixth largest automobile insurer in the USA, manufacturers of carpets, building products, clothing and footwear. There are service businesses (the training of aircraft and ship operators), retailers of home furnishings and fine jewellery, a daily and Sunday newspaper and the largest direct seller of housewear products in the USA.

The annual report of Berkshire Hathaway (2002) provides an insight into its rationale and management. Warren Buffett explains how he and his vice chairman run the business.

Charlie Munger and I think of our shareholders as owner-partners and of ourselves as managing partners. (Because of the size of our shareholdings we are also, for better or worse, controlling partners.) We do not view the company itself as the ultimate owner of our business assets but instead view the company as a conduit through which our shareholders own the assets. . . . Our long term economic goal . . . is to maximise Berkshire's average annual rate of gain in intrinsic business value on a per-share basis. We do not measure the economic significance or performance of Berkshire by its size; we measure by per-share progress.

Our preference would be to reach our goal by directly owning a diversified group of businesses that generate cash and consistently earn above average returns on capital. Our second choice is to own parts of similar businesses, attained primarily through purchases of marketable common stocks by our insurance subsidiaries. . . . Charlie and I are interested only in acquisitions that we believe will raise the per-share intrinsic value of Berkshire's stock.

Regardless of price we have no interest at all in selling any good businesses that Berkshire owns. We are also very reluctant to sell sub-par businesses as long as we expect them to generate at least some cash and as long as we feel good about their managers and labour relations. . . . Gin rummy managerial behaviour (discard your least promising business at each turn) is not our style. We would rather have our overall results penalised a bit than engaged in that kind of behaviour.

Buffett then explains how they manage their subsidiary businesses:

. . . we delegate almost to the point of abdication: though Berkshire has about 45,000 employees, only 12 of these are at headquarters. . . . Charlie and I mainly attend to capital allocation and the care and feeding of our key managers. Most of these managers are happiest when they are left alone to run their businesses and that is customarily just how we leave them. That puts them in charge of all operating decisions and of despatching the excess cash they generate to headquarters. By sending it to us, they don't get diverted by the various enticements that would come their way were they responsible for deploying the cash their businesses throw off. Further more, Charlie and I are exposed to a much wider range of possibilities for investing these funds than any of our managers could find in his/her own industry.

Source: Berkshire Hathaway Annual Report, 2002.

Questions

1 Berkshire Hathaway's businesses are very diverse, but exclude high-technology businesses. Why might that be, given the group's parenting style?

2 Using the checklist explained in section 7.4, suggest how and in what ways Berkshire Hathaway may or may not add value to its shareholders.

- *Countries with underdeveloped markets* can be fertile ground for conglomerates. Where external capital and labour markets do not yet work well, conglomerates offer a substitute mechanism for allocating and developing capital or managerial talent within their own organisational boundaries. For example, Korean conglomerates (the chaebol) were successful in the rapid growth phase of the Korean economy partly because they were able to mobilise investment and develop managers in a way that standalone companies in South Korea traditionally were unable to. Also, the strong cultural cohesion amongst managers in these chaebol reduced the coordination and monitoring costs that would be necessary in a Western conglomerate, where managers would be trusted less.[12] The same may be true today in other fast growing economies that still have underdeveloped capital and labour markets.

It is important also to recognise that the distinction between related and unrelated diversification is often a matter of degree. As in the case of Berkshire Hathaway, although there are very few operational relationships between the constituent businesses, there is a relationship in terms of similar parenting requirements. As in the case of the car manufacturers diversifying forwards into apparently related businesses such as repairs and servicing, operational relationships can turn out to be much less valuable than at first they appear. The boundary between related and unrelated diversification is blurred and it is easy to exaggerate relatedness.

7.3.3 Diversification and performance

Because most large corporations today are diversified, but also because diversification can sometimes be in management's self-interest, many scholars and policy-makers have been concerned to establish whether diversified companies really perform better than undiversified companies. After all, it would be deeply troubling if large corporations were diversifying simply to spread risk for managers, to save managerial jobs in declining businesses or to preserve the image of growth, as in the case of Enron.

Research studies of diversification have generally found some performance benefits, with *related diversifiers* outperforming both firms that remain *specialised* and those which have *unrelated* diversified strategies.[13] In other words, the diversification–performance relationship tends to follow an inverted (or upside down) U-shape, as in Exhibit 7.4. The implication is that some diversification is good – but not too much.

However, these performance studies produce statistical averages. Some related diversification strategies fail – as in the case of the vertically-integrating car manufacturers – while some conglomerates succeed – as in the case of Berkshire Hathaway. The case against unrelated diversification is not solid, and effective dominant logics or particular national contexts can play in its favour. The conclusion from the performance studies is that, although on

Exhibit 7.4 Diversity and performance

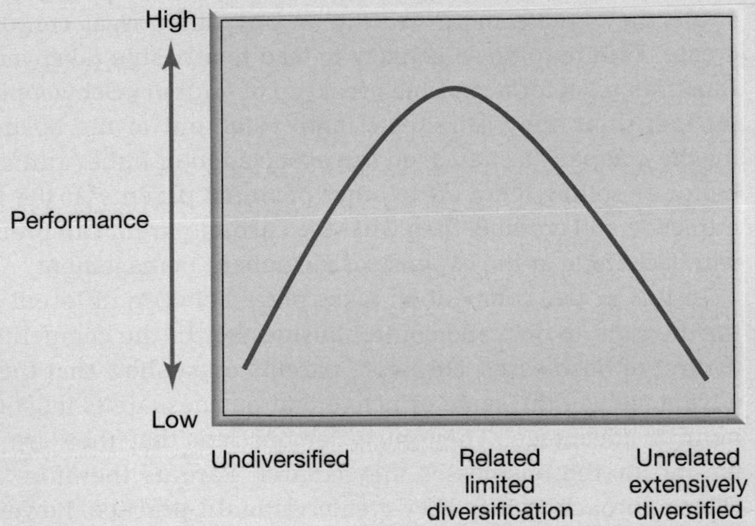

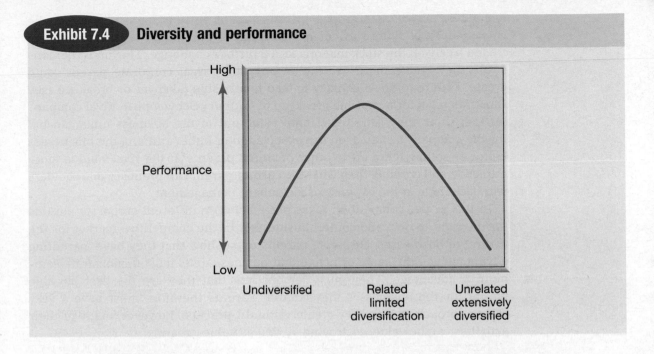

average related diversification pays better than unrelated, any diversification strategy needs rigorous questioning on its particular merits.

7.4 VALUE CREATION AND THE CORPORATE PARENT

Given the doubtful benefits of diversification, it is clear that some corporate parents do not add value. During 2006, two large US conglomerates, Tyco and Cendant, decided to break themselves up voluntarily, recognising that their subsidiary business units would be more valuable apart than together under their parenting. In the public sector too, units such as schools or hospitals are increasingly being given freedom from parenting authorities, because independence is seen as more effective. This section examines how corporate parents can both add and destroy value, and considers three different parenting approaches that can be effective.

7.4.1 Value-adding and value-destroying activities of corporate parents[14]

Any corporate parent needs to demonstrate that they create more value than they cost. This applies to both commercial and public sector organisations.

For public sector organisations, privatisation or outsourcing is likely to be the consequence of failure to demonstrate value. Companies whose shares are traded freely on the stock markets face a further challenge. They must demonstrate they create more value than any other rival corporate parent could create. Failure to do so is likely to lead to a hostile takeover or break-up (see Illustration 7.4 for a possible break-up of Cadbury Schweppes). Rival companies that think they can create more value out of the business units can bid for the company's shares, on the expectation of either running the businesses better or selling them off to other potential parents. If the rival's bid is more attractive and credible than what the current parent can promise, shareholders will back them at the expense of incumbent management.

In this sense, competition takes place between different corporate parents for the right to own and control businesses. In the competitive market for the control of businesses, corporate parents must show that they have 'parenting advantage', on the same principle that business units must demonstrate competitive advantage. They must demonstrate that they are the best possible parent for the businesses they control. Parents therefore must have a very clear approach to how they create value. In practice, however, many of their activities can be value-destroying as well as value-creating.

Value-adding activities[15]

There are four main types of activity by which a corporate parent can add value.

- *Envisioning*. The corporate parent can provide a clear overall vision or *strategic intent* for its business units.[16] This vision should guide and motivate the business unit managers in order to maximise corporate-wide performance through commitment to a common purpose. The vision should also provide stakeholders with a *clear external image* about what the organisation as a whole is about: this can reassure shareholders about the rationale for having a diversified strategy in the first place. Finally, a clear vision provides a *discipline* on the corporate parent to stop it wandering into inappropriate activities or taking on unnecessary costs.
- *Coaching and facilitating*. The corporate parent can help business unit managers *develop strategic capabilities*, by coaching them to improve their skills and confidence. They can also facilitate cooperation and sharing across the business units, so improving the *synergies* from being within the same corporate organisation. Corporate-wide management courses are one effective means of achieving these objectives, as bringing managers across the business to learn management skills also provides an opportunity for them to build relationships between each other and see opportunities for cooperation.
- *Providing central services and resources*. The centre is obviously a provider of capital for *investment*. The centre can also provide central services such as treasury, tax and human resource advice, which if centralised can have

Illustration 7.4

A sweet deal for Nelson Peltz?

Financiers can make money out of over-diversified corporations, and managers have to respond.

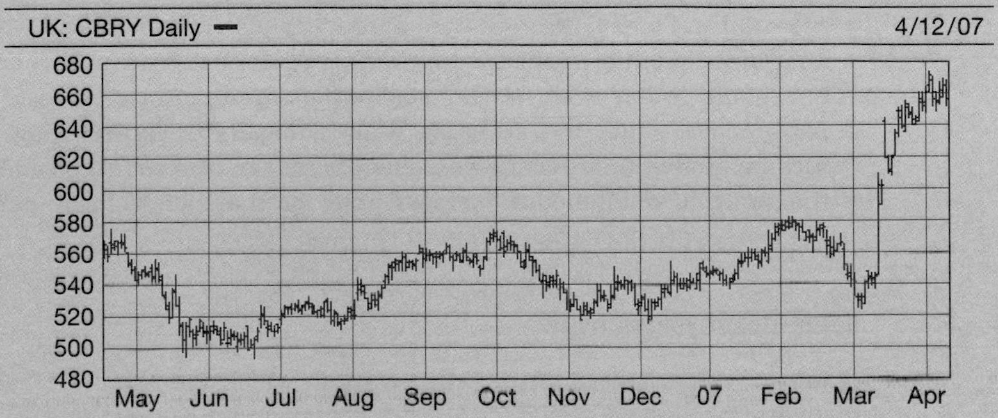

Figure 1 Cadbury Schweppes share price, 2006–2007

Source: www.bigcharts.com. Marketwatch.Online by BigCharts.com. Copyright 2007 by Dow Jones & Company, Inc. Reproduced with permission of Dow Jones & Company, Inc. in format Textbook via Copyright Clearance Center.

In March 2007, American financier Nelson Peltz used his hedge fund Trian Fund Management LP to take a 3 per cent stake in Cadbury Schweppes PLC. Peltz was known as an activist shareholder, keen to extract maximum shareholder value through pressuring management or breaking up underperforming groups. Over the next few days, the Cadbury Schweppes share price rose by 15 per cent (see Figure 1).

Since 1969, Cadbury Schweppes had combined the chocolate and confectionary businesses of the original Cadbury company (founded 1824) with the carbonated drinks business of Schweppes (founded 1790). Cadbury's major confectionary brands included Dairy Milk, Creme Eggs and Dentyne gum. The company was the largest confectionery producer in the world, with 10 per cent market share, just ahead of Mars and Nestlé. The Schweppes business owned 7 Up and Dr Pepper, as well as the original Schweppes drinks. However, in its main market of the USA, it was still a distant number three to Coca-Cola and PepsiCo, who together accounted for 75 per cent of the carbonated drinks market. Cadbury Schweppes management were investing substantially in the drinks business, having bought up major bottling facilities during 2006. Todd Stitzer, the Cadbury Schweppes Chief Executive, had played a leading role in acquiring Dr Pepper and 7 Up back in 1995.

Two days after the announcement of Peltz's stake, Cadbury Schweppes stated it was actively considering the demerger of its drinks business. Options that were being examined for the drinks business included: making it a stand-alone company; selling the business outright to another company or private equity house; and floating a minority stake in the business and, over time, selling the remaining shares.

Soon after, rumours began to emerge of a possible merger between Cadbury Schweppes and Hershey, the American confectioner with over 5 per cent of the world confectionery market. Such a deal would give the merged company a commanding lead over competitors and substantial leverage over powerful retailers. Cadbury was weak in the US confectionary market, while Hershey was weak in Europe.

Sources: Wall Street Journal and *Financial Times*, various dates.

Questions

1 Why has the Cadbury Schweppes share price behaved in the way it has?

2 Why do you think Cadbury Schweppes had not acted earlier on the demerger option?

sufficient scale to be efficient and to build up *relevant expertise*. Centralised services often have greater *leverage*: for example, combining the purchases of separate business units increases their bargaining power for shared inputs such as energy. This leverage can be helpful in *brokering* with external bodies, such as government regulators or other companies in negotiating alliances. Finally, the centre can have an important role in managing expertise within the corporate whole, for instance by *transferring managers* across the business units or by creating shared *knowledge management* systems.

- *Intervening*. Finally, the corporate parent can also intervene within its business units in order to ensure appropriate performance. The corporate parent should be able to closely *monitor* business unit performance and *improve performance* either by replacing weak managers or by assisting them in turning around their businesses. The parent can also *challenge and develop* the strategic ambitions of business units, so that satisfactorily performing businesses are encouraged to perform even better.

Value-destroying activities

However, there are also three broad ways in which the corporate parent can inadvertently destroy value:

- *Adding management costs*. Most simply, the staff and facilities of the corporate centre are expensive. The corporate centre typically has the best paid managers and the most luxurious offices. It is the actual businesses that have to generate the revenues that pay for them. If their costs are greater than the value they create, then the corporate centre's managers are net value-destroying.
- *Adding bureaucratic complexity*. As well as these direct financial costs, there is the 'bureaucratic fog' created by an additional layer of management and the need to coordinate with sister businesses. These typically slow-down managers' responses to issues and lead to compromises between the interests of individual businesses.
- *Obscuring financial performance*. One danger in a large diversified company is that the underperformance of weak businesses can be obscured. Weak businesses might be cross-subsidised by the stronger ones. Internally, the possibility of hiding weak performance diminishes the incentives for business unit managers to strive as hard as they can for their businesses: they have a parental safety net. Externally, shareholders and financial analysts cannot easily judge the performance of individual units within the corporate whole. Diversified companies' share prices are often marked down, because shareholders prefer the 'pure plays' of stand-alone units, where weak performance cannot be hidden.

These dangers suggest clear paths for corporate parents that wish to avoid value destruction. They should keep a close eye on centre costs, both financial and bureaucratic, ensuring that they are no more than required by their corporate strategy. They should also do all they can to promote financial transparency, so that business units remain under pressure to perform and shareholders are confident that there are no hidden disasters.

Overall, there are many ways in which corporate parents can add value. It is, of course, difficult to pursue them all and some are hard to mix with others. For example, a corporate parent that does a great deal of top-down intervening is less likely to be seen by its managers as a helpful coach and facilitator. Business unit managers will concentrate on maximising their own individual performance rather than looking out for ways to cooperate with other business unit managers for the greater good of the whole. For this reason, corporate parenting roles tend to fall into three main types, each coherent within itself but distinct from the others.[17] These three types of corporate parenting role are summarised in Exhibit 7.5.

Exhibit 7.5 Portfolio managers, synergy managers and parental developers

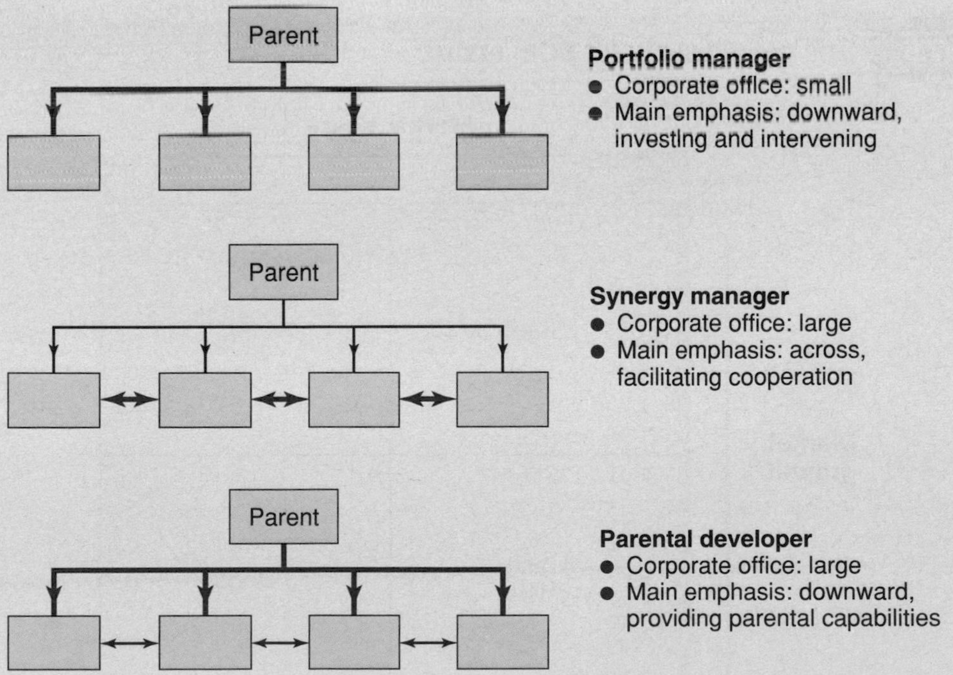

Source: Adapted from M. Goold, A. Campbell and M. Alexander, *Corporate Level Strategy*, Wiley, 1994.

7.5 PORTFOLIO MATRICES

The discussion in section 7.4 was about the rationales that corporate parents might adopt for the management of a multi-business organisation. This section introduces two models by which managers can manage the various parts of their portfolio differently, or add and subtract business units within the portfolio. Each model is concerned with two basic criteria:

- the *balance* of the portfolio, for example, in relation to its markets and the needs of the corporation.
- the *attractiveness* of the business units in terms of how strong they are individually and how profitable their markets or industries are likely to be.

7.5.1 The growth/share (or BCG) matrix[18]

www.pearsoned.co.uk/fos
KEY CONCEPT
Boston Consulting Group (BCG) and Portfolio Matrices

One of the most common and long-standing ways of conceiving of the balance of a portfolio of businesses is the Boston Consulting Group (BCG) matrix (see Exhibit 7.6). Here market share and market growth are critical variables for determining attractiveness and balance. High market share and high growth are, of course, attractive. However, the BCG matrix also warns that high growth

Exhibit 7.6 The growth share (or BCG) matrix

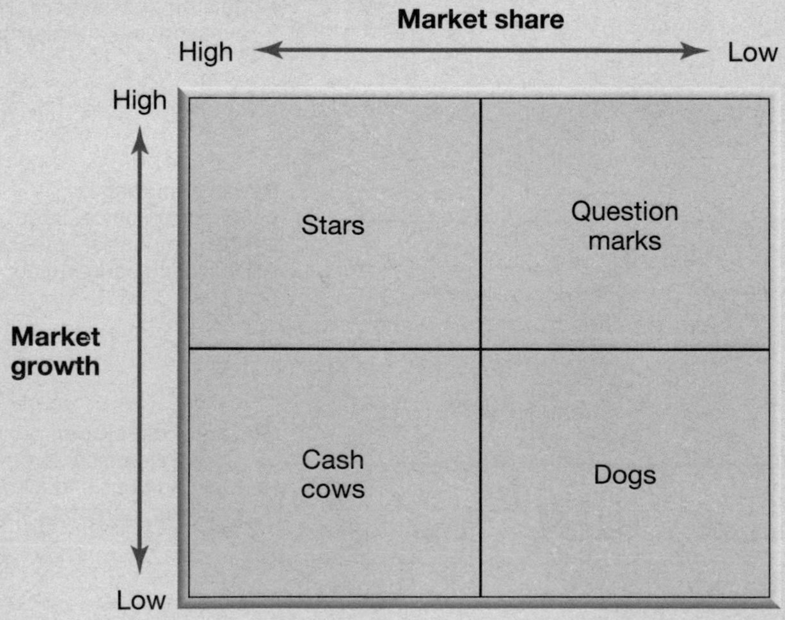

demands heavy investment, for instance to expand capacity or develop brands. There needs to be a balance within the portfolio, so that there are some low-growth businesses that are making sufficient surplus to fund the investment needs of higher-growth businesses.

The growth/share axes of the BCG matrix define four sorts of business:

A **star** is a business unit which has a high market share in a growing market

- A **star** is a business unit which has a high market share in a growing market. The business unit may be spending heavily to keep up with growth, but high market share should yield sufficient profits to make it more or less self-sufficient in terms of investment needs.

A **question mark** (or problem child) is a business unit in a growing market, but without a high market share

- A **question mark** (or problem child) is a business unit in a growing market, but not yet with high market share. Developing question marks into stars, with high market share, takes heavy investment. Many question marks fail to develop, so the BCG advises corporate parents to nurture several at a time. It is important to make sure that some question marks develop into stars, as existing stars eventually become cash cows and cash cows may decline into dogs.

A **cash cow** is a business unit with a high market share in a mature market

- A **cash cow** is a business unit with a high market share in a mature market. However, because growth is low, investments needs are less, while high market share means that the business unit should be profitable. The cash cow should then be a cash provider, helping to fund investments in question marks.

Dogs are business units with a low share in static or declining markets

- **Dogs** are business units with a low share in static or declining markets and are thus the worst of all combinations. They may be a cash drain and use up a disproportionate amount of company time and resources. The BCG usually recommends divestment or closure.

The BCG matrix has several advantages. It provides a good way of visualising the different needs and potential of all the diverse businesses within the corporate portfolio. It warns corporate parents of the financial demands of what might otherwise look like a desirable portfolio of high-growth businesses. It also reminds corporate parents that stars are likely eventually to wane. Finally, it provides a useful discipline to business unit managers, underlining the fact that the corporate parent ultimately owns the surplus resources they generate and can allocate them according to what is best for the corporate whole. Cash cows should not hoard their profits. Incidentally, surplus resources may not only be investment funds: the corporate parent can also reallocate business unit managers who are not fully utilised by low growth cash cows or dogs.

However, there are at least three potential problems with the BCG matrix:

- *Definitional vagueness*. It can be hard to decide what high and low growth or share mean in particular situations. Managers are often keen to define themselves as 'high share' by defining their market in a particularly narrow way (for example, ignoring relevant international markets).

- *Capital market assumptions*. The notion that a corporate parent needs a balanced portfolio to finance investment from internal sources (cash cows) assumes that capital cannot be raised in external markets, for instance by issuing shares or raising loans. The notion of a balanced portfolio may be more relevant in countries where capital markets are underdeveloped or in private companies that wish to minimise dependence on external shareholders or banks.
- *Unkind to animals*. Both cash cows and dogs receive ungenerous treatment: the first being simply milked, the second terminated or cast out of the corporate home. This treatment can cause *motivation problems*, as managers in these units see little point in working hard for the sake of other businesses. There is also the danger of the *self-fulfilling prophecy*. Cash cows will become dogs even more quickly than the model expects if they are simply milked and denied adequate investment. Finally, the notion that a dog can be simply sold or closed down also assumes that there are *no ties to other business units* in the portfolio, whose performance might depend in part on keeping the dog alive. This portfolio approach to dogs works better for conglomerate strategies, where divestments or closures are unlikely to have knock-on effects on other parts of the portfolio.

7.5.2 The directional policy (GE-McKinsey) matrix

The **directional policy matrix** positions SBUs according to (a) how attractive the relevant market is in which they are operating, and (b) the competitive strength of the SBU in that market

Another way to consider a portfolio of businesses is by means of the *directional policy matrix*[19] which categorises business units into those with good prospects and those with less good prospects. The matrix was originally developed by McKinsey & Co. consultants in order to help the American conglomerate General Electric manage its portfolio of business units. Specifically, the **directional policy matrix** positions business units according to (a) how attractive the relevant market is in which they are operating, and (b) the competitive strength of the SBU in that market. Attractiveness can be identified by PESTEL or five forces analyses; business unit strength can be defined by competitor analysis (for instance the strategy canvas): see Chapter 2. Some analysts also choose to show graphically how large the market is for a given business unit's activity, and even the market share of that business unit, as shown in Exhibit 7.7. For example, managers in a firm with the portfolio shown in Exhibit 7.7 will be concerned that they have relatively low shares in the largest and most attractive market, whereas their greatest strength is in a market with only medium attractiveness and smaller markets with little long-term attractiveness.

The matrix also provides a way of considering appropriate corporate-level strategies given the positioning of the business units, as shown in Exhibit 7.8. It suggests that the businesses with the highest growth potential and the greatest strength are those in which to invest for growth. Those that are the weakest and in the least attractive markets should be divested or 'harvested' (i.e. used to yield as much cash as possible before divesting).

Exhibit 7.7 Directional policy (GE–McKinsey) matrix

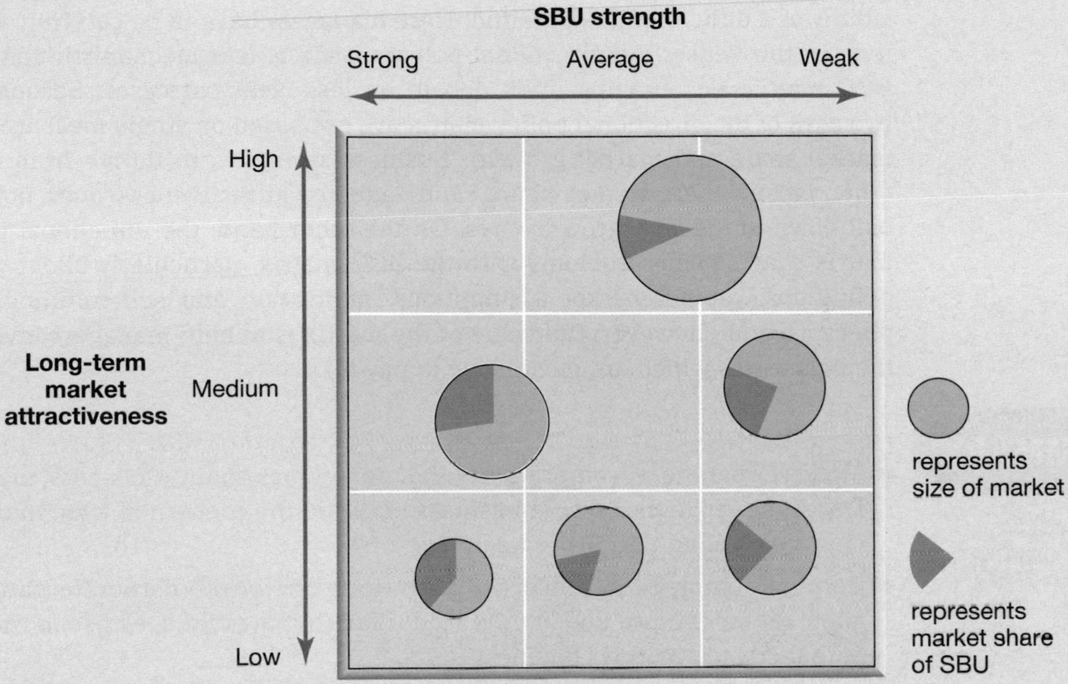

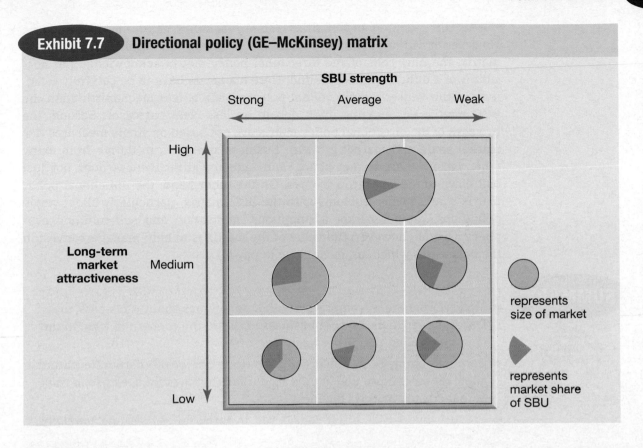

Exhibit 7.8 Strategy guidelines based on the directional policy matrix

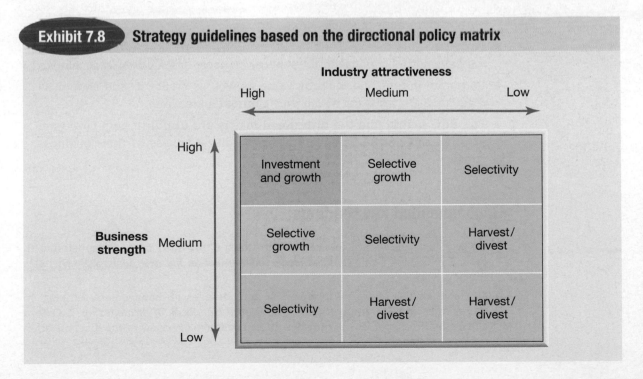

Business strength \ Industry attractiveness	High	Medium	Low
High	Investment and growth	Selective growth	Selectivity
Medium	Selective growth	Selectivity	Harvest/ divest
Low	Selectivity	Harvest/ divest	Harvest/ divest

The directional policy matrix is more complex than the BCG matrix. However, it can have two advantages. First, unlike the simpler four box BCG matrix, the nine cells of the directional policy matrix acknowledge the possibility of a difficult middle ground. Here managers have to be carefully selective. In this sense, the directional policy matrix is less mechanistic than the BCG matrix, encouraging open debate on less clear-cut cases. Second, the two axes of the directional policy matrix are not based on single measures (i.e. market share and market growth). Business strength can derive from many other factors than market share, and industry attractiveness does not just boil down to industry growth rates. On the other hand, the directional policy matrix shares some problems with the BCG matrix, particularly about vague definitions, capital market assumptions, motivation and self-fulfilling prophecy. Overall, however, the value of the matrix is to help managers invest in the businesses which are most likely to pay off.

SUMMARY

www.pearsoned.co.uk/fos AUDIO SUMMARY

- Many corporations comprise several, sometimes many, business units. Decisions above the level of business units are the concern of what in this chapter is called the *corporate parent*.
- Corporate strategy is concerned with decisions of the corporate parent about (a) the *product* and *market scope*, and (b) how they seek to *add value* to that created by their business units.
- Product diversity is often considered in terms of *related* and *unrelated* diversification.
- Performance tends to suffer if organisations become very diverse, or unrelated, in their business units.
- Corporate parents may seek to add value by adopting different *parenting roles*: the portfolio manager, the synergy manager or the parental developer.
- Corporate parents can destroy value as well as create it, and should be ready to *divest* units for which they cannot create value.
- The BCG matrix and the directional matrix are useful to help corporate parents manage the balance and overall attrativeness of their business portfolio.

Recommended key readings

- An accessible discussion of strategic directions is provided by A. Campbell and R. Park, *The Growth Gamble: When leaders should bet on big new businesses*, Nicholas Brealey, 2005.
- M. Goold and K. Luchs, 'Why diversify: four decades of management thinking' in D. Faulkner and A. Campbell (eds), *The Oxford Handbook of Strategy*, vol. 2, Oxford University Press, pp. 18–42, provides an authoritative overview of the diversification option over time.

- A summary of different portfolio analyses is provided in D. Faulkner, 'Portfolio matrices', in V. Ambrosini (ed.), *Exploring Techniques of Analysis and Evaluation in Strategic Management*, Prentice Hall, 1998.

References

1. This figure is an extension of the product/market matrix: see H.I. Ansoff, *Corporate Strategy*, 1988, chapter 6. The Ansoff matrix was later developed into the one show below:

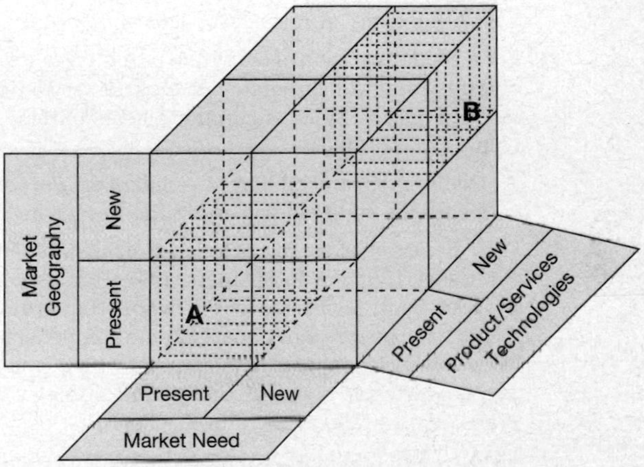

Source: H. Ansoff, *The New Corporate Strategy*, Wiley, 1988.

2. For the European Commission competition authority, http://ec.europa.eu/comm/competition; for the UK Competition Commission, see http://www.competition-commission.org.uk/.
3. See for example, J. Huang, M. Enesi, and R. Galliers, 'Opportunities to learn from failure with electronic commerce: a case study of electronic banking', *Journal of Information Technology*, vol. 18, no. 1 (2003), pp. 17–27.
4. For discussions of the challenge of sustained growth and diversification, see A. Campbell and R. Parks, *The Growth Gamble*, Nicholas Brearley (2005) and D. Laurie, Y. Doz and C. Sheer, 'Creating new growth platforms', *Harvard Business Review*, vol. 84, no. 5 (2006), pp. 80–90.
5. On economies of scope, see D.J. Teece, 'Towards an economic theory of the multi-product firm', *Journal of Economic Behavior and Organization*, vol. 3 (1982), pp. 39–63.
6. M. Goold and A. Campbell, 'Desperately seeking synergy', *Harvard Business Review*, vol. 76, no. 2 (1998), pp. 131–145.
7. See C.K. Prahalad and R. Bettis, 'The dominant logic: a new link between diversity and performance', *Strategic Management Journal*, vol. 6, no. 1 (1986), pp. 485–501; and R. Bettis and C.K. Prahalad, 'The dominant logic: retrospective and extension', *Strategic Management Journal*, vol. 16, no. 1 (1995), pp. 5–15.
8. For a theoretical discussion and empirical study of management interests and diversification, see M. Goranova, T. Alessandri, P. Brandes and R. Dharwadkar, 'Managerial ownership and corporate diversification: a longitudinal view', *Strategic Management Journal*, vol. 28, no. 3 (2007), pp. 211–226.
9. A. Pehrson, 'Business relatedness and performance: a study of managerial perceptions', *Strategic Management Journal*, vol. 27, no. 3 (2006), pp. 265–282.
10. A. Campbell and K. Luchs, *Strategic Synergy*, Butterworth/Heinemann, 1992.
11. See Prahalad and Bettis in references 7 above.

12. See C. Markides, 'Corporate strategy: the role of the centre' in A. Pettigrew, H. Thomas and R. Whittington (eds), *Handbook of Strategy and Management*, Sage, 2002. For a discussion of recent chaebol changes, see J. Chang and H.-H. Shin, 'Governance system effectiveness following the crisis: the case of Korean business group headquarters', *Corporate Governance: an International Review*, vol. 14, no. 2 (2006), pp. 85–97.
13. L.E. Palich, L.B. Cardinal and C. Miller, 'Curvilinearity in the diversification-performance linkage: an examination of over three decades of research', *Strategic Management Journal*, vol. 21 (2000), pp. 155–174. The inverted-U relationship is the research consensus, but studies often disagree, particularly finding variations over time and across countries. For recent context sensitive studies, see M. Mayer and R. Whittington, 'Diversification in Context: a Cross National and Cross Temporal Extension, *Strategic Management Journal*, vol. 24 (2003), pp. 773–781 and A. Chakrabarti, K. Singh and I. Mahmood, 'Diversification and performance: evidence from East Asian firms', *Strategic Management Journal*, vol. 28, (2007), pp. 101–120.
14. For a good discussion of corporate parenting roles, see Markides in reference 12 above. A recent empirical study of corporate headquarters is D. Collis, D. Young and M. Goold, 'The size, structure and performance of corporate headquarters', *Strategic Management Journal*, vol. 28, no. 4 (2007), pp. 383–406.
15. M. Goold, A. Campbell and M. Alexander, *Corporate Level Strategy*, Wiley 1994, is concerned with both the value-adding and value-destroying capacity of corporate parents.
16. For a discussion of the role of a clarity of mission, see A. Campbell, M. Devine and D. Young, *A Sense of Mission*, Hutchinson Business, 1990. However, G. Hamel and C.K. Prahalad argue in chapter 6 of their book, *Competing for the Future*, Harvard Business School Press, 1994, that mission statements have insufficient impact for the competence of a clarity of 'strategic intent'. This is more likely to be a brief but clear statement which focuses more on clarity of strategic direction (they use the word 'destiny') than on how that strategic direction will be achieved. See also Hamel and Prahalad on strategic intent in the *Harvard Business Review*, vol. 67, no. 3 (1989), pp. 63–76.
17. The first two rationales discussed here are based on a paper by Michael Porter, 'From competitive advantage to corporate strategy', *Harvard Business Review*, vol. 65, no. 3 (1987), pp. 43–59.
18. For a more extensive discussion of the use of the growth share matrix see A.C. Hax and N.S Majluf in R.G. Dyson (ed.), *Strategic Planning: Models and analytical techniques*, Wiley, 1990; and D. Faulkner, 'Portfolio matrices', in V. Ambrosini (ed.), *Exploring Techniques of Analysis and Evaluation in Strategic Management*, Prentice Hall, 1998; for source explanations of the BCG matrix see B.D. Henderson, *Henderson on Corporate Strategy*, Abt Books, 1979.
19. A. Hax and N. Majluf, 'The use of the industry attractiveness-business strength matrix in strategic planning', in R. Dyson (ed.), *Strategic Planning: Models and analytical techniques*, Wiley, 1990.

CASE EXAMPLE

The Virgin Group

Aidan McQuade

Introduction

The Virgin Group is one of the UK's largest private companies. The group included, in 2006, 63 businesses as diverse as airlines, health clubs, music stores and trains. The group included Virgin Galactic, which promised to take paying passengers into sub-orbital space.

The personal image and personality of the founder, Richard Branson, were highly bound up with those of the company. Branson's taste for publicity has led him to stunts as diverse as appearing as a cockney street trader in the US comedy *Friends*, to attempting a non-stop balloon flight around the world. This has certainly contributed to the definition and recognisability of the brand. Research has showed that the Virgin name was associated with words such as 'fun', 'innovative', 'daring' and 'successful'.

In 2006 Branson announced plans to invest $3bn (€2.4bn; £1.7bn) in renewable energy. Virgin, through its partnership with a cable company NTL, also undertook an expansion into media challenging publicly the way NewsCorp operated in the UK and the effects on British democracy. The nature and scale of both these initiatives suggests that Branson's taste for his brand of business remains undimmed.

Origins and activities

Virgin was founded in 1970 as a mail order record business and developed as a private company in music publishing and retailing. In 1986 the company was floated on the stock exchange with a turnover of £250m (€362.5m). However, Branson became tired of the public listing obligations: he resented making presentations in the City to people whom, he believed, did not understand the business. The pressure to create short-term profit, especially as the share price began to fall, was the final straw: Branson decided to take the business back into private ownership and the shares were bought back at the original offer price.

Photo: Steve Bell/Rex Features

The name Virgin was chosen to represent the idea of the company being a virgin in every business it entered. Branson has said that: 'The brand is the single most important asset that we have; our ultimate objective is to establish it as a major global name.' This does not mean that Virgin underestimates the importance of understanding the *businesses* that it is branding. Referring to his intent to set up a 'green' energy company producing ethanol and cellulosic ethanol fuels in competition with the oil industry, he said, 'We're a slightly unusual company in that we go into industries we know nothing about and immerse ourselves.'

Virgin's expansion had often been through joint ventures whereby Virgin provided the brand and its partner provided the majority of capital. For example, the Virgin Group's move into clothing and cosmetics required an initial outlay of only £1,000, whilst its partner, Victory Corporation, invested £20m. With Virgin Mobile, Virgin built a business by forming partnerships with existing wireless operators to sell services under the Virgin brand name. The carriers' competences lay in network management. Virgin set out to differentiate itself by offering innovative services. Although it did not operate its own network, Virgin won an award for the best wireless operator in the UK.

This case was updated and revised by Aidan McQuade, University of Strathclyde Graduate School of Business, based upon work by Urmilla Lawson.

Virgin Fuels appears to be somewhat different in that Virgin is putting up the capital and using the Virgin brand to attract attention to the issues and possibilities that the technology offers.

In 2005 Virgin announced the establishment of a 'quadruple play' media company providing television, broadband, fixed-line and mobile communications through the merger of Branson's UK mobile interests with the UK's two cable companies. This Virgin company would have 9 million direct customers, 1.5 million more than BSkyB, and so have the financial capacity to compete with BSkyB for premium content such as sports and movies.[1] Virgin tried to expand this business further by making an offer for ITV. This was rejected as undervaluing the company and then undermined further with the purchase of an 18 per cent share of ITV by BSkyB. This prompted Branson to call on regulators to force BSkyB to reduce or dispose of its stake citing concerns that BSkyB would have material influence over the free-to-air broadcaster.[2]

Virgin has been described as a 'keiretsu' organisation – a structure of loosely linked, autonomous units run by self-managed teams that use a common brand name. Branson argued that, as he expanded, he would rather sacrifice short-term profits for long-term growth of the various businesses.

Some commentators have argued that Virgin had become an endorsement brand that could not always offer real expertise to the businesses with which it was associated. However, Will Whitehorn, Director of Corporate Affairs for Virgin, stated, 'At Virgin we know what the brand means and when we put our brand name on something we are making a promise.'

Branson saw Virgin adding value in three main ways, aside from the brand. These were their public relations and marketing skills; its experience with greenfield start-ups; and Virgin's understanding of the opportunities presented by 'institutionalised' markets. Virgin saw an 'institutionalised' market as one dominated by few competitors, not giving good value to customers because they had become either inefficient or preoccupied with each other. Virgin believed it did well when it identified such complacency and offered more for less. The entry into fuel and media industries certainly conforms to the model of trying to shake up 'institutionalised' markets.

Corporate rationale

In 2006 Virgin still lacked the trappings of a typical multinational. Branson described the Virgin Group as 'a branded venture capital house'.[3] There was no 'group' as such; financial results were not consolidated either for external examination or, so Virgin claimed, for internal use. Its website described Virgin as a family rather than a hierarchy. Its financial operations were managed from Geneva.

In 2006 Branson explained the basis upon which he considered opportunities: they have to be global in scope, enhance the brand, be worth doing and have an expectation of a reasonable return on investment.[4] Each business was 'ring-fenced', so that lenders to one company had no rights over the assets of another. The ring-fencing seems also to relate not just to provision of financial protection, but also to a business ethics aspect. In an interview in 2006 Branson cricitised supermarkets for selling cheap CDs. His criticism centred on the supermarkets' use of loss leading on CDs damaging music retailers rather than fundamentally challenging the way music retailers do business. Branson has made it a central feature of Virgin that it shakes up institutionalised markets by being innovative. Loss leading is not an innovative approach.

Virgin has evolved from being almost wholly comprised of private companies to a group where some of the companies are publicly listed.

Virgin and Branson

Historically, the Virgin Group had been controlled mainly by Branson and his trusted lieutenants, many of whom had stayed with him for more than 20 years. The increasing conformity between personal interest and business initiatives could be discerned in the establishment of Virgin Fuels. In discussing his efforts to establish a 'green' fuel company in competition with the oil industry Branson made the geopolitical observation that non-oil-based fuels could 'avoid another Middle East war one day'; Branson's opposition to the Second Gulf War is well publicised.[5] In some instances the relationship between personal conviction and business interests is less clear cut. Branson's comments on the threat to British democracy posed by NewsCorp's ownership of such a large percentage of the British media could be depicted as either genuine concern from a public figure or sour grapes from a business rival just been beaten out of purchasing ITV.

More recently Branson has been reported as talking about withdrawing from the business 'which more or less ran itself now',[6] and hoping that his son Sam might become more of a Virgin figurehead.[7] However, while he was publicly contemplating this withdrawal from business, Branson was also launching his initiatives in media and fuel. Perhaps Branson's idea of early retirement is somewhat more active than most.

Corporate performance

By 2006 Virgin had, with mixed results, taken on one established industry after another in an effort to shake up 'fat and complacent business sectors'. It had further set its sights on the British media sector and the global oil industry.

Airlines clearly were an enthusiasm of Branson's. According to Branson, Virgin Atlantic, which was 49 per cent owned by Singapore Airways, was a company that he would not sell outright: 'There are some businesses you preserve, which wouldn't ever be sold, and that's one.' Despite some analysts' worries that airline success could not be sustained given the 'cyclical' nature of the business, Branson maintained a strong interest in the industry, and included airline businesses such as Virgin Express (European), Virgin Blue (Australia) and Virgin Nigeria in the group. Branson's engagement with the search for 'greener' fuels and reducing global warming had not led him to ground his fleets. but rather to prompt a debate on measures to reduce carbon emissions from aeroplanes.

At the beginning of the twenty-first century the most public problem faced by Branson was Virgin Trains, whose Cross Country and West Coast lines were ranked 23rd and 24th out of 25 train-operating franchises according to the Strategic Rail Authority's Review in 2000. By 2002 Virgin Trains was reporting profits and paid its first premium to the British government.

The future

The beginning of the twenty-first century also saw further expansion by Virgin, from airlines, spa finance and mobile telecoms in Africa, into telecoms in Europe, and into the USA. The public flotation of individual businesses rather than the group as a whole has become an intrinsic part of the 'juggling' of finances that underpins Virgin's expansion.

Some commentators have identified a risk with Virgin's approach: 'The greatest threat [is] that . . . Virgin brand . . . may become associated with failure.'[8] This point was emphasised by a commentator[9] who noted that 'a customer who has a bad enough experience with any one of the product lines may shun all the others'. However, Virgin argues that its brand research indicates that people who have had a bad experience will blame that particular Virgin company or product but will be willing to use other Virgin products or services, due to the very diversity of the brand. Such brand confidence helps explain why Virgin should even contemplate such risky and protracted turnaround challenges as its rail company.

Sarah Sands recounts that Branson's mother 'once proudly boasted that her son would become Prime Minster'. Sands futher commented that she thought his mother underestimated his ambition.[10] With Virgin's entry into fuel and media and Branson's declarations that he is taking on the oil corporations and NewsCorp, Sands may ultimately prove to have been prescient in her comment.

Notes

1. *Sunday Telegraph*, 4 December (2005).
2. *Independent*, 22 November (2006).
3. Hawkins (2001a, b).
4. PR Newswire Europe, 16 October (2006).
5. *Fortune*, 6 February (2006).
6. *Independent on Sunday*, 26 November (2006).
7. Ibid.
8. *The Times* 1998, quoted in Vignali (2001).
9. Wells (2000).
10. *Independent on Sunday*, 26 November (2006).

Sources: *The Economist*, 'Cross his heart', 5 October (2002); 'Virgin on the ridiculous', 29 May (2003); 'Virgin Rail: tilting too far', 12 July (2001). P. McCosker, 'Stretching the brand: a review of the Virgin Group', *European Case Clearing House*, 2000. *The Times*, 'Virgin push to open up US aviation market', 5 June (2002); 'Branson plans $1bn US expansion', 30 April (2002). *Observer*, 'Branson eyes 31bn float for Virgin Mobile', 18 January (2004). *Strategic Direction*, 'Virgin Flies High with Brand Extensions', vol. 18, no. 10, (October 2002). R. Hawkins, 'Executive of Virgin Group outlines corporate strategy' *Knight Ridder/Tribune Business News*, July 29 (2001a). R. Hawkins, 'Branson in new dash for cash', *Sunday Business*, 29 July (2001b); *South China Morning Post*, 'Virgin shapes kangaroo strategy aid liberalisation talks between Hong Kong and Australia will determine carrier's game-plan', 28 June (2002). C. Vignali, 'Virgin Cola', *British Food Journal*, vol. 103, no. 2 (2001), pp. 131–139. M. Wells, 'Red Baron', *Forbes Magazine*, vol. 166, no. 1, 7 March (2000).

Questions

1. What is the corporate rationale of Virgin as a group of companies?
2. Are there any relationships of a strategic nature between businesses within the Virgin portfolio?
3. How does the Virgin Group, as a corporate parent, add value to its businesses?
4. What were the main issues facing the Virgin Group at the end of the case and how should they be tackled?

8

International Strategy

LEARNING OUTCOMES

After reading this chapter, you should be able to:

→ Assess the internationalisation potential of different markets, sensitive to variations over time.

→ Identify sources of competitive advantage in international strategy, both through global sourcing and exploitation of local factors embodied in Porter's Diamond.

→ Distinguish between four main types of international strategy.

→ Rank markets for entry or expansion, taking into account attractiveness, cultural and other forms of distance and competitor retaliation threats.

→ Assess the relative merits of different market entry modes, including joint ventures, licensing and foreign direct investment.

Photo: (FREELENS Pool) Tack/STILL Pictures
The Whole Earth Photo Library

8.1 INTRODUCTION

The last chapter introduced market development as a strategy, in relation to the Ansoff matrix. This chapter focuses on a specific but important kind of market development, operating in different geographical markets. This kind of internationalisation raises choices about which countries to compete in, how far to modify the organisation's range of products or services and how to manage across borders. These kinds of questions are relevant to a wide range of organisations today. There are, of course, the large traditional multinationals such as Nestlé, Toyota and McDonalds. But increasingly new small firms are also 'born global', building international relationships right from the start. Public sector organisations are also having to make choices about collaboration, outsourcing and even competition with overseas organisations. European Union legislation requires public service organisations to accept tenders from non-national providers.

Exhibit 8.1 places international strategy as the core theme of the chapter. International strategy, however, depends ultimately on both the external environment (as in Chapter 2) and organisational capabilities (as in Chapter 3). On the environmental side, Exhibit 8.1 highlights internationalisation drivers; on the capabilities side, it emphasises international and national sources of advantage. The choice of international strategy in turn tends to shape the selection of country markets and the modes of market entry.

Exhibit 8.1 International strategy framework

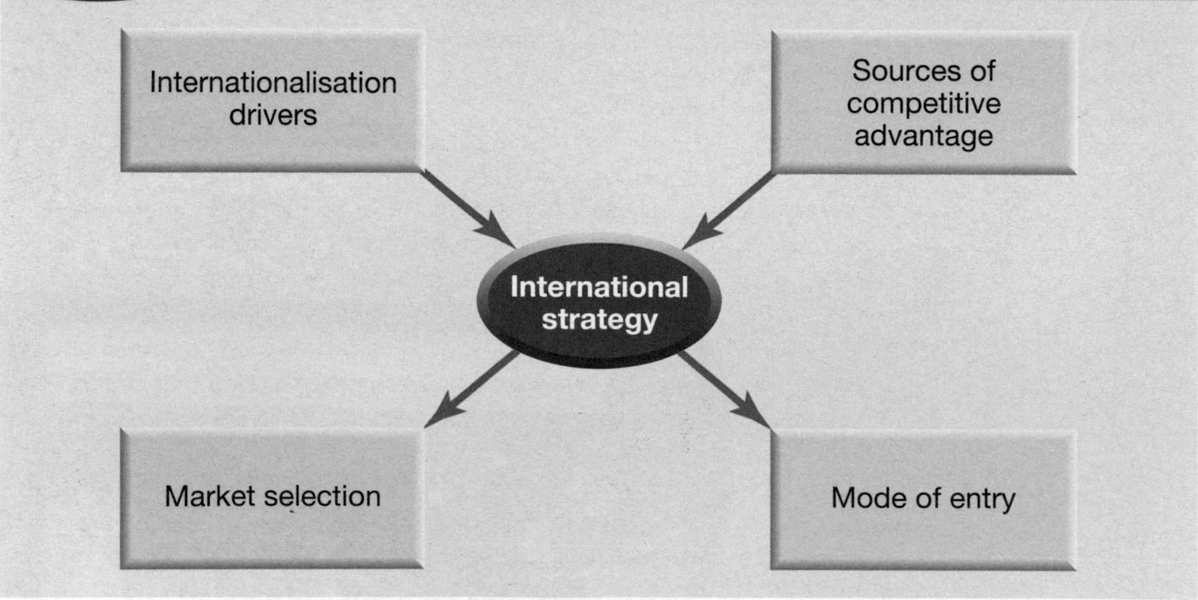

This chapter examines key issues in international strategy as follows. The next section introduces the *drivers of internationalisation*. The chapter then considers international and national sources of competitive advantage, particularly those located in *global sourcing* and those in the nationally-specific factors embodied in Michael Porter's *Diamond framework*. In the light of these drivers and sources of competitive advantage, the chapter describes different *types of international strategy*. As different geographical markets tend to demand significant product or service modifications, some international strategies take the organisation from simple market development to increasingly diversified strategies.[1] From here, the chapter moves to analyse market selection and market entry. Here, the chapter stresses the interdependence of market attractiveness with various kinds of *distance* and the threat of *competitor retaliation*. Finally, the chapter considers the relative advantages of different *entry modes*, including joint ventures, foreign direct investment and licensing. *Entry sequences* are discussed, including those for new firms and emerging market multinationals.

8.2 INTERNATIONALISATION DRIVERS

www.pearsoned.co.uk/ffos
KEY CONCEPT
Yip's internationalisation drivers

There are many general pressures increasing internationalisation. Barriers to international trade, investment and migration are all now much lower than they were a couple of decades ago. International regulation and governance have improved, so that investing and trading overseas is less risky. Improvements in communications – from cheaper air travel to the internet – make movement and the spread of ideas much easier around the world. Not least, the success of new economic powerhouses such as the so-called BRICs – Brazil, Russia, India and China – is generating new opportunities and challenges for business internationally.[2]

However, not all these internationalisation trends are one way; nor do they hold for all industries. For example, migration is now becoming more difficult between some countries. The Internet and cheap air travel are making it easier for expatriate communities to stick with home cultures, rather than merging into a single global 'melting pot' of tastes and ideas. Many so-called multinationals are concentrated in quite particular markets, for example, North America and Western Europe, or have a very limited set of international links, for example, supply or outsourcing arrangements with just one or two countries overseas. Markets vary widely in the extent to which consumer needs are standardising – compare computer operating systems to tastes in chocolate. In short, managers need to beware 'global baloney', by which economic integration into a single homogenised and competitive world is wildly exaggerated. As in the Chinese retail market (Illustration 8.1), international drivers are usually a lot more complicated than that.

Illustration 8.1

Chinese retail: global or local?

Internationalisation is not a simple process, as supermarket chains Carrefour and Wal-Mart have found in China.

At the start of the twenty-first century, China is a magnet for ambitious Western supermarket chains. Growing at 13 per cent a year, the Chinese market is predicted by Euromonitor to reach $747bn. (£418bn; €380bn) by 2010. Some 520 million people are expected to join the Chinese upper middle class by 2025. With the local industry fragmented and focused on particular regions, large Western companies might have an advantage.

In 1995, after six years' experience in neighbouring Taiwan, French supermarket chain Carrefour was the first to enter the Chinese market in a substantial fashion. By 2006, Carrefour was the sixth largest retailer in China, though the market being what it is, this meant only 0.6 per cent overall market share. The world's largest retailer, the American Wal-Mart, was close behind, especially with its acquisition in 2006 of a Taiwanese chain with outlets on the mainland. These two rivals are pursuing very different strategies. Wal-Mart is pursuing its standard centralised purchasing and distribution strategy, supplying as much as it can from its new, state-of-the-art distribution centre in Shenzen. Carrefour is following a decentralised strategy: except in Shanghai, where it has several stores, Carrefour allows its local store managers, scattered across the many different regions of China, to make their own purchasing and supply decisions.

The growth of companies such as Carrefour and Wal-Mart, as well as local chains, demonstrates that already there is a substantial market for the Western supermarket experience. Carrefour, for example, was a pioneer of 'private label' goods in China, while Wal-Mart brings logistical expertise. Growing wealth and exposure to foreign ideas will no doubt increase Chinese receptiveness. None the less, progress has been slow. Wal-Mart has yet to make a profit in China; Carrefour finally is, but its 2–3 per cent margins are significantly below the nearly 5 per cent margins it enjoys in France.

One early discovery for Wal-Mart was that Chinese consumers prefer frequent shopping trips, buying small quantities each time. While Wal-Mart assumed that Chinese consumers would drive to out-of-town stores and fill their cars with large frozen multi-packs on a once-a-week shop, much like Americans, in fact Chinese customers would break open the multi-packs to take just the smaller quantities they required. Now Wal-Mart supplies more of its frozen foods loose, offering customers a scoop so they can take exactly the amount they want. In 2006, moreover, Wal-Mart allowed trade unions into its stores, in marked contrast to its policy in the rest of the world.

Another discovery for Western retailers is the amount of regional variation in this vast and multi-ethnic country. In the north of China, soya sauces are important; in central China, chilli pepper sauces are required; in the South, it is oyster sauces that matter. For fruit, northerners must have dates; southerners want lychees. In the north, the cold means more demand for red meat and, because customers are wearing layers of clothing, wider store aisles. Northerners do not have much access to hot water, so they wash their hair less frequently, meaning that small sachets of shampoo sell better than large bottles.

Sources: *Financial Times*, *Wall Street Journal* and Euromonitor (various dates).

Questions

1 What are the pros and cons of the different China strategies pursued by Carrefour and Wal-Mart?

2 What might be the dangers for a large Western retailer in staying out of the Chinese market?

Exhibit 8.2 Drivers of internationalisation

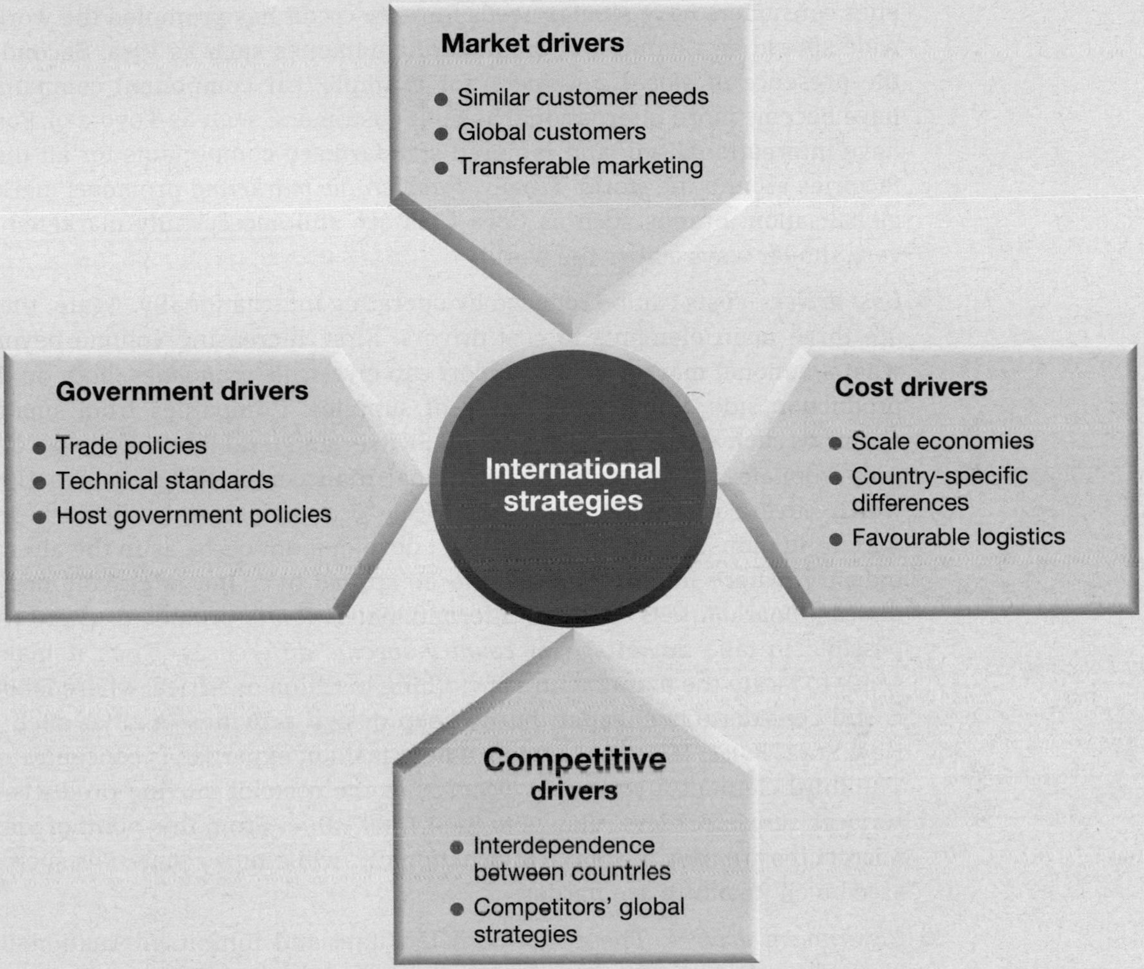

Source: Adapted from Yip, G.S. (2003), p. 10, Exhibit 1–4. Yip, George S., *Total Global Strategy II*, 2nd, © 2003. Electronically reproduced by permission of Pearson Education, Inc. Upper Saddle River, New Jersey.

Given internationalisation's complexity, international strategy should be underpinned by a careful diagnosis of the strength and direction of trends in particular markets. George Yip's 'drivers of globalisation' framework provides a basis for such a diagnosis (see Exhibit 8.2).[3] Note though that, while this framework refers to the need for a *global strategy*, with all parts of the business carefully coordinated around the world, most of these drivers also apply to broader *international strategies*, allowing for more limited overseas operations and looser coordination between them (see section 8.4). Accordingly, Yip's drivers can be thought of simply as 'internationalisation drivers'. The four internationalisation drivers are as follows:

- *Market drivers*. A critical facilitator of internationalisation is some standardisation of markets. There are three components underlying this driver. First, the presence of *similar customer needs and tastes*: the fact that in most societies consumers have similar needs for easy credit has promoted the worldwide spread of a handful of credit card companies such as Visa. Second is the presence of *global customers*: for example, car component companies have become more international as their customers, such as Toyota or Ford, have internationalised, and required standardised components for all their factories around the world. Finally, *transferable marketing* promotes market globalisation: brands such as Coca Cola are still successfully marketed in very similar ways across the world.
- *Cost drivers*: costs can be reduced by operating internationally. Again, there are three main elements to cost drivers. First, increasing volume beyond what a national market might support can give *scale economies*, both on the production side and in purchasing of supplies. Companies from smaller countries such as the Netherlands and Switzerland tend therefore to become proportionately much more international than companies from the USA, which have a vast market at home. Scale economies are particularly important in industries with high product development costs, as in the aircraft industry, where initial costs need to be spread over the large volumes of international markets. Second, internationalisation is promoted where it is possible to take advantage of *country-specific differences*. Thus it makes sense to locate the manufacture of clothing in China or Africa, where labour is still considerably cheaper, but to keep design activities in cities such as New York, Paris, Milan or London, where fashion expertise is concentrated. The third element is *favorable logistics*, or the costs of moving products or services across borders relative to their final value. From this point of view, microchips are easy to source internationally, while bulky materials such as assembled furniture are harder.
- *Government drivers*. These can both facilitate and inhibit internationalisation. The relevant elements of policy are numerous, including tariff barriers, technical standards, subsidies to local firms, ownership restrictions, local content requirements, controls over technology transfer, intellectual property (patenting) regimes and currency and capital flow controls. No government allows complete economic openness and openness typically varies widely from industry to industry, with agriculture and high-tech industries related to defence likely to be particularly sensitive. Nevertheless, the World Trade Organization continues to push for greater openness and the European Union and the North American Free Trade Agreement have made significant improvements in their specific regions.[4]
- *Competitive drivers*. These relate specifically to globalisation as an integrated worldwide strategy rather than simpler international strategies. Such drivers have two elements. First, *interdependence* between country operations increases the pressure for global coordination. For example, a business with

Illustration 8.2

Deutsche Post's increasing international diversity

Globalising markets and political and regulatory change are amongst the reasons for an organisation's increasing international diversity.

The internationalisation of Deutsche Post is closely linked to the opportunities and pressures resulting from the deregulation of national and international markets and the associated globalisation of the transport and logistics industries. The foundation was laid by the 'big bang' reform of the German postal system in 1990. The 'Law concerning the Structure of Posts and Telecommunication' retained Deutsche Post as a state-owned company but aimed to prepare the company for gradual privatisation (the firm went public in 2000 with an initial sale of 29 per cent of share capital). In the following years the company went through a period of consolidation and restructuring which saw the integration of the former East German Post. By 1997, a year which saw a liberalisation of the German postal market, the company had put into place the groundwork for a period of rapid international expansion.

The subsequent globalisation of Deutsche Post's activities was largely driven by the demands of a growing number of business customers for a single provider of integrated national and international shipping and logistics services. Over the next five years Deutsche Post responded by acquiring key players in the international transport and logistics market, notably Danzas and DHL, with the aim of 'becoming the leading global provider of express and logistics services'. This international expansion enabled Deutsche Post – renamed Deutsche Post World Net (DPWN) in order to highlight its global ambitions – to gain, for example, a major contract with fellow German company BMW for the transport, storage and delivery of cars to its Asian dealerships. As part of its so-called 'START' programme, DPWN initiated, in 2003, a programme aimed at harmonising its products and sales structures, creating integrated networks and implementing group-wide process management in order to realise the benefits of the economies of scale resulting from its global operations. At the same time DPWN implemented its 'One brand – One face to the customer' motto by making the DHL brand its global 'public face' with the expectation that this 'familiar and trusted brand name will aid us as we continue to develop globalised services'.

Deregulation and wider political changes, reflected in the elimination of trade restrictions, continued to drive international expansion. China's entry into the World Trade Organization enhanced the potential for growth in its international postal market. Accordingly, DPWN strengthened its commitment to this increasingly important market and was rewarded with a 35 per cent growth rate over the period from 2002 to 2004 and, through a joint venture with Sinotrans, gained a 40 per cent market share of Chinese cross-border express services. DPWN aimed to exploit regulatory changes closer to home as well. With its subsidiary Deutsche Post Global Mail (UK) gaining a long-term licence for unlimited bulk mail delivery from the British regulator 'Postcomm', DPWN saw further opportunity for growth in the UK and continued to expand its presence in the British postal market through the acquisition of postal operator Speedmail.

Sources: www.dpwn.de/enrde/press/news; DPWN Annual Report 2002.

Prepared by Michael Mayer, Bath University.

Questions

1. What were the internationalisation drivers associated with DPWN's strategy?
2. Evaluate the pros and cons of both a multidomestic strategy and a global strategy for DPWN.

a plant in Mexico serving both the American and the Japanese markets has to coordinate carefully between the three locations: surging sales in one country, or a collapse in another, will have significant knock-on effects on the other countries. The second element relates directly to competitor strategy. The presence of *globalised competitors* increases the pressure to adopt a global strategy in response because competitors may use one country's profits to cross-subsidise their operations in another. A company with a loosely-coordinated international strategy is vulnerable to globalised competitors, because it is unable to support country subsidiaries under attack from targeted, subsidised competition. The danger is of piecemeal withdrawal from countries under attack, and the gradual undermining of any overall economies of scale that the international player may have started with.[5]

The key insight from Yip's drivers framework is that internationalisation potential of industries is variable. There are many different factors that can support or inhibit it, and an important step in determining an internationalisation strategy is a realistic assessment of the true scope for internationalisation in the particular industry. Illustration 8.2 explains some of the reasons for Deutsche Post's increasing international diversity since the late 1990s.

8.3 NATIONAL AND INTERNATIONAL SOURCES OF ADVANTAGE

As is clear from the earlier discussion of cost drivers in international strategy, the location of activities is a crucial source of potential advantage and one of the distinguishing features of international strategy relative to other diversification strategies. As Bruce Kogut has explained, an organisation can improve the configuration of its *value chain and network*[6] by taking advantage of country-specific differences (see section 3.5.1). There are two principal opportunities available: the exploitation of particular *national advantages*, often in the company's home country, and sourcing advantages overseas via an *international value network*.

8.3.1 Porter's National Diamond[7]

www.pearsoned.co.uk/fos KEY CONCEPT Porter's Diamond

As for any strategy, internationalisation needs to be based on possession of some sustainable competitive advantage (see Chapter 3). This competitive advantage has usually to be substantial. After all, a competitor entering a market from overseas typically starts with considerable *dis*advantages relative to existing home competitors, who will usually have superior market knowledge, established relationships with local customers, strong supply chains and the like. A foreign entrant must have significant competitive advantages to overcome such disadvantages. The example of the American giant retailer

Exhibit 8.3 Porter's Diamond – the determinants of national advantages

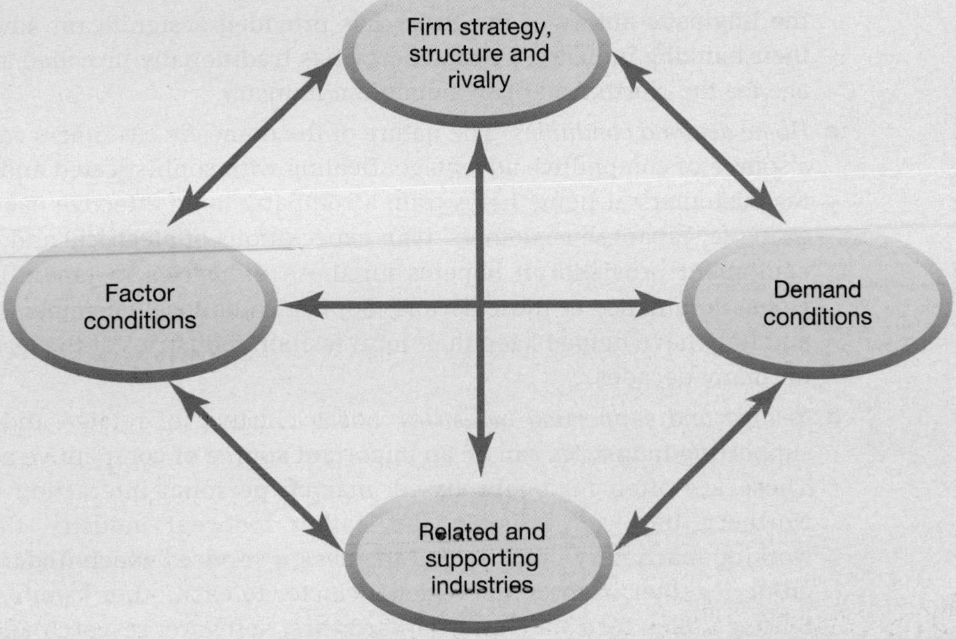

Source: Adapted with the permission of The Free Press, a Division of Simon & Schuster Adult Publishing Group, from *The Competitive Advantage of Nations* by Michael E. Porter. Copyright © 1990, 1998 by Michael E. Porter. All rights reserved.

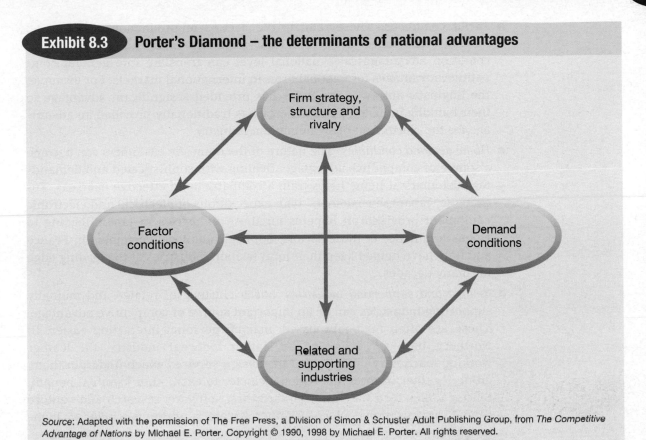

Wal-Mart provides an illustration: Wal-Mart has been successful in many Asian markets with relatively under-developed retail markets, but was forced to withdraw from Germany's maturer market after nearly a decade of failure in 2006. In Germany, unlike in most Asian markets, Wal-Mart had no significant competitive advantage over domestic retailers.

Chapter 3 addresses competitive advantage in general, but the international context raises specifically national sources of advantage that can be substantial and hard to imitate. Countries, and regions within them, often become associated with specific types of enduring competitive advantage: for example, the Swiss in private banking, the North Italians in leather and fur fashion goods, and the Taiwanese in computer laptops. Michael **Porter's Diamond** helps explain why some nations tend to produce firms with sustained competitive advantages in some industries more than others (See Exhibit 8.3). The degree of national advantage varies from industry to industry.

Porter's Diamond suggests that there are inherent reasons why some nations are more competitive than others, and why some industries within nations are more competitive than others

Porter's Diamond suggests there are four interacting determinants of national, or home-base, advantage in particular industries (these four determinants together make up a diamond-shaped figure). The home base determinants are:

- *Factor conditions*. These refer to the 'factors of production' that go into making a product or service (i.e. raw materials, land and labour). Factor condition advantages at a national level can translate into general competitive advantages for national firms in international markets. For example, the linguistic ability of the Swiss has provided a significant advantage to their banking industry. Cheap energy has traditionally provided an advantage for the North American aluminium industry.
- *Home demand conditions*. The nature of the domestic customers can become a source of competitive advantage. Dealing with sophisticated and demanding customers at home helps train a company to be effective overseas. For example, Japanese customers' high expectations of electrical and electronic equipment provided an impetus for those industries in Japan, leading to global dominance of those sectors. Sophisticated local customers in France and Italy have helped keep their local fashion industries at the leading edge for many decades.
- *Related and supporting industries*. Local 'clusters' of related and mutually supporting industries can be an important source of competitive advantage. These are often regionally based, making personal interaction easier. In Northern Italy, for example, the leather footwear industry, the leather working machinery industry and the design services which underpin them, group together in the same regional cluster to each other's mutual benefit. Silicon Valley forms a cluster of hardware, software, research and venture capital organisations which together create a virtuous circle of high-technology enterprise.
- *Firm strategy, industry structure and rivalry*. The characteristic strategies, industry structures and rivalries in different countries can also be bases of advantage. German companies' strategy of investing in technical excellence gives them a characteristic advantage in engineering industries and creates large pools of expertise. A competitive local industry structure is also helpful: if too dominant in their home territory, local organisations can become complacent and lose advantage overseas. Some domestic rivalry can actually be an advantage, therefore. For example, the long-run success of the Japanese car companies is partly based on government policy sustaining several national players (unlike in the UK, where they were all merged into one) and the Swiss pharmaceuticals industry became strong in part because each company had to compete with several strong local rivals.

Porter's Diamond has been used by governments aiming to increase the competitive advantage of their local industries. The argument that rivalry can be positive has led to a major policy shift in many countries towards encouraging competition rather than protecting home-based industries. Governments can also foster local industries by raising safety or environmental standards (i.e. creating sophisticated demand conditions) or encouraging cooperation between suppliers and buyers on a domestic level (i.e. building clusters of related and supporting industries in particular regions).

For individual organisations, however, the value of Porter's Diamond is to identify the extent to which they can build on home-based advantages to create competitive advantage in relation to others on a global front. For example, Dutch brewing companies – such as Heineken – have benefited from early globalisation resulting from the nature of the Dutch home market. Benetton, the Italian clothing company, has achieved global success by using its experience of working through a network of largely independent, often family-owned manufacturers to build its network of franchised retailers. Before embarking on an internationalisation strategy, managers should seek out sources of general national advantage to underpin their company's individual sources of advantage.

8.3.2 The international value network

However, the sources of advantage need not be purely domestic. For international companies, advantage can be drawn from the international configuration of their *value network*. Here the different skills, resources and costs of countries around the world can be systematically exploited in order to locate each element of the value chain in that country or region where it can be conducted most effectively and efficiently. This may be achieved both through foreign direct investments and joint ventures but also through **global sourcing**, i.e. by purchasing services and components from the most appropriate suppliers around the world, regardless of their location. For example, in the UK, the National Health Service has been sourcing medical personnel from overseas to offset a shortfall in domestic skills and capacity.

Global sourcing: purchasing services and components from the most appropriate suppliers around the world regardless of their location

Different locational advantages can be identified:

- *Cost advantages* include labour costs, transportation and communications costs and taxation and investment incentives. Labour costs are important. American and European firms, for example, are increasingly moving software programming tasks to India where a computer programmer costs an American firm about one-quarter of what it would pay for a worker with comparable skills in the USA. As wages in India have risen, Indian IT firms have already begun moving work to even more low-cost locations such as China with some predicting that subsidiaries of Indian firms will come to control as much as 40 per cent of China's IT service exports.
- *Unique capabilities* may allow an organisation to enhance its competitive advantage. A reason for Accenture to locate a rapidly expanding software development office in the Chinese city of Dalian was that communication with potential Japanese and Korean multinational firms operating in the region was easier than if an equivalent location in India or the Philippines had been chosen. Organisations may also seek to exploit advantages related to specific technological and scientific capabilities. Boeing, for example, located its largest engineering centre outside of the USA in Moscow to help

Illustration 8.3

Boeing's global R&D network

Organisations may seek to exploit locational advantages worldwide.

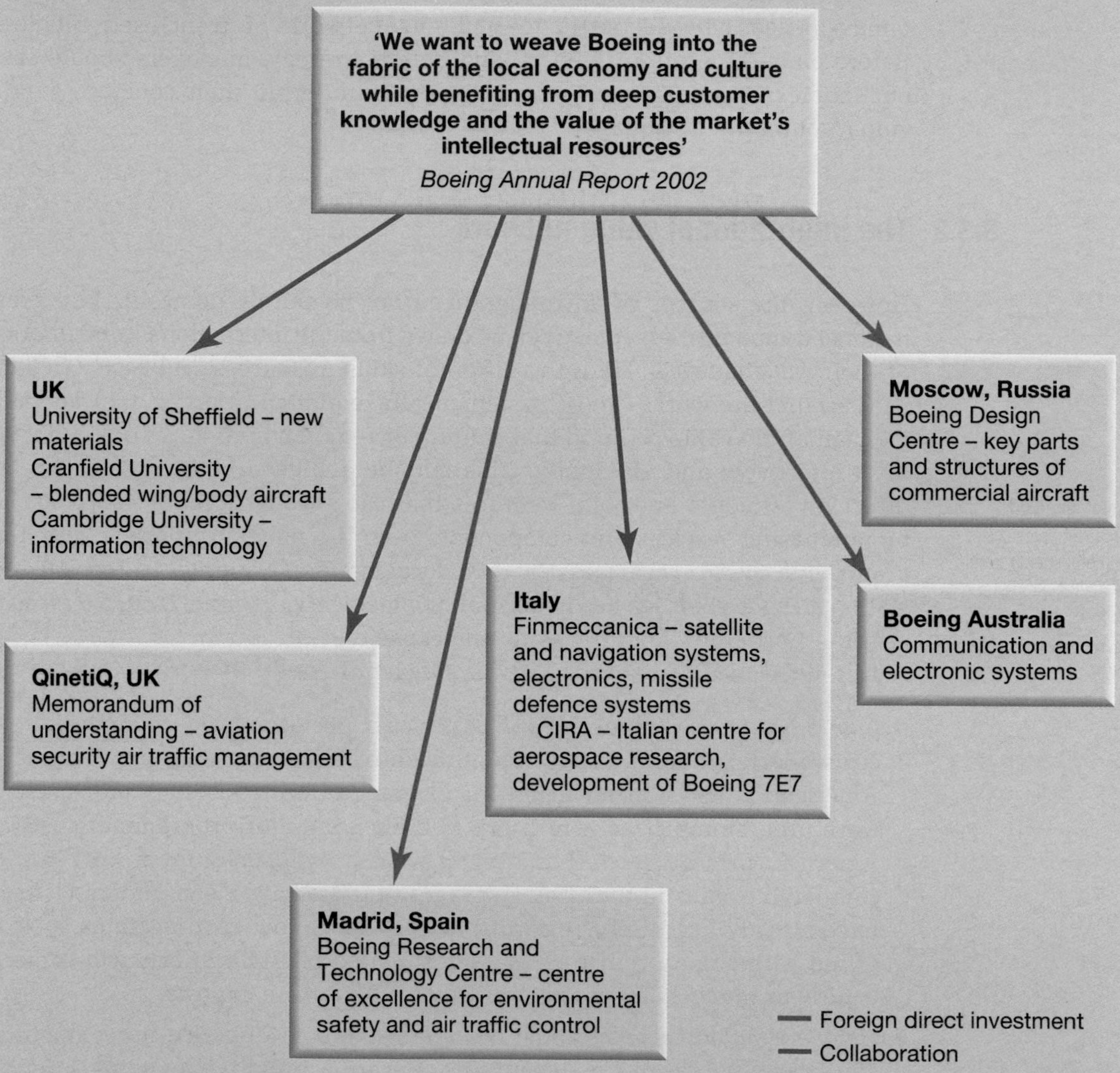

Sources: Boeing.com, Boeing Annual Report 2002, Aviation International News Online.

Prepared by Michael Mayer, Bath University.

Questions

1. What reasons might be driving the internationalisation of Boeing's R&D activities?
2. What challenges might Boeing face as it internationalises its R&D activities?

it access Russian know-how in areas such as aerodynamics. Organisations such as Boeing are thus increasingly leveraging their ability selectively to exploit locational advantages with a view to building on and enhancing their existing strategic capabilities. Put differently, internationalisation is increasingly not only about exploiting existing capabilities in new national markets, but about developing strategic capabilities by drawing on the capabilities elsewhere in the world.

- *National characteristics* can enable organisations to develop differentiated product offerings aimed at different market segments. American guitar-maker Gibson, for example, complements its US-made products with often similar, lower-cost alternatives produced in South Korea under the Epiphone brand. However, because of the American music tradition, Gibson's high-end guitars benefit from the reputation of still being 'made in the USA'.

Of course one of the consequences of organisations trying to exploit the locational advantages available in different countries' organisations can be that they create complex networks of intra- and inter-organisational relationships. Boeing, for example, has developed a global web of R&D activities through its subsidiaries and partnerships with collaborating organisations (see Illustration 8.3).

8.4 INTERNATIONAL STRATEGIES

The **global–local dilemma** relates to the extent to which products and services may be standardised across national boundaries or need to be adapted to meet the requirements of specific national markets

Given the ability to obtain sources of international competitive advantage through home-based factors or international value networks, organisations still face difficult questions about what kinds of strategies to pursue in their markets. Here the key problem is typically the so-called **global–local dilemma**. This relates to the extent to which products and services may be standardised across national boundaries or need be adapted to meet the requirements of specific national markets. For some products and services – such as televisions – markets appear similar across the world, offering huge potential scale economies if design, production and delivery can be centralised. For other products and services – such as television programming – tastes still seem highly nationally-specific, drawing companies to decentralise operations and control as near as possible to the local market. This global–local dilemma can evoke a number of responses from companies pursuing international strategies, ranging from decentralisation to centralisation, with positions in between.

This section introduces four different kinds of international strategy, based on choices about the international *configuration* of the various activities an organization has to carry out and the degree to which these activities are then

Exhibit 8.4 Four international strategies

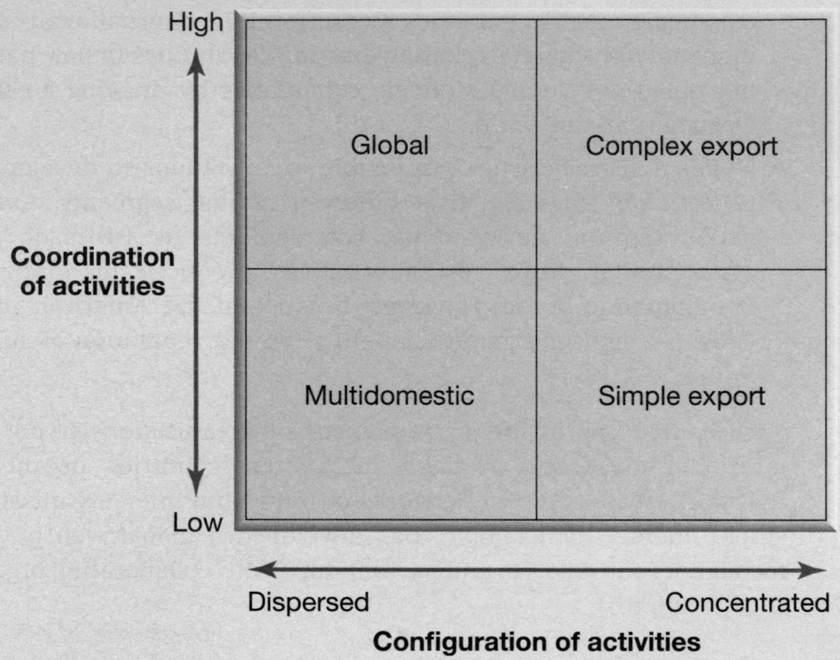

Source: Adapted from M.E. Porter, 'Changing patterns of international competition'. Copyright © 1986, by The Regents of the University of California. Reprinted from the *California Management Review*, vol. 28, no. 2. By permission of The Regents. NB Porter's strategies are relabelled for consistency with the rest of the book.

www.pearsoned.co.uk/fos KEY CONCEPT Four international strategies

coordinated internationally (see Exhibit 8.4). More precisely, configuration refers to the geographical dispersion or concentration of activities such as manufacturing and R&D, while coordination refers to the extent to which operations in different countries are managed in a decentralized way or a centrally coordinated way. The four basic international strategies are:[8]

- *Simple export*. This strategy involves a concentration of activities (particularly manufacturing) in one country, typically the country of the organisation's origin. At the same time, marketing of the exported product is very loosely-coordinated overseas, perhaps handled by independent sales agents in different markets. Pricing, packaging, distribution and even branding policies may be determined locally. This strategy is typically chosen by organisations with a strong locational advantage – as determined by the Porter Diamond, for example – but where the organisation either has insufficient managerial capabilities to coordinate marketing internationally or where coordinated marketing would add little value, for example in agricultural or raw material commodities.

- *Multidomestic*. This strategy is similarly loosely coordinated internationally, but involves a dispersion overseas of various activities, including manufacturing and sometimes product development. Instead of export, therefore, goods and services are produced locally in each national market. Each market is treated independently, with the needs of each local domestic market given priority – hence 'multidomestic'. Local adaptations can make the overall corporate portfolio increasingly diversified. This strategy is appropriate where there are few economies of scale and strong benefits to adapting to local needs. This multidomestic strategy is particularly attractive in professional services, where local relationships are critical, but it carries risks towards brand and reputation if national practices become too diverse.
- *Complex export*. This strategy still involves location of most activities in a single country, but builds on more coordinated marketing. Economies of scale can still be reaped in manufacturing and R&D, but branding and pricing opportunities are more systematically managed. The coordination demands are, of course, considerably more complex than in the simple export strategy. This is a common stage for companies from emerging economies, as they retain some locational advantages from their home country, but seek to build a stronger brand and network overseas with growing organisational maturity.
- *Global strategy*. This strategy describes the most mature international strategy, with highly coordinated activities dispersed geographically around the world. Using international value networks to the full, geographical location is chosen according to the specific locational advantage for each activity, so that product development, manufacturing, marketing and headquarters functions might all be located in different countries. For example, Detroit-based General Motors designed its Pontiac Le Mans at the firm's German subsidiary Opel, with its high engineering skills; developed its advertising via a British agency with the creativity strengths of London; produced many of its more complex components in Japan, exploiting its sophisticated manufacturing and technological capabilities; and assembled the car in South Korea, a location where a lower-cost, yet skilled, labour force was available.

In practice, these four international strategies are not absolutely distinct. Managerial coordination and geographical concentration are matters of degree rather than sharp distinctions. Companies may often oscillate within and between the four strategies. Their choices, moreover, will be influenced by changes in the internationalisation drivers introduced earlier. Where, for example, tastes are highly standardised, companies will tend to favour complex export or global strategies. Where economies of scale are few, the logic is more in favour of multidomestic strategies.

8.5 MARKET SELECTION AND ENTRY

Having decided on an international strategy built on significant sources of competitive advantage and supported by strong internationalisation drivers, managers need next to decide which countries to enter. Not all countries are equally attractive. To an extent, however, countries can initially be compared using the standard environmental analysis techniques, for example along the dimensions identified in the PESTEL framework (see section 2.2.1) or according to the industry Five Forces (section 2.3). However, there are specific determinants of market attractiveness that need to be considered in internationalisation strategy, and they can be analysed under two main headings: the intrinsic characteristics of the market and the nature of the competition. A key point here is how initial estimates of country attractiveness can be modified by various measures of *distance* and the likelihood of competitor *retaliation*. The section concludes by considering different *entry modes* into national markets.

8.5.1 Market characteristics

At least four elements of the PESTEL framework are particularly important in comparing countries for entry:

- *Political*. Political environments vary widely between countries and can alter rapidly. Russia since the fall of Communism has seen frequent swings for and against private foreign enterprise. Governments can of course create significant opportunities for organisations. For example, the official regional development agency Scottish Enterprise provided a subsidy in order to attract the 2003 MTV music awards to the Scottish capital Edinburgh, while political and regulatory changes can create opportunities for international expansion as with Deutsche Post (see Illustration 8.2 earlier). It is important, however, to determine the level of *political risk* before entering a country.
- *Economic*. Key comparators in deciding entry are levels of gross domestic product and disposable income which help in estimating the potential size of the market. Fast-growth economies obviously provide opportunities, and in developing economies such as China growth is translating into an even faster creation of a high-consumption middle class. However, companies must also be aware of the stability of a country's currency which may affect its income stream. There can be considerable *currency risk*.
- *Social*. Social factors will clearly be important, for example the availability of a well-trained workforce or the size of demographic market segments – old or young – relevant to the strategy. Cultural variations need to be considered, for instance in defining tastes in the marketplace.

- *Legal*. Countries vary widely in their legal regime, determining the extent to which businesses can enforce contracts, protect intellectual property or avoid corruption. Similarly, policing will be important for the security of employees, a factor that in the past has deterred business in some South American countries.

It is quite common to rank country markets against each other on criteria such as these and then to choose the countries for entry that offer the highest relative scores. However, Pankaj Ghemawat has pointed out that what matters is not just the attractiveness of different countries relative to each other, but also the compatibility of the possible countries with the internationalising firm itself.[9] The argument is that, for firms coming from any particular country, some countries are more 'distant' – or incompatible – than others. In other words, companies with different nationalities would not fit equally well in all the top-ranked countries. A South American market might rank the same as an East African market in terms of attractiveness, but a Spanish company would probably be more at home in the first than the second. As well as a relative ranking of countries, therefore, each company has to add its assessment of countries according to their 'closeness'.

In arguing that 'distance still matters', Ghemawat offers a 'CAGE framework', with each letter of the acronym highlighting different dimensions of distance:

- *Cultural distance*. The distance dimension here relate to differences in language, ethnicity, religion and social norms. Cultural distance is not just a matter of similarity in consumer tastes, but extends to important compatibilities in terms of managerial behaviours. Here, for example, American firms might be closer to Canada than to Mexico, which Spanish firms might find relatively compatible.
- *Administrative and political distance*. Here distance is in terms of incompatible administrative, political or legal traditions. Colonial ties can diminish difference, so that the shared heritage of France and its former West African colonies create certain understandings that go beyond linguistic advantages. Institutional weaknesses – for example slow or corrupt administration – can open up distance between countries. So too can political differences: Chinese companies are increasingly able to operate in parts of the world that American companies are finding harder, for example parts of the Middle East and Africa.
- *Geographical distance*. This is not just a matter of the kilometres separating one country from another, but involves other geographical characteristics of the country such as size, sea access and the quality of communications infrastructure. For example, Wal-Mart's difficulties in Europe relate to the fact that its logistics systems were developed in the geographically enormous space of North America, and proved much less suitable for the smaller and more dense countries of Europe. Transport infrastructure can shrink or

exaggerate physical distance. France is much closer to large parts of Continental Europe than to the UK, because of the barrier presented by the English Channel and Britain's relatively poor road and rail infrastructure.

- *Economic*. The final element of the CAGE framework refers particularly to wealth distances. Here, instead of simply assuming that a wealthy market is a good one to enter, and a poor market a bad one, the framework points to the differing capabilities of companies from different countries. Multinationals from rich countries are typically weak at serving consumers in poorer markets (see Illustration 8.4 for how Unilever approaches this problem). In developing countries, rich country multinationals often end up focusing on economic elites. In reverse, it often takes a long time for companies from developing countries to learn all the requirements that the middle classes from wealthy countries routinely expect.[10]

8.5.2 Competitive characteristics

Assessing the relative attractiveness of markets by PESTEL and CAGE analyses is only the first step. The second element relates to competition. Here, of course, Michael Porter's five forces framework can help (see section 2.3). For example, country markets with many existing competitors, powerful buyers (perhaps large retail chains such as in much of North American and Northern Europe) and low barriers to further new entrants from overseas would typically be unattractive. However, an additional consideration is the likelihood of retaliation from other competitors.

The five forces framework (see section 2.3.1) has already raised the issue of competitor retaliation under the heading of rivalry. With regard to international strategy, the likelihood and ferocity of potential competitor reactions are added to the simple calculation of relative country market attractiveness. As in Exhibit 8.5, country markets are aligned against two axes.[11] The first is *market attractiveness* to the new entrant, based on PESTEL, CAGE and five forces analyses, for example. In Exhibit 8.5, countries A and B are the most attractive to the entrant. The second is the *defender's reactiveness*, likely to be influenced by the market's attractiveness to the defender but also by the extent to which the defender is working with a globally-integrated, rather than multi-domestic, strategy. A defender will be more reactive if the markets are important to it and it has the managerial capabilities to coordinate its response. Here, the defender is highly reactive in countries A and D. The third element is the *clout* (i.e. power) that the defender is able to muster in order to fight back. Clout is typically a function of share in the particular market, but might be influenced by connections to other powerful local players, such as retailers or government. In Exhibit 8.5, clout is represented by the size of the bubbles, with the defender having most clout in countries A, C, D and F.

Choice of country to enter can be significantly modified by adding reactiveness and clout to calculations of attractiveness. Relying only on attractiveness,

Illustration 8.4

Strategic innovation at Hindustan Lever Ltd

Large multinational corporations may still need to tailor their products and services to local market needs.

Unilever is one of the world's biggest consumer products companies. It seeks to establish its brands on a global basis and support them with state-of-the-art research and development. However, it is acutely aware that markets differ and that, if it is to be global, it has to be prepared to adapt to local market conditions. It also recognises that if it is to have global reach, it has to be able to market its goods in poorer areas as well as richer areas. Indeed it estimates that by 2010 half of its sales will come from the developing world – an increase of over 30 per cent from the equivalent figure in 2000.

In the rural areas of India Hindustan Lever is setting about marketing Unilever's branded goods in ways suited to local conditions.

Much of the effort goes into marketing branded goods in local 'haats' or market places, where Unilever representatives sell the products from the back of trucks using loudspeakers to explain the brand proposition. Local executives argue that, poor as people are, they 'aren't naturally inclined to settle for throwaway versions of the real deal – if the companies that make the real deal bother to explain the difference'.

To help develop the skills to do this Lever management trainees in India begin their careers by spending weeks living in rural villages where they eat, sleep and talk with the locals: 'Once you have spent time with consumers, you realise that they want the same things you want. They want a good quality of life.'

The same executives have innovated further in the way goods are marketed. They have developed direct sales models where women, belonging to self-help groups that run micro credit operations, sell Lever products so as to make their collectives' savings grow. Where television viewing is uncommon, Hindustan Lever marketing executives have also mounted thousands of live shows at cattle and trade markets, employing rural folklore. The aim here is not just to push the Lever brands, it is to explain the importance of more frequent washing and better hygiene. Indeed sales personnel attend religious festivals and use ultraviolet light wands on people's hands to show the dangers of germs and dirt.

But it is not just the way the goods are marketed that is tailored to rural India. Product development is also different. For example, Indian women are very proud of the care of their hair and regard hair grooming as a luxury. However, they tend to use the same soap for body washing as for washing their hair. So Lever has dedicated research and development efforts into finding a low-cost soap that can be used for the body and for the hair and which is targeted to smaller towns and rural areas.

As Keki Dadiseth, a director of Hindustan Lever, puts it: 'Everyone wants brands. And there are a lot more poor people in the world than rich people. To be a global business . . . you have to participate in all segments.'

Source: Rekha Balu, 'Strategic innovation: Hindustan Lever Ltd', *FastCompany.com* (www.fastcompany.com/magazine), issue 47, June (2001).

Questions

1 What are the challenges a multinational such as Unilever faces in developing global brands whilst encouraging local responsiveness?

2 What other examples of local tailoring of global brands can you think of?

3 Multinationals have been criticised for marketing more expensive branded goods in poorer areas of developing countries. What are your views of the ethical dimensions to Hindustan Lever's activities?

Exhibit 8.5 International competitor retaliation

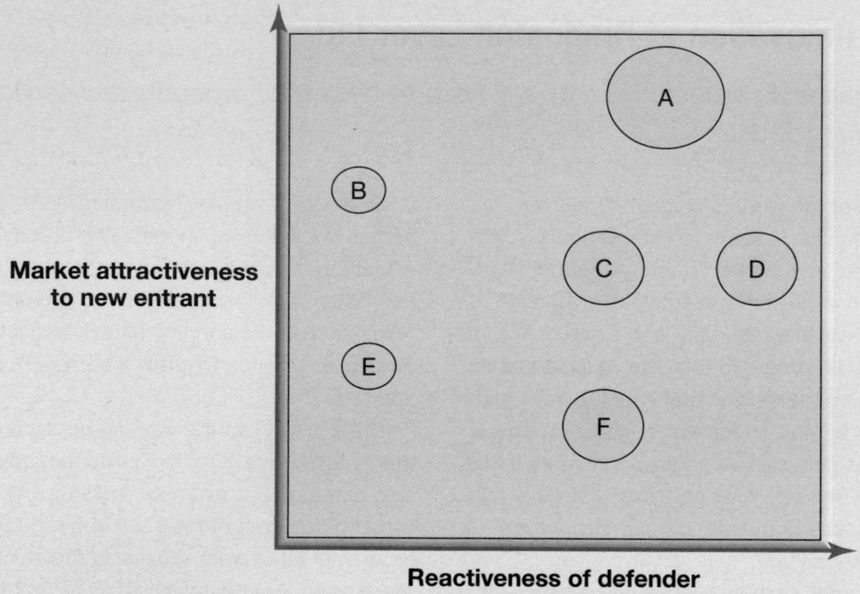

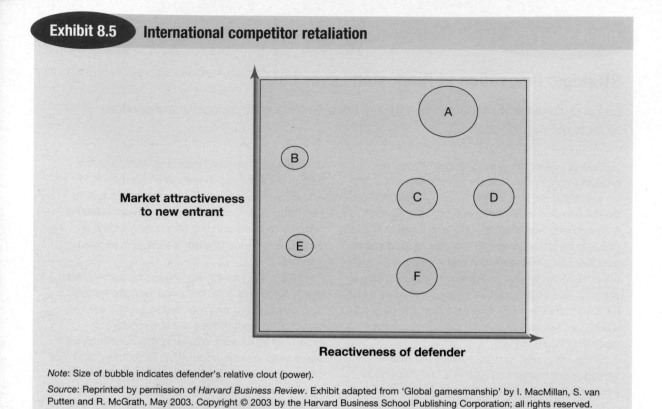

Note: Size of bubble indicates defender's relative clout (power).

Source: Reprinted by permission of *Harvard Business Review*. Exhibit adapted from 'Global gamesmanship' by I. MacMillan, S. van Putten and R. McGrath, May 2003. Copyright © 2003 by the Harvard Business School Publishing Corporation; all rights reserved.

the top ranked country to enter in Exhibit 8.5 is country A. Unfortunately, it is also one in which the defender is highly reactive, and the one in which it has most clout. Country B becomes a better international move than A. In turn, country C is a better prospect than country D, because, even though they are equally attractive, the defender is less reactive. One surprising result of taking defender reactiveness and clout into account is the re-evaluation of country E: although ranked fifth on simple attractiveness, it might rank overall second if competitor retaliation is allowed for.

This sort of analysis is particularly fruitful for considering the international moves of two interdependent competitors, such as Unilever and Procter & Gamble or British Airways and Singapore Airlines. In these cases the analysis is relevant to any aggressive strategic move, for instance the expansion of existing operations in a country as well as initial entry. Especially in the case of globally-integrated competitors, moreover, the overall clout of the defender must be taken into account. The defender may choose to retaliate in other markets than the targeted one, counter-attacking wherever it has the clout to do damage to the aggressor. Naturally, too, this kind of analysis can be applied to interactions between diversified competitors as well as international ones: each bubble could represent different products or services.

8.5.3 Entry modes

Once a particular national market has been selected for entry, an organisation needs to choose how to enter that market. Entry modes differ in the degree of resource commitment to a particular market and the extent to which an organisation is operationally involved in a particular location. The key entry mode types are: exporting; contractual arrangement through licensing and franchising; joint ventures and alliances; and foreign direct investment, which in turn may involve the acquisition of established companies or 'greenfield' investments, the development of facilities 'from scratch'. These alternative methods of strategy development are explained further in section 9.3 but the specific advantages and disadvantages for international market entry are summarised in Exhibit 8.6.

Entry modes are often selected according to stages of organisational development. Internationalisation brings organisations into new and often unknown territory, requiring managers to learn new ways of doing business.[12] Internationalisation is therefore traditionally seen as a sequential process whereby companies gradually increase their commitment to newly entered markets, accumulating knowledge and increasing their capabilities along the way. This strategy of **staged international expansion** means that firms begin by using entry modes such as licensing and exporting that allow them to acquire local knowledge whilst minimising the exposure of their assets. Once firms have sufficient knowledge and confidence, they can then sequentially increase their exposure, perhaps first by a joint venture and finally by direct foreign investment. An example is the entry of automobile manufacturer BMW into the American market. After a lengthy period of exporting from Germany to the USA, BMW set up a manufacturing plant in Spartanburg, South Carolina in order to strengthen its competitive position in the strategically important American market.

Staged international expansion: firms initially use entry modes that allow them to maximise knowledge acquisition whilst minimising the exposure of their assets

In contrast to the gradual internationalisation followed originally by many large and established firms, some small firms are now internationalising rapidly at early stages in their development using multiple modes of entry to several countries. These are the so-called 'born global' firms.[13] GNI, the mini-multinational in Illustration 8.5, illustrates this born-global process. In achieving this rapid internationalisation, born global firms need to manage simultaneously the process of internationalisation and develop their wider strategy and infrastructure, whilst often lacking the usually expected experiential knowledge to do so.

Emerging country multinationals too are often moving quickly through entry modes. Prominent examples are the Chinese white goods multinational Haier, the Indian pharmaceuticals company Ranbaxy Laboratories and Mexico's Cemex cement company. These companies' international strategies are not simply export and cost-based.[14] Typically they develop *unique capabilities* in their home market, in areas neglected by established multinationals. They then move on to establish outposts in more developed markets. For example,

Exhibit 8.6 Market entry modes: advantages and disadvantages

Exporting

Advantages	Disadvantages
• No operational facilities needed in the host country • Economies of scale can be exploited • By using Internet, small/inexperienced firms can gain access to international markets	• Does not allow the firm to benefit from the locational advantages of the host nation • Limits opportunities to gain knowledge of local markets and competitors • May create dependence on export intermediaries • Exposure to trade barriers such as import duties • Incurs transportation costs • May limit the ability to respond quickly to customer demands

Joint ventures and alliances

Advantages	Disadvantages
• Investment risk shared with partner • Combining of complementary resources and know-how • May be a governmental condition for market entry	• Difficulty of identifying appropriate partner and agreeing appropriate contractual terms • Managing the relationship with the foreign partner • Loss of competitive advantage through imitation • Limits ability to integrate and coordinate activities across national boundaries

Licensing

Advantages	Disadvantages
• Contractually agreed income through sale of production and marketing rights • Limits economic and financial exposure	• Difficulty of identifying appropriate partner and agreeing contractual terms • Loss of competitive advantage through imitation • Limits benefits from the locational advantages of host nation

Foreign direct investment

Advantages	Disadvantages
• Full control of resources and capabilities • Facilitates integration and coordination of activities across national boundaries • Acquisitions allow rapid market entry • Greenfield investments allow development of state-of-the-art facilities and can attract financial support from the host government	• Substantial investment in and commitment to host country leading to economic and financial exposure • Acquisition may lead to problems of integration and coordination • Greenfield entry time consuming and less predictable in terms of cost

Illustration 8.5

The mini-multinational

GNI, a biotechnology start-up, has fewer than 100 employees, but operates in five countries in four continents.

Christopher Savoie is an American entrepreneur who originally studied medicine in Japan, becoming fluent in Japanese and adopting Japanese citizenship. In 2001, he founded GNI, a biotechnology company that by 2006 had raised 3bn yen (€20m) in investment funds, including a stake from famed global investment bank Goldman Sachs. The company already has operations in Tokyo and Fukuoka, Japan; in Shanghai, China; in Cambridge and London, UK; and in San Jose in California. There is also collaboration with a laboratory in Auckland, New Zealand. Savoie comments: 'We take the best in each country and put them together.'

GNI's strategy is to focus on Asian ailments that have been neglected by big Western pharmaceutical companies, for example stomach cancer and hepatitis. According to Savoie: 'Asia has been getting the short end of the stick. As a small company, we had to choose a niche, and we thought that half of humanity was an acceptable place to start.'

GNI's scientists work on umbilical cords, providing genetic tissue that has been virtually unaffected by the environment. However, Japanese parents traditionally keep their children's umbilical cords. GNI therefore works with the Rosie Maternity Hospital in Cambridge to source its basic genetic materials. On the other hand, GNI in Japan has ready access to supercomputers, and Japanese scientists have worked out the algorithms required to analyse the genetic codes. Japan also has been the main source of investment funds, where regulations on start-ups are relaxed. China comes in as an effective place to test treatments on patients. Regulatory advantages mean that trials can be carried out more quickly in China, moreover for one-tenth of the cost in Japan. In 2005, GNI merged with Shanghai Genomics, a start-up run by two US-educated entrepreneurs. Meanwhile, in San Jose, there is a business development office seeking out relationships with the big American pharmaceutical giants.

Savoie describes the business model as essentially simple:

> We have a Chinese cost structure, Japanese supercomputers and, in Cambridge, access to ethical materials (umbilical cords) and top clinical scientists. This is a network we can use to take high-level science and turn it into molecules to compete with the big boys.

Sources: D. Pilling, 'March of the mini-multinational', *Financial Times*, 4 May (2006); www.gene-networks.com.

Questions

1. Analyse GNI's value network in terms of cost advantages, unique capabilities and national characteristics.
2. What managerial challenges will GNI face as it grows?

because of the needs of the Chinese market, Haier became skilled at very efficient production of simple white goods, providing a cost advantage that is transferable outside a Chinese manufacturing base. In 1999, Haier set up a manufacturing operation in South Carolina in the USA, competing head-on with Western giant multinationals such as General Electric and Whirlpool on their home territory.

SUMMARY

www.pearsoned.co.uk/fos
AUDIO SUMMARY

- *Internationalisation potential* in any particular market is determined by four drivers: market, cost, government and competitors' strategies.
- Sources of advantage in international strategy can be drawn from both global sourcing through the *international value network* and national sources of advantage, as captured in *Porter's Diamond*.
- There are four main types of international strategy, varying according to extent of *coordination* and *geographical configuration*: simple export, complex export, multidomestic and global.
- Market selection for international entry or expansion should be based on attractiveness, multidimensional measures of *distance* and expectations of competitor *retaliation*.
- Modes of entry into new markets include *export, licensing, joint ventures* and *alliances* and *foreign direct investment*.

Recommended key readings

- An eye-opening introduction to the detailed workings – and inefficiencies – of today's global economy is P. Rivoli, *The Travels of a T-Shirt in the Global Economy: an Economist Examines the Markets, Power and Politics of World Trade*, Wiley, 2006. A more optimistic view is in T. Friedman, *The World is Flat: the Globalized World in the Twenty First Century*, Penguin, 2006.
- An invigorating perspective on international strategy is provided by G. Yip, *Total Global Strategy II*, Prentice Hall, 2003. A comprehensive general textbook is A. Rugman and S. Collinson, *International Business*, 4th edition, FT Prentice Hall, 2006.

References

1. Indeed, many authors refer to internationalisation simple as 'international diversification': see N. Capar and M. Kotabe, 'The relationship between international diversification and performance in service firms', *Journal of International Business Studies*, vol. 34 (2003), pp. 345–355.
2. T. Friedman, *The World is Flat: the Globalized World in the Twenty First Century*, Penguin, 2006; and P. Rivoli, *The Travels of a T-Shirt in the Global Economy: an Economist Examines the Markets, Power and Politics of World Trade*, Wiley, 2006.
3. G. Yip, *Total Global Strategy II*, Prentice Hall, 2003.
4. Useful industry specific data on trends in openness to trade and investment can be found at the World Trade Organization's site, ww.wto.org.
5. G. Hamel and C.K. Prahalad, 'Do you really have a global strategy?', *Harvard Business Review*, vol. 63, no. 4 (1985), pp. 139–148.
6. B. Kogut, 'Designing global strategies: comparative and competitive value added changes', *Sloan Management Review*, vol. 27 (1985), pp. 15–28.
7. M. Porter, *The Competitive Advantage of Nations*, MacMillan, 1990.

8. This typology builds on the basic framework of M. Porter, 'Changing patterns of international competition', *California Management Review*, vol. 28, no. 2 (1987), pp. 9–39, but adapts its terms for the four strategies into more readily understandable terms: note particularly that here 'global' strategy is transposed to refer to the top left box, and the top right box is described as 'complex export'.
9. P. Ghemawat, 'Distance still matters', *Harvard Business Review*, September (2001), 137–147.
10. For a good analysis of developing country companies and their opportunities, see T. Khanna and K. Palepu, 'Emerging giants: building world-class companies in developing countries', *Harvard Business Review*, October (2006), pp. 60–69.
11. This framework is introduced in I. MacMillan, A. van Putten and R. McGrath, 'Global Gamesmanship', *Harvard Business Review*, vol. 81, no. 5 (2003), pp. 62–71.
12. For detailed discussions about the role of learning and experience in market entry see M.F. Guillén, 'Experience, imitation, and the sequence of foreign entry: wholly owned and joint-venture manufacturing by South Korean firms and business groups in China, 1987–1995', *Journal of International Business Studies*, vol. 83 (2003), pp. 185–198; and M.K. Erramilli, 'The experience factor in foreign market entry modes by service firms', *Journal of International Business Studies*, vol. 22, no. 3, (1991), pp. 479–501.
13. G. Knights and T. Cavusil, 'A taxonomy of born-global firms', *Management International Review*, vol. 45, no. 3 (2005), pp. 15–35.
14. For analyses of emerging country multinationals, see T. Khanna and K. Palepu, 'Emerging giants: building world-class companies in developing countries', *Harvard Business Review*, October (2006), pp. 60–69; and J. Sinha, 'Global champions from emerging markets', *McKinsey Quarterly*, no. 2 (2005), pp. 26–35.

CASE EXAMPLE

Lenovo computers: East meets West

Introduction

In May 2005, the world's thirteenth largest personal computer company, Lenovo, took over the world's third largest personal computer business, IBM's PC division. Lenovo, at that time based wholly in China, was paying $1.75bn (€1.4bn, £1bn) to control a business that operated all over the world and had effectively invented the personal computer industry back in 1981. Michael Dell, the creator of the world's largest PC company, commented simply: 'it won't work'.

Lenovo had been founded back in 1984 by Liu Chuanzhi, a 40-year-old researcher working for the Computer Institute of the Chinese Academy of Sciences. His early career had included disassembling captured American radar systems during the Vietnam War and planting rice during the Chinese Cultural Revolution. Liu Chuanzhi had started with $25,000 capital from the Computer Institute and promised his boss that he would build a business with revenues of $250,000. Working in the Computer Institute's old guardhouse, and borrowing its office facilities, one of Liu's first initiatives was reselling colour televisions. But real success started to come in 1987, when Lenovo was one of the first to package Chinese-character software with imported PCs.

Lenovo began to take off, with Liu using the support of his father, well placed in the Chinese government, to help import PCs cheaply through Hong Kong. During 1988, Lenovo placed its first job advertisement, and recruited 58 young people to join the company. Whilst the founding generation of Lenovo staff were in their forties, the new recruits were all in their twenties, as the Cultural Revolution had prevented any university graduates for a period of 10 years in China. Amongst the new recruits was Yang Yuanqing, who would be running Lenovo's PC business before he was 30, and later become Chairman of the new Lenovo–IBM venture at the age of 41. It was this new team which helped launch the production of the first Lenovo PC in 1990, and drove the company to a 30 per cent market share within China by 2005. The company had partially floated on the Hong Kong Stock Exchange in 1994.

Photo: Kim Cheung/AP/PA Photos

Lenovo's Chairman, Yang Yuanqing

The deal

Work on the IBM PC deal had begun in 2004, with Lenovo assisted by management consultancy McKinsey & Co. and investment banker Goldman Sachs. IBM wanted to dispose of its PC business, which had only 4 per cent market share in the USA and suffered low margins in a competitive market dominated by Dell and Hewlett Packard. Higher margin services and mainframe computers would be IBM's future. As well as Lenovo, IBM had private equity firm Texas Pacific Group in the bidding. Lenovo offered the best price, but Texas Pacific was persuaded enough to take a stake in the new group, while IBM took 13 per cent ownership. The government-owned Chinese Academy of Sciences still owned 27 per cent of the stock, the largest single shareholder.

The new Chairman, Yang Yuanqing, had a clear vision of what the company was to achieve, while recognising some of the challenges:

> In five years, I want this (Lenovo) to be a very famous PC brand, with maybe double the growth of the industry. I want to have a very healthy profit margin, and maybe some other businesses beyond PCs, worldwide. We are at the beginnings of this new company, so we can define some fundamentals about the culture. The three words I use to describe this are trust, respect, compromise.

He continued:

> As a global company maybe we have to sacrifice some speed, especially during our first phase. We need more communication. We need to take time to understand each other. But speed was in the genes of the old Lenovo. I hope it will be in the genes of the new Lenovo.

IBM was not leaving its old business to sink or swim entirely on its own. Lenovo had the right to use the IBM brand for PCs for five years, including the valuable ThinkPad name. IBM's salesforce would be offered incentives to sell Lenovo PCs, just as they had with IBM's own-brand machines. IBM Global Services was contracted to provide maintenance and support. IBM would have two non-voting observers on the Lenovo board. Moreover, Stephen Ward, the 51-year-old former head of IBM's PC division, was to become Lenovo's Chief Executive Officer.

Managing the new giant

Having an IBM CEO was not entirely a surprise. After all, the $13bn business was nearly 80 per cent ex-IBM and customers and employees had to be reassured of continuity. But there were some significant challenges for the new company to manage none the less.

Things had not started well. When the Chinese team first flew to New York to meet the IBM team, they had not been met at the airport as they had expected and was normal polite practice in China. Yang and Ward had disagreed about the location of the new headquarters, Yang wishing it to be shared between Beijing and near New York. Ward had prevailed, and Yang moved his family to the USA. The new organisation structure kept the old IBM business and the original Lenovo business as separate divisions. But still the new company needed considerable liaison with China, a 13-hour flight away, across 12 time zones. Teleconferencing between the East Coast and China became a way of life, with the Americans calling typically at either 6.00 in the morning or 11.00 at night to catch their Chinese colleagues. Calls were always in English, with many Chinese less than fluent and body language impossible to observe.

The Chinese nature of the company was an issue for some constituencies. IBM had had a lot of government business, and populist members of the US Congress whipped up a scare campaign about Chinese computers entering sensitive domains. In Germany, labour laws allowed a voluntary transition of IBM employees to Lenovo, and many German workers chose not to transfer, leaving the company short staffed. There was some discomfort amongst former IBM employees in Japan about Chinese ownership. Between the two dominant cultures, American and Chinese, there were considerable differences. Qiao Jian, Vice President for Human Resources, commented:

> Americans like to talk; Chinese people like to listen. At first we wondered why they kept talking when they had nothing to say. But we have learnt to be more direct when we have a problem, and the Americans are learning to listen.

Cultural differences were not just national. Lenovo was a new and relatively simple company – basically one country, one product. Multinational giant IBM Corporation, founded in 1924, was far more complex. The Lenovo management team, mostly in their thirties, were much younger than IBM's, and the average age of the company as a whole was just 28. IBM was famous for its management processes and routines. Qiao Jian commented: 'IBM people set a time for a conference call and stick to it every week. But why have the call if there is nothing to report?' On the other hand, IBM people had a tendency for being late for meetings, something that was strictly discouraged within Lenovo.

Some results

At first, the response to the new Lenovo was positive. IBM customers stayed loyal and the stock price began to climb (see Figure 1). Remaining IBM executives recognised that at least they were part of a business committed to PCs, rather than the Cinderella in a much larger IBM empire. The fact that a Lenovo PC manufactured in China had a labour cost of just $3.00 offered a lot of opportunity.

However, market leader Dell responded to the new company with heavy price cuts, offering $100 savings on the average machine. With market share in the crucial

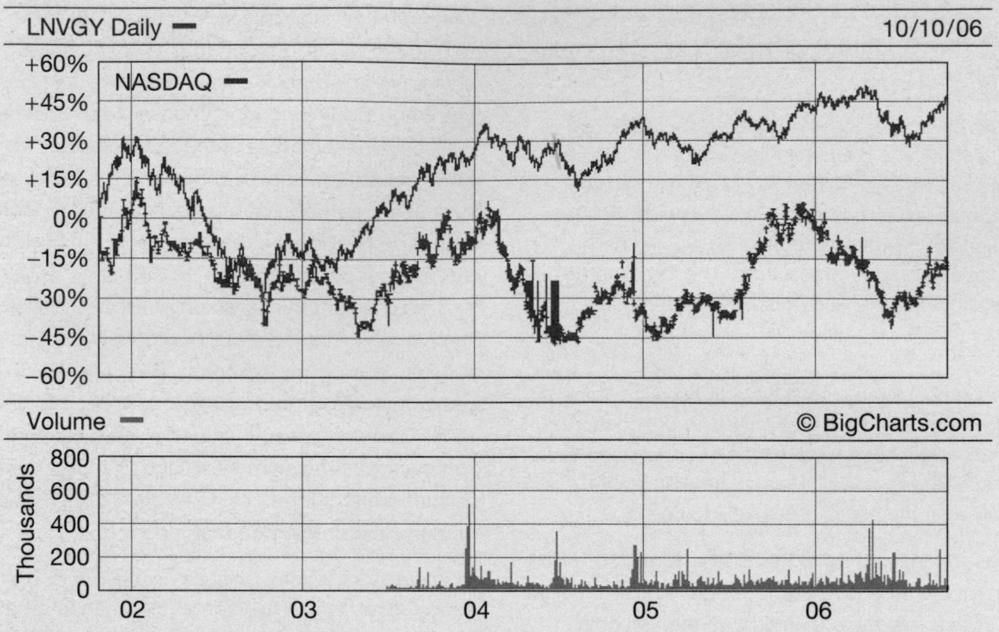

Figure 1 Lenovo Group's stock price, 2001–2006, compared with NASDAQ index

Source: www.bigcharts.com (11 October 2006). Marketwatch.Online by BigCharts.com. Copyright 2006 by Dow Jones & Company, Inc. Reproduced with permission of Dow Jones & Company, Inc. in the format Textbook via Copyright Clearance Center.

American market beginning to slip, ex-IBM CEO Stephen Ward was replaced in December 2005 by William Amelio. This was a coup for Lenovo, as Amelio had been running Dell's Asia–Pacific region. As well as knowing Lenovo's competitor from the inside, Amelio, based for several years in Singapore, had a good understanding of Asian business:

> In the five years I have been in Asia, one thing I have learned . . . is to have a lot more patience. I have to be someone who has a high sense of urgency and drive, but I have also learned how to temper that in the various cultures that I have dealt with in order to be more effective.

Amelio started by addressing costs, removing 1,000 positions, or 10 per cent, from Lenovo's non-China workforce. He integrated the IBM business and the old Lenovo business into a single structure. The company launched a new range of Lenovo-branded PCs for small and medium-sized American business, a market traditionally ignored by IBM. To improve its reach in this segment, Lenovo expanded sales to big American retailers such as Office Depot. US market share began to recover, pushing beyond 4 per cent again. Lenovo began to consider entry into the Indian market.

Amelio's actions seemed to pay off. After a precipitous slide during the first half of 2006, the stock price turned up. But there was no disguising that the stock price in the autumn of 2006 was still below where it was five years earlier, and that it continued to trail the hi-tech American NASDAQ index.

Sources: L. Zhijun, *The Lenovo Affair*, Wiley, Singapore, 2006; *Business Week*, 7 August (2006), 20 April (2006), 22 December (2005) and 9 May (2005); *Financial Times*, 8 November (2005), 9 November (2005) and 10 November (2005).

Questions

1 What national sources of competitive advantage might Lenovo draw from its Chinese base? What disadvantages derive from its Chinese base?

2 In the light of the CAGE framework and the MacMillan *et al.* Competitor Retaliation framework (Exhibit 8.5), comment on Lenovo's entry into the American market.

3 Now that Lenovo is international, what type of generic international strategy should it pursue – simple export, multidomestic, complex export or global?

9

Strategy Methods and Evaluation

LEARNING OUTCOMES

After reading this chapter you should be able to:

- Identify the *methods* by which strategies can be pursued: *organic development, mergers and acquisitions and strategic alliances.*
- Employ three *success criteria* for evaluating strategic options: *suitability, acceptability and feasibility.*
- Use a range of different *techniques for evaluating strategic options*.

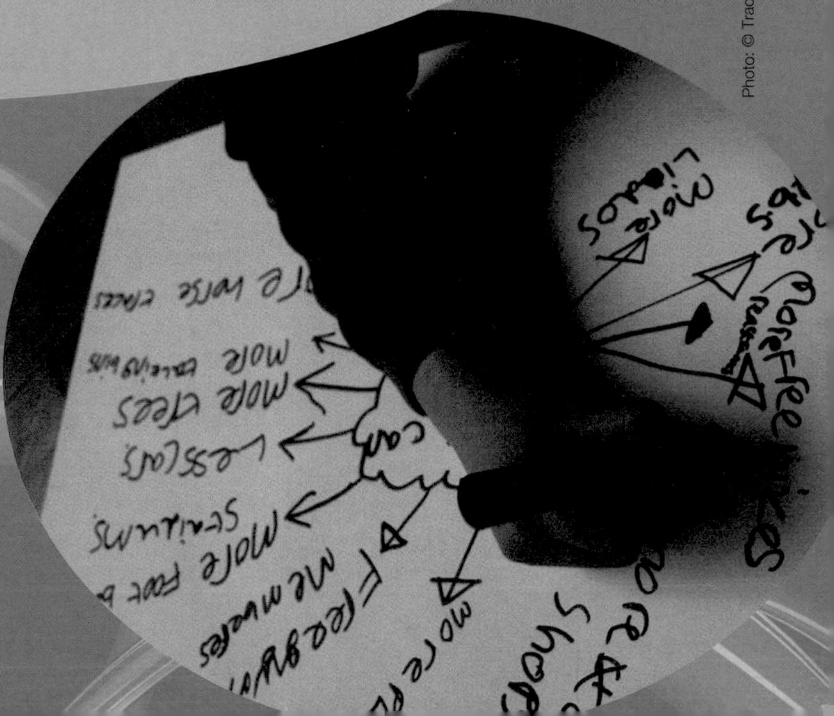

9.1 INTRODUCTION

Chapter 6 offered a range of choices about how to position the organisation in relation to competitors. Within this generalised choice about the basis of competitive strategy there are more specific choices to be made about the strategic direction of the organisation; in particular which markets and which products are most appropriate. These choices were set out in Chapter 7 and developed further in Chapter 8 in the context of international strategy. However, there is a third level of choice concerned with the *methods by which competitive strategy and strategic direction can be pursued*. This is the theme of section 9.2, the first half of this chapter.

Bearing in mind that the use of the concepts and tools introduced in Chapters 2 to 5 of the book will also have generated ideas about strategies that might be followed, the strategist may well need to consider many possible options. The second half of this chapter therefore discusses the *success criteria* by which they can be assessed and, building on these criteria, explains some of the *techniques for evaluating strategic options*.

Exhibit 9.1 summarises the overall structure of the chapter.

Exhibit 9.1 Strategy methods and evaluation: chapter structure

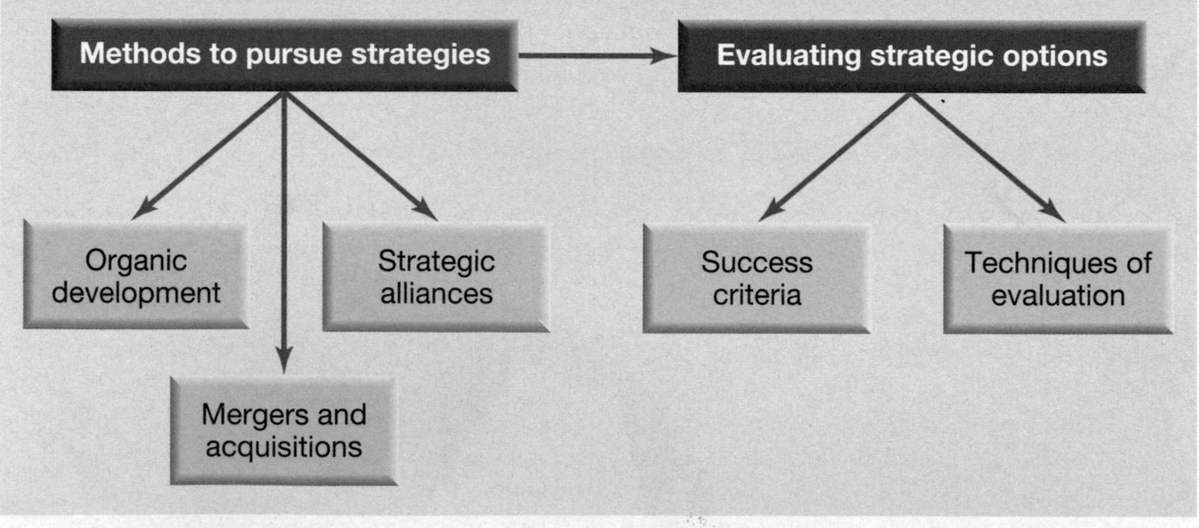

9.2 METHODS OF PURSUING STRATEGIES

A **strategic method** is the *means* by which a strategy can be pursued

Any of the strategy directions discussed in Chapters 6 to 8 may be undertaken in different ways or by different **strategic methods**: the *means* by which a strategy can be pursued. These methods can be divided into three types: organic development, acquisition (or disposal) and alliances.

9.2.1 Organic development[1]

Organic development is where strategies are developed by building on and developing an organisation's own capabilities

Organic development or internal development is where strategies are developed by building on and developing an organisation's own capabilities. For many organisations organic development has been the primary method of strategy development, and there are some compelling reasons why this should be so:

- *Highly technical products* in terms of design or method of manufacture lend themselves to organic development since the process of development may be the best way of acquiring the necessary capabilities to compete successfully. These competences may of course in turn spawn new products and create new market opportunities.
- *Knowledge and capability development* may be enhanced by organic development. For example, a business may feel that the direct involvement gained from having its own sales force rather than using sales agents gains greater market knowledge and therefore competitive advantage over other rivals more distant from their customers.
- *Spreading investment over time*. The final cost of developing new activities internally may be greater than that of acquiring other companies. However spreading these costs over time may be a more favourable option than major expenditure at a point in time required for an acquisition. This is a strong motive for organic development in small companies or many public services that may not have the resources for major one-off investments.
- *Minimising disruption*. The slower rate of change of organic development may also minimise the disruption to other activities and avoid the political and cultural problems of acquisition integration that can occur (see section 9.2.2).
- *The nature of markets* may dictate organic development. In many instances organisations breaking new ground may not be in a position to develop by acquisition or joint development, since they are the only ones in the field. Or there may be few opportunities for acquisitions, as for example, for foreign companies attempting to enter Japan.

www.pearsoned.co.uk/fos
KEY CONCEPT
Alliances, mergers and acquisitions

9.2.2 Mergers and acquisitions

An **acquisition** is where an organisation takes ownership of another organisation

A **merger** is a mutually agreed decision for joint ownership between organisations.

An **acquisition** is where an organisation takes ownership of another organisation, whereas a **merger** implies a mutually agreed decision for joint ownership between organisations. In practice, few acquistions are hostile and few mergers are the joining of equals. So both acquisitions and mergers typically involve the managers of one organisation exerting strategic influence over the other. Global activity in mergers is dominated by North America and Western Europe whereas it is much less common in other economies, for example, Japan. This reflects the influence of the differences in governance systems that exist (see section 4.2).

Motives for acquisitions and mergers

There are different motives for developing through acquisition or merger. A major reason can be the need to keep up with a changing *environment*:

- *Speed of entry*. Products or markets may be changing so rapidly that acquisition becomes the only way of successfully entering the market, since the process of internal development is too slow.
- The *competitive situation* may influence a company to prefer acquisition. In static markets and where market shares of companies are steady it can be difficult for a new company to enter the market, since its presence may create excess capacity. If entry is by acquisition the risk of competitive reaction may be reduced.
- *Consolidation opportunities*. Where there are low levels of industry concentration, there may be an opportunity for improving the balance between supply and demand by acquiring companies and shutting down excess capacity. In many countries, *deregulation* of public utilities has also created a level of fragmentation that was regarded as suboptimal. This was then an opportunity for acquisitive organisations to rationalise provision and/or seek to gain other benefits, for example, through the creation of 'multi-utility' companies offering electricity, gas, telecommunications and other services to customers.
- *Financial markets* may provide conditions that motivate acquisitions. If the share value or price/earnings (P/E) ratio of a company is high, it may see the opportunity to acquire a firm with a low share value or P/E ratio. Indeed, this is a major stimulus for the more opportunistic acquisitive companies. An extreme example is asset stripping, where the main motive is short-term gain by buying up undervalued assets and disposing of them piecemeal.

There may also be *capability considerations*:

- *Exploitation of strategic capabilities* can motivate acquisitions, for example, through buying companies overseas in order to leverage marketing or R&D skills internationally.
- *Cost efficiency* is a commonly stated reason for acquisitions typically by merging units so as to rationalise resources (for example, head office services or production facilities) or gain scale advantages.
- *Obtaining new capabilities* may also be achieved through acquisitions, or at least be a motive for acquisition. For example, a company may be acquired for its R&D expertise, or its knowledge of particular business processes or markets.

Acquisition can also be driven by the *stakeholder expectations*:

- *Institutional shareholder expectations* may be for continuing growth and acquisitions may be a quick way to deliver this growth. There are considerable dangers, however, that acquisitive growth may result in value destruction rather than creation – for some of the reasons discussed in Chapter 7.

- *Managerial ambition* may motivate acquisitions because they speed the growth of the company. In turn, this might enhance their self-importance, provide better career paths and greater monetary rewards.
- *Speculative motives* of some stakeholders may stimulate acquisitions that bring a short-term boost to share value. Other stakeholders are usually wary of such speculation since their short-term gain can destroy longer-term prospects.

Acquisitions and financial performance

Acquisitions are not an easy or guaranteed route to improving financial performance. As many as 70 per cent of acquisitions end up with lower returns to shareholders of both organisations. The most common mistake is in paying too much for a company – possibly through lack of experience in acquisitions, or poor financial advice (for example, from the investment bank involved). In addition the managers of the acquiring company may be over-optimistic about the benefits of the acquisition. An acquisition will probably include poor resources and competences as well as those which were the reason for the purchase; or it may be that the capabilities of the merging organisations are not compatible. This was the case, for example, in the 2004 acquisition in the UK of the Safeway supermarket chain by its competitor Morrisons. Amongst the problems was that Morrisons spent a year trying to integrate the IT systems of the two companies before abandoning the attempt. Indeed for this reason acquirers may attempt to buy products or processes rather than whole companies if possible. At the very best it may take the acquiring company considerable time to gain financial benefit from acquisitions.

Making acquisitions work

The implementation agenda following an acquisition or merger will vary depending on its purpose. Nonetheless there are four frequently occurring issues that account for success or failure of an acquisition/merger.

- *Adding value*. The acquirer may find difficulty in adding value to the acquired business (the parenting issue as discussed in section 7.4).
- *Gaining the commitment of middle managers* responsible for the operations and customer relations in the acquired business is important in order to avoid internal uncertainties and maintain customer confidence. Linked to this, deciding which executives to retain in the acquired business needs to be done quickly.
- *Expected synergies may not be realised*, either because they do not exist to the extent expected or because it proves difficult to integrate the activities of the acquired business. For example where the motive was the transfer of competences or knowledge it may be difficult to identify what these are (see section 3.4.3).

- *Problems of cultural fit.* This can arise because the acquiring business finds that 'everyday' but embedded aspects of culture (for example, organisation routines) differ in ways that prove difficult to overcome but are not readily identifiable before the acquisition. This can be particularly problematic with cross-country acquisitions.

9.2.3 Strategic alliances

A strategic alliance is where two or more organisations share resources and activities to pursue a strategy

www.pearsoned.co.uk/fos
KEY CONCEPT
Alliances, mergers and acquisitions

A **strategic alliance** is where two or more organisations share resources and activities to pursue a strategy. They vary from simple two-partner alliances co-producing a product to one with multiple partners providing complex products and solutions. By the turn of the century the top 500 global companies had an average of 60 alliances each. This kind of joint development of new strategies has become increasingly popular. This is because organisations cannot always cope with increasingly complex environments or strategies (such as globalisation) from internal resources and competences alone. They may need to obtain materials, skills, innovation, finance or access to markets but recognise that these may be as readily available through cooperation as through ownership. However about half of all alliances fail[2] so careful thought is needed as to reasons for success and failure.

Motives for alliances

A frequent reason for alliances is to obtain resources that an organisation needs but does not itself possess. For example banks need to gain access to the payment systems that allow credit cards to be used in retail outlets (for example, Visa or Mastercard) and to the automated teller machines (ATMs) to allow cash withdrawals. These resources do not, however, confer competitive advantage on members of the alliance; nor are they intended to do so – they are threshold requirements for modern banking. Such arrangements are '*infrastructure alliances*' that involve the sharing or pooling of resources and mechanism of cooperation, but which are not seeking to gain competitive advantage.[3] Here, however, we are concerned with *strategic alliances* that do seek to gain such advantage.

Motives for such alliances are of three main types:

- The need for *critical mass*, which alliances can achieve by forming partnerships with either competitors or providers of complementary products. This can lead to cost reduction and improved customer offering.
- *Co-specialisation* – allowing each partner to concentrate on activities that best match their capabilities: for example to enter new geographical markets where an organisation needs local knowledge and expertise in distribution, marketing and customer support. Similarly alliances with organisations in other parts of the value chain (for example, suppliers or distributors) are common.

- *Learning* from partners and developing competences that may be more widely exploited elsewhere. For example, first steps into e-business may be achieved with a partner that has expertise in website development. However, the longer-term intention might be to bring those activities in-house. Organisations may also enter alliances as a means of *experimentation* since it allows them to break out of a sole reliance on the exploitation of their own resources and capabilities. Indeed they may use alliances as a basis for developing strategic options different from those being developed in house organically.[4]

Types of alliance

There are different types of strategic alliance. Some may be formalised inter-organisational relationships. At the other extreme, there are loose arrangements of cooperation and informal networking between organisations, with no shareholding or ownership involved:

- *Joint ventures* are relatively formalised alliances and may take different forms themselves. Here organisations remain independent but set up a newly created organisation jointly owned by the parents. Joint ventures are a favoured means of collaborative ventures in China for example. Local firms provide labour and entry to markets; Western companies provide technology, management expertise and finance.
- *Consortia* may involve two or more organisations in a joint venture arrangement typically more focused on a particular venture or project. Examples include large civil engineering projects, or major aerospace undertakings, such as the European Airbus. They might also exist between public sector organisations where services (such as public transport) cross administrative boundaries.
- *Networks* are less formal arrangements where organisations gain mutual advantage by working in collaboration without relying on cross ownership arrangements and formal contracts. Carlos Jarillo suggests that characteristic of such network arrangements are a reliance on coordination through mutual adaptation of working relationships, mutual trust (see below) and, typically, a 'hub organisation' that may have promoted the network and maintains a proactive attitude to it.[5] Such networked arrangements may exist between competitors in highly competitive industries where some form of sharing is nonetheless beneficial: for example, in the Formula 1 industry, where state of the art know-how tends to flow between firms.

Other alliance arrangements exist usually of a contractual nature and are unlikely to involve ownership:

- *Franchising* involves the franchise holder undertaking specific activities such as manufacturing, distribution or selling, whilst the franchiser is responsible for the brand name, marketing and probably training. Perhaps the best-known examples are Coca-Cola and McDonald's.

Exhibit 9.2 Types of strategic alliance

	FORM OF RELATIONSHIP		
INFLUENCING FACTORS	**Loose (Market)** • Networks • Opportunistic alliances	**Contractual** • Licensing • Franchising • Subcontracting	**Ownership** • Consortia • Joint ventures
The Market			
• Speed of market change	Fast change	→	Slow change
Resources			
• Asset management	Managed separately by each partner	→	Managed together
• Partner's assets	Draws on 'parent's' assets	→	Dedicated assets for alliance
• Risk of losing assets to partner	High risk	→	Low risk
Expectations			
• Spreading financial risk	Maintains risk	→	Dilutes risk
• Political climate	Unfavourable climate	→	Favourable climate

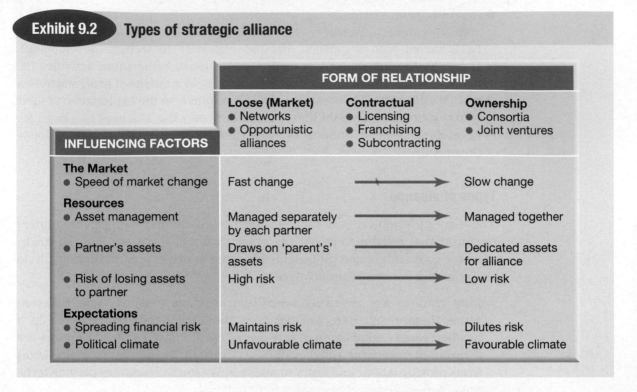

- *Licensing* is common in science-based industries where, for example, the right to manufacture a patented product is granted for a fee.
- With *subcontracting*, a company chooses to subcontract particular services or part of a process: for example, increasingly in public services responsibility for waste removal, cleaning and IT services may be subcontracted (or 'outsourced') to private companies.

Exhibit 9.2 shows three important factors that can influence types of alliance:

- *Speed of market change* will require strategic moves to be made quickly. So less formal and flexible network arrangements may be more appropriate than a joint venture, which could take too long to establish.
- *The management of resources and capabilities*. If a strategy requires separate, dedicated, resources then a joint venture will be appropriate. In contrast, if the strategic purpose and operations of the alliance can be supported by the current resources of the partners this favours a looser contractual relationship or network.
- The *expectations and motives* of alliance partners will play a part. For example if alliance partners see the alliance as a means of spreading their financial risk, this will favour more formal arrangements such as joint ventures.

Ingredients of successful alliances[6]

Although organisations may establish an alliance for one or more of the reasons outlined above, the benefits of alliances tend to evolve. It may, for example, be established to address a particularly complex technological opportunity, but yield new and unexpected opportunities. The success of alliances is therefore dependent on how they are managed and the way in which the partners foster the evolving nature of the partnership. Given this, success factors fall under three broad headings:

- *Strategic purpose*. A clear strategic purpose is likely to be helpful at the outset of an alliance. However alliance members will, quite likely, have differing if compatible reasons for being part of the alliance. As an alliance develops it is likely that their expectations and perceived benefits will evolve – not least because they are often built to cope with dynamic or complex environments. If the expectations of alliance members start to diverge the alliance may eventually disintegrate. If the evolving expectations remain compatible or converge then it is likely the alliance will continue. It is also possible that convergance could give rise to more formalised ownership arrangements such as a merger of the alliance partners.
- *Alliance expectations and benefits*. Similarly, given that the expectations of alliance partners may vary, managing those expectations as the alliance evolves is vital. At the most basic level, expectations cannot be met without a willingness to exchange information, including performance information that would not normally be shared between organisations. However, beyond this, given that many alliances are about learning and experimentation, the acceptance of these as benefits of themselves by alliance members may be important. If one of the partners does not buy into such benefits and attempts to impose a 'static' strategy on the alliance this may well lead to problems.[7] There are also indications that alliances that develop knowledge-based products and services (as distinct from physical product) tend to bind alliance partners more closely together since they are likely to be mutually dependent on shared tacit knowledge in the development of such products and services.[8]
- *Managing alliance relationships*. Senior management support for an alliance is important since alliances require a wider range of relationships to be built and sustained. This can create cultural and political hurdles that senior managers must help to overcome. In turn, strong interpersonal relationships to achieve *compatibility at the operational level* is also needed. In cross-country partnerships this includes the need to transcend national cultural differences. Consistently, however, research shows that *trust* is the most important ingredient of success and a major reason for failure if it is absent. But trust has two separate elements. Trust can be *competence based* in the sense that each partner is confident that the other has the resources and competences to fulfil their part in the alliance. Trust is also *character based*

and concerns whether partners trust each other's motives and are compatible in terms of attitudes to integrity, openness, discretion and consistency of behaviour. Overall the message is that it is the quality of the relationships in an alliance that are of prime importance; indeed to a greater extent than the physical resources in an alliance.

A consistent message that recurs, then, is that whilst it may be very helpful to ensure that an alliance has clear *goals, governance and organisational arrangements* concerning activities that cross or connect the partners, it is also important to keep the alliance *flexible*, such that it can *evolve and change*.

9.3 STRATEGY EVALUATION

Chapters 6 to 8 of the book have now introduced an array of strategic choices as summarised in Exhibit 9.3. This section of the chapter turns to how these might be evaluated by asking why some strategies might succeed better than

Exhibit 9.3 Strategic options

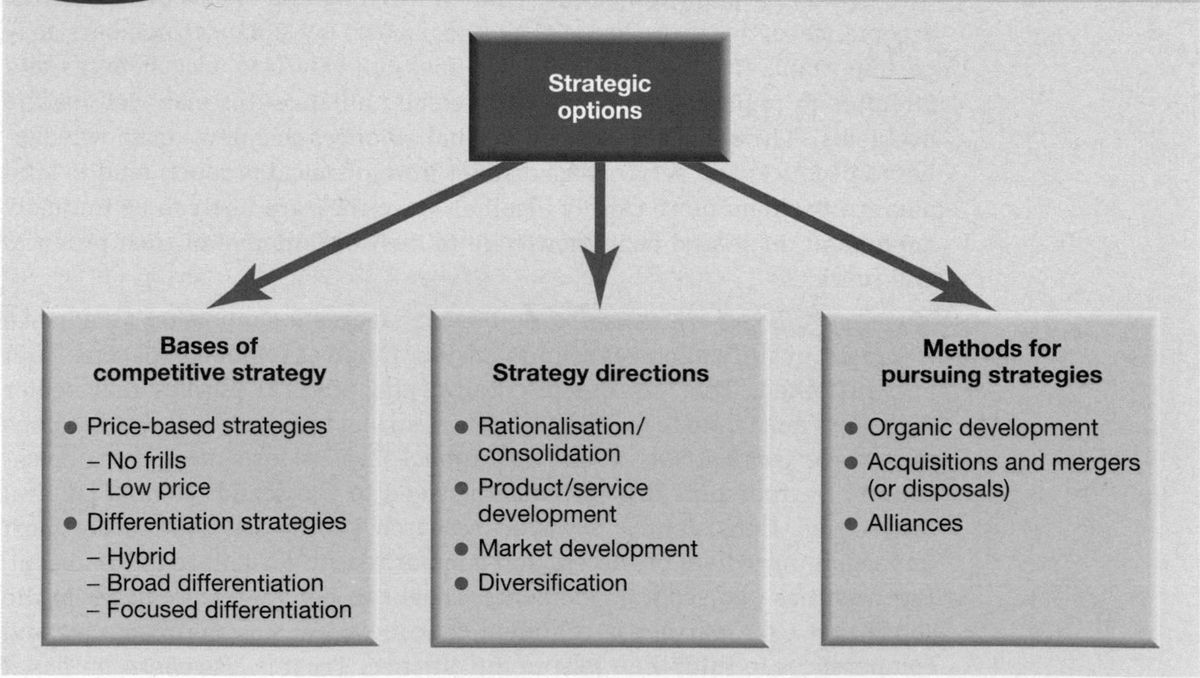

Success criteria are used to assess the viability of strategic options

others. It does this in terms of three key **success criteria** which can be used to assess the viability of strategic options:

- *Suitability* is concerned with whether a strategy addresses the key issues relating to the *strategic position* of the organisation (as discussed in Chapters 2 to 5).
- *Acceptability* is concerned with the expected *performance outcomes* (such as the *return* or *risk*) of a strategy and the extent to which these meet the *expectations* of stakeholders.
- *Feasibility* is concerned with whether a strategy could work in practice; therefore whether it has the capabilities to deliver a strategy.

9.3.1 Suitability

Suitability is concerned with whether a strategy addresses the key issues relating to the strategic position of the organisation

Suitability is concerned with whether a strategy addresses the key issues that have been identified in understanding the strategic position of the organisation. It is therefore concerned with the overall *rationale* of a strategy. In particular this requires an assessment of the extent to which any strategic option would fit with key drivers and expected changes in the *environment*, exploit *strategic capabilities* and be appropriate in the context of *stakeholder expectations and influence* and *cultural influences*. So the concepts and frameworks already discussed in Chapters 2 to 5 can be especially helpful in understanding suitability. Some examples are shown in Exhibit 9.4. However, there is an important point to bear in mind. It is very likely that a great many issues will have been raised if the concepts and tools discussed in Chapters 2 to 5 have been employed. It is therefore important that the really important issues are identified from amongst all these. Indeed a major skill of a strategist is to be able to discern these *key strategic issues*. Evaluating the suitability of a strategy is extremely difficult unless these have been identified.

The discussions about strategic directions in the preceding chapters in Chapters 6 to 8 and on strategy methods in section 9.2 above were concerned, not only with understanding what directions and methods were 'available' to organisations but also providing reasons why each might be considered. So the examples in those sections also illustrate why strategies might be regarded as *suitable*. Exhibit 9.5 summarises these points from earlier sections and provides examples of reasons why strategy directions or methods might be regarded as suitable.

There may be options 'available' to an organisation that are more or less suitable than others. A number of evaluation tools may be used to assess suitability. The following are useful frameworks that can assist in understanding better the relative suitability of different strategic options:

- *Ranking strategic options*. Options are assessed against key factors relating to the strategic position of the organisation and a score (or ranking) established for each option. See Illustration 9.1 for a detailed example

Exhibit 9.4 Suitability of strategic options in relation to strategic position

Concept	Exhibit Illustrations	Helps with understanding	Suitable strategies must address (examples)
PESTEL	Ill. 2.1	Key environmental drivers Changes in industry structure	Industry cycles Industry convergence Major environmental changes
Scenarios	Ill. 2.2	Extent of uncertainty/risk Extent to which strategic options are mutually exclusive	Need for contingency plans or 'low-cost probes'
Five-forces	Ex. 2.2 Ill. 2.3	Industry attractiveness Competitive forces	Reducing competitive intensity Development of barriers to new entrants
Strategic groups	Ill. 2.5	Attractiveness of groups Mobility barriers Strategic spaces	Need to reposition to a more attractive group or to an available strategic space
Core competences	Exs 3.1, 3.6 3.8	Industry threshold standards Bases of competitive advantage	Eliminating weaknesses Exploiting strengths
Value chain	Exs 3.6, 3.7	Opportunities for vertical integration or outsourcing	Extent of vertical integration or possible outsourcing
Stakeholder mapping	Ex. 4.5 Ill. 4.4a, b	Power and interest of stakeholders	Which strategic options are likely to address the interests of which stakeholders
Cultural web	Ex. 5.7 Ill. 5.4	The links between organisational culture and the current strategy	The strategic options most aligned with the prevailing culture

- *Decision trees* can also be used to assess strategic options against a list of key factors. Here options are 'eliminated' and preferred options emerge by progressively introducing requirements which must be met (such as growth, investment or diversity). See Illustration 9.2
- *Scenarios*. Here strategic options are considered against a range of possible future situations. This is especially useful where a high degree of uncertainty exists (as discussed in section 2.2.2 – see Illustration 2.2). Suitable options are ones that are sensible in terms of the various scenarios so several need to be 'kept open', perhaps in the form of contingency plans. Or it could be that a option being considered is found to be suitable in different scenarios.

Exhibit 9.5 Some examples of suitability

Strategic option	Why this option might be suitable in terms of: Environment	Capability	Stakeholder and/or cultural influences
Directions			
Consolidation	Withdraw from declining markets Maintain market share	Build on strengths through continued investment and innovation	Stick to what the organisation and its stakeholders know best
Market penetration	Gain market share for advantage	Exploit superior resources and competences	
Product development	Exploit knowledge of customer needs	Exploit R&D	Minimise the risk of alienating stakeholders with interests in preserving the status quo or making counter cultural decisions
Market development	Current markets saturated New opportunities for: geographical spread, entering new segments or new uses	Exploit current products and capabilities	
Diversification	Current markets saturated or declining	Exploit core competences in new arenas	Meet the needs of stakeholders with expectations for more rapid growth But potential for culture clash
Methods			
Organic development	Partners or acquisitions not available or not suitable	Building on own capabilities Learning and competence development	Cultural/political ease
Merger/acquisition	Speed Supply/demand P/E ratios	Acquire competences Scale economies	Returns: growth or share value But potential for culture clash
Joint development	Speed Industry norm Required for market entry	Complementary competences Learning from partners	Dilutes risk Fashionable

Illustration 9.1

Ranking options: Churchill Pottery

Ranking can usefully build on a SWOT analysis by comparing strategic options against the key strategic factors from the SWOT analysis.

In the 1990s Churchill Pottery, based in Stoke-on-Trent, UK, was one of the subjects of a BBC series entitled *Troubleshooter*, where the management teams of a number of companies were invited to discuss their organisation's strategic development with Sir John Harvey-Jones (ex-Chairman of ICI). Like many traditional manufacturing companies at the time, Churchill found itself under increasing pressure from cheaper imports in its traditional markets, and was considering whether to move 'up market' by launching a new range aimed at the design-conscious end of the market. The ranking exercise below was done by a group of participants on a management programme having seen the Churchill Pottery video.

The results of the ranking are interesting. First, they highlight the need to do *something*. Second, the radical departures in strategy – such as moves into retailing or diversification – are regarded as unsuitable. They do not address the problems of the core business, do not fit the capabilities of Churchill and would not fit culturally. This leaves related developments as the front runners – as might be expected in a traditional manufacturing firm like Churchill. The choice boils down to significant investments in cost reduction to support an essentially 'commodity' approach to the market (options 2 and 5) or an 'added value' attack on the growing 'up-market' segments. The company chose the latter and with some success – presumably helped by its wide television exposure through the *Troubleshooter* series.

Source: Based on the BBC *Troubleshooter* series.

Questions

1 Has option 4 been ranked above the others because:
   (a) It has the most ticks?
   (b) It has the least crosses?
   (c) A combination of these?
   (d) Other reasons?
   Justify your answer.

2 List the main strengths and limitations of ranking analysis.

Ranking exercise

	Key strategic factors						
Strategic options	Family ownership	Investment funds	Low-price imports	Lack of marketing/ design skills	Automation low	Consumer taste (design)	Ranking
1. Do nothing	✓	?	✗	?	✗	✗	**C**
2. Consolidate in current segments (investment/automation)	✓	✗	✓	?	✓	?	**B**
3. Expand overseas sales (Europe)	✗	✗	✗	✗	✗	?	**C**
4. Launch 'up-market' range	✓	✓	✓	✗	?	✓	**A**
5. Expand 'own-label' production (to hotel/ catering industry)	✓	✓	✓	?	✗	?	**B**
6. Open retail outlets	✗	✗	?	✗	?	?	**C**
7. Diversify	✗	✗	?	?	?	✓	**C**

✓ = favourable; ✗ = unfavourable; **?** = uncertain or irrelevant.
A = most suitable; **B** = possible; **C** = unsuitable.

Illustration 9.2

A strategic decision tree for a law firm

Decision trees evaluate future options by progressively eliminating others as additional criteria are introduced to the evaluation.

A law firm had most of its work related to house conveyancing where profits had been significantly squeezed. Therefore, it wanted to consider a range of new strategies for the future. Using a strategic decision tree it was able to eliminate certain options by identifying a few key criteria which future developments would incorporate, such as growth, investment (in premises, IT systems or acquisitions), and diversification (for example, into matrimonial law which, in turn, often brings house conveyancing work as families 'reshape').

Analysis of the decision tree reveals that if the partners of the firm wish growth to be an important aspect of future strategies, options 1–4 are ranked more highly than options 5–8. At the second step, the need for low-investment strategies would rank options 3 and 4 above 1 and 2, and so on.

The partners were aware that this technique has limitations in that the choice at each branch of the tree can tend to be simplistic. Answering 'yes' or 'no' to diversification does not allow for the wide variety of alternatives which might exist between these two extremes, for example *adapting the 'style' of the conveyancing service* (this could be an important variant of options 6 or 8). Nevertheless, as a starting point for evaluation, the decision tree provides a useful framework.

Questions

1. Try reversing the sequence of the three parameters (to diversification, investment and growth) and redraw the decision tree. Do the same eight options still emerge?
2. Add a fourth parameter to the decision tree. This new parameter is development by *internal methods* or by *acquisition*. List your 16 options in the right-hand column.

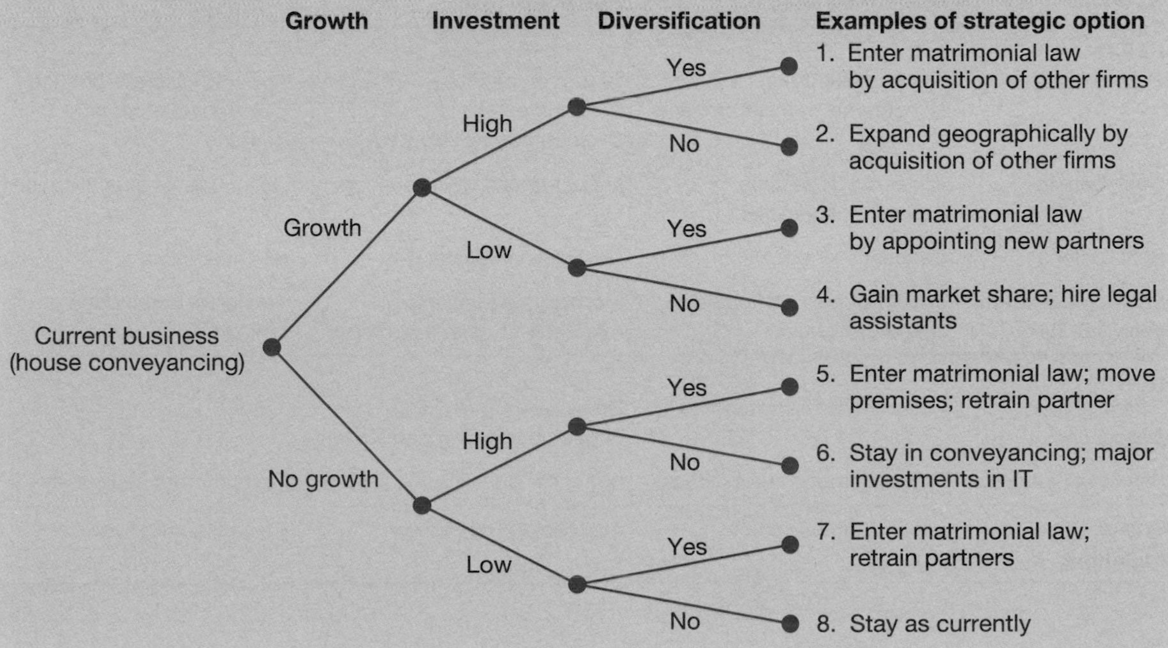

9.3.2 Acceptability

Acceptability is concerned with the expected performance outcomes of a strategy and the extent to which these meet the expectations of stakeholders.

Acceptability is concerned with the expected performance outcomes of a strategy. These can be of three types: *return, risk* and *stakeholder reactions*. Exhibit 9.6 summarises some frameworks that can be useful in understanding the acceptability of strategies, together with some of their limitations. It is probably sensible to use more than one approach in assessing the acceptability of a strategy.

Return

Returns are the benefits which stakeholders are expected to receive from a strategy

Returns are the benefits which stakeholders are expected to receive from a strategy. Measures of return are a common way of assessing proposed new ventures or major projects by managers within businesses. So an assessment of financial and non-financial returns likely to accrue from specific strategic options could be a key criterion of acceptability of a strategy – at least to some stakeholders. There are different approaches to understanding return. This section looks briefly at three of these. It is important to remember that there are no absolute standards as to what constitutes good or poor return. It will differ between industries, countries and between different stakeholders. Views

Exhibit 9.6 Some criteria for assessing the acceptability of strategic options

Criteria	Used to understand	Examples	Limitations
Return			
Profitability	Financial return on investments in major projects	Return on capital Payback period Discounted cash flow (DCF)	Apply to discrete projects Only tangible costs/benefits
Cost–benefit	Wider costs/benefits (including intangibles)	Major infrastructure projects	Difficulties of quantification
Real options	Sequence of decisions	Real options analysis	Quantification
Shareholder value analysis (SVA)	Impact of new strategies on shareholder value	Mergers/acquisitions Assessment of new ventures	Technical detail often difficult
Risk			
Financial ratio projections	Robustness of strategy	Break-even analysis Impact on gearing and liquidity	
Sensitivity analysis	Test assumptions/robustness	'What if?' analysis	Tests factors separately
Stakeholder reactions	Political dimension of strategy	Stakeholder mapping	Largely qualitative

also differ as to which measures give the best assessment of return, as will be seen below.

Financial analysis[9]

Traditional financial analyses are used extensively in assessing the acceptability of different strategic options. Three commonly used approaches are:

- Forecasting the *return on capital employed (ROCE)* for a specific time period after a new strategy is in place. For example, an ROCE of 15 per cent by year 3. This is shown in Exhibit 9.7(a). The ROCE is a measure of the earning power of the resources used in implementing a particular strategic option.
- Estimating the *payback period*. This is the length of time it takes before the cumulative cash flows for a strategic option become positive. In the example in Exhibit 9.7(b) the payback period is three and a half years. Payback is used as a financial criterion when a significant capital injection is needed to support a new venture. The judgement that has to be made is whether the payback period is too long and the organisation is prepared to wait. Payback periods vary from industry to industry. Public infrastructure projects such as road building may be assessed over payback periods exceeding 50 years.
- Calculating *discounted cash flows (DCF)*. This is a widely used investment appraisal technique. It is an extension of payback analysis. Once the cash inflows and outflows have been assessed for each of the years of a strategic option (see Exhibit 9.7(c)) they are discounted. This reflects the fact that cash generated early is more valuable than cash generated later. In the example, the cost of capital or discounting rate of 10 per cent (after tax) reflects the rate of return required by those providing finance for the venture – shareholders and/or lenders. The 10 per cent cost of capital *includes* an allowance for inflation of about 3–4 per cent. It is referred to as the 'money cost of capital'. By contrast, the 'real' cost of capital is 6–7 per cent *after* allowing for or *excluding* inflation.

  The projected after-tax cash flow of £2m at the start of year 2 is equivalent to receiving £1.82m now (£2m multiplied by 0.91 or 1/1.10). £1.82m is called the *present value* of receiving £2m at the end of year 1/start of year 2 at a cost of capital of 10 per cent. Similarly, the after-tax cash flow of £5m at the end of year 2/start of year 3 has a present value of £4.13m (£5m multiplied by 1/1.10 squared). The *net present value (NPV)* of the venture, as a whole, is calculated by adding up all the annual present values over the venture's anticipated life. In the example, this is 7 years. The NPV works out at £8.78m. Allowing for the time value of money, the £8.78m is the extra cash flow that a strategic option will generate during its entire lifetime. It is important to remember that DCF analysis is only as good as the assumptions on which it is based. For example, if sales volume increases of 3 per cent a year turn out to be unrealistic then the NPV calculation will be too optimistic. The *internal rate of return (IRR)* is that rate of return producing a zero NPV. For example in Exhibit 9.7(c) a cost of capital or discounting rate of about 32 per cent would produce a zero NPV.

Exhibit 9.7 Assessing profitability

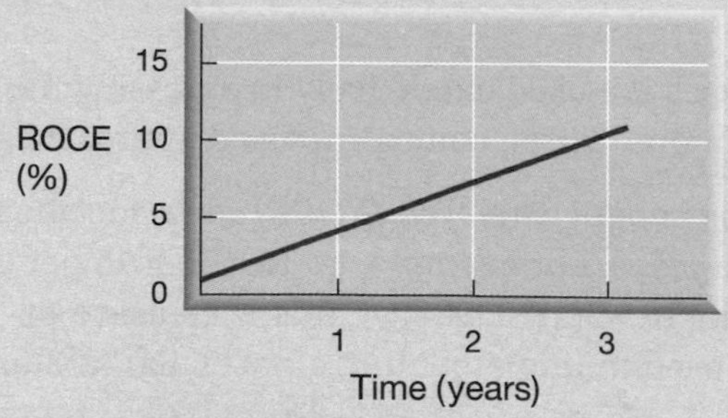

(a) Return on capital employed

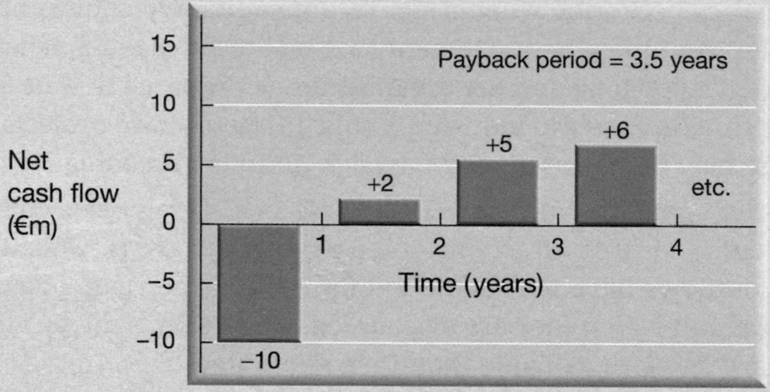

(b) Payback period

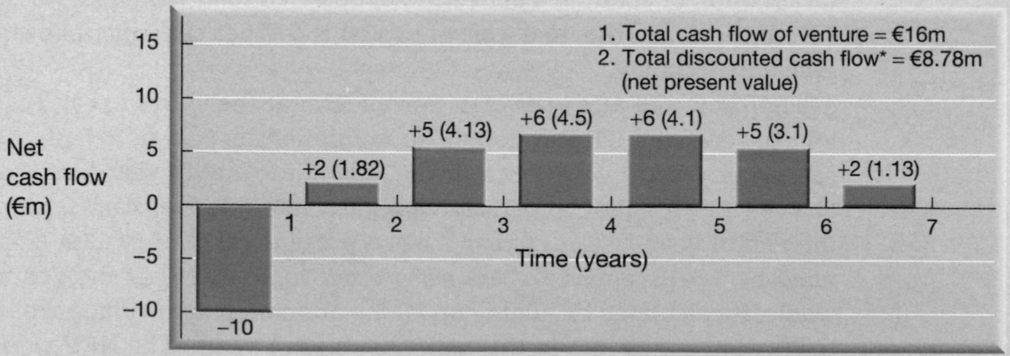

* Using a discounting rate of 10%.
Figures in brackets are discounted by 10% annually.

(c) Discounted cash flow (DCF)

There are also other considerations to be borne in mind when carrying out a financial analysis. In particular, do not be misguided by the apparent thoroughness of the various approaches. Most were developed for the purposes of investment appraisal. Therefore, they focus on discrete projects where the additional cash inflows and outflows can be predicted relatively easily: for example, a retailer opening a new store. Such assumptions are not necessarily valid in many strategic contexts. The precise way in which a strategy develops (and the associated cash flow consequences) tend to become clearer as the implementation proceeds rather than at the outset. Nor are strategic developments and the relevant cash flows easy to isolate from ongoing business activities.

Additionally, financial appraisals tend to focus on the direct *tangible* costs and benefits rather than the strategy more broadly. For example, a new product may look unprofitable as a single project. But it may make strategic sense by enhancing the market acceptability of other products in a company's portfolio. In an attempt to overcome some of these shortcomings, other approaches have been developed in an assessment of return.

Cost–benefit

In many situations, profit is too narrow an interpretation of return, particularly where intangible benefits are an important consideration. This is usually so for major public infrastructure projects for example, such as the siting of an airport or a sewer construction project, as shown in Illustration 9.3, or in organisations with long-term programmes of innovation (for example, pharmaceuticals or aerospace). The *cost–benefit* concept suggests that a money value can be put on all the costs and benefits of a strategy, including tangible and intangible returns to people and organisations other than the one 'sponsoring' the project or strategy.

Although in practice monetary valuation is often difficult, it can be done and, despite the difficulties, cost–benefit analysis is useful provided its limitations are understood. Its major benefit is in forcing managers to be explicit about the various factors that influence strategic choice. So, even if people disagree on the value that should be assigned to particular costs or benefits, at least they can argue their case on common ground and compare the merits of the various arguments.

Risk

Risk concerns the probability and consequences of the failure of a strategy

Another aspect of acceptability is the *risk* that an organisation faces in pursuing a strategy. **Risk** concerns the probability and consequences of the failure of a strategy. This risk can be high for organisations with major long-term programmes of innovation, where high levels of uncertainty exist about key issues in the environment or where there are high levels of public concern about new developments – such as genetically modified crops. Formal risk assessments are often incorporated into business plans as well as the investment appraisals

Illustration 9.3

Sewerage construction project

Investment in items of infrastructure – such as sewers – often requires a careful consideration of the wider costs and benefits of the project.

The UK's privatised water companies were monopolies supplying water and disposing of sewage. One of their priorities was investment in new sewerage systems to meet the increasing standards required by law. They frequently used cost–benefit analysis to assess projects. The figures below are from an actual analysis.

Cost/Benefit	£m	£m
Benefits		
Multiplier/linkage benefits		0.9
Flood prevention		2.5
Reduced traffic disruption		7.2
Amenity benefits		4.6
Investment benefit		23.6
Encouragement of visitors		4.0
Total benefits		42.8
Costs		
Construction cost	18.2	
Less: Unskilled labour cost	(4.7)	
Opportunity cost of construction	(13.5)	
Present value of net benefits (NPV)	29.3	
Real internal rate of return (IRR)	15%	

Note: Figures discounted at a *real* discount rate of 5% over 40 years.

Benefits

Benefits result mainly from reduced use of rivers as overflow sewers. There are also economic benefits resulting from construction. The following benefits are quantified in the table:

- The multiplier benefit to the local economy of increased spending by those employed on the project.
- The linkage benefit to the local economy of purchases from local firms, including the multiplier effect of such spending.
- Reduced risk of flooding from overflows or old sewers collapsing – flood probabilities can be quantified using historical records, and the cost of flood damage by detailed assessment of the property vulnerable to damage.
- Reduced traffic disruption from flooding and road closures for repairs to old sewers – statistics on the costs of delays to users, traffic flows on roads affected and past closure frequency can be used to quantify savings.
- Increased amenity value of rivers (for example, for boating and fishing) can be measured by surveys asking visitors what the value is to them or by looking at the effect on demand of charges imposed elsewhere.
- Increased rental values and take-up of space can be measured by consultation with developers and observed effects elsewhere.
- Increased visitor numbers to riverside facilities resulting from reduced pollution.

Construction cost

This is net of the cost of unskilled labour. Use of unskilled labour is not a burden on the economy, and its cost must be deducted to arrive at opportunity cost.

Net benefits

Once the difficult task of quantifying costs and benefits is complete, standard discounting techniques can be used to calculate net present value and internal rate of return, and analysis can then proceed as for conventional projects.

Source: G. Owen, formerly of Sheffield Business School.

Questions

1. What do you feel about the appropriateness of the listed benefits?
2. How easy or difficult is it to assign money values to these benefits?

of major projects. Importantly risks other than ones with immediate financial impact are included such as 'risk to corporate or brand image' or 'risk of missing an opportunity'. Developing a good understanding of an organisation's strategic position (Chapters 2 to 5 of this book) is at the core of good risk assessment. However some of the concepts below can also be used to establish the detail within a risk assessment.

Financial ratios

The projection of how key financial ratios might change if a strategy were adopted can provide useful insights into risk. At the broadest level, an assessment of how the *capital structure* of the company would change is a good general measure of risk. For example, strategies that would require an increase in long-term debt will increase the gearing (or 'leverage') of the company and, hence, its financial risk.

A consideration of the likely impact on an organisation's *liquidity* (cash position) is also important in assessing risk. For example, a small retailer eager to grow quickly may be tempted to fund the required shop-fitting costs by delaying payments to suppliers and increasing bank overdraft. The extent to which this increased risk of reduced liquidity threatens survival depends on the likelihood of either creditors or the bank demanding payments from the company – an issue that clearly requires judgement.

Sensitivity analysis

Sometimes referred to as *what if* analysis, sensitivity analysis allows each of the important assumptions underlying a particular strategy to be questioned and challenged. In particular, it tests how sensitive the predicted performance or outcome (for example, profit) is to each of these assumptions. For example, the key assumptions underlying a strategy might be that market demand will grow by 5 per cent per annum, or that the company will stay strike free, or that certain expensive machines will operate at 90 per cent loading. Sensitivity analysis asks what would be the effect on performance (in this case, profitability) of variations on these assumptions. For example, if market demand grew at only 1 per cent, or by as much as 10 per cent, would either of these extremes alter the decision to pursue that strategy? This can help develop a clearer picture of the risks of making particular strategic decisions and the degree of confidence managers might have in a given decision. Illustration 9.4 shows how sensitivity analysis can be used.

Stakeholder reactions

The discussion of *stakeholder mapping* in section 4.4.1 showed how it can be used to understand the political context and consider the political agenda in an organisation. However, stakeholder mapping can also be useful in understanding the likely reactions of stakeholders to new strategies, the ability to manage these reactions, and hence the acceptability of a strategy.

Illustration 9.4

Sensitivity analysis

Sensitivity analysis is a useful technique for assessing the extent to which the success of a preferred strategy is dependent on the key assumptions which underlie that strategy.

In 2007 the Dunsmore Chemical Company was a single-product company trading in a mature and relatively stable market. It was intended to use this established situation as a 'cash cow' to generate funds for a new venture with a related product. Estimates had shown that the company would need to generate some £4m (≈ €6m) cash (at 2007 values) between 2008 and 2013 for this new venture to be possible.

Although the expected performance of the company was for a cash flow of £9.5m over that period (the *base case*), management were concerned to assess the likely impact of three key factors:

- Possible increases in *production costs* (labour, overheads and materials), which might be as much as 3 per cent p.a. in real terms.
- *Capacity-fill*, which might be reduced by as much as 25 per cent due to ageing plant and uncertain labour relations.
- *Price levels*, which might be affected by the threatened entry of a new major competitor. This could squeeze prices by as much as 3 per cent p.a. in real terms.

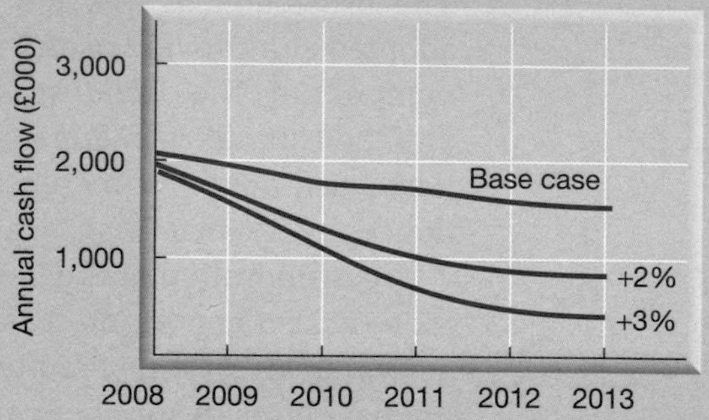

(a) Sensitivity of cash flow to changes in real production costs

It was decided to use sensitivity analysis to assess the possible impact of each of these factors on the company's ability to generate £4m. The results are shown in the graphs.

From this analysis, management concluded that their target of £4m would be achieved with *capacity utilisation* as low as 60 per cent, which was certainly going to be achieved. Increased *production costs* of 3 per cent p.a. would still allow the company to achieve

There are many situations where stakeholder reactions could be crucial. For example:

- *Financial restructuring*. A new strategy might require the financial restructuring of a business, for example an issue of new shares, which could be unacceptable to powerful groups of shareholders, since it dilutes their voting power.
- *An acquisition or merger* could be unacceptable to unions, government or some customers.
- *A new business model* might cut out channels (such as retailers), hence running the risk of a backlash, which could jeopardise the success of the strategy.
- *Outsourcing* is likely to result in job losses and could be opposed by unions.

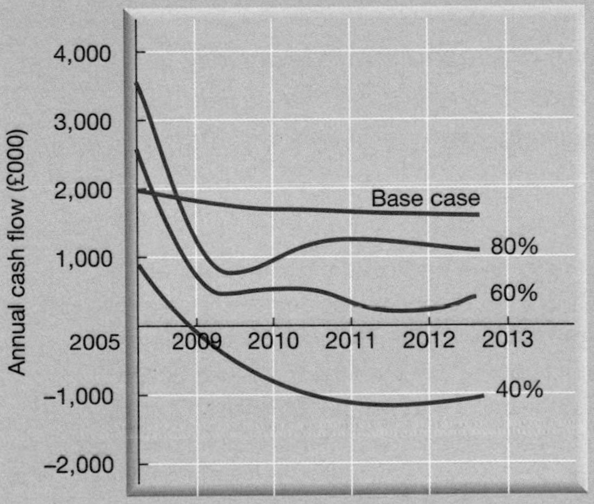

(b) Sensitivity of cash flow to changes in plant utilisation

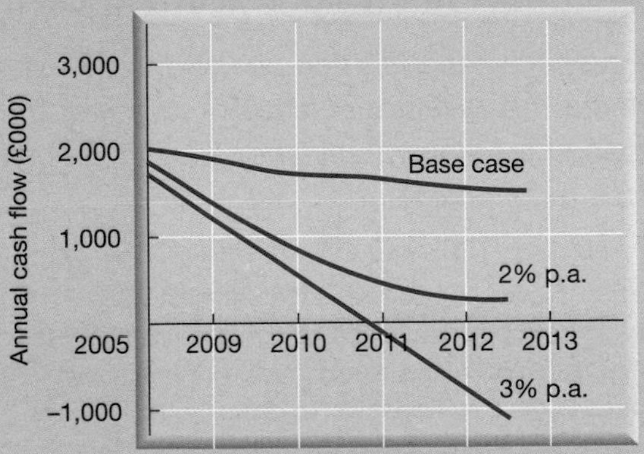

(c) Sensitivity of cash flow to reductions in real price

Source: The calculations for the sensitivity test utilise computer programs employed in the Doman case study by Peter Jones (Sheffield Business School).

the £4m target over the period. In contrast, *price* squeezes of 3 per cent p.a. would result in a shortfall of £2m.

Management concluded from this analysis that the key factor which should affect their thinking on this matter was the likely impact of new competition and the extent to which they could protect price levels if such competition emerged. They therefore developed an aggressive marketing strategy to deter potential entrants.

Question

What should the company do if its marketing campaigns fail to stop real price erosion:

(a) Push to achieve more sales volume/capacity fill?
(b) Reduce unit costs of production?
(c) Something else?

9.3.3 Feasibility

Feasibility is concerned with whether an organisation has the capabilities to deliver a strategy

Feasibility is concerned with whether an organisation has the resources and competences to deliver a strategy. A number of approaches can be used to understand feasibility.

Financial feasibility

A useful way of assessing financial feasibility is *cash flow analysis and forecasting*.[10] This seeks to identify the cash required for a strategy and the likely sources for obtaining that cash. These sources are sometimes referred to as *funding sources*. They are shown in Illustration 9.5. Cash flow forecasting is, of course, subject to the difficulties and errors of any method of forecasting.

Illustration 9.5

Cash flow analysis: a worked example

A cash flow analysis can be used to assess whether a proposed strategy is likely to be feasible in financial terms. It does so, first, by forecasting the cash that would be needed for the strategy and, second, identifying the likely sources of funding that cash requirement.

Kentex plc (a UK electrical goods retailer) was considering pursuing a strategy of expansion. In the immediate future, this would involve opening new stores in the Irish Republic. To evaluate the financial feasibility of this proposal and to establish the cash requirements and funding sources, the company decided to undertake a cash flow analysis.

Stage 1: Estimation of cash inflows

The opening of the new stores was estimated to increase revenues or sales from the current £30m (≈ €45m) to £31.65m over the following three years. In turn, this was expected to generate operating cash flows of £15m during the same time period.

Stage 2: Estimation of cash outflows

There would be a number of costs associated with the new stores. First, Kentex decided to purchase rather than lease property so capital investment would be required to purchase and then fit out the stores. The forecast was £13.25m. Also there would be additional working capital costs to cover extra stock etc. Forecasts for these were based on a simple pro rata estimate. On the previous sales level of £30m, a working capital level of £10m was required, so pro rata, additional sales of £1.65m would require an additional £0.55m in working capital. Tax liability and expected dividend payments were estimated at £1.2m and £0.5m respectively.

Stage 3: Estimation and funding of the cash shortfall

The calculations show a cash shortfall of £0.5m. The issue facing Kentex was how to finance this deficit. It could raise cash through the issue of new share capital but the company decided to seek a short-term loan of £0.65m. In turn, this would incur interest payments of £0.15m over the three-year period assuming simple interest at 7.5 per cent annually. Therefore, the net amount of cash raised would be £0.5m.

The overall cash flow analysis is summarised below:

Cash inflows	Cash outflows
Operating cash flows, £15m	Capital expenditure, £13.25m
	Further working capital, £0.55m
	Tax, £1.2m
	Subtotal of cash outflows, £15m
	Dividends, £0.5m
	Total cash outflows, £15.5m

Note: The shortfall between the cash inflows and the cash outflows is £500,000.

Questions

1. Which parts of this assessment are likely to have the greatest probability of error?
2. What are the implications of your answer to question 1 on how the analysis should be presented to the decision makers?
3. How might this uncertainty influence the management of the implementation phase if approval is given?

However, it should highlight whether a proposed strategy is likely to be feasible both in terms of cash generation and the availability and timing of new funding requirements.

Financial feasibility can also be assessed through break-even analysis.[11] This is a simple and widely used approach for judging the feasibility of meeting financial targets such as the ROCE and operating profit. In addition, it provides an assessment of the risks of various strategies particularly where different strategic options require markedly different cost structures.

Resource deployment

Although financial feasibility is important, a wider understanding of feasibility can be achieved by identifying the resources and competences needed for a specific strategy. Indeed the effectiveness of a strategy is likely to be dependent on whether such capabilities are available or can be developed or obtained. For example, geographical expansion in a market might be critically dependent on marketing and distribution expertise, together with the availability of cash to fund increased stocks. Or a strategy of developing new products to sell to current customers may depend on engineering skills, the capability of machinery and the company's reputation for quality in new products.

A resource deployment assessment can be used to judge: (a) the extent to which an organisation's current capabilities need to change to reach or maintain the *threshold* requirements for a strategy; and (b) if and how unique resources and/or core competences can be developed to sustain competitive advantage. The issue is whether these changes are *feasible* in terms of scale, quality of resource or time-scale of change.

Strategy in action

The question of feasibility is more generally raised by the issues discussed in the final chapter of the book. Here the concerns are not only with financial and resource deployment issues but with whether the strategy envisaged can be implemented in terms of:

- how a given strategy might be put into practice in terms of the way the organisation needs to be structured;
- what management processes (for example, in terms of planning and control systems) are needed and how effective they might be in delivering a strategy;
- how changes in strategy might be managed.

SUMMARY

- There are three broad *methods* of strategy development:
  - *Organic development* has the major benefit of building on the strategic capabilities of an organisation. However, it can result in overstretched resources and is likely to require the development of those capabilities.
  - *Mergers and acquisitions* may have advantages of speed and the ability to acquire competences not already held 'in-house'. However, the track record of acquisitions is not good.
  - Successful *alliances* appear to be those where partners have a positive attitude to the evolving nature of the alliance and where there is trust between partners.
- The success or failure of strategies will be related to three main *success criteria*:
  - *Suitability* is concerned with whether a strategy addresses the strategic position of the organisation, as discussed in Chapters 6 to 9 of this book. It is about the *rationale* of a strategy.
  - The *acceptability* of a strategy relates to three issues: the expected *return* from a strategy, the level of *risk* and the likely *reaction of stakeholders*.
  - *Feasibility* is concerned with whether an organisation has or can obtain the capabilities to deliver a strategy.

Recommended key readings

- A comprehensive book on mergers and acquisitions is P. Gaughan, *Mergers, Acquisitions and Corporate Restructurings*, 4th edition, Wiley, 2007.
- A useful book on strategic alliances is J. Child, *Cooperative strategy*, Oxford University Press, 2005.
- A companion book which explores techniques of strategy evaluation more fully is V. Ambrosini with G. Johnson and K. Scholes (eds), *Exploring Techniques of Analysis and Evaluation in Strategic Management*, Prentice Hall, 1998.

References

1. See J.F. Mognetti, *Organic Growth: Cost-Effective Business Expansion from Within*, Wiley, 2002.
2. But see J. Dyer, P. Kale and H. Singh, 'How to make strategic alliances work', *Sloan Management Review*, vol. 42, no. 4 (2001), pp. 37–43.
3. This definition is based on ul-Haq's explanation of infrastructure alliances, see R. ul-Haq, *Alliances and Co-Evolution: Insights from the Banking Sector*, Palgrave, 2005, pp. 6–9.
4. For a fuller discussion of the role of alliances and joint ventures in exploration versus exploitation see W. Kummerle, 'Home base and knowledge management in international ventures', *Journal of Business Venturing*, 17, no. 2 (2002), pp. 99–122.

5. These characteristics are based on J. Carlos Jarillo, 'On Strategic Networks', *Strategic Management Journal*, vol. 9, no. 1 (1988), pp. 31–41.
6. See Y. Doz and G. Hamel, *Alliance Advantage: The art of Creating value through partnering*, Harvard Business School Press, 1998; T. Pietras and C. Stormer, 'Making strategic alliances work', *Business and Economic Review*, vol. 47, no. 4 (2001), pp. 9–12; N. Kaplan and J. Hurd, 'Realising the promise of partnerships', *Journal of Business Strategy*, vol. 23, no. 3 (2002), pp. 38–42; A. Parkhe, 'Interfirm diversity in global alliances' *Business Horizons*, vol. 44, no. 6 (2001); R. ul-Haq (reference 3 above); I. Hipkin and P. Naude, 'Developing Effective Alliance Partnerships', *Long Range Planning*, vol. 39 (2006), pp. 51–69; A. Inkpen, 'Learning and Knowledge Acquisition Through International Strategic Alliances', *Academy of Management Executive*, vol. 2, no. 4 (1998), pp. 69–80; and 'Learning through joint ventures: a framework of knowledge acquisition', *Journal of Management Studies*, vol. 37, no. 7 (2000), pp. 1019–1045.
7. See I. Hipkin and P. Naude (reference 6).
8. Inkpen in the *Academy of Management Executive* (reference 6).
9. Most standard finance and accounting texts explain in more detail the financial analyses summarised here. For example see G. Arnold, *Corporate Financial Management*, 3rd edition, FT/Prentice Hall, 2005, chapter 4.
10. See G. Arnold, *Corporate Financial Management*, 3rd edition, FT/Prentice Hall, 2005, chapter 3, p. 108.
11. Break-even analysis is covered in most standard accountancy texts. See, for example, G. Arnold (reference 10), p. 223.

CASE EXAMPLE

Tesco conquers the world?

In 2006 Tesco, the UK's most successful grocery retailer (with about 30 per cent market share), again reported a record-breaking year. Over the previous four years it had almost doubled group sales (excluding VAT) and profits to £39bn (≈ €57bn) and £2.28bn respectively. The 'group statistics' painted a picture of what this growth meant on the ground: the number of stores had tripled to 2,672 and employee numbers had grown by about 60 per cent to 273,000. Significantly, sales to the rest of Europe had grown from 9 to 13 per cent of group sales and Asian sales were 11 per cent of group sales (up from 6 per cent in 2002). The company had also extended its product range significantly since 2002 – moving into non-food sectors and retailing services.

Not surprisingly the 2006 annual report was very 'upbeat' and the Chairman, David Reid, summarised the company achievements and prospects for the future:

UK Our sales performance in the UK core business has been strong, as we have invested in all parts of the customer offer.

International has delivered good growth in like-for-like sales, profits and returns. Our largest ever new store development programme delivered 5.4 million sq ft [500,000 m^2] of sales area, with a further 6.6 million sq ft planned in the current year.

Non-food has again made strong progress, with UK sales up by over 13%, against the background of cautious consumer spending. Our established areas such as health and beauty (up 10%) have done well and newer departments such as consumer electronics (34% growth) and clothing (16% growth) have performed particularly strongly.

Retailing services have also had a good year with tesco.com delivering record results, Tesco Personal Finance (TPF) performing well in a challenging personal finance sector and good growth in telecoms.

The report went on to explain in more detail exactly how each of the main parts of the business were changing and developing:

Photo: Richard Jones/Rex Features

Core UK business

'giving customers what they want 24/7'

Ranges
Because everyone is welcome at Tesco, we appreciate that our customers have different tastes and requirements. We work hard to give our customers a broad assortment of leading brands, a really good range of Tesco products – from *Finest* to *Value* lines – and lots of new ideas for feeding the family.

Instead of offering a standard product range everywhere, we have put a lot of effort into tailoring our offer for local customers. For example, our new *Extra* store in Slough, Berkshire features over 900 speciality Asian products, from new vegetarian and Halal ready meals to extensive ranges of bulk-pack rice, and even Bollywood DVDs.

Formats
Our store formats are a way of meeting the different needs of our customers wherever they live and however they want to shop – in large stores, in small stores or on-line. Tesco *Express* brings great food and low prices into the heart of neighbourhoods. . . . *Metro* offers the convenience of Tesco in town and city centres where people live and work. At Tesco *Superstores*, customers can find everything they need for their weekly shopping and at our *Extra* stores customers can not only find our full range of food and convenience lines, but also a comprehensive range of non-foods. *Homeplus* non-food only store was trialed in 2005.

NON-FOOD

'offering great quality, range, price and service'

More and more people are choosing to buy not just their household essentials but also bigger ticket items at Tesco, from clothing to TVs and fridges and from sports equipment to toys. They appreciate the convenience of being able to do all their shopping under one roof in our Extra stores.

We will be sourcing products that are common in all countries (UK, Ireland and Central Europe) together as a group. Each country will retain the responsibility of identifying the local needs of their customers and sourcing those products from the appropriate suppliers within their respected country.

RETAILING SERVICES

'making on-line shopping simple'

Tesco.com is the most successful on-line grocery shopping service in the world. What is remarkable about our on-line business is the diversity of customers using it, from busy urban families to people in rural communities. It has also allowed many house-bound people to shop properly for the first time.

DVDs to your door 60,000 customers have now signed up to our DVDs to rent service, giving them access to the 30,000 titles that are available through our on-line DVD service.

Energy We have enabled tens of thousands of customers to save money on their gas and electricity bills (by comparing prices of different suppliers). This service is fully comprehensive, fully independent and fully impartial.

Getting healthy on-line E–diets help customers to tailor their eating plans to what's right for them, taking into account lifestyles, food preferences and health recommendations.

'financial services that are simple'

Tesco Personal Finance now offers 21 financial products and services from loans and savings accounts to credit cards and insurance. We are Britain's third largest on-line car insurer with over 1.4 million active car insurance policies.

We are continually trying to improve our offer for customers and now offer the opportunity to purchase travel money in-store, by providing kiosks in seven stores. We have also made the purchase of premium bonds much more convenient for customers [through] the partnership with National Savings & Investments (NS&I).

Tesco Mobile is a virtual network formed as a joint venture with [the mobile network operator] O2.

International

With the exception of Ireland (91 stores) the company's international expansion had been in Eastern Europe (272 stores) and Asia (450 stores). The company planned to enter the US market in 2007 with a completely new local format for the American consumer modelled on *Express.* What was most interesting was the way that each development reflected local market conditions rather than working to a standard entry model. Some of the details from the 2006 annual report are shown in the box.

Where next from here?

Despite this rosy picture not everyone was convinced that Tesco was yet a major world player. The obvious comparison was with the world's biggest retailer, the US company Wal-Mart, whose turnover of US$312bn (≈ €250bn) was more than four times that of Tesco. Although Wal-Mart's US sales were flattening out it had a presence in some 70 countries with 2,285 stores outside the USA – this was almost three times Tesco's international 'footprint'. Importantly Wal-Mart won the race to enter India in the autumn of 2006 leaving Tesco with difficulties in finding a suitable local partner – crucial in that market.

Market research with UK consumers also highlighted issues for the company to think about. In particular, although Tesco had attracted a broad range of customers across demographics and age groups, there was evidence that the market was fragmenting. Tesco customers' loyalty seemed to be declining and in an analysis of people's favourite brands by age,[1] Tesco and other high street retailers did well among the over 55s, but did not feature at all in the top 10 brands of 16 to 24 year olds.

But the Tesco Chief Executive, Sir Terry Leahy, was clear about the Tesco 'formula' for success:

Tesco is about making the shopping experience better for customers and we've built our success and our growth by listening to them.

Note

1. Milward Brown research reported by Carlos Grande, *Financial Times*, 19 December (2006).

Source: *Tesco Annual Report 2006* at www.tesco.com

Tesco's international stores in 2006

China (39 stores)
We have begun to accelerate our expansion programme beyond the Yangtse delta and have teams working to develop our network in Beijing, Shenzhen and Guangzhou. We have also invested in capability, bringing Tesco systems and know-how into the business, focusing particularly on improving store design, the supply chain and store replenishment.

Japan (111 stores)
In Japan, we operate discount convenience supermarkets, typically 3,000 sq ft in size. We opened our first trial *Express* store in April 2006.

Malaysia (13 stores)
We are trialling our *Express* format in Malaysia with three stores, situated mainly in the area around Kuala Lumpur. We also opened our first *Value* store, a 3,000 sq m store in Banting. By offering a tailored hypermarket range in a smaller store which is cheaper to build, we have been able to bring a modern retail offer to a community which would not have been able to sustain a larger hypermarket.

South Korea (62 stores)
We opened eight new hypermarkets in South Korea this year, including three compact hypers. We have further adapted our *Express* model in South Korea, enabling us to focus on the key products which customers want to be able to buy, close to where they live and work.

Taiwan (6 stores)
[We have agreed an] asset swap deal with Carrefour . . . [which] will enable us to exit from Taiwan with minimal financial impact, allowing us to focus on investment in Central Europe and our other Asian businesses.

Thailand (219 stores)
[Through] the launch of our *Talad* format we have tailored our offer to customers who are used to shopping in local markets. We now have ten of these stores, which carry between 4,500 and 7,500 product lines in around 10,000 sq ft of selling space.

Czech Republic (35 stores)
We have accelerated our new store development programme, adding 20% to our sales area during the year, with eight new compact hypermarkets. (Also) we opened the Group's first 1,000 sq m, or '1K' store . . . [which] enables us to bring the Tesco offer to smaller towns, carrying a locally-tailored range of around 2,700 products.

Hungary (87 stores)
Customers are facing a more challenging economic and retail environment in Hungary, which has held back our growth but we have still made solid progress. Our customers have benefited from lower prices in store and from the roll-out of petrol stations, making it significantly cheaper to fill-up.

Poland (105 stores)
Customers love the convenience of our small format stores which bring many of the advantages of our larger hypermarkets closer to where they live and work.

Republic of Ireland (91 stores)
We continue to invest in bringing prices down for our Irish customers. . . . We are also focusing on extending our product ranges. With *Finest* growing in popularity, we have increased the number of lines in areas such as cheese, ready meals and wine.

Slovakia (37 stores)
In line with our other Central European businesses, Tesco Slovakia has introduced a price promise on 50 everyday items, guaranteeing that we won't be beaten by any local competitor. Our new store programme is now supported by the growth of our compact hypermarket format.

Turkey (8 stores)
In Turkey, Kipa delivered a very strong performance. . . . We successfully launched the *Kipa Value* brand in Turkey, with over 400 products so far and we plan to extend this in the coming year.

Questions

1. Using Exhibit 7.2 in Chapter 7 identify the strategic directions that Tesco had followed from its origins as a UK-based grocery retailer.
2. Identify the strategic directions 'available' to the company in the future and assess the relative suitability of each of these options by ranking them (using Illustration 9.1 as an example).
3. For each of the top four development directions in your ranking compare the relative merits of organic development, acquisition or strategic alliance.
4. Complete your evaluation of the options that now appear most suitable by applying the criteria of acceptability and feasibility (see sections 9.3.2 and 9.3.3 respectively).

10

Strategy in Action

LEARNING OUTCOMES

After reading this chapter you should be able to:

- → Analyse the main structural types of organisation in terms of their strengths and weaknesses.
- → Recognise how organisational processes (such as planning systems and performance targets) need to be designed to fit the circumstances in which strategies are delivered (such as an organisation's size, the type of the product/service and the nature of the markets).
- → Assess the impact of the *roles* and management *styles* of change agents.
- → Assess the value of different *levers* for strategic change.

Photo: © SuperStock/Alamy

10.1 INTRODUCTION

It was explained in Chapter 1 that strategic management can be thought of as having three main elements: understanding *the strategic position* of an organisation, making *strategic choices* for the future and managing *strategy in action* (see Exhibit 1.3). As this book is about the fundamentals of strategy, it mainly concentrates on the first two elements, position and choice. But even the most shrewdly-chosen strategy is valueless unless it can be turned into action. Although this book puts less emphasis on these management issues of strategy in action, this chapter will focus on three key issues (see Exhibit 10.1):

- The types of organisational *structure* that will best suit the strategies of the organisation. For example, whether people should be managed in business functions (finance, human resources, etc.) or in product or market divisions (such as geographical regions).
- The *organisational processes* needed to deliver the chosen strategy within any structure. For example, work supervision, planning processes and performance targets.
- The *managing of strategic change*, raising such issues as leadership, power and politics, and managerial tactics.

Other issues to do with strategy in action – such as strategy development processes, resourcing strategies and the practice of strategy – are dealt with more fully in *Exploring Corporate Strategy*.[1]

Exhibit 10.1 Strategy in action

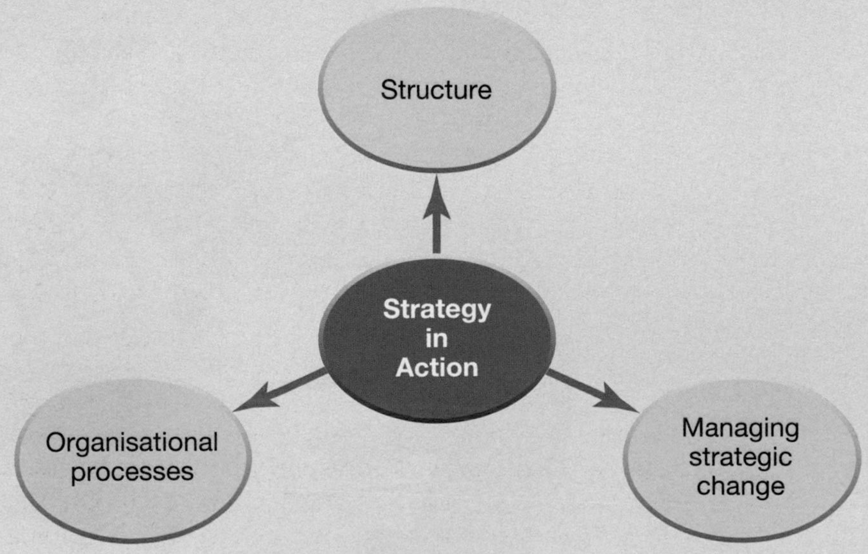

10.2 STRUCTURES

Managers often describe their organisation by drawing an organisation chart, mapping out its formal structure. These structural charts define the 'levels' and roles in an organisation. They are important to managers because they describe who is responsible for what. But formal structures matter in at least two more ways. First, structural reporting lines shape patterns of communication and knowledge exchange: people tend not to talk much to people much higher or lower in the hierarchy, or in different parts of the organisation. Second, the kinds of structural positions at the top suggest the types of skills required to move up the organisation. For example, a structure with functional specialists (such as marketing or finance) at the top indicates the importance of specialised functional disciplines rather than general business experience. In short, formal structures can reveal a great deal about the role of knowledge and skills in an organisation. Structures can therefore be hotly debated (see Illustration 10.1).

This section reviews three basic structural types: functional, multidivisional and matrix.[2] Broadly, the first two of these tend to emphasise one structural dimension over another, either functional specialisms or business units. In contrast the matrix structure tends to mix structural dimensions more evenly, for instance trying to give product and geographical units equal weight. However, none of these structures is a universal solution to the challenges of putting strategy into action. Rather, the right structure depends on the particular kinds of challenges each organisation faces.

10.2.1 The functional structure

Once an organisation grows beyond a very basic level of size and complexity, it has to start dividing up responsibilities. One fundamental kind of structure is the **functional structure**, which divides responsibilities according to the organisation's primary roles such as production, research and sales. Exhibit 10.2 represents a typical organisation chart for such a business. This structure is usually found in smaller companies, or those with narrow, rather than diverse, product ranges. Also, within a multidivisional structure (see below), the divisions themselves may be split up into functional departments (see Exhibit 10.3 later).

A functional structure is based on the primary activities that have to be undertaken by an organisation such as production, finance and accounting, marketing, human resources and research and development

www.pearsoned.co.uk/fos
KEY CONCEPT
Structures

Exhibit 10.2 also summarises the potential advantages and disadvantages of a functional structure. There are advantages in that it gives senior managers direct hands-on involvement in operations and allows greater operational control from the top. The functional structure provides a clear definition of roles and tasks, increasing accountability. Functional departments also provide concentrations of expertise, thus fostering knowledge development in areas of functional specialism.

Illustration 10.1

Volkswagen: a case of centralisation

A new chief executive introduces a more centralised structure over this multi-brand giant.

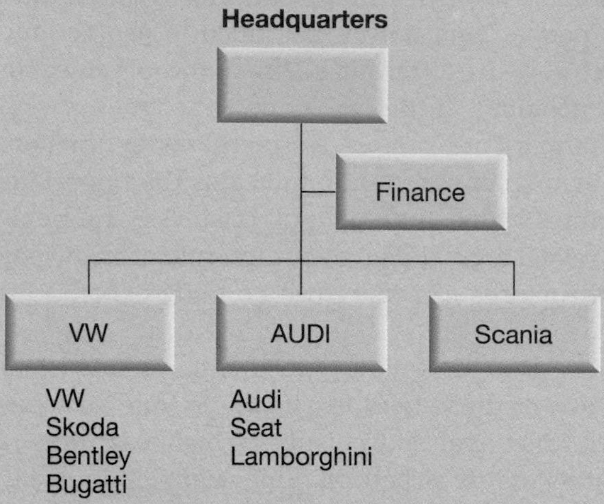

Figure 1 Volkswagen, November 2006 (simplified)

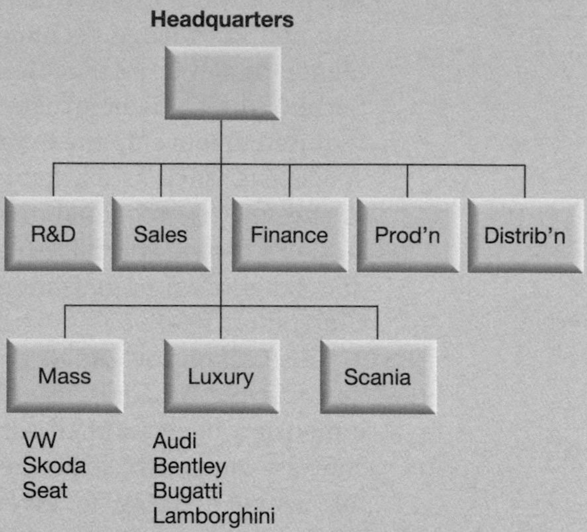

Figure 2 Volkswagen, January 2007 (simplifed)

In 2007, following the Porsche car company's building up of a controlling stake and the installation of a new chief executive, German car manufacturer Volkswagen announced a major reorganisation. For the previous few years, Volkswagen had been organised as two groups of brands under the main Volkswagen and Audi labels (see Figure 1), with technical and marketing expertise clustered around particular brands within these. Now the company was to be reorganised into two main groups, a mass market group (VW, Skoda, SEAT) and a more luxury market group (Audi, Bentley, Bugatti and Lamborghini). Volkswagen also had a large stake in truck company Scania. The company would be more centralised, with new corporate responsibilities for production, sales, distribution and R&D (see Figure 2). The new CEO, Martin Winterkorn, would also act as head of R&D and be directly responsible for the VW group of brands.

The stated aim of this more centralised structure was to increase synergies between the various brands. More centralised R&D would help ensure the sharing of engines and components, and centralisation of production would assist the optimisation of factory usage across the company. The departing head of the Volkswagen group took another view. He asserted that, in order to ensure cross-functional integration and motivation, expertise needed to identify closely with particular brands. According to him, the new structure mimicked the centralised Porsche structure, but Porsche was a much smaller company with just one main brand. Porsche's spokespersons responded by recalling that Porsche was the most profitable car company in the world, while Volkswagen was one of the least.

Questions

1. Which type of structure did the old decentralised structure resemble most and which type of structure is Volkswagen moving closer to?
2. What pros and cons can you see in the new Volkswagen structure?

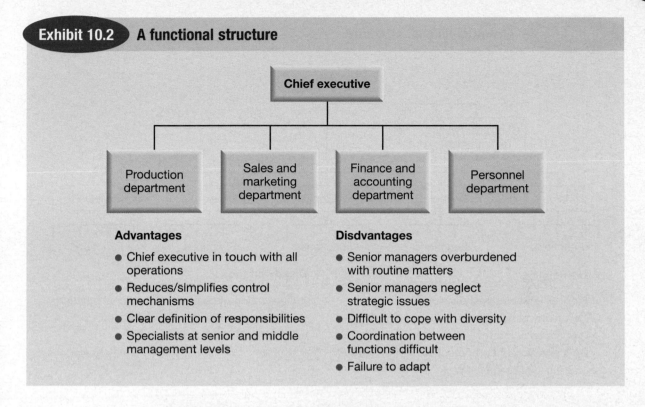

Exhibit 10.2 A functional structure

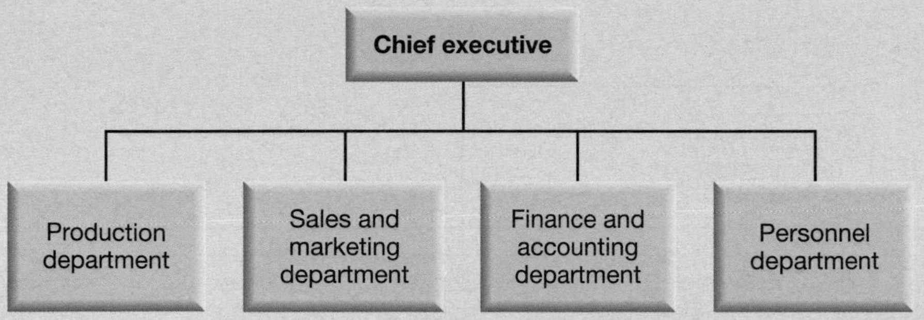

Advantages

- Chief executive in touch with all operations
- Reduces/simplifies control mechanisms
- Clear definition of responsibilities
- Specialists at senior and middle management levels

Disdvantages

- Senior managers overburdened with routine matters
- Senior managers neglect strategic issues
- Difficult to cope with diversity
- Coordination between functions difficult
- Failure to adapt

However, there are disadvantages, particularly as organisations become larger or more diverse. Perhaps the major concern in a fast-moving world is that senior managers focus on their functional responsibilities, becoming overburdened with routine operations and too concerned with narrow functional interests. As a result, they find it hard either to take a strategic view of the organisation as a whole or to manage coordinated responses quickly. Thus functional organisations can be inflexible. Separate functional departments tend also to be inward looking – so-called 'functional silos' – making it difficult to integrate the knowledge of different functional specialists. Finally, because they are centralised around particular functions, functional structures are not good at coping with product or geographical diversity. For example, a central marketing department may try to impose a uniform approach to advertising regardless of the diverse needs of the organisation's various SBUs around the world.

10.2.2 The multidivisional structure

A multidivisional structure is built up of separate divisions on the basis of products, services or geographical areas

A **multidivisional structure** is built up of separate divisions on the basis of products, services or geographical areas (see Exhibit 10.3). Divisionalisation often comes about as an attempt to overcome the problems that functional structures have in dealing with the diversity mentioned above.[3] Each division can respond to the specific requirements of its product/market strategy, using its own set of functional departments. A similar situation exists in many public

Exhibit 10.3 A multidivisional structure

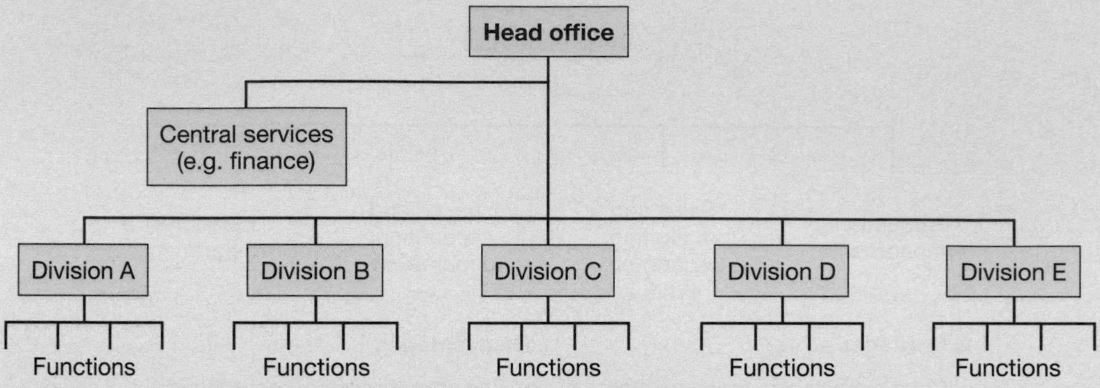

Advantages

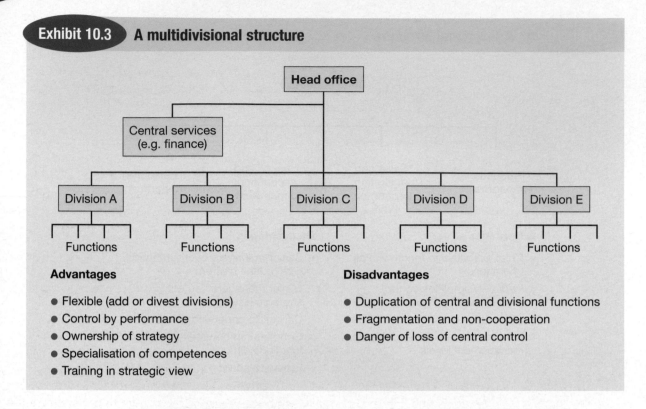

- Flexible (add or divest divisions)
- Control by performance
- Ownership of strategy
- Specialisation of competences
- Training in strategic view

Disadvantages

- Duplication of central and divisional functions
- Fragmentation and non-cooperation
- Danger of loss of central control

services, where the organisation is structured around *service departments* such as recreation, social services and education.

There are several potential advantages to divisional structures. They are flexible in the sense that organisations can add, close or merge divisions as circumstances change. As self-standing business units, it is possible to control divisions from a distance by monitoring business performance. Divisional managers have greater personal ownership for their own divisional strategies. Geographical divisions – for example, a European division or a North American division – offer a means of managing internationally. There can be benefits of specialisation within a division, allowing competences to develop with a clearer focus on a particular product group, technology or customer group. Management responsibility for a whole divisional business is good training in taking a strategic view for managers expecting to go on to a main board position.

However, divisional structures can also have disadvantages of three main types. First, divisions can become so self-sufficient that they are *de facto* independent businesses, but duplicating the functions and costs of the corporate centre of the company. So it may make more sense to split the company into independent businesses, and demergers of this type have been very common. Second, divisionalisation tends to get in the way of cooperation and knowledge sharing between business units: divisions can quite literally divide. Expertise is fragmented and divisional performance targets provide poor incentives to collaborate with other divisions. Finally, divisions may become too autonomous, especially where joint ventures and partnership dilute ownership. In these cases, multidivisionals degenerate into *holding companies*, where the corporate centre effectively 'holds' the various businesses in a largely financial sense, exercising little control and adding very little value. Exhibit 10.3 summarises these potential advantages and disadvantages of a multidivisional structure.

Large and complex multidivisional companies often have a second tier of *subdivisions* within their main divisions. Treating smaller strategic business units as subdivisions within a large division reduces the number of units that the corporate centre has to deal with directly. Subdivisions can also help complex organisations respond to contradictory pressures. For example, an organisation could have geographical subdivisions within a set of global product divisions.

10.2.3 The matrix structure

A **matrix structure** is a combination of structures which could take the form of product and geographical divisions or functional and divisional structures operating in tandem

A **matrix structure** combines different structural dimensions simultaneously, for example product divisions and geographical territories or product divisions and functional specialisms.[4] Exhibit 10.4 gives examples of such a structure.

Matrix structures have several advantages. They are effective at knowledge management because they allow separate areas of knowledge to be integrated across organisational boundaries. Particularly in professional service organisations, matrix organisation can be helpful in applying particular knowledge specialisms to different market or geographical segments. For example, to serve a particular client, a consulting firm may draw on people from groups with particular knowledge specialisms (for example, strategy or organisation design) and others grouped according to particular markets (industry sectors or geographical regions). Exhibit 10.4(b) shows how a school might combine the separate knowledge of subject specialists to create programmes of study tailored differently to various age groups. Matrix organisations are flexible, because they allow different dimensions of the organisation to be mixed together. They are particularly attractive to organisations operating globally, because of the possible mix between local and global dimensions. For example, a global company may prefer geographically defined divisions as the operating units for local marketing (because of their specialist local knowledge of customers). But at the same time it may still want global product divisions responsible for the worldwide coordination of product development and manufacturing, taking advantage of economies of scale and specialisation. In some organisations a matrix structure is created to support specific projects and is 'disbanded' when the project is finished. These *project structures* are common in civil engineering, events management and parts of the public services.

However, because a matrix structure replaces formal lines of authority with (cross-matrix) relationships, this often brings problems. In particular, it will

Exhibit 10.4 Two examples of matrix structures

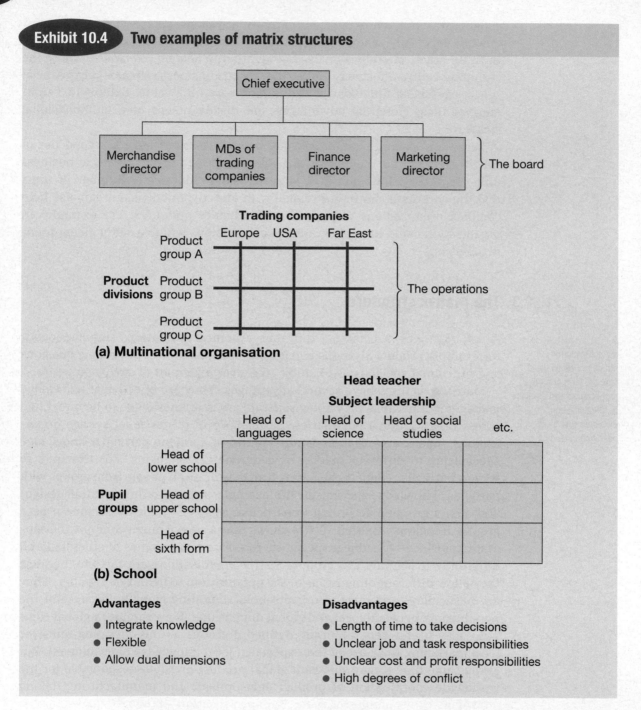

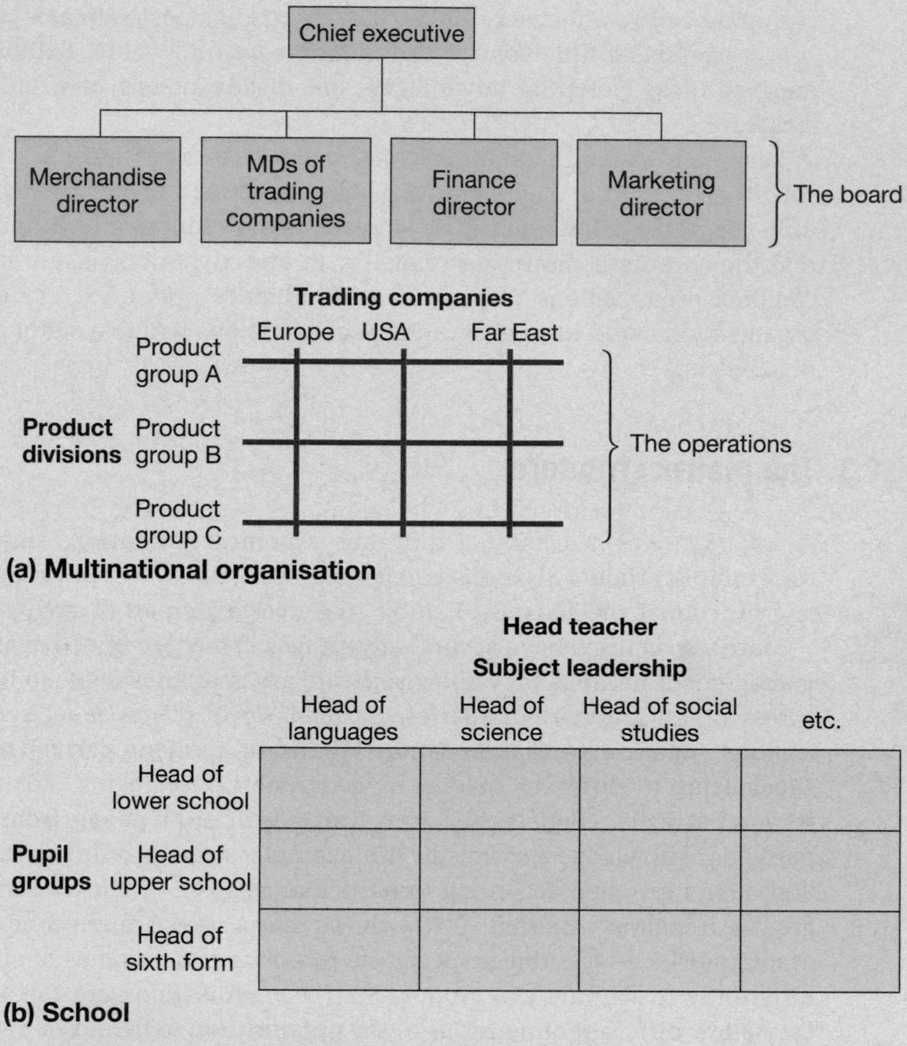

Advantages

- Integrate knowledge
- Flexible
- Allow dual dimensions

Disadvantages

- Length of time to take decisions
- Unclear job and task responsibilities
- Unclear cost and profit responsibilities
- High degrees of conflict

typically take *longer to reach decisions* because of bargaining between the managers of different dimensions. There may also be *conflict* because staff find themselves responsible to managers from two structural dimensions. In short, matrix organisations are hard to control.

As with any structure, but particularly with the matrix structure, the critical issue in practice is the way it actually works (i.e. the processes and relationships). The key ingredient in a successful matrix structure can be senior managers good at sustaining collaborative relationships (across the matrix) and coping with the messiness and ambiguity which that can bring. It is for this reason that Bartlett and Ghoshal describe the matrix as involving a 'state of mind' as much as a formal structure.

10.3 ORGANISATIONAL PROCESSES

Structure is a key ingredient of putting strategy into action. But within any structure, what makes organisations work are the formal and informal organisational processes. These processes can be thought of as controls on the organisation's operations and can therefore help or hinder the translation of strategy into action.

Control processes can be subdivided in two ways. First, they tend to emphasise either control over inputs or control over outputs. Input control processes concern themselves with the *resources* consumed in the strategy, especially financial resources and human commitment. Output control processes focus on ensuring satisfactory *results*, for example, the meeting of targets or achieving market competitiveness. The second subdivision is between direct and indirect controls. Direct controls involve *close supervision* or monitoring. Indirect controls are more *hands-off*, setting up the conditions whereby desired behaviours are achieved semi-automatically.

Organisations normally use a blend of these control processes, but some will dominate over others according to the strategic challenges. As we shall see, input measures tend to require that the controllers have high levels of knowledge of what the controlled are supposed to do. In many knowledge-intensive organisations, especially those generating innovation and change, controllers rarely have a good understanding of what their expert employees are doing, and tend to rely more on output controls. At least they can know when a unit has made its revenue or profitability targets. Direct control relies heavily on the physical presence of management, although now surveillance through information technology can be a substitute. For this reason, international organisations may make use of indirect controls for their geographically dispersed subsidiaries. On the other hand, direct control processes can be very effective for small organisations on a single site.

10.3.1 Direct supervision

Direct supervision is the direct control of strategic decisions by one or a few individuals

Direct supervision is the direct control of strategic decisions by one or a few individuals, typically focused on the effort put into the business by employees.

It is a dominant process in small organisations. It can also exist in larger organisations where little change is occurring and if the complexity of the business is not too great for a small number of managers to control the strategy *in detail* from the centre. This is often found in family businesses and in parts of the public sector with a history of 'hands-on' political involvement (often where a single political party has dominated for a long period).

Direct supervision requires that the controllers thoroughly understand what is entailed by the jobs they supervise. They must be able to correct errors, but not cramp innovative experiments. Direct supervision is easiest on a single site, although long-distance monitoring (for instance, of trading strategies in banking) is now possible through electronic means. Direct supervision can also be effective during a *crisis*, when autocratic control through direct supervision may be necessary to achieve quick results. Turnaround managers are often autocratic in style.

10.3.2 Planning processes

Planning processes plan and control the allocation of resources and monitor their utilisation

Planning processes are the archetypal administrative control, where the successful implementation of strategies is achieved through processes that plan and control the allocation of resources and monitor their utilisation. The focus is on controlling the organisation's inputs, particularly financial. A plan would cover all parts of the organisation and show clearly, in financial terms, the level of resources allocated to each area (whether that be functions, divisions or business units). It would also show the detailed ways in which this resource was to be used. This would usually take the form of a *budget*. For example, the marketing function may be allocated €5m (£3.45m) but will need to show how this will be spent, for example, the proportions spent on staff, advertising, exhibitions and so on. These cost items would then be monitored regularly to measure actual spend against plan.

One strength of this planned approach to strategic control is the ability to monitor the implementation of strategy. The detailed way in which planning can support strategy varies:

- Planning can be achieved by *standardisation of work processes* (such as product or service features). Sometimes these work processes are subject to a rigorous framework of assessment and review – for example, to meet externally audited quality standards (such as ISO 9000). In many service organisations such 'routinisation' has been achieved through IT systems leading to deskilling of service delivery and significant reductions in cost. This can give competitive advantage where organisations are positioning on low price with commodity-like products or services. For example, the cost of transactions in Internet banking are a fraction of transactions made through branches.
- *Enterprise resource planning (ERP) systems,*[5] supplied by software specialists such as SAP or Oracle, use sophisticated IT to achieve planning type control.

These systems aim to integrate the entire business operations, including human resources, finance, operations, distribution, etc. This started with the use of EPOS (electronic point of sale) systems in retail outlets, which linked back into stock control. Further advantage may be gained if these systems can stretch more widely in the value-system beyond the boundaries of the organisation into the supply and distribution chains – for example, in automatic ordering of supplies to avoid 'stockout'. E-commerce operations are taking the integrative capability further. Illustration 10.2 shows an example of enterprise resource planning.

- Centralised planning approaches often use a *formula* for controlling resource allocation within an organisation. For example, in the public services, budgets might be allocated on a per capita basis (for example, number of patients to doctors).

Planning processes work best in simple and stable conditions, where a budget or a formula can apply equally well to all the units in the organisation and where assumptions are likely to hold good for the whole of the budget or formula period. Where there is diversity in the needs of business units, standard budgets or formulae are likely to advantage some units, while handicapping others. Thus in the UK some argue that the government should no longer treat all hospitals and universities the same way: each has its own challenges and opportunities. Also budgets and formulae can be inflexible where changing circumstances contradict original assumptions. Organisations can be penalised unfairly for adverse changes in circumstances, or denied the resources to respond to opportunities unforeseen in the original budget.

Because of the dangers of insensitivity to diverse needs in the organisation, it is often helpful to involve those most directly involved in *bottom-up* planning. In 'bottom-up' planning, local business units at the 'bottom' of the organisation propose initial plans 'up' to the corporate headquarters. The role of the corporate headquarters is to set guidelines for these initial plans and review them when they arrive. Initial proposed plans are often incompatible both with other units' plans and with headquarter's expectations and resourcing capabilities. Incompatibilities are resolved through processes of *reconciliation*, typically involving bargaining and some revisiting of some of headquarter's original guidelines. There are sometimes several iterations of this proposal and review process and so, while it can take into account business unit needs better than simple central planning, bottom-up planning can be very time-consuming and political.

10.3.3 Cultural processes

With rapid change, increasing complexity and the need to exploit knowledge, employee motivation is increasingly important to performance. Under these pressures, promoting *self-control* and personal motivation can be an effective means of control, influencing the quality of employee input without direct

Illustration 10.2

Enterprise resource planning (ERP) at Bharat Petroleum

ERP systems were at the heart of Bharat Petroleum's strategic transformation as it prepared for deregulation in the Indian oil industry.

Bharat Petroleum is one of India's top three refining and distribution companies. It has 4,854 gas stations, some 1,000 kerosene dealers and 1,828 liquid petroleum gas (LPG) distributors scattered all over the vast country that is India. Facing deregulation of its markets, and possibly partial privatisation, Bharat Petroleum embarked upon enterprise integration through the implementation of an SAP R/3 ERP system. The aim was to gain control over the company's operations through improved information in areas such as inventory and product despatch, all working to support better customer service and satisfaction. The new system was to cover 200 sites and include a wide range of processes from financial accounting, to personnel administration, quality management, maintenance, plant management and sales. The finance director projected cost savings alone of £5m (€7.5m) per year.

The implementation of the ERP system was not conceived simply as an information systems project. It built upon a previous delayering and restructuring of the company around six new strategic business units. The ERP implementation itself was named project ENTRANS, short for Enterprise Transformation. The head of the project team was not an information systems specialist, but a human resource professional. Only 10 members of the 60-person project team were from information systems. A project steering group, meeting at least monthly, oversaw the whole process, with the heads of all six strategic business units, finance, human resources and IT represented. The head of IT at Bharat Petroleum commented himself: 'The unique thing about Bharat Petroleum's ERP implementation is that, right from its conception, it has been a business initiative. We (IT) just performed the necessary catalytic role.'

Implementation was carried out with assistance from PricewaterhouseCoopers, 24 SAP consultants, a team of 70 in-house SAP qualified consultants and six full-time change coaches. All users were involved in training, focused on improving 'organisational learning' and Visionary Leadership and Planning Programmes. Bharat Petroleum's chairman declared there would be no reduction in the workforce as a direct result of ERP, even though lower staff costs were included in the benefits case.

Implementation was scheduled over 24 months, with pilots selected carefully on the basis of proximity to the project team (based in Mumbai), salience of the processes involved, and business and IT-readiness. Many initial teething problems were encountered. Informal processes were not always fully incorporated into the new SAP system, with awkward consequences. However, plant managers felt that ERP's formalisation of processes did eventually contribute greatly to increasing discipline amongst staff. In the year after completion of the implementation, Bharat Petroleum achieved 24 per cent sales growth. SAP itself rated Bharat Petroleum as in the top quartile of SAP ERP implementations.

Source: A. Teltumbde, A. Tripathy and A. Sahu, 'Bharat Petrolem Corporation Limited', *Vikalpa*, vol. 27, no. 3 (2002), pp. 45–58.

Questions

1 What is the significance of the ERP implementation not being headed by an information systems expert?

2 What possible dangers might there be in the formalisation and embedding of detailed business processes in an ERP system?

3 What should a company like Bharat Petroleum do with the large team of specialised in-house consultants and coaches once the ERP implementation project is completed?

intervention. Many workers have naturally a strong degree of self-control and motivation that can help ensure appropriate kinds of performance for the strategy: for instance, musicians or doctors, who have strong commitment to craft or professional standards. However, craft or professional standards can also deviate from what the organisation's strategy demands, and some workers will shirk in any case. Here managers can use cultural processes to achieve appropriate kinds of performance.

Cultural processes are concerned with organisational culture and the *standardisation of norms*

Cultural processes are concerned with organisational culture and the *standardisation of norms* (as discussed in Chapter 5). Control is indirect, internalised as employees become part of the culture. Control is exerted on the input of employees, as the culture defines norms of appropriate effort and initiative. Three processes are particularly important in shaping appropriate cultures: *recruitment*, the selection of appropriate staff in the first place; *socialisation*, the integration of new staff through training, induction and mentoring programmes, for example, but also through informal influences such as role models; and *reward*, in other words, recognising appropriate behaviour through pay, promotion or symbolic processes (for example, public praise). These cultural processes often meet subtle kinds of resistance by employees, for example, cynicism and 'going-through-the-motions', and once instituted become hard to change as strategies evolve. Organisations have many cultural processes that are not within formal management control, such as peer group pressure not to respond to organisational strategies.

Nonetheless, cultural processes are particularly important in organisations facing complex and dynamic environments. Sometime these positive cultural processes happen without deliberate management intervention. Collaborative cultures can foster 'communities of practice', in which expert practitioners inside or even outside the organisation share their knowledge to generate innovative solutions to problems on their own initiative. These informal, self-starting communities range from the Xerox photocopying engineers who would exchange information about problems and solutions over breakfast gatherings at the start of the day, to the programmer networks which support the development of Linux 'freeware' internationally over the Internet.

10.3.4 Performance targeting processes

Performance targets relate to the *outputs* of an organisation (or part of an organisation), such as product quality, prices or profit

Performance targets focus on the *outputs* of an organisation (or part of an organisation), such as product quality, revenues or profits. These targets are often known as key performance indicators (KPIs). The performance of an organisation is judged, either internally or externally, on its ability to meet these targets. However, within specified boundaries, the organisation remains free on how targets should be achieved. This approach can be particularly appropriate in certain situations:

- *Within large businesses*, corporate centres may choose performance targets to control their business units without getting involved in the details of how they achieve them. These targets are often cascaded down the organisation as specific targets for subunits, functions and even individuals.

- In *regulated markets*, such as privatised utilities in the UK and elsewhere, government-appointed regulators increasingly exercise control through agreed *performance indicators* (PIs), such as service or quality levels, as a means of ensuring 'competitive' performance.
- In *the public services*, where control of resource inputs was the dominant approach historically, governments are attempting to move control processes towards outputs (such as quality of service) and, more importantly, towards outcomes (for example, patient mortality rates in health care).

Many managers find it difficult to develop a useful set of targets. One reason for this is that any particular set of indicators is liable to give only a partial view of the overall picture. Also, some important indicators (such as customer satisfaction) tend to get neglected because they are hard to measure, leaving the focus on easily available data such as financial ratios. In the last decade or so, *balanced scorecards* have been increasingly used as a way of widening the scope of performance indicators.[6] **Balanced scorecards** combine both qualitative and quantitative measures, acknowledge the expectations of different stakeholders and relate an assessment of performance to choice of strategy (as shown in Exhibit 10.5). Importantly, performance is linked not only to short-term outputs but also to the way in which processes are managed – for example, the processes of innovation and learning which are crucial to long-term success.

Balanced scorecards combine both qualitative and quantitative measures, acknowledge the expectations of different stakeholders and relate an assessment of performance to choice of strategy

www.pearsoned.co.uk/fos KEY CONCEPT Balanced scorecards

Exhibit 10.5 is an example of a balanced scorecard for a small start-up company supplying standard tools and light equipment into the engineering industry. The owner-manager's financial perspective was simply one of survival during this start-up period, requiring a positive cash flow (after the initial investments in plant, stock and premises). The strategy was to compete on customer service for both initial delivery and maintenance back-up. This required core competences in order processing and maintenance scheduling underpinned by the company's IT system. These core competences were open to imitation, so, in turn, the ability to improve these service standards continuously was critical to success.

10.3.5 Market processes

Market processes involve some formalised system of 'contracting' for resources

Market processes (or *internal markets*) can be brought inside organisations to control activities internally.[7] Here market processes typically involve some formalised system of 'contracting' for resources or inputs from other parts of an organisation and for supplying outputs to other parts of an organisation. Control focuses on outputs, for example, revenues earned in successful competition for internal contracts. The control is indirect: rather than accepting detailed performance targets determined externally, units have simply to earn their keep in competitive internal markets.

Exhibit 10.5 **The balanced scorecard: an example**

Financial perspective

CSF*	Measures
Survival	Cash flow

Customer perspective

CSF*	Measures
Customer service (standard products)	• Delivery time • Maintenance response time

Internal perspective

CSF*	Measures
IT systems development • Features • Cost	Performance per £ invested (vs. competitors)

Innovation and learning perspective

CSF*	Measures
Service leadership	• Speed to market (new standards) • Speed of imitation (robustness)

* CSF = critical success factor

Internal markets can be used in a variety of ways. There might be *competitive bidding*, perhaps through the creation of an internal investment bank at the corporate centre to support new initiatives. Also, a customer–supplier relationship may be established between a central service department, such as training or IT, and the operating units. Typically these internal markets are subject to considerable regulation. For example, the corporate centre might set rules for *transfer prices* between internal business units to prevent exploitative contract pricing, or insist on *service-level agreements* to ensure appropriate service by an essential internal supplier, such as IT, for the various units that depend on it.

Internal markets work well where complexity or rapid change make impractical detailed direct or input controls. But they can create problems as well. First, they can increase bargaining between units, consuming important management time. Second, they may create a new bureaucracy monitoring all of the internal transfers of resources between units. Third, an overzealous use of market mechanisms can lead to dysfunctional competition and legalistic contracting, destroying cultures of collaboration and relationships. These have all been complaints made against the internal markets and semi-autonomous foundation hospitals introduced in the UK's National Health Service. On the other hand, their proponents claim that these market processes free a traditionally over-centralised health service to innovate and respond to local needs, while market disciplines maintain overall control.

10.4 MANAGING STRATEGIC CHANGE

This section of the chapter is concerned with the role people play in managing strategic change and how they do it. It begins by considering the *roles* in strategic change played by strategic leaders, middle managers and the influence of outsiders such as consultants and external *stakeholders*. It then goes on to examine different *styles* of managing change and the *levers* for managing change.

10.4.1 Roles in managing change

A **change agent** is the individual or group that effects strategic change in an organisation

When it comes to managing strategic change, there is too often an over-emphasis on individuals at the top of an organisation. It is useful to think of *change agency* more broadly. A **change agent** is the individual or group that helps effect strategic change in an organisation. For example, the creator of a strategy may, or may not, be the change agent. He or she may need to rely on others to take a lead in effecting changes to strategy. It could be that a middle manager is a change agent in a particular context; or perhaps consultants, working together with managers from within the organisation.

Strategic leadership

Leadership is the process of influencing an organisation (or group within an organisation) in its efforts towards achieving an aim or goal

The management of change is, however, often directly linked to the role of a strategic leader.[8] More generally, however, **leadership** is the process of influencing an organisation (or group within an organisation) in its efforts towards achieving an aim or goal. So a leader is not necessarily someone at the top, but rather someone who is in a position to have influence in their organisation.

Leaders are often categorised in two ways:

- *Charismatic leaders*, who are mainly concerned with building a vision for the organisation and energising people to achieve it. The evidence suggests that these leaders have particularly beneficial impact on performance when the people who work for them see the organisation facing uncertainty.
- *Instrumental or transactional leaders*, who focus more on designing systems and controlling the organisation's activities.

However, ideally what is required is the ability to tailor the strategic leadership style to context and there is evidence[9] that the most successful strategic leaders are able to do just this. Indeed, with regard to the management of change, it would seem to be a problem if they cannot. After all, some approaches are more to do with creating strategy, or with control rather than the management of change, and might well lead to approaches to change not suited to the particular needs of the specific change context.

What is likely, however, is that those at the top of an organisation will be seen by others, not least those who work for them, but also other stakeholders and outside observers, as intimately associated with strategic change programmes when they occur. In this sense they are symbolically highly significant in the change process.

Middle managers

A top-down approach to managing strategy and strategic change sees middle managers as implementers of strategy. However, they have multiple roles in relation to the management of strategy.[10] In the context of managing strategic change there are five roles they play:

- The *implementation and control* role. Here they are, indeed, the implementers of top management plans by making sure that resources are allocated and controlled appropriately, monitoring performance and behaviour of staff and, where necessary, explaining the strategy to those reporting to them.
- '*Sense making*' of strategy. Top management may set down a strategic direction, but how it is made sense of in specific contexts (for example, a region of a multinational or a functional department) may, intentionally or not, be left to middle managers. If misinterpretation of that intended strategy is to be avoided, it is therefore vital that middle managers understand and feel an ownership of it.
- *Reinterpretation and adjustment* of strategic responses as events unfold (for example, in terms of relationships with customers, suppliers, the workforce and so on). This is a vital role for which middle managers are uniquely qualified because they are in day-to-day contact with such aspects of the organisation and its environment.
- A crucial *relevance bridge* between top management and members of the organisation at lower levels. They are in a position to translate change initiatives into a message that is locally relevant.
- *Advisors* to more senior management on what are likely to be blockages and requirements for change.

When it comes to strategic change, middle managers are therefore in a key 'mediating' role between those trying to direct from the top and the operating level. A number of researchers have made the point that, in this role, how they make sense of top-down strategy and how they talk about and explain it to others becomes critically important.

Outsiders

Whilst managers in the organisation have important roles to play, 'outsiders' can also be important. For example these could include:

- A *new chief executive* from outside the organisation may be introduced into a business to enhance the capability for change. This is especially so in turnaround situations. He or she changes the context for change by bringing a fresh perspective on the organisation, not bound by the constraints of the past, or the embedded routines that can prevent strategic change.
- *New management from outside the organisation* can also increase the diversity of ideas, help break down cultural barriers to change and increase the experience of and capability for change. However, their successful influence is likely to depend on how much explicit *visible backing* they have from the chief executive. Without such backing they may be seen as lacking authority and influence.
- *Consultants* are often used to help formulate strategy or to plan the change process. They are also increasingly used as facilitators of change processes: for example, in a coordinating capacity, as project planners for change programmes, as facilitators of project teams working on change, or of strategy workshops used to develop strategy and plan means of strategic change. The value of consultants is threefold. First, they too do not inherit the cultural baggage of the organisation and can therefore bring a dispassionate view to the process. Second, as a result, they may ask questions and undertake analyses which challenge taken for granted ways of seeing or doing things. Third, they signal symbolically the importance of a change process, not least because their fees may be of a very high order.
- *Other stakeholders* may be key influencers of change. For example government, investors, customers, suppliers and business analysts all have the potential to act as change agents on organisations.

10.4.2 Styles of managing change

Whoever the change agent is needs to consider the style of management they adopt. Different styles are likely to be more or less appropriate according to context. These styles are summarised in Exhibit 10.6.[11]

Education involves the explanation of the reasons for and means of strategic change

- **Education** involves the explanation of the reasons for and means of strategic change. This might be appropriate when the problem in managing change is because of misinformation or lack of information and if there is adequate time to persuade people of the need for change. However, there are problems here. Assuming that reasoned argument in a top-down fashion will overcome perhaps years of embedded assumptions about what 'really matters' could be naïve. Change may be more effective if those affected by it are involved in its development and planning.

Exhibit 10.6 **Styles of managing strategic change**

Style	Means/context	Benefits	Problems	Circumstances of effectiveness
Education	Group briefings assume internalisation of strategic logic and trust of top management	Overcoming lack of (or mis)information	Time consuming Direction or progress may be unclear	Incremental change or long-time horizontal transformational change
Participation	Involvement in setting the strategy agenda and/or resolving strategic issues by taskforces or groups	Increasing ownership of a decision or process May improve quality of decisions	Time consuming Solutions/outcome within existing paradigm	
Intervention	Change agent retains co-ordination/control: delegates elements of change	Process is guided/controlled but involvement takes place	Risk of perceived manipulation	Incremental or non-crisis transformational change
Direction	Use of authority to set direction and means of change	Clarity and speed	Risk of lack of acceptance and ill-conceived strategy	Transformational change
Coercion/edict	Explicit use of power through edict	May be successful in crises or state of confusion	Least successful unless crisis	Crisis, rapid transformational change or change in established autocratic cultures

Participation in the change process is the involvement of those who will be affected by strategic change in the change agenda

- **Participation** in the change process is the involvement of those affected by strategic change in the change agenda; for example, in the identification of strategic issues, the strategic decision-making process, the setting of priorities, the planning of strategic change or the drawing up of action plans. Such involvement can foster a more positive attitude to change; people see the constraints the organisation faces as less significant and feel increased ownership of, and commitment to, a decision or change process. It may therefore be a way of building readiness and capability for change. However, there is the inevitable risk that solutions will be found from within the existing culture so anyone who takes this approach may need to retain the ability to intervene in the process.

Intervention is the coordination of and authority over processes of change by a change agent who delegates elements of the change process

- **Intervention** is the coordination of and authority over processes of change by a change agent who delegates *elements* of the change process. For example, particular stages of change, such as ideas generation, data collection, detailed planning, the development of rationales for change or the identification of critical success factors, may be delegated to project teams or taskforces. Such teams may not take full responsibility for the change process, but become involved in it and see their work building towards it. The change agent retains responsibility for the change, ensures the monitoring of progress and that change is seen to occur. An advantage is that it involves members of the organisation, not only in originating ideas, but also in the *partial implementation* of solutions, giving rise to commitment to the change.

Direction is the use of personal managerial authority to establish a clear strategy and how change will occur

- **Direction** involves the use of personal managerial authority to establish a clear strategy and how change will occur. It is top-down management of strategic change associated with a clear vision or strategic intent and may also be accompanied by similar clarity about critical success factors and priorities.

Coercion is the imposition of change or the issuing of edicts about change

- **Coercion** is direction in its most extreme form. It is the imposition of change or the issuing of edicts about change. This is the explicit use of power and may be necessary if the organisation is facing a crisis, for example.

There are some overall observations that can be made about the appropriateness of these different styles in different contexts:

- *Different styles for different stages*. Styles of managing change may need to differ according to stages in a change process. Clear direction may be vital to motivate a desire or create a *readiness* to change; participation or intervention can help in gaining wider commitment across the organisation and developing *capabilities* to identify blockages to change, plan and implement specific action programmes.
- *Time and scope*. Participative styles are most appropriate for incremental change within organisations, but where transformational change is required, directive approaches may be more appropriate. (It is worth noting that even where top management see themselves adopting participative styles, their subordinates may perceive this as directive and, indeed, may welcome such direction.)
- *Power*. In organisations with *hierarchical power structures* a directive style may be common and it may be difficult to break away from it, not least because people expect it. On the other hand, in *'flatter' power structures* (or an adhocracy, a more networked or learning organisation), it is likely that collaboration and participation will be common and desirable.
- *Personality types*. Different styles suit different managers' personality types. However, those with the greatest *capability* to manage change may have the ability to adopt different styles in different circumstances.
- *Styles of managing change are not mutually exclusive*. For example, clear direction on overall vision might aid a more collaborative approach to more detailed strategy development. Education and communication may be appropriate for some stakeholders, such as financial institutions; participation may be appropriate for groups in parts of the organisation where it is necessary to build *capability and readiness*; whereas if there are parts of the

organisation where change has to happen fast, *timing* may demand a more directive style.

Illustration 10.3 shows how chief executives may use different styles in different contexts.

10.4.3 Levers for managing change

Challenging the taken for granted

One of the major challenges in achieving strategic change can be the need to change often long-standing mindsets or taken-for-granted assumptions – the paradigm (see section 5.3.5). This may be difficult since long-standing assumptions may be very resistant to change. There are different ways such challenge may be attempted:

- Strategic analysis, using the sort of tools in this book, may itself serve to challenge and therefore change the paradigm.
- Scenario planning (see section 2.2.2) is similarly advocated as a way of overcoming individual biases and cultural assumptions by getting people to see possible different futures and the implications for their organisations.[12]
- Others argue that people's assumptions need to be challenged by surfacing them specifically and encouraging people to question and challenge each other.[13] The idea is that making visible such assumptions means that they are more likely to be questioned.

Changing operational processes and routines

In the end, strategies are delivered through day-to-day processes and routines of the operations of the organisation. There is therefore a need for *planning operational change*: the identification of the key changes in the routines of the organisation. In effect, strategic change needs to be considered in terms of the re-engineering of organisational processes.[14] This can also be another way in which taken-for-granted assumptions are challenged because it may have the effect of getting people to question and challenge deep-rooted beliefs and assumptions in the organisation. The overall lesson is that changes in routines may appear to be mundane, but they can have significant impact.

Power and political processes[15]

Section 4.4.1 discussed the importance of understanding stakeholder relationships in and around the organisation. There is also a need to consider the management of strategic change within this 'political' context. This may also be important because, to effect change, powerful support may be required from an individual or groups. This may be the chief executive, a powerful member

Illustration 10.3

Leadership styles for managing change

Successful top executives have different leadership styles.

Don't noodle

I have always been a pretty good listener, and I am quick to admit that I do not have all the answers. So I am going to listen. But shortly after I listen, the second piece is to pull the trigger. I have all the input, and here is what we are going to do. People need closure on a decision. If you listen and then noodle on it, people get confused, and that's not effective leadership.

Terry Lundgren, CEO of Federated Department Stores (Interviewed by Matthew Boyle, in *Fortune*, 12 December 2005, vol. 152, no. 12, pp. 126–127.)

Coach but don't coddle

My approach to leadership is to raise aspiration and then achieve great execution . . . communicate priorities clearly, simply and frequently . . . to a large degree our division leaders must define their own future. I play the role of coach; but coaching doesn't mean coddling. I expect our managers to make choices . . . to help managers make these strategic choices leaders must sometimes challenge deeply held assumptions. . . . Being a role model is vital . . . I know that I must be ready for moments of truth that alert the organisation to my commitment.

Allan G. Laffley, Chief Executive of Procter & Gamble (in *Leadership Excellence*, November 2006, vol. 23, no. 11, pp. 9–10)

Be dedicated

Sir Terry Leahy of Tesco has overseen one of the biggest retail transformations in the world. Yet he is 'disarmingly ordinary. . . . His speech is serious and straightforward. He's no showman . . . you are not confronted with some huge presence. . . . He talks only about Tesco; . . . it's like meeting a religious leader faithfully reciting a creed.' And strategically: 'He is a combination of the very smart – he's always seeing over the hill – and the very simple. . . . You give him a problem and he'll go off and work until he's solved it. His co-workers respect him for his decision-making but he doesn't make his moves on a whim. . . . Everything is analysed, taken apart, discussed and put back together. . . . He's gathered around him senior managers who've been with him and the group for years. He's in charge but he's also collegiate.' He also likes to talk and listen to people in the stores: 'What makes Leahy different is the extraordinary degree to which he chats with junior staff and absorbs their views and the attention he pays to customers.'

Chris Blackhurst 'Sir Terry Leahy' *Management Today*, February 2004, p. 32.

Build on the key influencers

William Bratton was the police commissioner of New York City responsible for the Zero Tolerance campaign that reduced crime in the city. Bratton's belief was that once 'the beliefs and energies of a critical mass of people are engaged, conversion to another idea will spread like an epidemic, bringing about fundamental change very quickly'. He put key managers face-to-face with detailed operational problems so that they could not evade reality and put them 'under a spotlight'. For example, he brought together senior policemen and required them to face questions from senior colleagues about the performance of their precinct and how it contributed to overall strategy. The aim was to introduce a 'culture of performance': to allow success to be applauded but to make it very clear that underperformance was not tolerated.

W.C. Kim and R. Mauborgne, 'Tipping point leadership', *Harvard Business Review*, April 2003, pp. 60–69.

Questions

1 What might be the benefits and problems of each of the leadership styles? In what circumstances?

2 Only some stakeholders are specifically mentioned in the examples. Does this mean that the style should be the same towards all stakehoders of the organisation?

Exhibit 10.7 Political mechanisms in organisations

Activity areas	Mechanisms: Resources	Elites	Subsystems	Symbolic	Key problems
Building the power base	Control of resources Acquisition of/identification with expertise Acquisition of additional resources	Sponsorship by an elite Association with an elite	Alliance building Team building	Building on legitimation	Time required for building Perceived duality of ideals Perceived as threat by existing elites
Overcoming resistance	Withdrawal of resources Use of 'counter-intelligence'	Breakdown or division of elites Association with change agent Association with respected outsider	Foster momentum for change Sponsorship/reward of change agents	Attack or remove legitimation Foster confusion, conflict and questioning	Striking from too low a power base Potentially destructive: need for rapid rebuilding
Achieving compliance	Giving resources	Removal of resistant elites Need for visible 'change hero'	Partial implementation and collaboration Implantation of 'disciples' Support for 'Young Turks'	Applause/reward Reassurance Symbolic confirmation	Converting the body of the organisation Slipping back

of the board or an influential outsider. Exhibit 10.7 shows some of the mechanisms associated with managing change from a political perspective.

- *Acquiring resources* or being identified with important resource areas or areas of expertise. In particular the ability to withdraw or allocate such resources can be a valuable tool in overcoming resistance or persuading others to accept change or build readiness for change.
- *Association with powerful stakeholder groups (elites)*, or their supporters, can help build a power base. Similarly, association with a change agent who is respected or visibly successful can help a manager overcome resistance to change. Or a change agent facing resistance to change may seek out and win over someone highly respected from within the very group resistant to change. It may also be necessary to *remove individuals or groups* resistant to change. Who these are can vary – from powerful individuals in senior positions to whole layers of resistance, perhaps in the form of senior executives in a threatened function or service.

- *Building alliances* and *networks* of contacts and sympathisers, may be important in overcoming the resistance of more powerful groups. Attempting to convert the whole organisation to an acceptance of change is difficult, but there may be parts of the organisation or individuals in it more sympathetic to change than others, with whom a change agent might build support. He or she may also seek to marginalise those who are resistant to change. However, the danger is that powerful groups in the organisation may regard the building of such a team, or acts of marginalisation, as a threat to their own power, leading to further resistance to change. An analysis of power and interest using stakeholder mapping (section 4.4.1.) can, therefore, be useful to identify bases of alliance and likely resistance.

However, the political aspects of change management are also potentially hazardous. Exhibit 10.7 also summarises some of the problems. In overcoming resistance, the major problem may simply be the lack of power to undertake such activity. Trying to break down the status quo may become so destructive and take so long that the organisation cannot recover from it. If the process needs to take place, its replacement by some new set of beliefs and the implementation of a new strategy is vital and needs to be speedy. Further, as already identified, in implementing change, gaining the commitment of a few senior executives at the top of an organisation is one thing; it is quite another to convert the body of the organisation to an acceptance of significant change.

Change tactics

There are also more specific tactics of change which might be employed to facilitate the change process.

Timing

The importance of timing is often neglected in thinking about strategic change. But choosing the right time tactically to promote change is vital. For example:

- *Building on actual or perceived crisis* is especially useful the greater the degree of change needed. If there is a higher perceived risk in maintaining the status quo than in changing it, people are more likely to change. Indeed, it is said that some chief executives seek to elevate problems to achieve perceived crisis in order to galvanise change. For example, a threatened takeover may be used as a catalyst for strategic change.
- *Windows of opportunity* in change processes may exist. The arrival of a new chief executive, the introduction of a new, highly successful product, or the arrival of a major competitive threat on the scene may provide opportunities to make more significant changes than might normally be possible. Since change will be regarded nervously, it may also be important to choose the time for promoting such change to avoid unnecessary fear and nervousness. For example, if there is a need for the removal of executives, this may be best done before rather than during the change programme. In such a way,

the change programme can be seen as a potential improvement for the future rather than as the cause of such losses.

- *The symbolic signalling of timeframes* may be important. Change agents should avoid conflicting messages about the timing of change. For example, if rapid change is required, they should avoid the maintenance of procedures and signals that suggest long time horizons, such as maintaining long-established control and reward procedures or routines.

Visible short-term wins

A strategic change programme will require many detailed actions and tasks. It is important that some are seen to be successful quickly. This could take the form, for example, of a retail chain quickly developing a new store concept and demonstrating its success in the market; the effective breaking down of old ways of working and the demonstration of better ways; the speeding up of decisions by doing away with committees and introducing clearly defined job responsibilities; and so on. In themselves, these may not be especially significant aspects of a new strategy, but they may be visible indicators of a new approach associated with that strategy. The demonstration of such wins will therefore galvanise commitment to the strategy.

One reason given for the inability to change is that resources are not available to do so. This may be overcome if it is possible to identify 'hot spots' on which to focus resources and effort. For example, William Bratton, famously responsible for the Zero Tolerance policy of the New York Police Department, began by focusing resource and effort on narcotics-related crimes. Though associated with 50–70 per cent of all crimes he found they only had 5 per cent of the resources allocated by NYPD to tackle them. Success in this field led to the roll-out of his policies into other areas and to gaining the resources to do so.

SUMMARY

www.pearsoned.co.uk/ftos AUDIO SUMMARY

- There are many *structural types* (such as functional, divisional, matrix). Each structural type has its own strengths and weaknesses and responds differently to the challenges of an organisation's specific context.
- There is a range of different *organisational processes* to facilitate the implementation of strategy. These processes can focus on either inputs or outputs and be direct or indirect.
- There may be a range of change agents including leaders, middle managers and outsiders.
- Change agents may need to adopt different *styles* of managing strategic change according to different contexts.
- *Levers for managing strategic change* need to be considered in terms of the type of change and context of change. Such levers include changing *operational processes* and *routines*, the importance of *political processes* and other change *tactics*.

Recommended key readings

- The best single coverage of issues about structuring and management processes is in R. Daft, *Organisation Theory and Design*, 9th edition, South-Western, 2006.
- Issues of managing change are well covered in the companion book to this text: J. Balogun, V. Hope Hailey, *Exploring Strategic Change*, Prentice Hall, 3rd edition, 2008.

References

1. G. Johnson, K. Scholes and R. Whittington, *Exploring Corporate Strategy*, 8th edition (2008), Pearson.
2. A good review of new and old types can be found in G. Friesen, 'Organisation design for the 21st century', *Consulting to Management – C2M*, vol. 16, no. 3 (2005), pp. 32–51.
3. This view of divisionalisation as a response to diversity was originally put forward by A.D. Chandler, *Strategy and Structure*, MIT Press, 1962. See R. Whittington and M. Mayer, *The European Corporation: Strategy, Structure and Social Science*, Oxford University Press, 2000, for a summary of Chandler's argument and the success of divisional organisations in contemporary Europe.
4. For a review of current experience with matrix structures, see S. Thomas and L. D'Annunzio, 'Challenges and strategies of matrix organisations: top-level and mid-level managers' perspectives', *Human Resource Planning*, vol. 28, no. 1 (2005), pp. 39–48.
5. For readers who would like to read more about ERP the following are useful: P. Binngi, M. Sharma and J. Godia, 'Critical issues affecting an ERP implementation', *Information Systems Management*, vol. 16, no. 3 (1999), pp. 7–14; T. Grossman and J. Walsh, 'Avoiding the pitfalls of ERP system implementation', *Information Systems Management*, vol. 21, no. 2 (2004), pp. 38–42.
6. See R. Kaplan and D. Norton, 'The balanced scorecard: measures that drive performance', *Harvard Business Review*, vol. 70, no. 1 (1992), pp. 71–79; for a recent development, see R. Kaplan and D. Norton, 'Having trouble with your strategy? Then map it', *Harvard Business Review*, vol. 78, no. 5 (2000), pp. 167–176; and R. Kaplan and D. Norton, *Alignment: How to Apply the Balanced Scorecard to Strategy*, Harvard Business School Press, 2006.
7. Companies like Royal Dutch Shell have been experimenting with internal markets to stimulate innovation. See Gary Hamel, 'Bringing Silicon Valley inside', *Harvard Business Review*, vol. 77, no. 5 (1999), pp. 70–84. For a discussion of internal market challenges, see A. Vining, 'Internal market failure', *Journal of Management Studies*, vol. 40, no. 2 (2003), pp. 431–457.
8. Indeed John Kotter defines leadership as being about the management of change: see J. Kotter, 'What Leaders Really Do', *Harvard Business Review*, pp. 85–96, December, 2001.
9. The discussion on different approaches of strategic leaders and evidence for the effectiveness of the adoption of different approaches can be found in D. Goleman, 'Leadership that gets results', *Harvard Business Review*, vol. 78, no. 2 (March–April 2000), pp. 78–90; and C.M. Farkas and S. Wetlaufer, 'The ways chief executive officers lead', *Harvard Business Review*, vol. 74, no. 3 (May–June 1996), pp. 110–112.
10. See S. Floyd and W. Wooldridge, *The Strategic Middle Manager: How to create and sustain competitive advantage*, Jossey-Bass, 1996.
11. Different authors explain change styles in different ways. This section is based on the typologies used by J. Balogun and V. Hope Hailey, *Exploring Strategic Change*, 3rd edition, Prentice Hall, 2007, section 2.4, pp. 31–36; and D. Dunphy and D. Stace, 'The strategic management of corporate change', *Human Relations*, vol. 46, no. 8 (1993), pp. 905–920. For an alternative framework see R. Caldwell, 'Models of change agency: a fourfold classification', *British Journal of Management*, vol. 14, no. 2 (2003), pp. 131–142.

12. For a discussion of the psychological context, thinking flaws, and the impact that these have for managers as they consider the future, see K. van der Heijden, R. Bradfield, G. Burt, G. Cairns and G. Wright, *The Sixth Sense: Accelerating organisational learning with scenarios*, John Wiley, 2002, chapter 2.

13. For an example of this approach see J.M. Mezias, P. Grinyer and W.D. Guth, 'Changing collective cognition: a process model for strategic change', *Long Range Planning*, vol. 34, no. 1 (2001), pp. 71–95. Also for a systematic approach to strategy making and change based on such surfacing, see F. Ackermann and C. Eden with I. Brown, *The Practice of Making Strategy*, Sage, 2005.

14. See M. Hammer and J. Champy, *Reengineering the Corporation: A manifesto for business revolution*, Harper Collins, 2004.

15. This discussion is based on observations of the role of political activities in organisations by, in particular, H. Mintzberg, *Power in and around organisations*, Prentice Hall, 1983; and J. Pfeffer, *Power in Organisations*, Pitman, 1981. However perhaps the most interesting book on political management remains Niccolo Machiavelli's sixteenth-century work, *The Prince* (available in Penguin Books, 2003). It is also the basis of a management book by Gerald Griffin, *Machiavelli on Management: Playing and winning the corporate power game*, Praeger, 1991.

CASE EXAMPLE

NHS Direct – a gateway to health

Alex Murdock

The National Health Service (NHS) in the United Kingdom is one of the largest public sector organisations of its kind in the world. It is the largest single employer in the United Kingdom. Making major change in such an organisation is challenging and often frustratingly slow. The case study is concerned with how resourcing issues can enable or frustrate the success of strategy.

NHS Direct has been a leading example of the new modernised NHS based around the needs of patients. In five years it has grown from a small pilot scheme to a unique national service.

(Recruitment Material for NHS Direct)

In May 2006 The *Guardian* Newspaper reported that NHS Direct, the nurse-led health helpline in England and Wales, planned to axe more than 1,000 staff in a comprehensive restructuring of branches and business objectives. It was to close 12 call centres across England and shed more than a quarter of the workforce to avert a forecast £15m [€22m] deficit for 2006–07.[1]

Scarcely a month or so later Audit Scotland, the body which audits NHS 24, the Scottish equivalent of NHS Direct, reported positively on the way in which NHS 24 in Scotland had opened up more local call centres and noted some concerns about whether the service would recruit more staff to operate them.

NHS Direct and its Scottish equivalent, NHS 24, provide people with help and advice on health issues over the telephone. It also offers Internet-based services and covers emergency out-of-hours services. The original model of a telephone help-line had thus been considerably extended.

Every month NHS Direct and NHS Direct Online each handle over 500,000 telephone calls and online visits respectively. This probably makes it the largest e-health service in the world. It had added Digital TV to its provision which already has about 500,000 contacts per month.[2] So the service had grown in both remit and complexity.

Although there were differences in operation and governance of NHS Direct and NHS 24 the service needed to function on a national level in respect of policies, networks, systems, performance and planning. The government regarded it as a national 'brand' which contributed to the development of the NHS.

The introduction of NHS Direct[3]

NHS Direct was the first step in a process that seeks to reconfigure radically the delivery of health care services and health care information. It provided both opportunities and challenges. The UK government hoped that NHS Direct would become a well-used and well-regarded '24×7' gateway to the NHS from people's own homes.

NHS Direct call centres recruited nurses with a range of experience in hospital and community settings. About 60 per cent of the nurses worked part time for the service – often combining it with work elsewhere in the NHS. The provision of flexible hours and, in one case, a workplace crèche also had a positive impact on staff recruitment. A national competency framework had been developed together with a planned rotation of staff between call centres and walk in centres.

NHS Direct was supported by considerable technology including extensive use of diagnostic software which prompted advisors to ask particular questions of callers and suggested possible diagnoses and recommended action.

This case was prepared by Alex Murdock of London South Bank University. It is intended as a basis of class discussion and not as an illustration of good or bad practice.

The NHS and NHS Direct: size, finance and growth projections

The NHS is one of the largest public sector organisations in Europe. In September 2004 there were over 1.3 million staff in the NHS Hospital and Community Health Services The size and workforce trends are shown in Appendix 1.

Chancellor Gordon Brown in his 2006 budget identified NHS expenditure as £96bn. This made it the second biggest area of government spending after social security. Furthermore NHS spending is planned to increase further to over £100bn in 2007–2008 (see Exhibit 1).

The proportion of GDP spent on the NHS will thus converge on the (higher) proportion of GDP spent on health by most other European countries.

In 2001 a university study assessed the cost of an NHS Direct call and calculated the impact on subsequent usage of other services. This suggested that NHS Direct saved about 45 per cent of its running costs through reduced usage of other services (see Exhibit 2).

NHS Direct: implementation and service relationships

The implementation of NHS Direct has been regarded as successful. The Public Accounts Committee Report noted that:

NHS Direct has quickly established itself as the world's largest provider of telephone healthcare advice, and is proving popular with the public. It has a good safety record, with very few recorded adverse events. Departments should

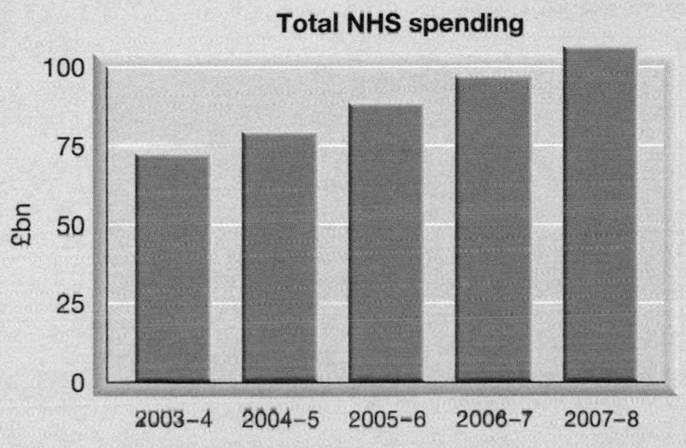

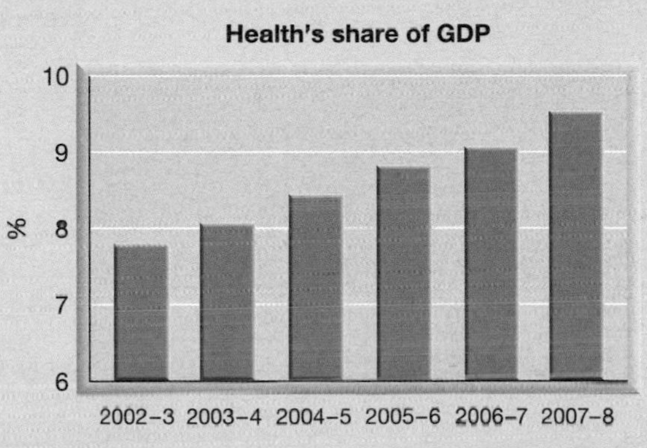

Exhibit 1 Projected NHS spending and share of gross domestic product (GDP)

Source: Derived from HM Treasury sources, reported in 'NHS Five Year Spending Plans 2003–2008' in *The Guardian*, 26 April 2002 (and October 2003). Copyright Guardian News and Media Ltd, 2002.

Exhibit 2 NHS Direct (England): costs and usage of various primary care services, 2001

	Cost without calling NHS Direct (£)	Cost including call to NHS Direct (£)	Usage without NHS Direct advice (%)	Usage with NHS Direct advice (%)
Self-care		15.11	17	35
GP in-hours contact	15.70	30.81	29	19
GP out-of-hours (urgent) contact	22.66	37.77	22	15
Accident and Emergency Hospital attendance	64.96	80.77	3	3
Ambulance Journey	141.54	156.65	8	8

Source: Derived from National Audit Office Report, 'NHS Direct in England', January 2002, HC 505.

consider what wider lessons they could learn from the successful introduction of this significant and innovative service on time.

(40th Report of Public Accounts Committee of House of Commons, 'NHS Direct in England', 2002)

The importance of the relationship to other parts of the NHS and related services is shown by Exhibit 3 which illustrates how NHS Direct functioned as a gateway.

The original intention that NHS Direct would have a significant impact upon reducing the demands upon GP (Family Doctor), Accident and Emergency Hospital and Ambulance services has not been entirely fulfilled.

However, the Public Accounts Committee noted the challenge of integration with other NHS services. It cautioned the Department of Health to set a clear strategic direction for the service to avoid its trying to do too many things at once. Callers were waiting too long and the service needed to improve both its capacity and technical competence.

The NHS Direct Special Health Authority worked with Primary Care Health Trusts to ensure that locally relevant services were delivered.

In Scotland the service developed in a different direction. It had adopted a different name: NHS24. This could be seen as a departure from the UK government image of developing a 'brand' for the service. The service was integrated into existing provision using a number of sites. The service in Scotland had developed

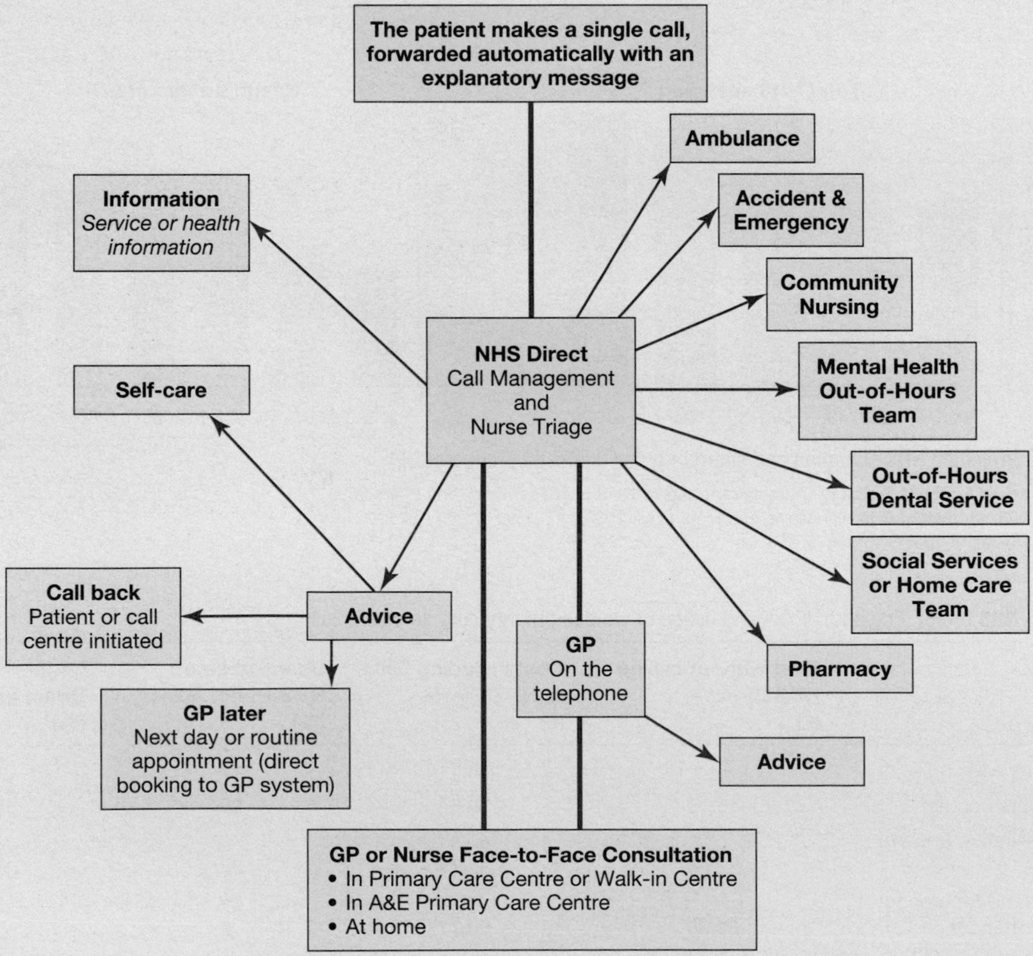

Exhibit 3 The NHS gateway to services

Source: 40th Report of Public Accounts Committee of House of Commons, 'NHS Direct in England', 2002.

in close collaboration with health agencies and doctors while elsewhere it was heavily 'nurse led'.

NHS Direct Online

The growth of the Internet-based service has been particularly significant. This may be associated with the increased use of the internet and growth of home-based broadband access in the UK.

NHS Direct Online forms one element of the NHS's new National Knowledge Service. It is aimed primarily at the public, whereas the National electronic Library for Health is aimed at health professionals.

The users of the Online service are not necessarily the same as the users of the telephone service. Quite naturally the Online service may be reaching a more IT literate user. It was quite likely (though NHS Direct does not provide any data) that the user group also includes health professionals.

NHS Direct has also developed a digital TV presence which expected to reach over 6 million households. This was launched in December 2006.

The extension of the service

The UK is a multicultural and multilingual society. NHS Direct (at least in England) has demonstrated an ability to reach users whose first language is not English through its Non-English language services focusing on most used languages. In Wales the service is provided in Welsh though the actual usage of this facility was relatively limited accounting for some 1.5 per cent of total calls.

The experience in recent years of health scares has had an impact on NHS Direct locally and nationally. It regards its role to be a source of information, advice and reassurance. The service has a particular role in responding to health alerts and possible epidemics as the key organisation in both identifying the problem and also disseminating information to a worried population.

The further development of NHS Direct and NHS24

The development of NHS Direct in England and Wales was associated with significant staff reductions in 2005–2006. This raised some concerns about the capacity of the service in the light of restrictions of spending which were generally affecting the NHS. There was a reduction of some 13 per cent in the number of Nurse Advisors in NHS Direct in 2006.

Nevertheless the success of the service has led to the Department of Health to plan an ambitious programme for expansion. The plan was to increase capacity to deal with 1.3 million calls per month (in England) by early 2007.

A review of the service in England by the National Audit Office focused on the need to address three key areas

- Capacity – to meet the new demands the service will have to develop new human resource strategies, develop networks to deal with variations in demand between centres and be able to provide a justification for additional funding.
- Safety – to maintain or even improve on the current safety record whilst expanding services.

The future?

The continuing reorganisation of the health services in the UK will impact on NHS Direct and NHS 24. The technological bias in England and Wales with the development of more online provision is well established. However, Scotland has laid more emphasis upon locally focused provision and avoidance of delay in responding to telephone enquiries.

As the service expands into new areas such as dentistry, management of patient appointments and emergency service cover it is going to prove more complicated to deliver the prompt, safe and integrated service set for it by key government reports. The increasingly complex and fast-moving technological milieu within which it has chosen to move is not always conducive to consolidation and reflection. In Scotland the plan for the electronic linking of patient records enabling wider access by medical (and some other) NHS staff may prove to be a stumbling point.

The warning note sounded by a manager quoted in an article in *Primary Care* in 2003 has proven to be prophetic:

> NHS Direct has achieved a 20 per cent growth in capacity with the same number of staff. And there is more of that to come. But being a telephone service, the demand is there and then. When we've got the capacity we give a good service but if the capacity isn't there, then you can quickly cross the line, so it's going to be challenging.
>
> (*Primary Care*, June 2003)

Notes

1 NHS Direct dispute the *Guardian* figures.
2 *Source*: NHS Direct Annual Report and Accounts 2006.
3 The author acknowledges J.F. Munro *et al.*, 'Evaluation of NHS Direct first wave sites', 2nd Interim Report to Dept of Health, March 2000, as a background source.
4 *Source*: *The Scotsman*, 6 October (2005).
5 See Audit Scotland: http://www.audit-scotland.gov.uk/publications/pdf/auditreports/05h12asg.pdf.

Questions

1 Looking at Exhibit 3 what structures and management processes are needed to manage the relationship between NHS Direct and the NHS as a whole?

2 What were the main issues about managing change as NHS Direct? (List these under the categories of: roles, styles and levers for change).

Appendix 1 Size and trends in NHS workforce: NHS staffing changes, 1999–2004

Increase in staff

	Sept. 1999	Sept. 2004	Increase since NHS plan[1]
Front-line staff of which:	926,200	1,119,600	193,400 (21%)
All doctors (excluding retainers)	94,000	117,000	23,100 (25%)
Nurses (including midwifery practice nurses and health visiting staff)	329,600	397,500	67,900 (21%)
Ambulance staff	14,800	17,300	2,500 (17%)
Scientific, therapeutic and technical staff	102,400	128,900	26,500 (26%)
Support to clinical staff	296,600	368,300	71,700 (24%)
Other frontline staff[2]	88,800	90,600	1,800 (2.1%)
NHS infrastructure support[3]	171,200	211,500	40,300 (24%)
Total NHS workforce	1,097,400	1,331,100	233,700 (21%)

Increase in training numbers

	In 1999/2000	In 2004/5	Increase since NHS plan[1]
Medical school intake	3,970	6,290[4]	2,320 (58%)
Nursing and midwifery training commissions	18,710	25,020	6,310 (34%)

1. Change since the NHS plan takes as a baseline the nearest annual figure before July 2000, compared with the latest annual position.
2. Includes practice staff (other than nurses) and other non-medical staff.
3. Includes central functions, properties and estates, and managers and senior managers.
4. Provisional Information as July 2005 student numbers have not yet been confirmed.

Source: Chief Executive's report to the NHS: December 2005.

Glossary

Acceptability is concerned with the expected performance outcomes of a strategy and the extent to which these meet the expectations of stakeholders (p. 246)

An **acquisition** is where an organisation takes ownership of another organisation (p. 233)

Backward integration is development into activities concerned with the inputs into the company's current business (p. 182)

Balanced scorecards combine both qualitative and quantitative measures, acknowledge the expectations of different stakeholders and relate an assessment of performance to choice of strategy (p. 274)

Barriers to entry are factors that need to be overcome by new entrants if they are to compete successfully (p. 30)

Business-level strategy is about how to compete successfully in particular markets (p. 7)

Buyers are the organisation's immediate customers, not necessarily the ultimate consumers (p. 33)

A **cash cow** is a business unit with a high market share in a mature market (p. 193)

A **change agent** is the individual or group that effects strategic change in an organisation (p. 276)

Coercion is the imposition of change or the issuing of edicts about change (p. 280)

Competences are the skills and abilities by which resources are deployed effectively through an organisation's activities and processes (p. 62)

Competitive rivals are organisations with similar products and services aimed at the same customer group (p. 35)

Competitive strategy is concerned with the basis on which a business unit might achieve competitive advantage in its market (p. 149)

Complementors are products or services for which customers are prepared to pay more if together than if they stand alone (p. 38)

Consolidation is where organisations focus defensively on their current markets with current products (p. 175)

Convergence is where previously separate industries begin to overlap in terms of activities, technologies, products and customers (p. 38)

Core competences are the skills and abilities by which resources are deployed through an organisation's activities and processes such as to achieve competitive advantage in ways that others cannot imitate or obtain (p. 65)

Corporate governance is concerned with the structures and systems of control by which managers are held accountable to those who have a legitimate stake in an organisation (p. 91)

Corporate-level strategy is concerned with the overall purpose and scope of an organisation and how value will be added to the different parts (business units) of the organisation (p. 7)

The **corporate parent** refers to the levels of management above that of the business units, and therefore without direct interaction with buyers and competitors (p. 172)

Corporate social responsibility is concerned with the ways in which an organisation exceeds its minimum obligations to stakeholders specified through regulation (p. 100)

Critical success factors (CSFs) are those product features that are particularly valued by a group of customers and, therefore, where the organisation must excel to outperform competition (p. 48)

Cultural processes are concerned with organisational culture and the *standardisation of norms* (p. 273)

The **cultural web** shows the behavioural, physical and symbolic manifestations of a culture that inform and are informed by the taken-for-granted assumptions, or paradigm (p. 134)

A **differentiation strategy** seeks to provide products or services that offer benefits that are different from those of competitors and that are widely valued by buyers (p. 153)

Direct supervision is the direct control of strategic decisions by one or a few individuals (p. 269)

Direction is the use of personal managerial authority to establish a clear strategy and how change will occur (p. 280)

The **directional policy matrix** positions SBUs according to (i) how attractive the relevant market is in which they are operating, and (ii) the competitive strength of the SBU in that market (p. 194)

Diversification is defined as a strategy that takes an organisation away from both its existing markets and its existing products (p. 177)

Dogs are business units with a low share in static or declining markets (p. 193)

Dynamic capabilities are an organisation's abilities to renew and recreate its strategic capabilities to meet the needs of a changing environment (p. 73)

Education as a style of managing change involves the explanation of the reasons for and means of strategic change (p. 278)

Feasibility is concerned with whether an organisation has the capabilities to deliver a strategy (p. 253)

The **five forces framework** helps identify the attractiveness of an industry or sector in terms of competitive forces (p. 30)

A **focused differentiation** strategy seeks to provide high perceived product/service benefits justifying a substantial price premium, usually to a selected market segment (niche) (p. 156)

Forward integration is development into activities which are concerned with a company's outputs (p. 182)

A **functional structure** is based on the primary activities that have to be undertaken by an organisation such as production, finance and accounting, marketing, human resources and research and development (p. 263)

The **global–local dilemma** relates to the extent to which products and services may be standardised across national boundaries or need to be adapted to meet the requirements of specific national markets (p. 215)

Global sourcing: purchasing services and com-ponents from the most appropriate suppliers around the world regardless of their location (p. 213)

Horizontal integration is development into activities which are complementary to present activities (p. 182)

A **hybrid strategy** seeks simultaneously to achieve differentiation and a price lower than that of competitors (p. 155)

An **industry** is a group of firms producing the same principal product or service (p. 30)

Intangible resources are non-physical assets such as information, reputation and knowledge (p. 61)

Intervention is the coordination of and authority over processes of change by a change agent who delegates elements of the change process (p. 279)

The **key drivers for change** are environmental factors that are likely to have a high impact on the success or failure of strategy (p. 27)

Leadership is the process of influencing an organisation (or group within an organisation) in its efforts towards achieving an aim or goal (p. 276)

A **low-price strategy** seeks to achieve a lower price than competitors whilst trying to maintain similar perceived product or service benefits to those offered by competitors (p. 152)

Market development is where existing products are offered in new markets (p. 177)

Market penetration is where an organisation gains market share (p. 174)

Market processes involve some formalised system of 'contracting' for resources (p. 274)

A **market segment** is a group of customers who have similar needs that are different from customer needs in other parts of the market (p. 46)

A **matrix structure** is a combination of structures which could take the form of product and geographical divisions or functional and divisional structures operating in tandem (p. 267)

A **merger** is a mutually agreed decision for joint ownership between organisations (p. 233)

A **mission statement** aims to provide employees and stakeholders with clarity about the overall purpose and *raison d'être* of the organisation. (p. 112)

A **multidivisional structure** is built up of separate divisions on the basis of products, services or geographical areas (p. 265)

A **'no frills' strategy** combines a low price, low perceived product/service benefits and a focus on a price-sensitive market segment (p. 152)

Objectives are statements of specific outcomes that are to be achieved (p. 114)

Operational strategies are concerned with how the component parts of an organisation deliver effectively the corporate- and business-level strategies in terms of resources, processes and people (p. 8)

Organic development is where strategies are developed by building on and developing an organisation's own capabilities (p. 233)

Organisational culture is the 'basic *assumptions and beliefs* that are shared by members of an organisation, that operate unconsciously and define in a basic taken-for-granted fashion an organisation's view of itself and its environment' (p. 128)

A **paradigm** is the set of assumptions held relatively in common and taken for granted in an organisation (p. 131)

Participation in the change process is the involvement of those who will be affected by strategic change in the change agenda (p. 279)

Performance targets relate to the *outputs* of an organisation (or part of an organisation), such as product quality, prices or profit (p. 273)

The **PESTEL framework** categorises environmental influences into six main types: political, economic, social, technological, environmental and legal (p. 25)

Planning processes plan and control the allocation of resources and monitor their utilisation (p. 270)

Porter's Diamond suggests that there are inherent reasons why some nations are more competitive than others, and why some industries within nations are more competitive than others (p. 211)

Primary activities are directly concerned with the creation or delivery of a product or service (p. 74)

Product development is where organisations deliver modified or new products to existing markets (p. 176)

Profit pools refer to the different levels of profit available at different parts of the value network (p. 79)

A **question mark** (or problem child) is a business unit in a growing market, but without a high market share (p. 193)

Related diversification is corporate development beyond current products and markets, but within the capabilities or value network of the organisation (p. 182)

The **resource-based view** of strategy: the competitive advantage and superior performance of an organisation is explained by the distinctiveness of its capabilities (p. 60)

Returns are the benefits which stakeholders are expected to receive from a strategy (p. 246)

Risk concerns the probability and consequences of the failure of a strategy (p. 249)

Rituals are activities or events that emphasise, highlight or reinforce what is especially important in a culture (p. 135)

Routines are 'the way we do things around here' on a day-to-day basis (p. 135)

Scenarios are detailed and plausible views of how the business environment of an organisation might develop in the future based on key drivers for change about which there is a high level of uncertainty (p. 27)

Staged international expansion: firms initially use entry modes that allow them to maximise knowledge acquisition whilst minimising the exposure of their assets (p. 223)

Stakeholder mapping identifies stakeholder expectations and power and helps in understanding political priorities (p. 107)

Stakeholders are those individuals or groups who depend on an organisation to fulfil their own goals and on whom, in turn, the organisation depends (p. 90)

A **star** is a business unit which has a high market share in a growing market (p. 193)

A **strategic alliance** is where two or more organisations share resources and activities to pursue a strategy (p. 236)

A **strategic business unit** is a part of an organisation for which there is a distinct external market for goods or services that is different from another SBU (p. 8)

Strategic capability is the resources and competences of an organisation needed for it to survive and prosper (p. 61)

Strategic choices involve understanding the underlying bases for future strategy at both the business unit and corporate levels and the options for developing strategy in terms of both the directions and methods of development (p. 15)

The **strategic customer** is the person(s) at whom the strategy is primarily addressed because they have the most influence over which goods or services are purchased (p. 47)

Strategic drift is the tendency for strategies to develop incrementally on the basis of historical and cultural influences but fail to keep pace with a changing environment (p. 123)

A **strategic gap** is an opportunity in the competitive environment that is not being fully exploited by competitors (p. 50)

Strategic groups are organisations within an industry with similar strategic characteristics, following similar strategies or competing on similar bases (p. 42)

Strategic lock-in is where an organisation achieves a proprietary position in its industry; it becomes an industry standard (p. 160)

Strategic management includes understanding *the strategic position* of an organisation, *strategic choices* for the future and organising *strategy in action* (p. 12)

A **strategic method** is the *means* by which a strategy can be pursued (p. 232)

The **strategic position** is concerned with the impact on strategy of the external environment, an organisation's strategic capability (resources and competences) and the expectations and influence of stakeholders (p. 14)

Strategy is the *direction* and *scope* of an organisation over the *long term*, which achieves *advantage* in a changing *environment* through its configuration of *resources and competences* with the aim of fulfilling *stakeholder expectations* (p. 3)

Strategy in action is concerned with ensuring that strategies are working in practice (p. 16)

Substitution reduces demand for a particular 'class' of products as customers switch to the alternatives (p. 33)

Success criteria are used to assess the viability of strategic options (p. 241)

Suitability is concerned with whether a strategy addresses the key issues relating to the strategic position of the organisation (p. 241)

Suppliers supply the organisation with what is required to produce the product or service, and include labour and sources of finance (p. 34)

Support activities help to improve the effectiveness or efficiency of primary activities (p. 75)

SWOT summarises the key issues from the business environment and the strategic capability of an organisation that are most likely to impact on strategy development (p. 81)

Symbols are objects, events, acts or people that convey, maintain or create meaning over and above their functional purpose (p. 135)

Synergy refers to the benefits that are gained where activities or assets complement each other so that their combined effect is greater than the sum of the parts (p. 179)

Tangible resources are the physical assets of an organisation such as plant, labour and finance (p. 61)

Threshold capabilities are those capabilities needed for an organisation to meet the necessary requirements to compete in a given market (p. 63)

Unique resources are those resources that critically underpin competitive advantage and that others cannot easily imitate or obtain (p. 63)

Unrelated diversification is the development of products or services beyond the current capabilities and value network (p. 184)

A **value chain** describes the categories of activities within and around an organisation, which together create a product or service (p. 74)

The **value network** is the set of interorganisational links and relationships that are necessary to create a product or service (p. 77)

Vertical integration is backward or forward integration into adjacent activities in the value network (p. 182)

A **vision statement** is concerned with what the organisation aspires to be (p. 112)

Index of Names

General Index

Publisher's Acknowledgements

We are grateful to the following for permission to reproduce copyright material:

Illustration 2.2 Figure adapted from *The Future of BioSciences: Four Scenarios for 2020 and Their Implications for Human Healthcare*, co-edited by Paul J.H. Schoemaker and Michael S. Tomczyk, Mack Center for Technological Innovation and DSI, 2006 (Schoemaker, P.J.H. and Tomcyzk, M.S. 2006); Exhibit 2.2 adapted from *Competitive Strategy: Techniques for Analyzing Industries and Competitors*, The Free Press, a Division of Simon & Schuster Adult Publishing Group (Porter, M.E. 1980); Exhibit 2.7 adapted from Charting your company's future from *Harvard Business Review*, Vol. 80, No. 6, reprinted by permission of *Harvard Business Review* (Kim, C. and Mauborgne, R. 2002); Chapter 2 Case Example, Tables 1 and 2 from www.brewersofeurope.org, reprinted by permission of The Brewers of Europe; Chapter 2 Case Example, Table 3 from Euromonitor International, *The World Brewing Industry*, reprinted by permission of Euromonitor International; Exhibits 3.5 and 3.6 from *Competitive Advantage: Creating and Sustaining Superior Performance*, The Free Press, a Division of Simon & Schuster Adult Publishing Group (Porter, M.E. 1985); Exhibit 4.2 adapted from David-Pitt Watson, Hermes; Chapter 4 Case Example, screen shot from http://joinred.com/manifesto.asp reproduced by permission of (RED); Illustration 5.3 courtesy of Anne McCann; Exhibit 5.5 adapted from *Turnaround: Managerial Recipes for Strategic Success*, pub. Associated Business Press, reprinted by permission of Peter H. Grinyer and J.-C. Spender (Grinyer, P.H. and Spender, J.-C. 1979); Exhibit 6.3 from Strategies to fight low-cost rivals in *Harvard Business Review*, Vol. 84, Issue 12, December 2006, reprinted by permission of *Harvard Business Review* (Kumar, N. 2006); Exhibit 7.2 adapted from *Corporate Strategy*, pub. Penguin, reprinted with permission of the Ansoff Family Trust (Ansoff, H. 1988); Illustration 7.4, Figure 1 reproduced with the permission of Dow Jones & Company, Inc., from www.bigcharts.com, 2007; permission conveyed through Copyright Clearance Center, Inc.; Exhibit 7.5 adapted from *Corporate Level Strategy*, Copyright © 1994 John Wiley & Sons, Inc., reprinted with permission of John Wiley & Sons, Inc. (Goold, M. *et al.* 1994); Chapter 7 References, p. 197 Figure from *The New Corporate Strategy*, Copyright © 1988, reprinted with permission of John Wiley & Sons, Inc. and the Ansoff Family Trust (Ansoff, H. 1988); Exhibit 8.2 adapted from *Total Global Strategy II*, reprinted by permission of Pearson Education, Inc. (Yip, G.S. 2003); Exhibit 8.3 adapted from Michael E. Porter, *The Competitive Advantage of Nations*, 1990, Palgrave Macmillan, reproduced with permission of Palgrave Macmillan and The Free Press, a Division of Simon & Schuster Adult Publishing Group (Porter, M.E. 1990); Exhibit 8.4 adapted from Changing patterns of international competition in *California Management Review*, Vol. 28, No. 2, by permission of The Regents of the University of California (Porter, M.E. 1986); Exhibit 8.5 adapted from Global gamesmanship in *Harvard Business Review*, May 2003, reprinted by permission of *Harvard Business Review* (Macmillan, I. *et al.* 2003); Chapter 8 Case Example, Figure 1 reproduced with the permission of Dow Jones & Company, Inc., from www.bigcharts.com, 11 October 2006; permission conveyed through Copyright Clearance Center, Inc.; Chapter 10 Case Example, Exhibit 1 from NHS five year spending plans 2003–2008 in *The Guardian*, 26 April 2002, Copyright Guardian News & Media Ltd. 2002; Chapter 10 Case Example, Table 1 from *Chief Executive's report to the NHS: December 2005*, reproduced under the terms of the

Click-Use Licence (Department of Health 2005); Chapter 10 Case Example, Figure 2 from *NHS Direct in England*, 40th Report of the Public Accounts Committee of the House of Commons (2002), Crown copyright material is reproduced with the permission of the Controller of HMSO and the Queen's Printer for Scotland.

Photographs: AB Electrolux, p. 20; actionplus sports images, p. 59; Alamy Ltd., p. 23, p. 54, p. 89, p. 231 and p. 261; BAA Aviation Photo Library, p. 147; Britain on View, p. 121; Corbis, p. 86; Dynamic Graphics, Inc., p. 171; Getty Images, p. 142; PA Photos, p. 118, p. 168 and p. 228, © PA Photos; Rex Features Ltd., p. 199 and p. 258; Still Pictures Ltd., p. 203; VIEW Pictures Ltd., p. 1.

We are grateful to the following for permission to reproduce the following texts:

Illustration 1.2 extract from Kingston University Plan, 2006–2010, www.kingston.ac.uk, reprinted by permission of Kingston University; Chapter 1 Case Example, extracts from Electrolux *Annual Report 2005* and www.electrolux.com reprinted by permission of AB Electrolux; Illustration 2.4 updated from Global influences on the public sector in *Exploring Public Sector Strategy* edited by G. Johnson and K. Scholes, pub. FT/Prentice Hall, reprinted by permission of D.J. Eppink and S. de Waal (Eppink, D.J. and de Waal, S. 2001); Illustration 3.1 extract © *Freeport-McMoRan Copper and Gold, Inc. Annual Report 2006*. All Rights Reserved; Illustration 3.1 extract from *Royal Opera House Annual Review 2005/6*, reprinted by permission of Royal Opera House; Illustration 4.4 The Metropolitan Police mission and values statements, reprinted by permission of Metropolitan Police Service; Illustration 4.4 Villeroy & Boch vision and values statements, reprinted by permission of Villeroy & Boch AG; Chapter 4 Case Example, extract from http://joinred.com/blogspot.com/ reprinted by permission of (PRODUCT) RED; Chapter 4 Case Example, extracts from Mind the Gap – with this attack on globalization in *The Times*, 24 October, © Gerard Baker/NI Syndication Ltd., 24.10.06 (Baker, G. 2006); Illustration 5.1 adapted from Why smart executives fail: four case histories of how people learn the wrong lessons from history in *Business History*, Vol. 48, No. 2, reprinted by permission of the publisher Taylor and Francis Ltd., http://www.tandf.co.uk/journals and Sydney Finkelstein (Finkelstein, S. 2006); Illustration 5.2 extracts from When in China . . . in *Management Today*, May, Haymarket Business Publications Ltd. (Slater, D. 2006); Illustration 6.4 extracts from Response from the AHRC to the Lambert Review of Business-University Collaboration, http://www.ahrc.ac.uk, reprinted by permission of Arts and Humanities Research Council (AHRC 2003); Illustration 7.3 extracts from *Annual Report 2002* reprinted by permission of Berkshire Hathaway, Inc. and Warren E. Buffett; Chapter 9 Case Example, extracts from *Tesco Annual Report 2006*, www.tesco.com, reprinted by permission of Tesco Stores Ltd.

In some instances we have been unable to trace the owners of copyright material, and we would appreciate any information that would enable us to do so.